CANCUN
HANDBOOK

MEXICO'S CARIBBEAN COAST

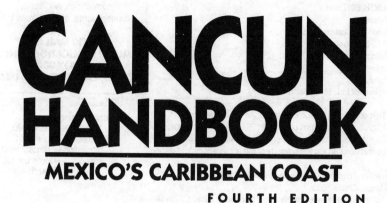

CANCUN
HANDBOOK

MEXICO'S CARIBBEAN COAST

FOURTH EDITION

CHICKI MALLAN

**PHOTOS BY
OZ MALLAN**

MOON
PUBLICATIONS INC.

CANCUN HANDBOOK: MEXICO'S CARIBBEAN COAST
FOURTH EDITION

Published by
Moon Publications, Inc.
P.O. Box 3040
Chico, California 95927-3040, USA

Printed by
Colorcraft Ltd., Hong Kong

Please send all comments,
corrections, additions,
amendments, and critiques to:

**CHICKI MALLAN
MOON PUBLICATIONS, INC.
P.O. BOX 3040
CHICO, CA 95927-3040, USA**

Printing History
1st edition—March 1990
2nd edition—June 1991
3rd edition—February 1993
4th edition—December 1994
Reprinted March 1995

Library of Congress Cataloging-in-Publication Data
Mallan, Chicki, 1933-
  Cancun Handbook and Mexico's Caribbean Coast/Chicki Mallan
  photos by Oz Mallan.--4th ed.
    p. cm.
  Includes bibliographical references and index.
  ISBN 1-56691-050-1
  1. Yucatán Peninsula--Guidebooks. 2. Cancún (Mexico)--Guidebooks.
  I. Mallan, Oz. II. Title. III. Title: Cancun handbook.
  F1376.M26 1994   94-4896
  917.2'67--dc20   CIP

Editor: Beth Rhudy
Copy Editors: Elizabeth Kim, Nicole Revere, Valerie Sellers
Production & Design: Nancy Kennedy
Cartographers: Bob Race, Brian Bardwell, Anne Hikido
Index: Deana Corbitt

Cover Art by Chuck Place
All photos by Oz Mallan unless otherwise noted.
Distributed in U.S. by Publishers Group West
Printed in Hong Kong

To Barbara and Bruce

ACKNOWLEDGMENTS

I wish there were a way to thank the entire population of the Yucatán Peninsula for their help in bringing the fourth edition of *Cancún Handbook* together, but since that's impossible, special thanks go to the Sectur Office in Mexico City, Cecilia Morfin in the Los Angeles Mexican Government Tourism Office, the State Tourism Office in Mérida, Linda Schramm with Mayaland Tours, Fernando Barbachana and his great white VW bug.

Last, thanks to all eight kids and 18 grandkids who are my best critics. I especially thank the other half of this team, Oz Mallan, photographer/husband/pal, who continues to provide dazzling photos—in good humor—even if it means hanging onto the side of a vine-covered pyramid for an hour and 23 minutes, waiting for the sun to come out from behind the tropical clouds.

CONTENTS

MAPS

MAP SYMBOLS

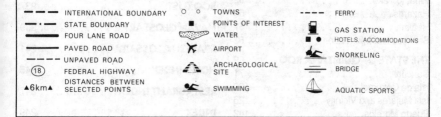

- - - INTERNATIONAL BOUNDARY
- ·- STATE BOUNDARY
——— FOUR LANE ROAD
——— PAVED ROAD
- - - UNPAVED ROAD
(18) FEDERAL HIGHWAY
▲6km▲ DISTANCES BETWEEN SELECTED POINTS

○ ○ TOWNS
■ POINTS OF INTEREST
WATER
✕ AIRPORT
ARCHAEOLOGICAL SITE
SWIMMING

- - - FERRY
GAS STATION
HOTELS, ACCOMMODATIONS
SNORKELING
BRIDGE
AQUATIC SPORTS

ABBREVIATIONS

a/c—air-conditioning
C—Centigrade
d—double occupancy
km—kilometer

OW—one-way
pp—per person
RT—roundtrip
s—single occupancy

s/n—sin número (without a
    street number)
t—triple occupancy
tel.—telephone

CHARTS

SPECIAL TOPICS

IS THIS BOOK OUT OF DATE?

We strive to keep our book as up to date as possible and would appreciate your help. If you find a hot new resort or attraction, or if we have neglected to include an important bit of information, please let us know. Our mapmakers take extraordinary care to be accurate, but if you find an error, let us know that as well.

We're especially interested in hearing from female travelers, RVers, outdoor enthusiasts, expatriates, and local residents. We're interested in any comments from the Mexican tourist industry, including hotel owners and individuals who specialize in accommodating visitors to their country.

If you have outstanding photos or artwork that you feel could be used in an upcoming edition, send us duplicate slides or drawings. You will be given full credit and a free book if your work is published. Materials will be returned only if you include a self-addressed, stamped envelope. Moon Publications will own all rights. Address your letters to:

Cancún Handbook
Moon Publications, Inc.
P.O. Box 3040
Chico, CA 95927, USA

FROM THE AUTHOR

Most people who enjoy Mexico are aware that many changes are taking place, mostly with the fluctuating peso. Even while producing this book, we were aware that prices would be out of date before the book was published. Prices are listed mostly in dollars—which change more slowly. Even dollar prices will change, but not as radically as peso prices. Most travelers want an idea of what to put in the pocketbook when planning a trip. However, please use the prices in this book as a *general guide only*—we have tried to supply addresses where you can check for the most current prices available.

KATHY ESCOVEDO SANDERS

INTRODUCTION
THE LAND

Cancún is located on the east coast of Mexico's Yucatán Peninsula in the state of Quintana Roo, which is bordered by the state of Yucatán to the northwest, Campeche to the west, and the country of Belize to the south. Quintana Roo occupies 50,350 square km and has a population of almost 200,000. Mostly flat, this long-isolated state is covered with tropical forest and boasts the most beautiful white-sand beaches on the Peninsula. Several islands lie offshore and a magnificient 250-km-long reef runs parallel to the Quintana Roo coast from the tip of Isla Mujeres to the Bay of Honduras, whose undersea life provides a world-class attraction. Chetumal, capital of the state, borders Belize, formerly known as British Honduras.

Geologically this area is a flat shelf of limestone and coral composition, which is like a stone sponge: rain is absorbed into the ground and delivered to natural stone-lined sinks and underground rivers. The abundant limestone provided the early Maya with sturdy material to create the mammoth structures that survived hundreds of years to become one of the re-

gion's chief attractions. The soft rock was readily cut with hand-hewn implements but created a problem in the Maya's search for water. In the northern region of Quintana Roo there are few rivers and lakes. Only in the extreme south does a sizeable river exist, the Río Hondo, which cuts a natural boundary between Belize and Quintana Roo, at the city of Chetumal. Four lakes at Cobá are scattered between ancient ruins.

Cenotes (Natural Wells)
Limestone and coral create eerie shorelines, caves, and, fortunately, waterholes. When flying over the Peninsula you can see circular ground patterns caused by the hidden movement of underground rivers and lakes. The water level rises and falls with the cycle of rain and drought. The constant ebb and flow erodes the underground limestone and earth in the water's path, creating steep-walled caverns; the surface crust eventually caves in, exposing the water below. Around these water sources Maya villages grew. Some of the wells are shallow, seven meters below the jungle floor; some are treacherously

deep, with the surface of the water as much as 90 meters below. In times of drought, the Maya fetched water by carving stairs into slick limestone walls or by hanging long ladders into abysmal hollows that lead to underground lakes.

John Stephens's book, *Incidents of Travel in The Yucatán,* covers his 1841 expedition with Frederick Catherwood. Catherwood's realistic art reproduces accurately how the Indians in the northern part of the Peninsula survived from year to year with little or no rainfall by burrowing deep into the earth to retrieve water. The two American explorers observed long lines of naked Indian men carrying calabash containers of the precious liquid from deep holes.

The Peninsula Coast

The Quintana Roo Coast is composed of many lagoons, sandbars, and mangrove swamps and is edged with coral reefs; several islands lie off shore—Cozumel, Isla Mujeres, and Contoy. The fifth-largest reef in the world, the Belize Reef extends from the tip of Isla Mujeres 250 km south to the Bay of Honduras. Many varieties of coral—including rare black coral found at great depths—grow in the hills and valleys of the often-deep reef that protects Quintana Roo. Diving for coral is prohibited in many places along the reef, and where permitted it makes for a dangerous, but lucrative, occupation. Since tourists are willing to buy it, the local divers continue to retrieve it from the crags and crevices of underwater canyons. In addition to attracting profit-seekers, the coral

ridges of the reef draw thousands of sport divers from all over the world each year.

CLIMATE

The weather in Quintana Roo falls into a wet season May-October and a dry season November-April. Though most travelers prefer the milder conditions of the dry season, you can enjoy the area any time of year. Travelers to the area in the dry season can expect hot days, occasional brief storms called *nortes,* and plenty of other tourists. Travel in the wet season can be more difficult, with regular rains and hot, muggy air. May and June are infamous in the Yucatán for heat and humidity both on the sweaty side of 90°.

Hurricane season runs July-November with most activity occurring from mid-August to mid-September. Though tropical storms are common this time of year and sometimes disrupt travel plans, full-fledged hurricanes, like Hurricane Gilbert, are relatively rare. However, don't make the mistake of thinking you can tough out one of these monsters! Leave the area quickly if a hurricane is headed your way.

Hurricane Gilbert

On 13 September 1988, a hurricane of extreme force hit the Yucatán Peninsula. Strong winds and high waves washed across the coast, uprooting trees, destroying buildings, and tearing away roadways and coastline. Some locations

suffered more damage than others. Cancún probably lost more glass than anything else. Certain areas of sandy beach were swallowed by the sea at Cancún, while in other areas sand was dumped as though by the truckload, creating high sand dunes where not needed. The eye of the hurricane passed between Playa del Carmen and Puerto Morelos. While a few buildings were totally washed away, others were destroyed on the inside (in one case two stories were gutted), with the outside walls left intact. Even today, the wounds are fresh, and stories abound. One woman in Puerto Morelos tells of taking refuge in a friend's house near the jungle after evacuating her beachfront home. While walking through a dark hall one night (the electricity was off for 15 days in this area), she was struck by two tropical snakes, which were obviously trying to escape their flooded jungle environment. After treatment in a Mérida hospital, she returned to find her house and everything in it gone. However, like most Yucatecans she has rebuilt and is back in business. (See "Amar Suites" in "Puerto Morelos.")

FLORA

The Forests

Quintana Roo is home to mangroves, bamboo, and swamp cypresses. Ferns, vines, and flowers creep from tree to tree and create a dense growth. On topmost limbs, orchids and air ferns reach for the sun. The southern part of the Yucatán Peninsula, with its classic tropical rainforest, hosts tall mahoganies, *campeche, zapote,* and *kapok,* also covered with wild jungle vines.

Palms

A wide variety of palm trees and their relatives grows on the Peninsula—tall, short, fruited, and even oil-producing varieties. Though similar, various palms have distinct characteristics. Royal palms are tall with smooth trunks. Queen palms are often used for landscaping and bear a sweet fruit. Thatch palms are called *chit* by the Indians, who use its frond extensively for roof thatch. The coconut palm serves the Yucatecan well; one of the most useful trees in the world, it produces oil, food, drink, and shelter. The tree matures in six to seven years and then for five to seven years bears coconuts, a nutritious food that is also used for copra and valued by locals as a money crop. Presently, this source of income has all but disappeared on much of the Quintana Roo coast due to the "yellowing" disease, a condition that's attacked palm trees from Florida to Central America. Henequen is a cousin to the palm tree; from its fiber come twine, rope, matting, and other products. New uses are sought constantly since this plant is abundant in the area.

From Fruit To Flowers

Quintana Roo grows delicious sweet and sour oranges, limes, and grapefruit. Avocado is abundant, and the papaya tree is practically a weed. The mamey tree grows tall (15-20 meters) and full, providing not only welcome shade but also an avocado-shaped fruit, brown on the outside with a vivid, salmon-pink flesh that makes a sweet snack (the flavor similar to a sweet yam's). Another unusual fruit tree is the guaya, a member of the litchi nut family. This rangy evergreen thrives on sea air and is commonly seen along the coast and throughout the Yucatán Peninsula. Its small, green, leathery pods grow in clumps like grapes and contain a sweet, yellowish, jellylike flesh—tasty! The calabash tree, a friend to the Indian for many years, provides gourds used for containers.

The tall ceiba is a very special tree to those close to the Maya religion. Considered the tree of life, even today locals leave it undisturbed, even if it sprouts in the middle of a fertile *milpa* (cornfield).

When visiting in the summer, you can't miss the beautiful *flamboyanes* (royal poinciana). As its name implies, when in bloom it is the most flamboyant tree around, with wide-spreading branches covered in clusters of brilliant orange-red flowers. These trees line sidewalks and plazas and when clustered together present a dazzling show.

Orchids

In remote areas of Quintana Roo one of the more exotic blooms, the orchid, is often found on the highest limbs of tall trees. Of the 71 species

WHAT IS A BIOSPHERE RESERVE?

The biosphere is the thin mantle of the earth in which we live. It consists of parts of the lithosphere, hydrosphere, and atmosphere. The biosphere maintains our life and that of all organisms. We need to protect it and keep it liveable.

The program *Man and Biosphere* was created by UNESCO in 1971, and it deals with the interaction of man with his environment. The program contains various projects, among which the concept of biosphere reserve has gained popularity and has become very important worldwide.

The idea of a biosphere reserve is new in conservation. It promotes the protection of different natural ecosystems of the world, and at the same time allows the presence of human activities through the rational use and development of natural resources on an ecological basis.

A biosphere reserve has a nucleus which is for conservation and limited scientific investigation only. A buffer zone would surround this nucleus in which people may live and use the resources on a regulated, ecological basis. Conservation in a biosphere reserve is the challenge of good use rather than prohibiting use. This concept sets it apart from the national parks in which people are only observers. Biosphere reserves are especially appropriate in Mexico where conservation and economic development are equally important.

—from the bulletin of the
Amigos de Sian Ka'an

reported on the Yucatán Peninsula, 20% are terrestrial and 80% are epiphytic, attached to host trees and deriving moisture and nutrients from the air and rain. Both types grow in many sizes and shapes: tiny buttons spanning the length of a long branch, large-petaled blossoms with ruffled edges, or intense, tiger-striped miniatures. The lovely flowers come in a wide variety of colors, some subtle, some brilliant.

Nature's Hothouse
In spring, flowering trees are a beautiful sight—and sound: hundreds of singing birds gather in the treetops throughout the mating season. While wandering through jungle landscapes, you'll see, thriving in the wild, a gamut of plants that we so carefully nurture and coax to survive on windowsills at home. Here in its natural environment, the croton exhibits wild colors, the pothos grows 30-cm leaves, and the philodendron splits every leaf in gargantuan glory.

White and red ginger are among the more exotic herbs that grow on the Peninsula. Plumeria (in the South Pacific called frangipani) has a wonderful fragrance and appears in many colors. Hibiscus and bougainvillea bloom in an array of bright hues. A walk through the jungle will introduce you to many delicate strangers in the world of tropical flowers. But you'll find old friends too, such as the common morning glory creeping and climbing for miles over bushes and trees. Viny coils thicken daily. Keeping jungle growth away from the roads, utility poles, and wires is a constant job for local authorities, because warm, humid air and ample rainfall encourage a lush green wonderland.

SIAN KA'AN

With the growing number of visitors to Quintana Roo and the continual development of its natural wonders, there's a real danger of decimating the wildlife and destroying the ancient culture of its people. In 1981, authorities and scientists collaborated on a plan to stem that threat. In 1986 the culmination of this group effort, the **Sian Ka'an Biosphere Reserve,** came to fruition. The plan takes into account land titles, logging, hunting, agriculture, cattle ranching, and tourist development. The local people feel comfortable with it, and in October 1986 Sian Ka'an was officially incorporated into UNESCO's World Network of Biosphere Reserves.

Several important issues were addressed, among them deforestation, which is becoming commonplace in Quintana Roo as the growing population clears more land for farms and ranches. Even in traditional fishing villages, growth is affecting the environment. In Punta Allen, to supplement their income fishermen were turning to the ancient method of slash-and-burn agriculture that for centuries had worked fine for the small groups of people inhabiting the Quintana Roo region. But with the continued systematic destruction of the forest to create new growing fields, the entire rainforest along the Caribbean could be destroyed in just a few years.

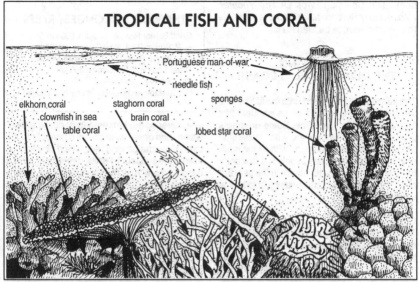

TROPICAL FISH AND CORAL

Portuguese man-of-war

needle fish

sponges

elkhorn coral

clownfish in sea

staghorn coral

brain coral

table coral

lobed star coral

DIANA LASICH HARPER

The people need an alternative means to support their families. The Amigos de Sian Ka'an and reserve administrators along with the local population have been working in the field (thanks to support from the World Wildlife Fund U.S.) and have come up with an experimental farm called "El Ramona," which consists of one acre of land farmed using crop rotation and interplanting of various fruit and vegetables. This ecologically sound procedure uses biodegradable pesticides and a minimum of fertilizers, allowing for constant production of diverse crops. The fishermen at Punta Allen were able to observe an operating prototype and have seen that the new method works. The cost of the farm, including a drip irrigation system, construction of a well, plus the purchase of a gas pump and plastic tubing, was US$2000, within the means of the Punta Allen fishermen. This compromise provides the fishermen with produce, slows deforestation, and creates a self-supporting farm.

Among other problems receiving attention is the plight of the palm tree. The palm is an important part of the cultural and practical lifestyle of the indigenous people of Quintana Roo. The Maya have for years used two particular types of palm, *Thrinax radiata* and *Coccothrinax readdi,*

as thatch for the roofs of their houses, and in the past 10 years fishermen have been cutting *Thrinax* to construct lobster traps. This palm is growing increasingly rare in the reserve today. Amigos de Sian Ka'an, with the World Wildlife Fund, is studying the palms' growth patterns and rates, anticipating a management plan that will encourage future growth. Other projects on the table include limiting commercial fishing, relocating an entire fishing village to an area that will better support the families, halting tourist development where it would endanger the ecology, and studying the lobster industry and its future. A number of other worthwhile projects are waiting in line. Like most ambitious endeavors, these take a lot of money. If you're interested in helping out, join the booster club. Your donation will help a worthy cause, and you'll get a newsletter with fascinating facts about the area and its people as well as updates on current projects. For more detailed information write to: Amigos de Sian Ka'an, Apto. Postal 770, Cancún, Quintana Roo 77500, Mexico.

Ecology Publications

For birders or any visitor intrigued with wildlife and interested in helping the ecological preservation of the Yucatán Peninsula, a fairly new book, *100 Common Birds Of The Yucatán Peninsula* by Barbara MacKinnon, is available through the Amigos de Sian Ka'an.

REEFS ALONG THE QUINTANA ROO COAST

The sea is a magical world unto itself. Humans are just beginning to learn of the wonders that take place within its depths. Some dreamers predict that a time is coming when oceans of the world will provide humans with all the nutrients they need, and that people will live comfortably side by side with the fish in the sea. For now, men and women are content just to look at what's there.

Coral

The spectacular coral reefs that grace the Yucatán's east coast are made up of millions of tiny carnivorous organisms called polyps. A type of limestone, coral grows in innumerable shapes: delicate lace, trees with reaching branches, pleated mushrooms, stovepipes, petaled flowers, fans, domes, heads of cabbage, and stalks of broccoli. The polyps can be less than a centimeter long or as big as 15 cm in diameter. Related to the jellyfish and sea anemone, polyps need sunlight and clear salt water no colder than 20° C to survive. Coral polyps have cylinder-shaped bodies. One end is attached to a hard surface (the bottom of the ocean, the rim of a submerged volcano, or the reef itself) and the other, the mouth, is circled with tiny tentacles that capture its minute prey with a deadly sting.

Coral reefs are formed when polyps attach themselves to each other. Stony coral, for example, makes the connection with a flat sheet of tissue between the middle of both bodies. They develop their limestone skeletons by extracting calcium out of the seawater and depositing calcium carbonate around the lower half of the body. They reproduce from buds or eggs. Occasionally small buds appear on the adult polyp; when mature, they separate from the adult and add to the growth of existing colonies. Eggs, on the other hand, grow into tiny forms that swim away and settle on the ocean floor. When developed, the egg begins a new colony.

As these small creatures continue to reproduce and die, their sturdy skeletons accumu-

THE WORLD'S LONGEST REEFS

Great Barrier Reef, Australia: 1,600 km
S.W. Barrier Reef, New Caledonia: 600 km
N.E. Barrier Reef, New Caledonia: 540 km
Great Sea Reef, Fiji Islands: 260 km
Belizean Reef: 250 km
S. Louisiade Archipelago Reef, PNG: 200 km

late. Over eons, broken bits of coral, animal waste, and granules of soil all contribute to the strong foundation for a reef, which slowly rises toward the surface. To grow, a reef must have a base no more than 25 meters below the water's surface, and in a healthy environment it can grow four to five cm a year. One small piece of coral represents millions of polyps and many years of construction.

Reefs are divided into three types: atoll, fringing, and barrier. An atoll can be formed around the crater of a submerged volcano. The polyps begin building their colonies on the round edge of the crater, forming a circular coral island with a lagoon in the center. Thousands of atolls occupy tropical waters of the world. A fringing reef is coral living on a shallow shelf that extends outward from shore into the sea. A barrier reef runs parallel to the coast. Water separates it from the land, and it can be a series of reefs

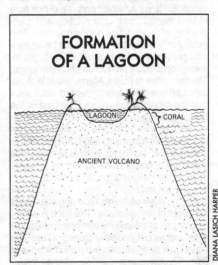

FORMATION OF A LAGOON

LAGOON
CORAL
ANCIENT VOLCANO

DIANA LASICH HARPER

SHELLS ON THE BEACH

horse conch	queen conch	West Indian fighting conch
cowrie	olive	West Indian top
prickly cockle	cut-ribbed ark	turkey wing

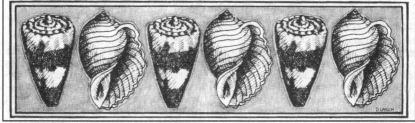

DIANA LASICH HARPER

with channels of water in between. This is the case with some of the largest barrier reefs in the Pacific and Indian oceans.

The Yucatán Peninsula's Belize Reef (the most common of several names) extends from the tip of Isla Mujeres to Sapodilla Caye in the Gulf of Honduras. This reef is 280 km long, fifth longest in the world. The beauty of the reef attracts divers and snorkelers from distant parts of the world to investigate its unspoiled marinelife.

The Meaning Of Color

Most people interested in a reef already know they're in for a brilliant display of colored fish. In the fish world, color isn't only for exterior decoration. Fish change hues for a number of reasons, including anger, protection, and sexual attraction. This is still a little-known science. For example, because of the many colors grouper appear in, marine biologists are uncertain how many species (or moods) there are. A male damselfish clearly imparts his aggression—and his desire for love—by turning vivid blue. Some fish have as many as 12 different recognizable color patterns, and they can change within seconds.

These color changes, along with other body signals, combine to make communication simple between species. Scientists have discovered that a layer of color-bearing cells lies just beneath a fish's transparent scales. These cells contain orange, yellow, black, or red pigments: some fish combine their colors to make yellow or green. A crystalline tissue adds white, silver, or iridescence. Color changes when the pigmented cells are revealed, combined, or masked.

Fish communicate in many other surprising ways, including electrical impulses and flashing bioluminescence (cold light). If fish communication intrigues you, read Robert Burgess's book, *Secret Languages of the Sea* (Dodd, Mead and Company).

Conservation

The Mexican government has strict laws governing the reef, to which most divers are more than willing to comply in order to preserve this natural treasure and its inhabitants. It takes hundreds of years to form large colonies, so please don't break off pieces of coral for souvenirs. After a very short time out of water the polyps lose their color and you have only a piece of chalky white coral—just like the pieces you can pick up beachcombing. Stiff fines await those who remove anything from the reef.

Spearfishing is allowed in some areas along the Yucatán coast, but not on the reef. The spear must be totally unmechanical and used freehand or with a rubber band only (no spear guns). If you plan on fishing, a Mexican fishing license is required. You can obtain one from sportfishing operations and bait and tackle shops in Cancún and Cozumel. If you're visiting a remote fishing lodge, ask if they supply licenses. For further information write to Oficina de Pesca, 2550 Fifth Ave., Suite 101, San Diego, CA 92103-6622; tel. (619) 233-6956.

FAUNA

Many exotic animals are found in the thick jungles and flatlands of Quintana Roo, many that aren't found elsewhere in Mexico. With patience it's possible to observe animals not normally seen in the wild. If you're serious about this venture, bring a small folding stool (unless you prefer to sit in a tree), a pair of binoculars, a camera, and plenty of bug repellent. The distribution of animals and plantlife is a direct result of the climatic zones, which in turn are affected by different elevations and proximity to the sea.

REPTILES

Although reptiles thrive in Yucatán's warm, sunny environment, humans are their worst enemy. Though against the laws of most countries today, in the past some species were greatly reduced in number because they were hunted for their unusual skin. A few black marketeers still take their toll on the species.

Iguana

This species—American lizards of the family Iguanidae—includes various large plant-eaters typically dark in color. Seen frequently in Quintana Roo, they come in many sizes with slight variations in color. The young iguana is bright emerald green. This common lizard grows to one meter long and has a blunt head and long flat tail. Bands of black and gray circle its body, and a serrated column reaches down the middle of its back almost to the tail.

The lizard's forelimbs hold the front half of its body up off the ground while its two back limbs are kept relaxed and splayed alongside its hindquarters. However, when the iguana is frightened, its hind legs do everything they're supposed to, and the iguana crashes quickly (though clumsily) into the brush searching for its burrow and safety. This reptile is not aggressive, but if cornered it will bite and use its tail in self-defense. The iguana mostly enjoys basking in the bright sunshine along the Caribbean. Though they are herbivores, the young also eat insects and larvae. Certain varieties in some areas of the Peninsula are almost hunted out—for example, the spiny-tailed iguana in the central valley of Chiapas. A moderate number is still found in the rocky foothill slopes and thorn-scrub woodlands. In Quintana Roo it is not unusual to see locals along dirt paths carrying sturdy specimens by the tail to put in the cookpot.

From centuries past, recorded references attest to the medicinal value of this lizard, which partly explains the active trade of live iguana in the marketplaces of some parts of the Peninsula.

iguana

Iguana stew is believed to cure or relieve various human ailments such as impotence. Another reason for their popularity at the market is their delicate white flesh, which tastes a lot like chicken but is much more expensive.

Other Lizards

You'll see a great variety of lizards, from the skinny two-inch miniature gecko to the chameleonlike black anole that changes colors to match its environment, either when danger is imminent or as subterfuge to fool the insects that it preys on. At mating time, the male anole's bright-red throat-fan is puffed out to make sure that all female lizards will see it. Some lizards are brightly striped in various shades of green and yellow; others are earth colors that blend with the gray and beige limestone that dots the landscape. Skinny as wisps of thread running on hind legs, or chunky and waddling with armorlike skin, the range is endless and fascinating!

Coral Snakes

The coral snakes found from the southern part of the Yucatán Peninsula to Panama grow much larger (1-1.5 meters) than the ones in the southern U.S. The body is slender, with no pronounced distinction between head and neck. In North and South America are several genera of true coral snakes, which are close relatives of cobras. Many false coral snakes with similar coloring are around, though harmless. Nocturnal, coral snakes spend the day in mossy clumps under rocks or logs.

Note: The two North American coral snakes have prominent rings around their bodies in the same sequence of black, yellow or white, and red. They don't look for trouble and seldom strike, but will bite if stepped on; their short fangs, however, can be stopped by shoes or clothing. Even though the Mexicans call this the "20-minute snake," meaning if you are bitten and don't get antivenin within 20 minutes, you die, it's actually more like a 24-hour period. According to Mexico's Instituto Nacional de Higiene, an average of 135 snake-bite deaths per year (mostly children) are reported for the country, the number declining as more villages receive antivenin.

Chances of the average tourist being bitten by a coral (or any other) snake are slim. However, if you plan on extensive jungle exploration, check with your doctor before you leave home. Antivenin is available in Mexico, and it's wise to be prepared for an allergic reaction to the antivenin by bringing antihistimine and Adrenalin. The most important thing to remember if bitten: *don't panic and don't run*. Physical exertion and panic cause the venom to travel through your body much faster. Lie down and stay calm; have someone carry you to a doctor.

Tropical Rattlesnakes

Called *cascabel* in Mexico and Mesoamerica, this species is the deadliest and most treacherous of all rattlers. It differs slightly from other species by having vividly contrasting neck bands. Contrary to popular myth, this serpent doesn't always rattle a warning of its impending strike. It grows 2-2.5 meters long and is found mainly in higher, drier areas of the tropics.

Caymans

The cayman is part of the crocodilian order. Its habits and appearance are similar to those of crocodiles; the main difference is its underskin. The cayman's skin is reinforced with bony plates on the belly, making it useless for the leather market. (Alligators and crocodiles, with smooth belly skin and sides, have been hunted almost to extinction in some parts of the globe.)

Of the five species of cayman, several frequent the brackish inlet waters near the estuaries on the north edge of the Yucatán Peninsula along the Río Lagartos (loosely translated to mean "River of Lizards"). They are broad-snouted and often look as though they sport a pair of spectacles. A large cayman can be 2.5 meters long and very dark gray-green with eyelids that look swollen and wrinkled. Some species have eyelids that look like a pair of blunt horns. They are quicker than alligators and have longer, sharper teeth. Their disposition is vicious and treacherous; don't be fooled by the old myth that on land they're cumbersome and slow. When cornered they move swiftly and are known for their viciousness toward people. The best advice you can heed is to give the cayman a wide berth when you spot one.

Sea Turtles

At one time many species of giant turtles meandered the coastal regions of Quintana Roo, laying their eggs in the warm Caribbean sands.

Though many didn't survive birds, crabs, and sharks, thousands of hatchlings managed to return each year to their birthplace. The Sea Turtle Rescue Organization claims that in 1947, during one day, over 40,000 sea turtles (Kemp's ridleys) nested on the one Mexican beach to which instinct returns them each year. In 1984 fewer than 500 Kemp's ridleys nested during the entire season.

In spite of concentrated efforts by the Mexican government, the number of turtles is still decreasing. They were a valuable source of food for the Maya Indians for centuries. But only in recent years has the wholesale theft of turtle eggs, coupled with the senseless slaughter of the hawksbill for its beautiful shell, begun to deplete the species. Refrigeration and freezer holds enable large fishing boats to capture thousands of turtles at one time and smuggle meat by the ton into various countries to be canned as soup or frozen for the unwary consumer: processors often claim the turtle meat in their product is from the legal freshwater variety.

Another problem is the belief that turtle eggs cure impotence. Despite huge fines for anyone possessing turtle eggs, every summer nesting grounds along the Yucatán Peninsula are raided. There is no hunting season for these threatened creatures, and the meat is illegal on menus throughout the state, though some restaurants ignore the law and verbally offer turtle meat. The eggs are kept much more secretively.

Ecological organizations are trying hard to save the dwindling turtle population. Turtle eggs are kept in captivity; when the hatchlings break through their shells, they are brought to a beach and allowed to rush toward the sea, hopefully imprinting a sense of belonging there so that they will later return to the spot. After a while at the beach, the hatchlings are scooped up and placed in tanks to grow larger before being released into the open sea. All of these efforts are in the experimental stage; the results will not be known for years. The government is enforcing tough penalties for people who take turtle eggs or capture, kill, sell, or imprison animals on the endangered list.

Pronatura is a grassroots Yucatecan organization valiantly working against the tide, looking after certain species that are heading toward extinction. A few current projects: sea turtle protection, a deer reproduction center, coastal and reef management planning, a toucan habitat study, a jaguar population study, and general conservation funds. For more information about donations write Pronatura, Calle 1d #254a, entre 36 y 38, Col. Campestre, Mérida, Yucatán 97120, Mexico; tel. and fax 44-2290. Specify your interest. Donations made out to "Friends of Pronatura" are U.S. tax deductible.

MAMMALS

Nine-banded Armadillos

This strange creature looks like a miniature prehistoric monster. The size of a small dog, its most unusual feature is the tough coat of plate armor which encases it. Even the tail has its own armor! Flexibility comes from nine bands (or external "joints") that circle the midsection. Living on a diet of insects, the armadillo's extremely keen sense of smell can locate grubs 15 cm underground. Its front paws are sharp, enabling it to dig easily into the earth and build underground burrows. After digging the hole, the animal carries down as much as a bushel of grass to make its nest. Here it bears and rears its young and sleeps during the day. Unlike some armadillos that roll up into a tight ball when threatened, this species will race for the burrow, stiffly arch its back, and wedge in so that it cannot be

armadillo DIANA LASICH HARPER

The raccoon has the curious habit of washing its food before eating it. A strictly nocturnal creature, it eats most anything that comes along, and can ruin an Indian milpa (cornfield) in no time. It's related to two other familiar jungle creatures, the coati and kinkajou.

pulled out. The tip of the Yucatán Peninsula is a favored habitat due to its scant rainfall and warm temperatures; too much rain floods the burrow and can drown young armadillos.

Giant Anteaters

This extraordinary cousin of the armadillo measures two meters long from the tip of its tubular snout to the end of its bushy tail. Its body is colored shades of brown-gray; the hindquarters become darker in tone, while a contrasting wedge-shaped pattern of black outlined with white decorates the throat and shoulders. This creature walks on the knuckles of its paws, keeping the foreclaws razor sharp. It's claws allow it to rip open the leathery mud walls of termite or white ant nests, the contents of which are a main food source. After opening the nest, the anteater begins flicking its tongue. Ants don't have a chance; the long, viscous tongue quickly transfers them to a toothless, elongated mouth.

While particularly dangerous to ants, its longs claws make the anteater a deadly beast when threatened, capable of injuring humans.

Tapirs

South American tapirs are found from the southern part of Mexico to southern Brazil. A stout-bodied animal, it has short legs and tail, small eyes, and rounded ears. The nose and upper lip extend into a short but very mobile proboscis. Totally herbivorous, tapirs usually live near streams or rivers in the forest. They bathe daily and also use the water as an escape when hunted either by humans or by their prime predator, the jaguar. Shy and unaggressive, these nocturnal animals have a definite home range, wearing a path between the jungle and their feeding area. If attacked, the tapir lowers its head and blindly crashes off through the forest; they've been known to collide with trees and knock themselves out in their chaotic attempt to flee!

Peccaries

Next to deer, peccaries are the most widely hunted game on the Yucatán Peninsula. Other names for this piglike creature are musk hog and javelina. Some compare peccaries to the wild pigs found in Europe, though in fact they're part of an entirely different family.

Two species found on the Peninsula are the collared and the white-lipped peccaries. The feisty collared peccary stands 50 cm at the shoulder and can be one meter long, weighing as much as 30 kilograms. It is black and white with a narrow, semicircular collar of white hair on the shoulders. In Spanish *javelina* means "spear," descriptive of the two spearlike tusks that protrude from its mouth. This more familiar peccary is found in the desert, woodlands, and rainforests, and travels in groups of 5-15. Also with tusks, the white-lipped peccary is reddish brown to black and has an area of white around its mouth. This larger animal, which can grow to 105 cm long, is found deep in tropical rainforests and lives in herds of 100-plus.

Cats

Seven species of cats are found in North America, four tropically distributed. The jaguar is heavy-chested with sturdy, muscled forelegs. It has small, rounded ears and its tail is relatively short. Color ranges from tan on top and white on the underside to pure black. The male can weigh 65-115 kilograms, females 45-85 kilograms. Largest of the cats on the Peninsula, the jaguar is about the same size as a leopard. Other cats found in Quintana Roo are the ocelot and puma. In tropical forests of the past the large cats were the only predators capable of controlling the populations of hoofed game such as deer, peccaries, and tapirs. If hunting is poor and times are tough, the jaguar (el tigre) will go into rivers and scoop up fish with its large paws. The river is also one of the jaguar's favorite spots for hunting the large tapir when it comes to drink.

Manatee

Probably the most unusual mammal, the manatee is an elephantine creature of immense proportions with gentle manners and the curiosity of a kitten. Though today seldom seen, this enormous animal, often referred to as the sea cow, at one time roamed the shallow inlets, bays, and estuaries of the Caribbean in large numbers. The manatee is said to be the basis for seamen's myths of mermaids. In South America this particular mammal is revered by certain Indian tribes. The manatee image is frequently seen in the art of the ancient Maya, who hunted it for its flesh. In modern times, the population has been reduced by the encroachment of large numbers of people in the manatees' habitats along the riverways and shorelines. Ever-growing numbers of motorboats inflict often-deadly gashes on the nosy creatures.

At birth the manatee weighs 30-35 kilograms; it can grow up to four meters long and weigh over a ton. Gray with a pinkish cast and shaped like an Idaho potato, it has a spatulate tail, two forelimbs with toenails, pebbled coarse skin, tiny sunken eyes, numerous fine-bristled hairs scattered sparsely over its body, and a permanent Mona Lisa smile.

The head of the mammal seems small for its gargantuan body, and its preproboscidean lineage includes dugongs (in Australia), hyrax, and elephants. The manatee's truncated snout and prehensile lips help push food into its mouth. The only aquatic mammal that exists on vegetation, the manatee grazes on bottom-growing grasses and other aquatic plantlife. It ingests as much as 225 kilograms per day, cleaning rivers of oxygen-choking growth. It is unique among mammals in that it constantly grows new teeth—to replace worn ones, which fall out regularly. Posing no threat to any other living thing, it has been hunted for its oil, skin, and flesh, which is said to be tasty.

The mammal thrives in shallow, warm water; in Quintana Roo and coves of Belize the manatee has been reported in shallow bays between Playa del Carmen and Punta Allen, but very infrequently anymore. One recent spring evening, in a small bay in Belize near the Chetumal border, a curious manatee spent about an hour lazily swimming the cove, lifting its truncated snout, and often its entire head, out of the water about every four minutes. The few people (this author included) standing on a small dock in the bay were thrilled to be seeing the shy animal.

In neighboring Guatemala, the government is sponsoring a manatee reserve in Lago de Izabal. In the U.S. the mammal is found mostly in the inshore and estuarine areas of Florida. It is protected under the Federal U.S. Marine Mammal Pro-

giant anteater   DIANA LASICH HARPER

a close-up of the truncated snout and prehensile lips of the manatee, which surprisingly is a distant relative of the elephant

tection Act of 1972, the Endangered Species Act of 1973, and the Florida Manatee Sanctuary Act of 1978. It is estimated that its total population numbers about 2,000.

BIRDS

Since a major part of the Yucatán Peninsula is still undeveloped and covered with trees and brush, it isn't surprising to find exotic, rarely seen birds all across the landscape. The Mexican government is beginning to realize the great value in this (almost) undiscovered treasure trove of nature and is making initial efforts to protect nesting grounds. The birds of the Yucatán, which attract scientists and laypeople alike, have until recent years been free from pesticides, smog, and human beings' encroachment. If you're a serious birdwatcher, you probably know all about Quintana Roo. Undoubtedly, however, change is coming as more people intrude into the rangeland of the birds, exploring these still undeveloped tracts on the Yucatán Peninsula. Hopefully, stringent regulations will take hold before many of these lovely birds are chased away or destroyed.

Cobá, with its marshy-rimmed lakes, nearby cornfields, and relatively tall, humid forest, is worth a couple of days to the ornithologist. One of the more impressive birds to look for is the keel-billed toucan, often seen perched high on a bare limb in the early hours of the morning. Others include chachalacas (held in reverence by the Maya), screeching parrots, and occasionally the ocellated turkey. For an excellent bird book that deals with the Yucatán Peninsula, check out *100 Common Birds of the Yucatán Peninsula*, written by Barbara MacKinnon. A well-known birdwatcher, Barbara has lived in the Cancún area for many years, and is donating all the profits of her book to the Sian Ka'an Reserve. Available for US$30 through Amigos de Sian Ka'an, Apto. Postal 770, Cancún, Quintana Roo 77500, Mexico.

Sooty Terns
In Cancún, on a coral island just offshore from the Camino Real Hotel, a breeding colony of sooty terns has been discovered. The sooty tern is one of several seabirds that lack waterproof feathers. It is the only one that will not venture to land on a passing ship or drifting debris. Feeding on tiny fish and squid that swim near the ocean surface, the bird hovers close to the water, snatching unsuspecting prey.

The sooty tern nests from April till September. The Camino Real Hotel is being urged to warn guests to stay away from the rocky island. Humans are the sooty tern's only predator. If frightened, the parent birds panic, leaving the eggs exposed to the hot tropical sun, or knocking the young into the sea where they drown immediately.

Flamingos
The far north end of the Peninsula at Río Lagartos plays host to thousands of long-necked, long-legged flamingos during the nesting season (June-August). They begin arriving around the end of May, when the rains begin. This homecoming is a breathtaking sight: a profusion of pink/salmon colors clustered together on the white sand, or sailing across a blue sky, long, curved necks straight in flight, the flapping movement exposing contrasting black and pink on the undersides of their wings. The estimated flamingo population on the Yucatán Peninsula is 30,000. This wildlife refuge, called **El Cuyo,** protects the largest colony of nesting American flamingos in the world.

Many of these flamingos winter in Celestún, a small fishing village on the northwest coast a few kilometers north of the Campeche-Yucatán state border. Celestún lies between the Gulf of Mexico and a long tidal estuary known as La Cienega. Since the disruption of Hurricane Gilbert, a flock of flamingos has found a new feeding ground near Chicxulub. If you're visiting Mérida and want to see flamingos during the winter season, it's a closer drive to Celestún or Chicxulub (about one hour) than to Río Lagartos (about three hours). don't forget your camera and color film!

Estuary Havens
Estuaries play host to hundreds of bird species. A boat ride into one of them will give you an opportunity to see a variety of ducks; this is a wintering spot for many North American flocks. Among others, you'll see the blue-winged teal, northern shoveler, and lesser scaup. You'll also see a variety of wading birds feeding in the shallow waters, including numerous types of heron, snowy egret, and, in the summer, white ibis. Seven species of birds are endemic to the Yucatán Peninsula: ocellated turkey, Yucatán whippoorwill, Yucatán flycatcher, orange oriole, black catbird, yellow-lored parrot, and the quetzal.

Quetzals
Though the ancient Maya made abundant use of the dazzling quetzal feathers for ceremonial costumes and headdresses, they hunted other fowl in much larger quantities for food; nonetheless, the quetzal is the only known bird from the pre-Columbian era that is almost extinct. The Guatemalan government has established a quetzal sanctuary not too far from the city of Cobán. The

kingfisher

LOUISE FOOTE

beautifully designed reserve is open to hikers, with several kilometers of good trails leading up into the cloud forest. For the birder this could be a worthwhile detour to search out the gorgeous quetzal. The tourist office in Cobán, INGUAT, hands out an informative leaflet with a map and description of the quetzal sanctuary.

FISH

The fish and other sealife of the Yucatán coast are world-famous among divers and snorkelers. The barrier reef that runs the length of the Peninsula from Isla Mujeres to Belize is home to myriad fish species, including parrot fish, candy bass, moray eels, spotted scorpionfish, turquoise angelfish, fairy basslets, flame fish, and gargantuan manta rays. Several species of shark thrive in the waters off Quintana Roo, though they're not considered a major threat to swimmers and divers.

Sport fish including sailfish, marlin, and bluefin tuna inhabit the outer Caribbean waters. Check with a hotel or tourist office to arrange a fishing trip. Hard-fighting bonefish and pompano can be found in the area's lagoons.

In the shark caves off Isla Mujeres, sharks "sleep" on the cave floor due to low water salinity. Though some brave divers boast of petting the sluggish predators, most choose not to disturb them.

FISH IN THE CARIBBEAN

blue chromis	trumpetfish
toadfish	sand tilefish
porkfish	triggerfish
trunkfish	sergeant major
queen angelfish	big eye
grouper	bluestriped grunt
stoplight parrot fish	butterfly indigo
French grunt	hamlet
spotted drum	barracuda
angelfish	hogfish
barred cardinal	

The clear waters of the cenotes, or giant wells, of the Yucatán are home to several species of blind fish, which live out their existence in darkness.

INSECTS AND ARACHNIDS

Those pesky air-breathing invertebrates are unavoidable in any tropical locale. Some are annoying (mosquitoes and gnats), some are dangerous (black widows, bird spiders, and scorpions), and others can cause pain when they bite (red ants), but many are beautiful (butterflies and moths), and *all* are fascinating studies in evolved socialization and specialization. Note: Cockroaches also live in the jungle, so don't be surprised if you run into one.

Butterflies And Moths

The Yucatán has an abundance of beautiful moths and butterflies. Of the 90,000 types of butterflies in the world, a large percentage is seen in Quintana Roo. You'll see, among others, the magnificent blue morpho, orange-barred sulphur, copperhead, cloudless sulphur, malachite, admiral, calico, ruddy dagger-wing, tropical buckeye, and emperor. The famous monarch is also a visitor during its annual migration from the Florida Peninsula. It usually makes a

MOTHS AND BUTTERFLIES

1. Butterflies fly during the day; moths fly at dusk or at night.

2. Butterflies rest with their wings folded straight up over their bodies; most moths rest with their wings spread flat.

3. All butterflies have bare knobs at the end of both antennae (feelers); moths' antennae are either plumy or hairlike and end in a point.

4. Butterflies have slender bodies; moths are plump. Both insects are of the order Lepidoptera. So, lepidopterists, you are in butterfly heaven in the jungle areas of the Yucatán Peninsula.

stopover on Quintana Roo's east coast, including Cancún and Cozumel, on its way south to the Central American mountains and Mexican highlands where it spends the winter. Trying to photograph a live butterfly is a testy business. Just when you have it in your crosshairs, the comely critter flutters off to another spot!

HISTORY

ANCIENTS

Earliest Humans
People and animals from Asia crossed the Bering land bridge into North America in the Pleistocene Epoch about 50,000 years ago, when sea levels were much lower. The epic human trek south continued until only 3,000 years ago, when anthropologists say people first reached Tierra del Fuego, at the tip of South America.

As early as 10,000 B.C., Ice Age humans hunted woolly mammoth and other large animals roaming the cool, moist landscape of central Mexico. Between 7000 and 2000 B.C., society evolved from hunters and gatherers to farmers. After about 6000 B.C., corn, squash, and beans were independently domesticated in widely separated areas of Mexico. The remains of clay figurines from the Preclassic period, presumed to be fertility symbols, marked the rise of religion in Mesoamerica, beginning around 2000 B.C.

Around 1000 B.C. the Olmec Indian culture, believed to be the region's earliest, began to spread throughout Mesoamerica. Large-scale ceremonial centers grew along Gulf coast lands, and much of Mesoamerica was influenced by these Indians' religion of worshipping jaguar-like gods. Also at this time, the New World's first calendar and a beginning system of writing were developed.

Classic Period
The Classic period, beginning about A.D. 300, is now hailed by many as the peak of cultural development among the Maya Indians and other cultures throughout Mexico. Until A.D. 900, phenomenal progress was made in the development of artistic, architectural, and astronomical skills. Impressive buildings were constructed during this period, and codices (folded bark books) were written and filled with hieroglyphic symbols that detailed complicated mathematical calculations of days, months, and years. Only the priests and the privileged held this knowledge, and continued to learn and develop it until, for an unknown reason, the growth halted suddenly.

Post-Classic
After A.D. 900, the Toltec influence took hold, marking the end of the most artistic era and the birth of a new militaristic society built around a blend of ceremonialism, civic and social organization, and conquest.

COLONIAL HISTORY

Hernán Cortés

Following Columbus's arrival in the New World, other adventurers traveling the same seas soon found the Yucatán Peninsula. In 1519, 34-year-old Hernán Cortés sailed from Cuba against the wishes of the Spanish governor. With 11 ships, 120 sailors, and 550 soldiers he set out to search for slaves, a lucrative business with or without the government's blessing. His search began on the Yucatán coast and would eventually encompass most of Mexico. However, he hadn't counted on the ferocious resistance and cunning of the Maya Indians. The fighting was destined to continue for many years—a time of bloodshed and death for many of his men. (This "war" didn't really end on the Peninsula until the Chan Santa Cruz Indians finally signed a peace treaty with the Mexican federal government in 1935, over 400 years later.) By the time Cortés died in 1547 (while exiled in Spain), the Spanish military and Franciscan

Hernán Cortés

friars were well entrenched in the Yucatán Peninsula.

Diego De Landa

The Franciscan priests were shocked by Mayan religious customs such as body mutilation and human sacrifice, which they believed to be influences of the devil. The Franciscans believed it their holy duty to eliminate the Maya religion and convert the Indians.

Diego de Landa arrived in Mexico in 1549 as a 25-year-old friar, and was instrumental in the destruction of many thousands of Maya idols. He oversaw the burning of 27 codices filled with characters and symbols that he could not understand, but which he believed contained only superstitions and the devil's lies. Since then, only three codices have been found and studied, and only parts of them have been completely deciphered. While Landa was directly responsible for destroying the history of these ancient people, his reputation is partly redeemed by his writing the most complete and detailed account of Maya life in his book *Relaciones de las Cosas de Yucatán*. Landa's book describes daily living in great detail, including the growth and preparation of food, the structure of society, the priesthood, and the sciences. Although he was aware of the sophisticated "count of ages," he didn't understand it. Fortunately, he left a one-line formula which, used as a mathematical and chronological key by later researchers, opened up the science of Maya calculations and their great knowledge of astronomy.

Landa was called back to Spain in 1563 after colonial civil and religious leaders accused him of "despotic mismanagement." He spent a year in prison, and while his fate was being decided, he wrote the book as a defense against the charges. During his absence, his replacement, Bishop Toral, acted with great compassion toward the Indians. Landa was ultimately cleared and was allowed to return to the New World in 1573, where he became a bishop and resumed his previous methods of proselytizing. He lived in the Yucatán until his death in 1579.

Franciscan Power

Bishop Toral was cut from a different cloth. A humanitarian, he was appalled by the unjust treatment of Indians. Though Toral, after Landa's imprisonment, tried to impose sweeping changes, he was unable to make inroads into the power held by the Franciscans in the Yucatán. Defeated, he retired to Mexico. However, shortly before his death in 1571, his reforms were implemented with the "Royal Cedula," which prohibited friars from shaving the heads of Indians against their will, flogging them, or keeping prison cells in monasteries. It also called for the immediate release of all Indian prisoners.

Catholicism

Over the years, the majority of Indians were baptized into the Catholic faith. Most priests did their best to educate the people, teach them to read and write, and protect them from the growing number of Spanish settlers who used them as slaves. The Indians, then and now, practice Catholicism in their own manner, combining their ancient beliefs, handed down through centuries, with Christian doctrine. These mystic yet Christian ceremonies are performed in baptism, courtship, marriage, illness, farming, housebuilding, and fiestas.

Further Subjugation

While all of Mexico dealt with the problems of economic colonialism, the Yucatán Peninsula had an additional one: harassment by vicious pirates who made life on the Gulf coast unstable. Around 1600, when silver production began to wane, Spain's economic power faltered. In the following years, haciendas (self-supporting estates or small feudal systems) began to thrive, overrunning communal villages jointly owned by the Maya. But later, between 1700 and 1810 as Mexico endured the backlash of several government upheavals in Europe, Spanish settlers on the Peninsula began exploiting the native Maya in earnest. The passive Indians were ground down, their lands taken away, and their numbers greatly reduced by the white man's epidemics and mistreatment.

Caste War

The Spaniards grabbed the Maya land and planted it with tobacco and sugarcane year after year until the soil had worn out. Added to the other abuses, it was inevitable that the Indians' rage would eventually explode in a furious attack. This bloody uprising in the 1840s was

CHRONOLOGICAL TABLE

DATES	PERIODS
2000 B.C.	ARCHAIC
800 B.C.	EARLY PRECLASSIC
300 B.C.	MIDDLE PRECLASSIC
250 A.D.	LATE PRECLASSIC
600 A.D.	EARLY CLASSIC
900 A.D.	LATE CLASSIC
1200 A.D.	EARLY POST-CLASSIC
1530 A.D.	LATE POST-CLASSIC

called the Caste War. Though the Maya were farmers, not soldiers, this savage war saw them taking revenge on every white man, woman, and child by means of rape and murder. European survivors made their way to the last Spanish strongholds of Mérida and Campeche. The governments of the two cities appealed for help to Spain, France, and the United States. No one answered the call, and it was soon apparent that the remaining two cities would be wiped out. But fate would not have it that way; just as the governor of Mérida was about to begin evacuating the city, the Maya picked up their primitive weapons and walked away.

Attuned to the signals of the land, the Maya knew that the appearance of the flying ant was the first sign of rain and signaled the time to plant corn. When, on the brink of destroying the enemy, the winged ant made an unusually early appearance, the Indians turned their backs on certain victory and returned to their villages to plant corn.

This was just the breather the Spanish settlers needed. Help came from Cuba and Mexico City, as well as 1,000 U.S. mercenary troops. Vengeance was merciless. Most Maya were killed indiscriminately. Some were taken prisoner and sold to Cuba as slaves; others left their villages and hid in the jungles, in some cases for decades. Between 1846 and 1850, the population of the Yucatán Peninsula was reduced from 500,000 to 300,000. Quintana Roo along the Caribbean coast was considered a dangerous no-man's-land for almost another hundred years.

Spanish-style ship

Growing Maya Power

Many Maya Indians escaped slaughter during the Caste War by fleeing to the isolated territory known today as Quintana Roo. The Maya revived the "Talking Cross," a pre-Columbian oracle representing gods of the four cardinal directions. This was a religious/political marriage. Three determined survivors of the Caste War—a priest, a master spy, and a ventriloquist—all wise leaders, knew their people's desperate need for divine leadership. As a result of the words from the "talking cross," shattered Indians came together in large numbers and began to organize. The community guarded the cross's location, and advice from it continued to strengthen the Maya.

They called themselves Chan Santa Cruz (meaning "People of the Holy Cross"). As their confidence developed, so did the growth and power of their communities. Living in dense forests very close to the border with British Honduras (now Belize), they found they had something their neighbors wanted: timber. The Chan Santa Cruz Maya began selling timber to the British and were given arms in return. These weapons gave the Maya even more power. From 1855 to 1857 internal strife weakened the relations between Campeche and Mérida. While the Spaniards were dealing with the problem on the Gulf coast, the Maya took advantage of the vulnerability of Fort Bacalar and in 1857 took it over, gaining control of the entire Caribbean coast from Cabo Catouche in the far north to the border of British Honduras in the south. In three years they destroyed all of the Spanish settlements while slaughtering or capturing thousands of whites.

The Indians of the coastal community of Chan Santa Cruz, also known as Cruzobs, for years had murdered their captives. But starting in 1858 they took lessons from the colonials and began to keep whites for slave labor in the fields and forest; women were put to work doing household chores and some became concubines. For the next 40 years, the Chan Santa Cruz Indians kept the east coast of the Yucatán for themselves; a shaky truce with the Mexican government endured. The Indians were financially independent, self-governing, and, with no roads in, totally isolated from technological advancements beginning to take place in other parts of the

Peninsula. They were not at war as long as everyone left them alone.

The Last Stand

Only when President Porfirio Diáz took power in 1877 did the Mexican federal government began to think seriously about the Yucatán Peninsula. Over the years, Quintana Roo's isolation and the strength of the Maya in their treacherous jungle had foiled repeated efforts by Mexican soldiers to capture the Indians. The army's expeditions were infrequent, but it rankled Diáz that a handful of Indians had been able to keep the Mexican federal army at bay for so long. An assault in 1901, under the command of general Ignacio Bravo, broke the government's losing streak. The general captured a village, laid railroad tracks, and built a walled fort. Supplies arriving by rail kept the fort stocked, but the Indian army held the fort under siege for an entire year. When reinforcements arrived from the capital, the upstarts were finally put down. Thus began another cycle of brutal Mexican occupation until 1915. The scattered Indians didn't give up. They persisted with guerilla raids from the rainforest until the Mexicans, finally defeated once again, pulled out and returned Quintana Roo to the Maya.

From 1917 till 1920, hundreds of thousands of Indians died from influenza and smallpox epidemics introduced by the Spanish. An Indian leader, General May, took stock of his troops, and saw clearly that the old soldiers were fading. They had put up a long tough battle to hold onto their land and culture. The year 1920 marked the end of their independent reign in Quintana Roo's jungle. Foreign gummakers initiated the chicle boom, bringing *chicleros* to work the trees. It was then that General May demanded (and received) a negotiated settlement. In 1935 the Chan Santa Cruz Indians signed a peace treaty with the Mexican Federals.

MODERN TIMES

Meanwhile, in the northern part of the Peninsula, international demand for the henequen plant brought prosperity to Mérida, capital of the state of Yucatán. Twine and rope made from the sword-shaped leaves of this variety of agave plant were in demand all over the world. Soon after the henequen boom began in 1875, Mérida had become the jewel of the Peninsula. Spanish haciendas staffed by Indian slaves cultivated the easily grown plant, and for miles the outlying areas were planted with the henequen, which required little rainfall and thrived in the Peninsula's thin, rocky soil. Beautiful mansions were built by entrepreneurs who led the gracious life, sending their children to school in Europe, cruising with their wives to New Orleans in search of new luxuries and entertainment. Port towns were developed on the Gulf coast, and a two-km-long wharf named Progreso was built to accommodate the large ships that came for sisal (hemp from the henequen plant).

The only thing that didn't change was the lifestyle of the *peones*. The Indian peasants' life was still devoid of human rights. They labored long, hard hours, living in constant debt to the company store, where their meager peso wage was spent before it was received. The Indians were caught up in a cycle of bondage that endured for many years in Mérida. One story holds than it was during this time that the lovely *huipil* (Indian dress) was mandated to be worn by all Indians and mestizos (those of mixed blood) on the Peninsula. There would then be no problem distinguishing Indians from pure-blooded Spaniards.

Hacienda Wealth

The outside world was becoming aware of the Peninsula, its newly found economic activity, and its rich *patrones*. In 1908, an American journalist, John Kenneth Turner, stirred things up when he documented the difficult lives of the Indian plantation workers, and the accompanying opulence enjoyed by the owners. From this time forward, reform was inevitable. In 1915, wealthy hacienda owners were compelled to pay an enormous tax to then-President Venustiano Carranza. This tax was forcibly extracted under the watchful eye of General Alvarado and 7,000 armed soldiers, who needed the money to put down revolutionaries Emiliano Zapata and Pancho Villa in the northern regions of Mexico. Millions of pesos changed hands.

The next thorn in the side of the hacienda owners was upstart Felipe Carrillo Puerto, the first socialist governor of Mérida. Under his tutelage the Indians set up a labor union, educational center, and political club that amounted to

Hacienda Yaxcopoil dates back to the turn of the century

leagues of resistance. These leagues gave the *peones* the first secular hope ever held out to them. Through them, workers wielded a power that wealthy Yucatecans were forced to acknowledge. Carrillo pushed on, making agrarian reforms at every turn. He decreed that abandoned haciendas were up for appropriation by the government. He was so successful that his opponents began to worry seriously about the power he was amassing. With the number of his followers growing, conservatives saw only one way to stop him. In 1923, Felipe Carrillo Puerto was assassinated.

The Revolution
The fight against wealthy landowners and the power elite did not die with Carrillo. In the south, Emiliano Zapata was demanding land reform; shortly thereafter, the revolution put an end to the elitist control of wealth in the country. The constitution of 1917 had made some inroads. It was instrumental in dividing up the large haciendas, giving the country back to the people (*some* of the people), and making sweeping political changes. The education of all children was mandated and many new schools were built. Power of the church was curtailed and church land redistributed.

In this war of ideals, however, Indian villages were broken up along with the large haciendas, and turmoil continued. Again it was the rich against the poor; a whole new class of rich had been created, those who had the new power. In 1936, President Lázaro Cárdenas (1934-40)

declared Quintana Roo a territory of the Mexican government. It wasn't until later years that some of the Indians received favorable treatment, when President Cárdenas gave half the usable land in Quintana Roo to the poor. In 1974, with the promise of tourism, the territory was admitted to the Federation of States of Mexico.

Mexican Unity
Between 1934 and 1940, the Mexican government nationalized most foreign companies, which were taking more out of the country than they were putting in. Mexico suffered through a series of economic setbacks but gained unity and national self-confidence. Like a child learning to walk, the country took many falls. But progress continued; the people of the country saw more jobs, fairer wages, and more products on the market. The progress lasted until the 1970s, when inflation began to rise. By 1976 it was totally out of hand. Mexico was pricing itself out of the market, both for tourists and capital investors. Eventually, a change in the monetary policy let the peso float, finding its own value against the dollar. The policy brought back tourists and investors.

The condition of the peso is a boon for visitors, but a burden for the people. The belief is that enough tourism will create more jobs so that the economic condition will ultimately remedy itself. Smart Mexican businesspeople began developing the natural beauty of the Caribbean coast, and indeed visitors are coming from all over the world.

GOVERNMENT

Theoretically, Mexico enjoys a constitutional democracy modeled after that of the United States. A president, a two-house congress, and a judiciary branch see to the business of running the country. Theoretically, Mexico's elections are free. Realistically, for 66 years the country has been controlled by one party, the PRI (Partido Revolución Institutional, or Institutional Revolution Party). Political dissent—represented primarily by PAN (Partido Acción Nacional) and PMS (Partido Mexicano Socialista)—has never had much voice. The president, who can serve only a single six-year term, hand-picks the next PRI candidate who historically has been guaranteed the office through use of the state-controlled media and dubious election procedures.

In addition to Mexico's 32 states, the country has the *Distrito Federal,* or Federal District in Mexico City, which encompasses the government center. The states are allowed a small measure of autonomy, but the reach of the federal government is long. City mayors, called *presidentes municipales,* appoint federal *delegatos* to represent the national government at the municipal level.

Fraud and corruption have been ugly mainstays of Mexican government from its beginning. In the 1988 presidential election, PRI candidate Carlos Salinas Gortari officially garnered 51% of the vote, a figure many critics believe was invented by the PRI after polls closed. (A suspicious "breakdown" in the election computer delayed the results for several days.)

But Salinas's term will likely be remembered as a time of historic reforms, such as expanding the number of Senate seats to allow more for the opposition, limiting campaign spending, and changing the rules of the body that oversees Mexican elections.

The only certainty in Mexico's tumultuous political arena is that, after decades of a government static in its ways, things are changing fast. The U.S. Congress's passage of NAFTA in 1993 sealed a free-trade deal between Mexico, the U.S., and Canada that will likely change Mexico's economic landscape forever—the political ramifications of which are still unclear. The March 1994 election-year shooting of PRI presidential candidate Luis Donaldo Colosio in Tijuana was Mexico's first major political assassination since 1928. Soon after, Colosio's campaign manager, technocrat Ernesto Zedillo, was nominated to fill the candidacy. Mexico's political future is anyone's guess.

ECONOMY

Mexico's chief industries are oil, mining, and tourism. Mexican oil is produced by Pemex, the national corporation, and most is shipped at OPEC prices to the U.S. (its number-one customer), Canada, Israel, France, and Japan. Rich in natural gas, the country sends the U.S. 10% of its total output. Two-thirds of Mexico's export revenue comes from fossil fuels.

The Yucatán
The leading industry on the Yucatán Peninsula is the oil business. Along the Gulf coast from Campeche south into the state of Tabasco, the oil industry is booming. Yucatán cities are beginning to show signs of good financial health.

Yucatecan fisheries are abundant along the Gulf coast. At one time fishing was not much more than a ma-and-pa business here, but today fleets of large purse seiners with their adjacent processing plants can be seen on the Gulf of Mexico just south of the city of Campeche and on Isla del Carmen. With the renewed interest in preserving fishing grounds for the future, the industry could continue to thrive for many years.

Tourism is developing into the number-two contributor to the economy. Going with a good thing, the government has set up a national trust to finance a program of developing beautiful areas of the country to attract visitors. Cancún is the most successful thus far.

Cancún
Until the 1970s Quintana Roo's economy amounted to very little. For a few years the chi-

henequen leaves

Agriculture

The land in the northernmost part of the Yucatán was described by Diego de Landa, an early Spanish priest, as "a country with the least earth ever seen, since all of it is one living rock." Surprisingly, the thin layer of soil is enough to support agriculture. This monotonous landscape is dotted with a multitude of sword-shaped plants called henequen. At the turn of the century, Spanish settlers on the Peninsula made vast fortunes growing and selling henequen, which was used for rope-making. However, it was the Maya who showed the Spanish its many valuable uses, especially for building their houses. Without nails or tools, houses were tied together with handmade henequen twine. Wherever palapa-style structures are built today by the Indians, the same nail-free method is used.

With careful nurturing of the soil, the early Indians managed to support a large population of people on the land. Though rainfall is spotty and unreliable, the land is surprisingly fertile and each year produces corn and other vegetables on small farms. The northern tip of the Peninsula can be dry and arid. On the northwest edge where trade winds bring more rain, the land is slightly greener. As you travel south, the desert gradually becomes green until you find yourself in a jungle plain at Quintana Roo fringed by the turquoise Caribbean and the Río Hondo.

Along the coast of Quintana Roo, remnants of large coconut plantations, now broken up into small tracts and humble ranchitos, are being developed by farmers with modest government assistance. At one time it was commonplace to see copra lining the roadside, drying in the sun. The number of coconut trees afflicted with "yellowing disease" in the Yucatán has greatly decreased the output of copra in the state. The disease and Hurricane Gilbert combined to turn what was once a mixture of thick, lush coconut trees and rich, verdant jungle into what looks like a war zone, with dead limbs and topless coconut trees. Fortunately the jungle rejuvenates quickly, and within a few more years nature will cover the dead with new growth. As for the coconut trees, new strains are being planted that are resistant to this dreadful disease.

Different parts of the Peninsula produce different crops. In most areas juicy oranges grow,

cle boom brought a flurry of activity up and down the state. At that time chicle, used to make chewing gum, was shipped from the harbor of Isla Cozumel. Native and hardwood trees have always been in demand; coconuts and fishing were the only other natural resources that added to the economy—but neither on a large scale. With the development of an offshore sandbar—Cancún—into a multimillion-dollar resort, tourism is now its number-one money-maker. Cancún is one of Mexico's most modern and popular resorts. Construction is continuing south along the coast. Other naturally attractive sites are earmarked for future development, and the corridor south of Cancún is already showing signs of growth with several new resorts, a marina, an 18-hole golf course, and talk of another international airport. New roads give access to previously unknown beaches and often-unseen Maya structures. Extra attention is going to archaeological zones ignored for hundreds of years, and to building restrooms, ticket offices, and fences to keep out vandals.

which you can find for sale everywhere; in the marketplace and at roadside stands, vendors often remove the green peel, leaving the sweet fruit ready to eat. The earliest chocolate drink was developed by the Indians in Mexico and presented to the Spanish. Today chocolate manufactured in Mexico is shipped all over the world. Bananas of many kinds, from finger-size to 15-inch red plantains, are grown in thick groves close to the Gulf coast. Tabasco bananas are recognized worldwide as among the finest.

Many of the crops now produced by American farmers were introduced by the Maya and Aztecs, including corn, sweet potatoes, tomatoes, peppers, squash, pumpkin, and avocados. Many other products favored by Americans are native to the Yucatán Peninsula: papaya, cotton, tobacco, rubber, vanilla, and turkey.

PEOPLE

Today, 75-80% of the entire population of Mexico is estimated to be mestizo (mixed blood, mostly Indian and Spanish), with 10-15% pure Indian. For comparison, as recently as 1870, pure-blooded Indians made up over 50% of the population. While no statistics are available, it's believed most of the country's pure Indians live on the Peninsula (including the state of Chiapas).

Language
The farther you go from a city, the less Spanish and more Mayan, or a dialect of Mayan, you'll hear. The government estimates that of the 10 million Mexican Indians in the country, about 25% speak only an Indian dialect. Of the original 125 native languages, 70 are still spoken, 20 of which are classified as Maya languages, including Tzeltal, Tzotzil, Chol, and Yucatec Mayan. Mexican education was made compulsory in 1917, though like most laws this one didn't reach the Yucatán Peninsula till quite recently. Despite efforts to integrate the Indian into Mexican society, many remain content with the status quo. Schools throughout the Peninsula use Spanish-language books, even though many children speak only a Maya dialect. In some of the smaller, more rural, schools (such as in Akumal), bilingual teachers are recruited to help children make the transition.

Higher Education
Though education is free, many rural parents need their children to help with work on the ranchito. That and the cost of books still prevent many Yucatecan children from getting a higher education. For years, Peninsula students wanting an education had to travel to the university at Mérida. Now though the number of students going on to college grows with each generation, and universities are slowly being built, the state of Quintana Roo still does not have a university. College is available in Campeche and Tabasco, and another one has been built in Mérida.

Housing And Family
The major difference in today's rural housing is the growth of the ranchito. Only one hut sits on a family farm that raises corn, sometimes a few pigs and turkeys, and maybe even a few head of cattle. While far from posh, the Indians' homes have become slightly more comfortable than their ancestors', commonly furnished with a table and chairs, a lamp, and maybe a metal bathtub. In southern Quintana Roo huts are often built of planks and have tin roofs. In the north many are constructed with stucco walls. Many huts have electric lighting and TV antennae and some even have refrigerators.

Until recently families usually had many children. A man validated his masculinity and gained respect by having a large family. The labor around the family plot was doled out to children as they came along.

The Maya
Maya men and women average 1.62 (five feet six inches) and 1.5 (four feet eleven inches) meters tall respectively. Muscular bodied, they have straight black hair, round heads, broad faces with pronounced cheekbones, aquiline noses, almond-shaped dark eyes, and eyelids with the epicanthic or Mongolian fold.

Bishop Diego de Landa writes in his *Relaciones* that when the Spanish arrived, the Maya still practiced the ancient method of flattening a newborn's head with a wooden press. By pressing the infant's forehead, the fronto-nasal portion of the face was pushed forward, as can be seen

teacher and students

in carvings and other human depictions from the pre-Columbian period. This was considered a beautiful trait by the Maya. They also dangled a bead in front of a baby's eyes to encourage cross-eyedness, another Maya beauty mark. Dental mutilation was practiced by filing the teeth to give them different shapes or by inlaying carvings with pyrite, jade, or turquoise. Tattooing and scarification were accomplished by lightly cutting a design into the skin and purposely infecting it, creating a scar of beauty. Adult noblemen often wore a phony nosepiece to give the illusion of an even longer nose sweeping back into the long, flat forehead.

ANCIENT CULTURE OF THE YUCATAN PENINSULA

ORIGINS OF THE MAYA

The origins of the Maya world lie in the Pacific coastal plains of Chiapas and Guatemala. From here, Maya culture slowly moved north and west to encompass all of Guatemala, the Yucatán Peninsula, most of the states of Chiapas and Tabasco, and the western parts of Honduras and El Salvador. The earliest traces of human presence found in this area are obsidian spear points and stone tools dating back to 9000 B.C. The Loltún caves in the Yucatán contain a cache of extinct mammal bones, including mammoth and early horse, which were probably dragged there by a roving band of hunters. As the region dried out and large game disappeared over the next millennia, tools of a more settled way of life appeared, like grinding stones for preparing seeds and plant fibers. The first sedentary villages began to appear after 2000 B.C. With them came the hallmarks of a more developed culture: primitive agriculture and ceramics.

PROTO-MAYA

Archaeologists believe that the earliest people we can call Maya, or proto-Maya, lived on the Pacific coast of Chiapas and Guatemala. These tribes lived in villages that may have held over 1,000 inhabitants and made beautiful painted and incised ceramic jars for food storage. After 1000 B.C. this way of life spread north to the highlands site of Kaminaljuyú (now part of Guatemala City) and, over the next millennium, to the rest of the Maya world. Meanwhile, in what are now the Mexican states of Veracruz and Tabasco to the northwest, another culture, the Olmecs, was developing what is now considered Mesoamerica's first civilization. Its influence was felt throughout Mexico and Central America. Archaeologists believe that before the Olmecs disappeared around 300 B.C. they contributed two crucial cultural advances to the Maya: the long-count calendar and the hieroglyphic writing system, though some researchers think the latter may have actually originated in the Zapotec culture of Oaxaca.

During the Late Preclassic era (after 300 B.C.), that same Pacific coastal plain saw the rise of a Maya culture at a place called Izapa near Tapachula, Chiapas. The Izapans worshipped gods that are obviously precursors of the Classic Maya pantheon and commemorated religious and historical events in bas-relief carvings that emphasized costume and finery. All that was missing were long-count dates and hieroglyphs. Those appeared as the Izapan style spread north into the Guatemalan highlands. This was the heyday of Kaminaljuyú, which grew to enormous size, with over 120 temple-mounds and numerous stelae. The earliest calendar inscription that researchers are able to read comes from a monument found at El Baúl to the southwest of Kaminaljuyú; it has been translated as A.D. 36. The Izapan style's northernmost reach was Yucatán's Loltún caves, where an Izapan warrior-relief is carved out of the rock at the cave entrance.

In the Petén jungle region just north of the highlands, the dominant culture was the Chicanel, whose hallmarks are elaborate temple-pyramids lined with enormous stucco god-masks (as in Kohunlich). The recently excavated Petén sites of Nakbé and El Mirador are the most spectacular Chicanel cities yet found. El Mirador contains a 70-meter-tall temple-pyramid complex that may be the most massive structure in Mesoamerica. Despite the obvious prosperity of this region, there is almost no evidence of long-count dates or writing systems in either the Petun jungle or the Yucatán Peninsula just to the north.

The great efflorescense of the southern Maya world stops at the end of the Late Preclassic (A.D. 250). Kaminaljuyú and other cities were abandoned, and researchers believe that the area was invaded by Teotihuacano warriors extending the reach of their Valley of Mexico-based empire. In the Yucatán Peninsula, there is evidence of Teotihuacano occupation at the Río Bec site of Becán and at Acanceh near Mérida. You can see Teotihuacano-style costumes and gods in carvings at the great Petún city of Tikal and at Copán in Honduras. By A.D. 600, the Teotihuacano empire had collapsed, and the stage was set for the Classic Maya era.

MAYA HEARTLAND

The heartland of the Classic Maya (A.D. 600-800) runs from Copán in Western Honduras through the Petun region to Tikal, and ends at Palenque in Chiapas. The development of these city-states, which also included Yaxchilán and Bonampak, almost always followed the same pattern. Early in this era, a new and vigorous breed of rulers founded a series of dynasties across the region bent on deifying themselves and their ancestors. All the arts and sciences of the Maya world, from architecture to astronomy, were focused on this goal. The long-count calendar and the hieroglyphic writing system were the most crucial tools in this effort, as the rulers needed to recount the stories of their dynasty and of their own glorious careers. During the Classic era, painting, sculpture, and carving reached their climax; objects like Lord Pacal's sarcophagus lid from Palenque are now recognized as among the finest pieces of world art.

Royal monuments stood at the center of large and bustling cities. Cobá and Dzibilchaltún each probably hosted 50,000 inhabitants, and there was vigorous inter-city trade. In the northern area, the largest Classic era cities, including the Río Bec sites and Cobá, are more obscure to travlelers due to their relatively poor state of preservation. Each Classic city-state reached its apogee at a different time—the southern cities generally peaked first—but by A.D. 800 nearly all of them had collapsed and were left in a state of near-abandonment.

The Classic Maya decline is one of the great enigmas of Mesoamerican archaeology. There are a myriad of theories—disease, invasion, etc.—but many researchers now believe the collapse was caused by starvation brought on by over-population and destruction of the environment. With the abandonment of the cities, the Classic Maya's cultural advances disappeared as well. The last long-count date was recorded in 909, and many religious customs and beliefs were never seen again.

NORTHERN YUCATAN

However, Maya culture was far from dead; the new heartland was the northern end of the Yucatán Peninsula. Much archaeological work remains to be done in this area, and there are a number of controversies now raging as to who settled it where and when. For a brief period between A.D. 800 and 925, it was the Puuc region's turn to prosper. The art of architecture reached its climax in city-states like Uxmal, where the Nunnery Quadrangle and the Governor's Palace are considered among the finest Maya buildings. After the Puuc region was abandoned, almost certainly due to a foreign invasion, the center of Maya power moved east to Chichén Itzá. The debate rages as to who built (or re-built) Chichén, but the possibilities have narrowed to two tribes: Putún Maya warrior-traders and/or Toltecs escaping political strife in their Central Mexican homeland. Everyone agrees that there is Mexican influence at Chichén; the question is, was it carried by the Putún or by an invading Toltec army?

During the Early post-Classic era (A.D. 925-1200), Chichén was the great power of northern Yucatán. Competing city-states either bowed before its warriors or, like the Puuc cities and Cobá, were destroyed. After Chichén's fall in 1224—probably due to an invasion—a heretofore lowly tribe calling themselves the Itzá became the Late Post-Classic (1200-1530) masters of Yucatecan power politics. The Itzá's ruling Cocom lineage was finally toppled in the mid-15th century.

Northern Yucatán dissolved into an unruly group of jealous city-states ready to go to war with each other at a moment's notice. By the time of the Spanish conquest, culture was once again being imported from outside the Maya world. Putún Maya seafaring traders brought new styles of art and religious beliefs back from their trips to Central Mexico. Their influence may be seen in the Mixtec-style frescoes at Tulúm on the Quintana Roo coast.

MAYAPAN

Kukulcán II of Chichén Itzá founded Mayapán between A.D. 1263 and 1283. After his death and the abandonment of Chichén, an aggressive Itzá lineage named the Cocom seized power and used Mayapán as a base to subjugate northern Yucatán. They succeeded through wars using Tabascan mercenaries and intermarrying with other powerful lineages. Foreign lineage heads were forced to live in Mayapán where they could easily be controlled. At its height, the city covered 6.5 square km within a defensive wall that contained over 15,000 inhabitants. Architecturally, Mayapán leaves much to be desired; the city plan was haphazard, and its greatest monument was a sloppy, smaller copy of Chichén's Pyramid of Kukulcán.

The Cocom ruled for 250 years until A.D. 1441-1461, when an upstart Uxmal-based lineage named the Xiu rebelled and slaughtered the Cocom. Mayapán was abandoned and Yucatán's city-states weakened themselves in a series of bloody intramural wars that left them hopelessly divided when it came time to face the conquistadors.

RELIGION AND SOCIETY

The Earth

The Maya saw the world as a layered flat square. At the four corners (each representing a cardinal direction) stood four bearded gods called Becabs who held up the skies. In the underworld, four gods called Pahuatuns steadied the earth. The layered skies and underworld were divided by a determined number of steps up and down. Each god and direction was associated with a color: black for west, white for north, yellow for south, and most important, red for east. In the center of the earth stood the Tree of Life, "La Ceiba." Its powerful roots reached the underworld, and its lofty foliage swept the heavens, connecting the two. The ceiba tree was associated with the color blue-green (*yax*) along with all important things—water, jade, and new corn.

The Indians were terrified of the underworld and what it represented: odious rivers of rotting flesh and blood and evil gods such as Jaguar, god of the night, whose spotty hide was symbolized by the starry sky. Only the priests could communicate with and control the gods. For this reason, the populace was content to pay tribute to and care for all the needs of the priests.

Ceremonies

Ceremony appears to have been a vital part of the daily lives of the Maya. Important rituals took place on specific dates of their accurate calendar; everyone took part. These activities were performed in the plazas, on the platforms, and around the broad grounds of the temple-cities. Sweat baths apparently were incorporated into the religion. Some rituals were secret and only priests took part within the inner sanctums of the temple. Other ceremonies included fasts, abstinences, purification, dancing, prayers, and simple sacrifices of food, animals, or possessions (jewelry, beads, and ceramics) amid clouds of smoky incense.

The later Maya took part in self-mutilation. Carvings found at several sites depict an Indian pulling a string of thorns through a hole in his tongue or penis. The most brutal ceremonies involved human sacrifice. Sacrificial victims were thrown into a sacred well; if they didn't drown within a certain length of time (often overnight), they were rescued and then expected to relate the conversation of the spirits who lived in the bottom of the well. Other methods of sacrifice were spearing, beheading, or removing the heart of the victim with a knife and offering it still beating to the spirits.

Although old myths and stories say young female virgins were most often sacrificed in the sacred cenotes, anthropological dredging and diving in the muddy water in various Peninsula ruins has turned up evidence suggesting most of the victims were young children, both male and female.

Time

The priests of the Classic period represented time as a parade of gods who were really numbers moving through Maya eternity in careful mathematical order. They were shown carrying heavy loads with tumplines around their heads. The combination of the gods and their burdens reflected the exact number of days gone by since the beginning of the Maya calendar count. Each god has particular characteristics; number nine, an attractive young man with the spots of a serpent on his chin, sits leaning forward, jade necklace dangling on one knee, right hand reaching up to adjust his tumpline. His load is the screech

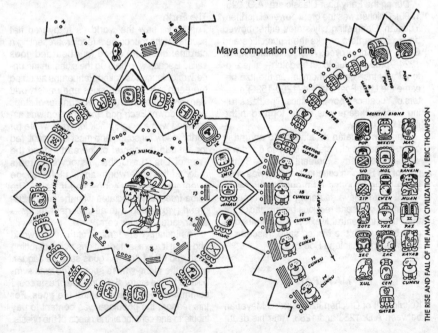

Maya computation of time

THE RISE AND FALL OF THE MAYA CIVILIZATION, J. ERIC THOMPSON owl of the *baktun* (the 144,000-day period). Together, the two represent nine times 144,000, or 1,296,000 days—the number of days elapsed since the beginning of the Maya day count and the day the glyph was carved, maybe 1,275 years ago. Archaeologists call this a long-count date. Simpler methods also were used, including combinations of dots and bars (ones and fives, respectively, with special signs for zero). Most Mayanists agree that the date of the beginning of the long count was 10 August 3114 B.C.

Status

If the Maya's sophisticated calendar sounds complicated, so will the complex, stratified society that made up the Maya civilization. Their society of many classes was headed by the elite, who controlled matters of warfare, religion, government, and commerce. Also in this group were architects who designed the magnificent temples and pyramids. Skilled masons belonged to a class that included servants of royalty. Priests directed the people in the many rites and festivals demanded by a pantheon of gods.

Farmers were instrumental in maintaining the social order. They battled a hostile environment, constantly fighting the jungle and frequent droughts. Creativity enabled them to win out most of the time. They slashed fields from rainforest, constructed raised plots in swampy depressions, and built irrigation canals. In some areas farmers terraced the land to conserve soil and water. The results of working by hand and using stone and wood tools were sufficient to feed a growing population. All aspects of Maya life were permeated by the society's religion.

THE ARTS

Pottery

The Maya were outstanding potters. Some of the earliest Maya pottery, found at Izapan, dates to 36 B.C. Evidence of artistic advancement is apparent in the variety of new forms, techniques, and artistic motifs that developed during the Classic period. Growth has been traced from simple monochrome ceramics of early periods to bichrome and later to rich polychrome. Polychrome drawings on pottery work have been found with recognizable color still visible. Three-legged plates with a basal edge and small con-

ical supports, as well as covered and uncovered vessels, were prevalent. A jar with a screw-on lid was found recently in Río Azul, a Maya site in an isolated corner of Guatemala.

Figurines, especially those found in graves on the island of Jaina, were faithful reproductions of the people and their times. Many decorated pottery vessels used for everyday purposes tell us something about these people who enjoyed beauty even in mundane objects. Decorative motifs ranged from simple geometric designs to highly stylized natural figures to simple true-to-life reproductions. We have learned much from Maya artists' realistic representations of body alterations, garments, and adornments typical of their time. All social classes are represented: common men and women, nobility, priests, musicians, craftspeople, merchants, warriors, ball players, even animals. Many of these clay figurines were used as flutes, whistles, ocarinas, rattles, or incense holders. Noteworthy is the quantity of female figurines that represent the fertility goddess Ixchell.

Sculpture

The Maya used their great talent for sculpture almost exclusively to decorate temples and sanctuaries. They employed a number of techniques, which varied depending on the area and the natural resources available. They excelled in freestanding stone carving, such as the stelae and altars. In areas such as Palenque, where stone wasn't as available, stucco art is outstanding. The Indians added rubber to the plaster-and-water mixture, creating an extremely durable surface that would polish to a fine luster. In Palenque you'll see marvelous examples of stucco bas-reliefs adorning pyramids, pillars, stairways, walls, friezes, masks, and heads. Sculpting was done not only in stone but also in precious materials such as gold and silver. Some of the Maya's finest work was done in jade, a substance they held in great reverence.

Painting

Paints were of mineral and vegetable origin in hues of red, yellow, brown, blue, green, black, and white. Mural painting was highly refined by the Maya. Murals found in several ancient sites depict everyday life, ceremonies, and battle scenes in brilliant colors. Bright color was also applied to the carved stone structures, pyramids,

Maya art

where on the Yucatán Peninsula, in carved temple panels, on pyramid steps, and in stelae commonly installed in front of the great structures, carrying pertinent data about the buildings and people of that era. The most important examples of the system are the three codices that survived the coming of the conquistadors. In the codices, symbols were put carefully on pounded fig bark with brushes and various dyes developed from plants and trees. As with all fine Maya art, it was the upper class and priests who learned, developed, and became highly skilled in hieroglyphics. Science and artwork ceased suddenly with the end of the Classic period, around A.D. 900.

MAYA "BASKETBALL"

Ball courts were prevalent in the ceremonial centers located throughout the Yucatán Peninsula. Though today's Maya are peaceful, at one time bloody games were part of the ancient culture, as may be seen from the remaining artwork (for example the panel in Chichén Itzá's Temple of the Bearded Man). The carvings graphically show that the losing (or as a few far-out researchers have suggested, the winning) team was awarded a bloody death. The players were heavily padded with leather, and the object of the game was to hit a hard rubber ball into a cement ring attached to a wall eight meters off the ground. Legend says the game went on for hours and the winners (or losers) were awarded clothes and jewelry from the spectators.

and stelae. Today all color has disappeared from the outside of these buildings along with most of the finishing plaster that was used as a smooth coating over large building stones. When Cortés's men first viewed the coast of Tulúm, it must have been quite a sight to behold: brilliantly colored buildings in the midst of lush green jungle overlooking a clear turquoise sea.

HOUSING

SCIENCE

Maya inscriptions relate to calculations of time, mathematics, and the gods. Astronomy was also a highly developed science. The Maya shared their calendar system and concept of zero with other Mesoamerican groups, but they went on to perfect and develop their sophisticated calendar, more exact to a ten-thousandth of a day than the Gregorian calendar in use today.

Hieroglyphics
The hieroglyphics the Maya used in scientific calculations and descriptions are seen every-

Thanks to remaining stone carvings, we know that the ancient Maya lived in houses almost identical to the palapa huts that many Yucatán residents still live in today. These huts were built with tall, thin sapling trees placed close together to form the walls, then topped with a palapa roof. This type of house provided circulation through the walls, and the thick palapa roof allowed the rain to run off easily, keeping the inside snug and dry. In the early years there were no real doors, and furnishings were sparce. Then as now, families slept in hammocks, the coolest way to sleep. For the rare times when it

CHAC, THE MAYA RAIN GOD

Families today still maintain a small *milpa*, or cornfield. It is handled in much the same manner as in their ancestors' days, even down to a Chac ritual. Performed at the end of each April, the ceremony arouses Chacs from their seasonal sleep. Bowls of corn porridge are left at the four corners of a family's *milpa* for the Chacs—age-old deities, who are still treated with great respect. To anger the Chacs could bring a drought and without the yearly rains the corn crop fails. Today, corn is not the critical staple that it was before the days of stores and supermarkets; however, many poor villages still rely only on what the people raise in their fields to survive.

Corn, the sustenance of Maya life, was more than food. Legendary beliefs of human beginnings were intertwined with the magic of corn. This is seen in many of the remaining carvings and drawings (such as a fresco at the ruins of Tulúm showing human feet as corn). The crop was so significant to the Maya that everything else would stop when the signs implied it was time to plant the fields. In ancient times, it was Maya priests who calculated the perfect time to fire the fields before the rains. They did this by relating the ritual calendar to the solar year, as at Chichén Itzá during the vernal equinox. Today the farmer observes nature's phenomena such as the swarming of flying ants and the rhythm and frequency of croaking frogs—a Maya version of a Farmer's Almanac. However, many Maya still refer to the calendar keeper of the village.

Corn is still planted in the centuries-old method of the Maya. First trees and grasses are cut and left in the field to dry before being set aflame. The fire is allowed to burn until all is reduced to ash. A stick is used to poke a hole in the ash-covered earth, where seeds are then dropped one by one.

turned cold, tiny fires were built on the floor below the hammocks to keep the family warm. Most of the cooking was done either outdoors or in another hut. Often a small group of people—extended family—built their huts together on one plot and lived an almost communal lifestyle. If one member of the group brought home a deer, everyone shared in this trophy. Though changing, this is still commonplace throughout the rural areas of the Peninsula.

EARLY AGRICULTURE

Enriching The Soil

Scientists believe Maya priests studied celestial movements. A prime function performed in the elaborate temples, which were built to strict astronomical guidelines, may have been charting the changing seasons and deciding when to begin the planting cycle. Farmers used the slash-and-burn method of agriculture, and still do today. Before the rains began in the spring, Indians cut the trees on a section of land, leaving stumps about a half meter above ground. Downed trees were spread evenly across the landscape in order to burn uniformly; residual ash was left to nourish the soil. At the proper time, holes were made with a pointed stick, and precious maize kernels were dropped into the earth, one by one. At each corner (the cardinal points) of the cornfield, offerings of *pozole* (maize stew) were left to encourage the gods to give forth great rains. With abundant moisture, crops were bountiful and rich enough to provide food even into the following year.

The Maya knew the value of allowing the land to lay fallow after two seasons of growth, and each family's *milpa* (cornfield) was moved from place to place around the villages scattered through the jungle. Often, squash and tomatoes were planted in the shade of towering corn stalks to make double use of the land. Today, you see windmills across the countryside (many stamped "Chicago, Inc."); with the coming of electricity to the outlying areas, pumps are being

tortilla-makers from Los Almendros in Mérida

TORTILLAS

In the public market the fascinating tortilla shop is always the busiest place. Folks line up to buy two, four, or six kilograms of tortillas every day. The staple of the Mexican diet, they are still made by hand in many homes, but a large percentage of people buy them for a reasonable price, saving hours of work on the *metate* (grinder) and the *tornal* (griddle). One traveler tells of spending 20 minutes in fascinated concentration observing the whole operation: 50-pound plastic sacks of shucked corn kernels stacked in a corner of the stall, the machinery that grinds it, the pale yellow dough, the unsophisticated conveyor belt that carries the dough across the live-flame cooking surface, the patrons who patiently line up for the fresh results, and the baker who hands the traveler several tortillas hot off the fire along with a friendly smile that says thanks for being interested.

used to bring water from underground rivers and lakes to irrigate crops. Outside of irrigation methods, the Maya follow the same ancient pattern of farming their ancestors did.

Maize

Corn was the heart of Maya nutrition, eaten at each meal. From it the Indians made tortillas, stew, and beverages—some of them alcoholic. Corn cultivation was such a vital part of Maya life that it is represented in drawings and carvings along with other social and religious symbols. In their combination of beans and corn, the Maya enjoyed all the protein they needed. They did not raise livestock until Spanish times.

Corn tortillas are still a main staple of the Mexican people. Native women in small towns can be seen early in the morning carrying bowls of corn kernels on their heads to the tortilla shop for grinding into tortilla dough. This was done by hand for centuries—and still is in isolated places. With the advent of electricity on the Peninsula, it's become much quicker to pay a peso or two to grind dough automatically. Others pay a few more pesos (price is controlled by the government) and buy their tortillas by the kilo hot off the griddle.

ENTER THE SPANIARDS

When the conquistadors arrived in 1517, the Maya of northern Yucatán were too divided to put up a successful long-term resistance. Nevertheless, they fought fiercely, and Francisco de Montejo was not able to establish his capital, Mérida, until 1542. Sporadic revolts by Yucatecan Maya have continued over the centuries, with the last ending only in the early 1900s. In the late 19th century, the Chiapan Maya fought several pitched battles with the Mexican army. The Guatemalan Maya city-states were conquered by the brutal Pedro de Alvarado, ending almost all resistance by 1541. However, one tribe managed to evade the conquistadors and settled deep in the jungle on an island in the middle of Lake Petén. Their traditional Maya city-state, called Tayasol, thrived until 1697, when a Spanish army finally penetrated that remote zone.

KATHY ESCOVEDO SANDERS

OUT AND ABOUT
RECREATION

BULLFIGHTING

The bullfight is not for everyone. Many foreigners feel it's inhumane treatment of a helpless animal. The bullfight is a bloodsport; if you can't tolerate this sort of thing, you'd probably be happier not attending. Bullfighting is big business in Mexico, Spain, Portugal, and South America. The *corrida de toros* (running of the bulls) is made up of a troupe of (now) well-paid men all playing an important part in the drama. On Sundays and holidays, 50,000 people fill the country's largest arena in Mexico City for each performance. The afternoon starts off promptly at 4 p.m. with music and a colorful parade of solemn pomp with matadors, picadores on horseback, and banderilleros, plus drag mules and many ring attendants. The matadors ceremoniously circle the crowded arena to the roar of the crowd. The afternoon has begun!

Traditional customs of the ring have not changed in centuries. The matador is the star of the event. This ceremony is a test of a man and his courage. He's in the arena for one purpose, to kill the bull—but bravely and with artful moves. First the preliminary *quites* and then a series of graceful veronicas heighten the excitement brushing the treacherous horns with each move. The matador wills the animal to come closer with each movement of the muleta. An outstanding bullfighter performs his ballet as close to the bull's horns as possible, to the crowd's wild cheers. He must elude the huge beast with only a subtle turn of his body. To add to the excitement, he does much of this on his knees. At the hour of truth, the judge gives the matador permission to dedicate the bull to a special person in the crowd. He throws his *montera* (hat) to the honored person and prepares for his final, deadly maneuvers.

At just the right moment, he slips the *estoque* (sword) into the bull's neck. A perfect blow will sever the aorta, killing the huge animal instantly. If the matador displays extraordinary grace, skill, and bravery, the judge awards him the ears and the tail, and the crowd their uncontrollable respect.

Bullfighting has long been one of the most popular events in Mexico. Aficionados of this Spanish artform thrill to the excitement of the crowd, the stirring music, the grace and courage of a noble matador, and the bravery of a good bull. A student of Mexican culture will want to take part in the corrida, to learn more about this powerful art.

Art is the key word. A bullfight is not a fight, it is an artistic scene of pageantry and ceremony, handed down from the Middle Ages, that was once celebrated all over Europe.

Records of the first primitive bullfight come to us from the island of Crete, 2,000 years before the time of Christ. At the same time in Spain, savage wild bulls roamed the Iberian Peninsula. When faced with killing one of these vicious animals, young men, not to be outdone by the Cretans, would "dance" as close as possible to the brute to show their bravery before finally killing the animal with an axe.

The Romans began importing Spanish wild bulls for Colosseum spectacles and the Arabs in Spain encouraged *tauromaquia* (bullfighting). In 1090, El Cid (Rodrigo Díaz de Vivar), the hero of Valencia and subject of romantic legend, is believed to have fought in the first organized bull festival. He lanced and killed a wild bull from the back of his horse. In that era, only noblemen were allowed to use a lance, and the corrida soon became the sport of kings. Even Julius Caesar is said to have gotten in the ring with a wild bull. Bullfighting quickly became popular, and stood out as the daring event for the rich. In Spain, bullfights were held in that country's ancient Roman colosseums. A feast day celebration wasn't complete without a *corrida de toros.* Predictably, the number of noblemen killed while participating in this wild event began to grow and the bullfight soon became the subject of controversy.

In the 16th century, Pope Pius V issued a papal ban threatening to excommunicate anyone killed while bullfighting. This didn't dull the enthusiasm of the Spanish; the pope withdrew the ban, and the fights continued. Queen Isabella and then King Philip ordered the bullfights halted, and the fights ceased.

Since the lance was forbidden, commoners intrigued with the event began fighting bulls on foot, using a cape to hide the sword (*estoque*) and confuse the bull. This was the beginning of the corrida as we know it today.

The corrida has changed little in the past 200 years. The beautiful clothes originally designed by the famous artist Goya are still used. Richly embroidered silk capes draped over the arena railing add a festive touch. Even in the smallest Yucatán village corrida, the costume design persists. Though made of simple cotton, rather than rich satin and gold-trimmed silk, delicately embroidered with typical designs of the Yucatán, the torero's garb is striking.

Gone are the wild bulls; the animals, all of Spanish ancestry, are bred on large Mexican ranches just for the bullring. Only the finest, those showing superior strength, cunning, and bravery, are sent to the ring. *El toro* is trained for one shining day in the arena.

The season begins in December and lasts three months. The rest of the year the *novilleros* (neophyte matadors) are seen in plazas across the country. They must prove themselves in the arena before they are acknowledged as respected and highly paid matadors. Bullfighting is as dangerous now as when the pope tried to have it banned in the 16th century. Almost half of the most renowned matadors in the past 250 years have died in the ring.

Bullfights usually take place on Sunday afternoons; the best seats on the shady side of the arena (*la sombra*) cost more. Ask at your hotel or local travel agency for ticket information. But remember, the corrida is not for everyone.

DIVING AND SNORKELING

Not everyone who travels to the Yucatán Peninsula is a diver or even a snorkeler—at first! One peek through the "looking glass"—a diving mask—changes that. The Caribbean is one of the most notoriously seductive bodies of water in the world. Turquoise blue and crystal clear with perfect tepid temperature, Yucatán coastal waters, protected by offshore reefs, are ideal for a languid float during hot, humid days.

Snorkeling
You'll find that the sea is where you'll want to spend a good part of your trip. So even if you never considered underwater sports in the past, you'll probably be eager to learn. First-timers should have little trouble learning to snorkel. Once you master breathing through a tube, it's

snorkeling in Xelha Lagoon, Quintana Roo

large plate, thereby performing the duties of a solar collector. The sponge is another curious underwater creature and it comes in all sizes, shapes, and colors, from common brown to vivid red.

Choosing A Dive Company

Diving lessons are offered at nearly all the dive shops on the Peninsula. Before you make a commitment, ask about the instructor and check his accident record, then talk to the harbormaster, or if you're in a small village, ask at the local cantina. Most of these divers (many are American) are conscientious, but a few are not, and the locals know whom to trust.

Bringing your own equipment to Mexico might save you a little money, depending on the length of your trip and means of transportation. But if you plan on staying just a couple of weeks and want to join a group on board a dive boat by the day, it's generally not much more to rent a tank, which will save you the hassle of carrying your own.

Choose your boat carefully. Look it over first. Some aren't much more than fishing boats, with little to make the diver comfortable. Ask questions; most of the divemasters speak English. Does it have a platform for getting in and out of the water? How many tanks of air may be used per trip? How many dives? Exactly where are you going? How fast does the boat go and how long will it take to get there? Remember, some of the best dive spots might be farther out at sea. A more modern boat, while more expensive, might get you extra diving time.

Detailed information is available for divers and snorkelers who wish to know about the dive sites you plan to visit. Once you're on the Yucatán Peninsula, you'll find pamphlets and books available in dive shops. Look for Ric Hajovsky's detailed pamphlet on reefs, depths, and especially currents. Wherever diving is good, you'll almost always find a dive shop. There are a few high-adventure dives where diving with an experienced guide is recommended (see "Water Sports" in "Isla de Cozumel").

Underwater Hazards And First Aid

A word here about some of the less inviting aspects of marine society. Anemones and sea urchins are everywhere. Some can be dangerous if touched or stepped on. The long-spined,

simply a matter of relaxing and floating. Time disappears once you are introduced, through a four-inch glass window, to a world of fish in rainbow colors of garish yellow, electric blue, crimson, and a hundred shades of purple. The longer you look, the more you'll discover: underwater caverns, tall pillars of coral, giant tubular sponges, shy fish hiding on the sandy bottom, and delicate wisps of fine grass.

Scuba Diving

For the diver, there's even more adventure. Reefs, caves, and rugged coastline harbor the unknown. Ships wrecked hundreds of years ago hide secrets as yet undiscovered. Swimming among the curious and brazen fish puts you into another world. This is raw excitement!

Expect to see an astounding variety of fish, crustaceans, and corals. Even close to shore, these amazing little animals create exotic displays of shape and form, dense or delicate depending on species, depth, light, and current. Most need light to survive; in deeper, low-light areas, some species of coral take the form of a

black sea urchin can inflict great pain and its poison can cause an uncomfortable infection. Don't think that you're safe in a wetsuit and booties or even if wearing gloves. The spines easily slip through the rubber. In certain areas, such as around the island of Cozumel, the urchin is encountered at all depths and is very abundant close to shore where you'll probably be wading in and out; keep your eyes open. If diving at night, use your flashlight. If you should run into one of the spines, remove it quickly and carefully, disinfect the wound, and apply antibiotic cream. If you have difficulty removing the spine, or if it breaks, see a doctor—pronto!

Cuts from coral, even if just a scratch, will often cause an infection. Antibiotic cream or powder will usually take care of it. If you get a deep cut, or if minute bits of coral are left in the wound, a serious and long-lasting infection can ensue. See a doctor.

Wise divers watch out for the color red, as many submarine hazards bear that hue. If you scrape against red coral, or "fire coral," you'll feel a burning sensation that lasts anywhere from a few minutes to five days. On some, it causes an allergic reaction and will raise large red welts. Cortisone cream will reduce inflammation and discomfort.

Fire worms (also known as bristle worms), if touched, will deposit tiny, cactuslike bristles in the skin. They can cause the same reaction as fire coral. *Carefully* scraping the skin with the edge of a sharp knife (as you would to remove a bee stinger) might remove the bristles. Any leftover bristles will ultimately work their way out, but you can be very uncomfortable in the meantime. Cortisone cream helps relieve this inflammation, too.

Several species of sponges have fine, sharp spicules (hard, minute, pointed calcareous or siliceous bodies that support the tissue) that you should not touch with a bare hand. The attractive red fire sponge can cause great pain; a mild solution of vinegar or ammonia (or urine if there's nothing else) will help. The burning lasts a couple of days, and cortisone cream soothes. But don't be fooled by dull-colored sponges. Many have the same sharp spicules, and touching them with a bare hand is risky at best.

Some divers feel the need to touch the fish they swim with. A few beginners want an underwater picture taken of them feeding the fish—bad news! When you offer fish a tasty morsel from your hand, you could start an underwater riot. Fish are always hungry and always ready for a free meal. Some of those denizens of the deep may not be so big, but in the frenzy to be first in line, their very efficient teeth have been known to miss the target. Another way to save your hands from unexpected danger is to keep them out of cracks and crevices, where moray eels live. A moray will usually leave you alone if you do likewise, but their many needle-sharp teeth can cause a painful wound that's apt to get infected.

A few seagoing critters resent being stepped on, and they can retaliate with a dangerous wound. The scorpion fish, hardly recognizable with its natural camouflage, lies hidden most of the time on a reef shelf or the bottom of the sea. If you should step on or touch it you can expect a painful, dangerous sting. If this happens, see a doctor immediately.

Another sinister fellow is the ray. There are several varieties in the Caribbean, including the yellow and southern stingrays. If you leave them alone they're generally peaceful, but if you step on them they will zap you with a tail that carries a poisonous sting, which can cause anaphylactic shock. Symptoms include respiratory difficulties, fainting, and severe itching. Go quickly to the doctor and tell him what caused the sting. One diver suggests a shuffling, dragging-of-the-feet gait when walking on the bottom of the ocean. If bumped rather than stepped on, the ray will quickly flee. Jellyfish can also inflict a miserable sting. Avoid particularly the long streamers of the Portuguese man-of-war, though some of the smaller jellyfish are just as hazardous.

Whatever you do, don't let these what-ifs discourage you from an underwater adventure. Thousands of people dive in the Caribbean every day of the year and only a small number of accidents occur.

Note: Please don't touch the coral; doing so is a death sentence to the polyps!

OTHER ACTIVITIES

Water-skiing, Parasailing, Windsurfing
With so many fine beaches, bays, and coves along the Caribbean, all water sports are available. Because so many beaches are protected

SAFETY REFERENCES

Check with your divemaster about emergency procedures before your boat heads out to sea. A safety recompression chamber is located on Isla de Cozumel, tel. (987) 2-0140. Here are some other useful numbers:

La Costera (Coast Guard): Radio channel 16 (canal número diez y seis)

Divers Alert Network (DAN): tel. (919) 684-8111. Dial this number for information about Cozumel's recompression chamber or for assistance in locating a chamber in the U.S.

Air-Evac International: tel. (619) 278-3822. Located in San Diego, CA.

Life Flight: tel. (713) 797-4011, (800) 392-4357; in the U.S. tel. (800) 231-4357. Air ambulance service located in Houston, TX. Check with your medical insurance company; generally speaking, they will pay for these emergency services.

by the reef that runs parallel to Quintana Roo's east coast, calm **swimming beaches** are easy to find. Also, many hotels have pools. Waterskiing is good on Nichupté Bay in Cancún, and parasailing is popular there also. Windsurfing lessons and rental boards are available at most resort areas: Cozumel, Cancún, Akumal, and Playa del Carmen.

Fishing

A fishing license is required for all anglers 16 years or older. Good for three days, one month, or a year, licenses are available for a small fee at most fresh- and saltwater fishing areas. Ask in the small cafes at the more isolated beaches. Check with the closest Mexican consulate about where you can get a permit for your sportfishing craft; you can also get current information there on fishing seasons and regulations which vary from area to area. Fishing gear may be brought into Mexico without customs tax; however, the customs officials at the border crossing from Brownsville, Texas, into Mexico are notorious for expecting to have their palms greased before allowing the RVer or boater to cross the border. If you find yourself in this position, start with dollar bills (bring lots of them with you); several people

need to be soothed before you can cross. If you choose not to pay the bribe, they can keep you hanging around for hours, even days, before they will allow you to cross. Sadly, it's a no-win situation. For more fishing information write to: General de Pesca, Av. Alvaro Obregón 269, Mexico 7, D.F.

Birdwatching

Birdwatching is wonderful throughout the Yucatán. From north to south the variety of birds is broad and changes with the geography and the weather. Bring binoculars and wear boots and lightweight trousers if you plan on watching in jungle areas. Studying **tropical flora** is also a popular activity. For this you most certainly will be in the backcountry—don't forget bug repellent, and be prepared for an occasional rain shower, even in the dry season. For most orchids and bromeliads, look up in the trees, but remember, the Yucatán also has ground orchids. And please, don't take anything away with you except pictures.

Photography

There's a world of beauty to photograph here, what with the sea, the people, and the natural landscape of the Peninsula. If you plan on **videotaping,** check with your local Mexican tourist office for information on what you can bring into the country. Most archaeological zones prohibit tripods. For the photographer who wants to film *everything,* small planes are available for charter in the larger cities and resorts. In Cancún, for instance, you can take pictures from a plane that tours for about 15 minutes over Cancún and the surrounding coast. Per-person price is US$30-40. (For further info see "Photography" under "Services and Information," below.)

Sports

Tennis courts are scattered about Quintana Roo; the large hotels at Cancún, Akumal, Cozumel, and Puerto Aventuras have them. Bring your own racket. **Golf courses** are few, but you can plan on playing in Cancún and Puerto Aventuras. Another course is under construction at the new Playacar resort in Playa del Carmen.

ACCOMMODATIONS AND FOOD

The Yucatán Peninsula offers a wide variety of accommodations. There's a myriad of hotels to choose from in cities, villages, beach resorts, and offshore islands, in all price ranges. If you like the idea of light housekeeping and preparing your own food, condos are available in many locales. If your lifestyle is suited to outdoor living, beach camping is wonderful along the Caribbean, and the number of small bungalows for tourists is growing rapidly.

CAMPING

If you are traveling in your own vehicle, you must obtain a vehicle permit when entering the country. Camping with a vehicle allows you to become a "luxury camper," bringing all the equipment you'll need (and more!). A van or small camper truck will fit on almost any road you'll run into. With an RV you can "street camp" in the city. Parking lots of large hotels (check with the manager) or side streets near downtown activities are generally safe and offer easy access to entertainment.

Vehicle Supplies
A few reminders and some common-sense planning make a difference when traveling and camping with a vehicle. Near the Caribbean coast are many swampy areas, so check for marshy ground before pulling off the road. When beach camping, park above the high-tide line. Remember that gas stations are not as frequently found on the Peninsula as in most parts of Mexico. If you plan on traveling for any length of time, especially in out-of-the-way places, carry extra gas, and fill up whenever the opportunity arises. Along with your food supply, always carry enough water for both the car and passengers. Be practical and come prepared with a few necessities (see our checklist).

Sleeping Outdoors
Sleeping under a jeweled sky in a warm clime can be either a wonderful or an excruciating experience. (Two factors that will make or break it are the heat and the mosquito population in the immediate vicinity.) Some campers sleep in tents to get away from biting critters, which helps but is no guarantee; also, heat hangs heavily inside a closed tent. Sleeping bags cushion the ground but tend to be much too warm. If you have a bag that zips across the bottom, it's cooling to let your feet hang out (well marinated in bug repellent or wearing a pair of socks—a dark color the mosquitoes might not notice). An air mattress or foam pad softens the ground (bring along a patch kit). Mexican campers often just roll up in a lightweight blanket, covering all skin, head to toe, to defy possible bug attacks.

The most comfortable option (according to Yucatecans and backpackers) is to sling a hammock between two palm trees, protecting yourself with a swath of mosquito netting and bug repellent. Some put a lightweight blanket between themselves and the hammock strings. For a very small fee, many rural resorts provide palapa hammock-huts that usually include water (for washing only); these places are great if you want to meet other backpackers. Though they are fast giving way to bungalow construction, a few hammock-huts are still found along the Caribbean coast and in Palenque, Chiapas.

HOTELS

In many Peninsula cities, modern hotels are springing up faster than any guidebook can track, especially in Cancún. All are trying to outdo themselves in luxury, service, amenities, and beauty. As a result, by 1998, Cancún will probably offer a high concentration of world-class hotels. Today 18,000 rooms are available in the hotel zone; by 1998 Cancún is expected to have 26,000 rooms available to visitors from around the world.

Reservations
Traveling during the peak season (15 Dec.-15 April) requires a little planning if you wish to stay at the popular hotels. Make reservations in advance. Many hotels can be contacted through an 800 number, travel agency, or auto club. Many well-known American chains are

Some beach huts offer little more than sapling walls, thatch roof, and hammock hooks; this one goes further with hanging beds and mosquito netting.

represented in the larger resorts (Cancún, Isla Mujeres, Playa del Carmen, Mérida, Villahermosa), and their international desks can make reservations for you. Many now have fax numbers, much quicker than regular mail. If not, write to them direct and enclose a deposit check for one night (if you don't know how much, guess). Ask (and allow plenty of time) for a return confirmation. If you're traveling May-June or Sept.-Oct., rooms are generally available. Many parts of the coast are quiet in the summer. However, in July Cancún is the destination for many vacationing Mexican families, so reservations are suggested.

Luxury

Some of the familiar hotel names found in Quintana Roo are the Presidente, Camino Real, Hyatt, Sheraton, Omni, Holiday Inn Crowne Plaza, and Hilton. They offer endless luxuries, including lovely bathrooms—some with hair dryers, marble fixtures, separate showers, and

thick, fluffy towels—in-room safes, cable television, mini-bars, a/c, good beds, suites, junior suites, balconies, terraces, gorgeous ocean views, green garden areas, pools (one is a kilometer long) with swim-up bars, nightclubs and fabulous restaurants, entertainment, travel agents, car rentals, gift shops, and delicatessens; almost all accept credit cards. Refunds are handled on an individual basis.

Moderate

In most cities on the Peninsula it's not difficult to find moderate hotels; even in downtown Cancún and a few scattered locations within the hotel zone, moderate hotels are available. They aren't nearly as glitzy, probably don't have telephones or multiple restaurants and bars, maybe not even a swimming pool, and they are not on the beach. However, the better ones provide transportation or are close to a bus stop. Prices can be one-third the cost of those in the hotel zone.

Budget

Travelers looking to spend nights cheaply can find a *few* overnight accommodations in Cancún (the downtown area); more in Cozumel, Isla Mujeres, Playa del Carmen, Mérida, Villahermosa, Campeche, Tuxtla Gutiérrez, and San Cristóbal de las Casas; and many more along the Caribbean and Gulf of Mexico coast. During the peak season in Cancún it takes a little (sometimes a lot of) nosing around (starting out early in the day helps), but inexpensive hostelry is available, and searching for one offers a good way to see the city and meet friendly locals as well.

For the adventurer in small rural villages, ask at the local cantina, cafe, or city hall for hotel or boardinghouse-type accommodation. These hotels are *usually* clean, and more than likely you'll share a toilet and (maybe) a shower. Sometimes you'll share the room itself, a large area with enough hammock hooks scattered around the walls to handle several travelers. The informed budget traveler carries his or her hammock (buy it on the Yucatán Peninsula if you don't already have one—they're the best made) when wandering around the Caribbean. When staying in the cheaper hotels in out-of-the-way places, come prepared with toilet paper, towel, soap, and bug repellent, and expect to buy bottled drinking water. Most of the villages have a small cantina that serves a *comida cor-*

YOUTH HOSTELS

CREA Cancún
Km 3, 200 Boulevard Kukulcán,
Zona Hotelera Cancún,
Quintana Roo, Mexico

CREA Playa del Carmen
Take the road that goes behind the Pemex
station, look for the sign.

CREA Campeche
Av. Agustín Melgar s/n, Col. Buenavista
Campeche, Campeche, Mexico

CREA Chetumal
Alvaro Obregón y General Anaya s/n
Chetumal, Quintana Roo, Mexico

CREA Tuxtla Gutiérrez
Calz. Angel Albino Corzo #1800
Tuxtla Gutiérrez, Chiapas, Mexico

For more information write to:
CREA, Agencia Nacional de
Juvenil Glorieta Metro Insurgentes,
Local CC-11, Col. Juárez,
C.P. 06600 Mexico, D.F.,
tel. 5-25-2548, 5-25-2974

rida (set lunch), or ask your host; credit cards are *not* the norm. However, the price will be right and the family that runs it will offer a cultural experience you won't forget.

Youth hostels, though few and far between, are good bargains on the Peninsula, especially in Cancún.

Condominiums

Cancún has hundreds of condos lining the beach and many under construction. Isla Mujeres, Cozumel, Playa del Carmen, and Akumal have a few condominiums,
and others are sprouting up along the southern coastal beaches as well. If you're vacationing with family or a group, condo living can be a real money-saver while still providing the fine services of a luxury hotel. Fully equipped kitchens make cooking a snap. In many cases the price includes daily maid service. Some condos (like the Condumel on Isla Cozumel) welcome you with a refrigerator stocked with food basics; you pay only for the foods and beverages that you use each day. Details are given in the appropriate travel sections.

Time Shares

Time-share mania is putting down roots. One of the biggest complaints from travelers to Cancún, Puerto Aventuras, and Cozumel in the last couple of years concerns the salespeople who pester visitors to buy condos and time-share accommodations. Their come-on is an offer for a free breakfast and often a free day's rental of a motorbike, or some other freebies. After the breakfast or lunch, they give a sales presentation, a tour of the facilities, and then each guest gets a hard pitch from a very experienced salesperson. These people have learned American sales methods down to the nitty-gritty. If you succumb to the offer of free breakfast and aren't interested in buying, better practice saying *"No."*

FOOD

Taste as many different dishes as possible! You'll be introduced to spices that add a new dimension to your diet. Naturally, you won't be wild about everything—it takes a while to become accustomed to squid served in its own black ink, for instance! A hamburger might not taste like one from your favorite fast-food place back home. It should also not come as a shock to find that your favorite downhome Tex-Mex enchiladas and tacos are nothing like those you order in Mexican restaurants.

Seafood

You won't travel far before realizing that one of Yucatán's specialties is fresh fish. All along the Caribbean and Gulf coasts are opportunities to indulge in piscine delicacies: lobster, shrimp, red snapper, sea bass, halibut, barracuda, and lots more. Even the tiniest cafe will prepare sweet fresh fish à la Veracruz, using ripe tomatoes, green peppers, and onions. Or if you prefer, ask for the fish *con ajo,* sautéed in garlic and butter—scrumptious! Most menus offer an opportunity to order *al gusto* (cooked to your pleasure).

Try the unusual conch (*kaahnk*), which has been a staple in the diet of the Maya along the Caribbean coast for centuries. It's often used in ceviche. Some consider this dish raw; actually, the conch or fish is marinated in a lime dressing with onions, peppers, and a host of spices—very tasty! Often conch is pounded, dipped in egg and cracker crumbs, and sautéed quickly

KATHY ESCOVEDO-SANDERS

(like abalone steak in California), with a squirt of fresh lime. (If it's cooked too long it becomes tough and rubbery.)

If you happen to be on a boat trip during which the crew prepares a meal of fresh fish on the beach, more than likely you'll be served *tik n' chik* cooked over an open fire. The whole fish (catch of the day) is placed on a wire rack and seasoned with onions, peppers, and *achiote,* a fragrant red spice grown on the Peninsula since the time of the early Maya. Bishop Diego de Landa identified *achiote* in his *Relaciones,* written in the 1500s.

Wild Game

The Yucatecans are hunters, and if you explore the countryside very much, you'll commonly see men and boys on bicycles, motorscooters, or horses with rifles slung over their shoulders and full game bags tied behind them. Game found in the jungle varies. *Pato* (wild duck) is served during certain times of the year and is prepared in several ways that must be tried.

Restaurants

Most small cafes that cater to Mexican families are open all day and late into the night. The Mexican custom is to eat the heavier meal of the day 1-4 p.m. In most of these family cafes a

generous *comida corrida* (set lunch) is served at this time. If you're hungry and want an economical (but filling) meal, that's what to ask for; though you don't know exactly what's coming, you get a tableful of delights. Always expect a large stack of tortillas, and five or six small bowls filled with the familiar and the unfamiliar: it could be black beans, a cold plate of tomatoes and the delicious Yucatán avocado, or *pollo pibil* (chicken in banana leaves). Cafes in the larger hotels that cater to tourists don't serve this set meal. Late in the evening, a light supper is served 9-11 p.m. Hotels with foreign tourists offer dinner earlier to cater to British, Canadian, and American tastes. Some restaurants add a service charge onto the bill. If so, the check will say *incluido propina*. It's still gracious to leave a few coins for the waiter. If the tip isn't added to the bill, leaving 10-15% is customary.

Strolling musicians are common in Mexican cafes. If you enjoy the music, 10 pesos is a considerate gift.

In certain cities, cafes that cater to Mexicans will commonly serve free snacks in the afternoon with a beer or cocktail. The Café Prosperidad (Calle 56 #456A) in downtown Mérida is very generous with its *antojitos* (snacks). The place is always packed with locals ordering the *comida corrida,* complete with live entertainment and waitresses wearing a long version of the *huipil*. Here you'll get the real essence of the city, and you may be the only gringo present. Remember, we didn't say the cafe is spotless!

Yucatán has its own version of junk food. You'll find hole-in-the-wall stands selling *tortas* (sandwiches), tacos, tamales, or *licuados* (fruit drinks), as well as corner vendors selling mangos on a stick, slices of pineapple, peeled oranges, candies of all kinds (including tall pink fluffs of cotton candy), and barbecued meat. The public markets have foods of every description, usually very cheap. In other words, there's a huge variety to choose from, so have fun.

A ploy used by many seasoned adventurers when they're tired of eating cold food from their backpacks: In a village where there isn't a cafe of any kind, go to the local cantina (or grocery store, church, or city hall) and ask if there's a woman in town who (for a fee) would be willing to include you at her dinner table. Almost always you'll find someone, usually at a fair price (determine price when you make your deal). With any luck you'll find a woman renowned not only for her *tortillas por manos* but also for

fruit vendor

the tastiest *poc chuc* this side of Ticul. You gain a lot more than food in this arrangement; the culture swap is priceless.

Food Safety

When preparing your own food in the backcountry, a few possible sources of bacteria are fresh fruit and vegetables, especially those with thin skins that don't get peeled, like lettuce or tomatoes. When washing these foods in local water (and they should definitely be washed thoroughly before consuming), add either bleach or iodine (8-10 drops per quart) to the water. Soaking vegetables together in a container or plastic bag for about 20 minutes is easy; carrying along Ziploc bags is essential. If at the beach and short of water, substitute seawater (for everything but drinking). Remember not to rinse the bleached food with contaminated water, just pat dry, and if they have a distasteful lingering flavor, a squirt of lime juice tastes great and is very healthy. Some foods nature has packaged hygienically; a banana has its own protective seal so is considered safe (luckily, since they're so abundant on the Peninsula). Foods that are cooked and eaten immediately are also considered safe.

women with bowls of corn

BOB RACE

FIESTAS

Mexico knows how to give a party! Everyone who visits the Yucatán should take advantage of any holidays falling during the visit. Workers are given a day off on legal holidays. See the special topic "Holidays and Fiestas" for dates of the biggest fiestas.

As well as the public festivities listed, a birthday, baptism, saint's day, wedding, departure, return, good crop, and many more reasons than we'd ever think of are good excuses to celebrate with a fiesta. One of the simplest but most charming celebrations is Mother's Day in Playa del Carmen, Mérida, and many other colonial cities. Children both young and old serenade mothers (often with a live band) with beautiful music outside their windows on the evening of the holiday. If invited to a fiesta, join in and have fun.

Village Festivities

Half the fun of any fiesta is watching preparations, which generally take all day and involve everyone. Fireworks displays are set up by *especialistas* who wrap and tie bamboo poles together with packets of paper-wrapped explosives. At some point this often-tall *castillo* (structure holding the fireworks) will be tilted up and set off with a spray of light and sound followed by appreciative cheers of delight.

Village fiestas are a wonderful time of dancing, music, noise, colorful costumes, good food, and usually lots of drinking. A public fiesta is generally held in the central plaza surrounded by temporary stalls where you can get Mexican fast food: tamales (both sweet and meat), *buñuelos* (sweet rolls), tacos, *refrescos* (soft drinks), *churros* (fried dough dusted with sugar), *carne asada* (barbecued meat), and plenty of beer chilling in any convenient ice-filled container.

Beware "The Egg"

You'll find innocent-looking little old ladies selling eggshells filled with confetti, ready to be smashed on an unsuspecting head. So be prepared if you're the only gringo around! The more you respond good-naturedly, the more you will continue to be the target—and what the heck, whether the headache is from too much beer or too many eggs doesn't matter. (Besides, it might be time for you to plunk out a few pesos for your own bombs!)

A Marriage Of Cultures

Many festivals in Mexico honor religious feast days. You'll see a unique combination of religious fervor and ancient beliefs mixed with plain old good times. In the church plaza, dances passed down from family to family since before

Yucatecan dancers

HOLIDAYS AND FIESTAS

Jan. 1: **New Year's Day.** Legal holiday.

Jan. 6: **Día de los Reyes Magos.** Day of the Three Kings. On this day Christmas gifts are exchanged.

Feb. 2: **Candelaria.** Candlemas. Many villages celebrate with candlelight processions.

Feb. 5: **Flag Day.** Legal holiday.

Feb./March: **Carnival.** The week before Ash Wednesday, the beginning of Lent. Some of the best planned festivals of the year are held this week. In Mérida, Isla Mujeres, Cozumel, Campeche: Easter parades with colorful floats, costume balls, and sporting events. Chetumal: a parade with floats, music, and folk dances from all over Mesoamerica.

March 21: **Birthday of Benito Juárez** (1806). Legal holiday.
Vernal Equinox. Chichén Itzá: A phenomenon of light and shadow displays the pattern of a serpent slithering down the steps of the Pyramid of Kukulcán.

May 1: **Labor Day.** Legal holiday.

May 3: **Day of the Holy Cross.** Dance of the Pig's Head performed during fiestas at Celestún, Felipe Carrillo Puerto, and Hopelchén.

May 5: **Battle of Puebla,** also known as **Cinco de Mayo.** In remembrance of the 1862 defeat of the French. Legal holiday.

May 12-18: **Chankah Veracruz** (near Felipe Carrillo Puerto). Honors the Virgin of the Immaculate Conception. Maya music, bullfights, and religious procession.

May 15: **San Isidro Labrador.** Festivals held at Panaba (near Valladolid) and Calkini (southwest of Mérida).

May 20-30: **Becal.** Jipi Fiesta in honor of the plant *jipijapa,* used in making Panama hats, the big money-maker for most of the population.

June 29: **Day Of San Pedro.** All towns with the name of San Pedro. Fiestas held in Sanah-cat and Cacalchen (near Mérida), Tekom, and Panaba (near Valladolid).

Early July: **Ticul** (near Uxmal). Weeklong fiesta celebrating the establishment of Ticul. Music, athletic events, dancing, and fireworks.

Sept. 15: **Independence Day.** Legal holiday.

Sept. 27-Oct. 14: **El Señor de las Ampollas** in Mérida. Religious holiday. Big fiesta with fireworks, religious services, music, and dancing.

Oct. 4: **Feast Day of San Francisco de Asisi.** Usually a weeklong fiesta precedes this day in Uman, Hocaba, Conkal, and Telchac Pueblo (each near Mérida).

Oct. 12: **Columbus Day.** Legal holiday.

Oct. 18-28: **Izamal.** Fiesta honoring El Cristo de Sitilpech. A procession carries an image of Christ from Sitilpech to the church in Izamal. Religious services, fireworks, music, and dancing. Biggest celebration on the 25th.

Oct. 31: **Eve of All Souls' Day.** Celebrated all through the Yucatán. Flowers and candles placed on graves, the beginning of an eight-day observance.

Nov. 1-2: **All Souls' Day and Day of the Dead.** Graveside and church ceremonies. A partylike atmosphere in all the cemeteries. Food and drink vendors do a lively business, as well as candy makers with their sugar skulls and skeletons. A symbolic family meal is eaten at the gravesite.

Nov. 8: **Conclusion of El Día de Muerte.** Day of the Dead.

Nov. 20: **Día de la Revolución.** Revolution Day of 1910. Legal holiday.

Dec. 8: **Feast of the Immaculate Conception.** Fiestas at Izamal, Celestún (including a boat procession), and Chompotón (boat procession carrying a statue of Mary, water-skiing show, other aquatic events, dancing, fair).

Dec. 12: **Our Lady of Guadalupe.**

Dec. 25: **Christmas.** Legal holiday.

Cortés introduced Christianity to the New World continue for hours. Dancers dress in symbolic costumes of bright colors, feathers, and bells, reminding local onlookers about their Maya past. Inside the church is a constant stream of the candle-carrying devout, some traveling long distances on their knees to the church, repaying a promise made to a deity months before in thanks for a personal favor, a healing, or a job found.

Some villages offer a corrida (bullfight) as part of the festivities. Even a small town will have a simple bullring; in the Yucatán these rings are frequently built of bamboo. In Maya fashion, no nails are used—only henequen twine to hold together a two-tiered bullring! The country corrida has a special charm. If celebrating a religious holiday, a procession carrying the image of the honored deity might lead off the proceedings. The bull has it good here; there are no bloodletting ceremonies and the animal is allowed to live. Only a tight rope around its middle provokes sufficient anger for the fight. Local young men perform in the arena with as much heart and grace as professionals in Mexico City. And the crowd shows its admiration with shouts, cheers, and of course *música!*—even if the band is composed only of a drum, a trumpet, and a guitar. Good fun for everyone, even those who don't understand the art of the corrida.

Religious Feast Days

Christmas and Easter are wonderful holidays. The *posada* (procession) of Christmas begins nine days before the holiday, when families and friends take part in processions that portray Mary and Joseph and their search for lodging before the birth of Christ. The streets are alive with people, bright lights, and colorful nativity scenes. Families provide swinging piñatas (pottery covered with papier-mâché in the shape of a popular animal or perky character and filled with candy and small surprises); children and adults alike enjoy watching the blindfolded small fry swing away with a heavy board or baseball bat while an adult moves and sways the piñata with a rope, making the fun last, giving everyone a chance. Eventually, someone gets lucky and smashes the piñata with a hard blow (it takes strength to break it), and kids skitter around the floor retrieving the loot. Piñatas are common, not only for Christmas and Easter but also for birthdays and other special occasions in the Mexican home.

The Fiesta And Visitors

A few practical things to remember about fiesta times. Cities will probably be crowded. If you know in advance that you'll be in town, make hotel and car reservations as soon as possible. Easter and Christmas at any of the beach hotels will be crowded, and you may need to make reservations as far as six months in advance. Some of the best fiestas are in more isolated parts of the Yucatán and neighboring states. Respect the privacy of people; the Indians have definite feelings and religious beliefs about having their pictures taken, so ask first and abide by their wishes.

TRANSPORTATION

For centuries, getting to the Yucatán Peninsula required a major sea voyage to one of the few ports on the Gulf of Mexico, followed by harrowing and uncertain land treks limited to mule trains and narrow paths through the tangled jungle. Today the Peninsula is accessible from anywhere in the solar system! Arrive via modern airports, a network of new (good) highways, a reasonably frequent train system (very limited), or an excellent bus service that reaches large cities as well as an incredible number of small villages in remote areas.

BY CAR

Renting a car in Mexico is usually a simple matter but can cost much more than in the U.S.— and is always subject to Murphy's Law. If you know exactly when you want the car and where, it's helpful to make reservations in the States in advance. If you wait until you get to Mexico, you pay the going rate, which can add up to about $60 per day for a small car; most offices give little or no weekly discount. This is not to say that you can't take part in the favorite Mexican pastime, bargaining.

Car Rental

If it's just before closing time, and if someone has cancelled a reservation, and if it's off-season on the Peninsula, it's possible to get a car for a good rate. However, that's a lot of ifs to count on when you want and need a car as soon as you arrive. Also, it's often difficult to get a car without reservations; you may have to wait around for one to be returned.

Hertz, Avis, and Budget franchise representatives can be found in many parts of Mexico. United States corporate offices will honor a contract price made in the States before your arrival in Mexico. Avis is currently the cheapest of the big three (Avis, Hertz, and Budget all list 800 numbers in the Yellow Pages; ask for the international desk). Make your arrangements before you leave home. Always ask for the best deal, usually a weekly arrangement. Even if you only plan to use the car for four or five days, use your calculator; it might still be a better deal, especially with unlimited mileage thrown in. Hertz offers **Affordable Mexico,** which in the past was a good deal, but of late can't beat Avis's deal. If you belong to AAA or other auto clubs, the car rental agency might give you a 10-20% discount (be sure you bring your membership card), but not in conjunction with another special deal.

Another advantage to making advance reservations is the verification receipt. Hang onto it; when you arrive at the airport and show your verification receipt (be sure you get it back), a car will almost always be waiting for you. Once in a while you'll even get an upgrade for the same fee if your reserved car is not available. On the other side of the coin, be sure that you go over the car carefully before you take it far. Drive it around the block and check the following:

- Make sure there's a spare tire and working jack.
- All doors lock and unlock, including trunk.
- The seats move forward, have no sprung backs, etc.
- All windows lock, unlock, roll up and down properly.
- The proper legal papers are in the car, with address and phone numbers of associate car rental agencies in cities you plan to visit (in case of an unexpected car problem).
- Horn, emergency brake, and foot brakes work properly.
- Clutch, gearshift, all gears (including reverse) work properly.
- Get directions to the nearest gas station; the gas tank may be empty. If it's full it's wise to return it full, since you'll be charged top dollar per liter of gas. Ask to have any damage, even a small dent, missing doorknob, etc., noted on your contract, if it hasn't been already.
- Note the hour you picked up the car and try to return it before that time: a few minutes over will cost you another full day's rental fee.

When you pick up your rental car, the company makes an imprint of your credit card on a blank bill, one copy of which is attached to the papers you give the agent when you return the car. Keep in mind that the car agency has a limit on how much you can charge on one credit card at one time. If you go over the limit, be prepared to pay the balance in cash or with another credit card. If you pick up a car in one city and return it to another, there's a hefty drop-off fee (per km). Most agents will figure out in advance exactly how much it will be so that there aren't any surprises when you return the car.

In 99 cases out of 100, all will go smoothly. However, if you run into a problem or are overcharged, don't panic—charge everything and save all your paperwork; when you return to the States, make copies of everything and call the company; chances are very good that you'll get a refund.

Insurance
Rental car insurance runs about US$6 per day and covers only 80% of the damages (which many travelers are unaware of). However, it's dangerous to skip insurance; in most cases in Mexico, when there's an accident the police take action first and ask questions later. With an insurance policy, most of the problems are eased over. Rental agencies also offer medical insurance for US$4 per day. Your private medical insurance should cover this (check). Also, ask your credit-card provider exactly what insurance they provide when you rent a car.

Documents
An international driver's license is not required to drive or rent a car in Mexico. However, if you feel safer with it, get one from an auto club. At AAA in California you will need two passport pictures and US$10, along with a current driver's license from your home state. The international license is another good form of identification if you should have an accident or other driving problems.

When you cross the border from the U.S. into Mexico, your car insurance is no longer valid. You can buy insurance from AAA or an auto club before you leave home. Numerous insurance agencies at most border cities sell Mexican insurance: Sanborn's is one of the largest. Ask Sanborn's for their excellent free road maps of the areas you plan to visit. For more information write: Sanborn's Mexican Insurance Service, P.O. Box 1210, McAllen, TX 78501; tel. (512) 682-3401.

In the last 15 years highway construction has been priority work on the Peninsula. A growing number of well-engineered roads throughout the area provide access to cities and towns—many of them expensive toll roads. However, before taking your car into the country, consider the manufacturer and the condition of the car. Will parts be available in the event of a breakdown? Volkswagen, Renault, Ford, General Motors, and Chrysler have Mexican branches and parts should be available. If you drive an expensive foreign sports car or a large luxury model, you might be better off making other arrangements. Repairs might be unavailable and you could be stranded in an unlikely place for days waiting for a part. It's always wise to make sure you and the mechanic understand the cost of repairs before he begins—just like at home! **Note:** Selling your car in Mexico is illegal.

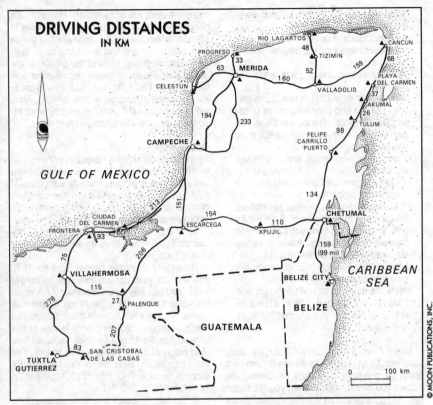

DRIVING DISTANCES
IN KM

RIO LAGARTOS
PROGRESO   48   CANCUN
33   TIZIMIN   68
63   MERIDA   159
CELESTUN   160   52   PLAYA
DEL CARMEN
VALLADOLID   37
AKUMAL
194   233   26
TULUM
FELIPE   98
CAMPECHE   CARRILLO
PUERTO

GULF OF MEXICO

213   151   154   134   CHETUMAL
CIUDAD   ESCARCEGA   110
DEL CARMEN   XPUJIL
FRONTERA   93
159
(99 mi)
75   206   CARIBBEAN
BELIZE CITY   SEA
VILLAHERMOSA
115   BELIZE
278   27   PALENQUE
GUATEMALA
83   SAN CRISTOBAL
TUXTLA   DE LAS CASAS
GUTIERREZ   0   100 km

© MOON PUBLICATIONS, INC.

Highways To Yucatán

In California, main highways cross the Mexican border from San Diego to Tijuana and from Calexico to Mexicali. From Arizona, go through Tucson to Nogales. From Texas, El Paso leads to Juárez, Eagle Pass to Piedras Negras, Laredo to Nuevo Laredo, and Brownsville to Matamoros. From each of these gateways, good highways bring you to the capital of the country, Mexico City.

From the capital the easiest and most direct route to Mérida and other Peninsula cities is Mex. 190D, a toll road to Puebla. At Puebla there's an interchange with Mex. 150D, another tollway that parallels the older free road (Mex. 150). On 150D you cross the plateau climbing to 2,385 meters at the summit of the Cumbres de Maltrata, after which a 22.5-km curving road drops you down quickly. Though this road is

often foggy, it beats the alternative—Mex. 150, which hairpins through the Cumbres de Acultzingo, a narrow, heart-thumping drop of 610 meters in only 11 km. Mexico 150D eliminates going through Mt. Orizaba; the old road (150) takes it in. In Cordoba 150D ends and the two roads meet; continue on 150 to the humid coastal plain. At Paso del Toro turn southeast onto 180, which leads to Veracruz, then continues through Coatzacoalcos to Villahermosa. From here you can continue on 186, which loops southeast, close to Palenque, and then north through Escarcega where the road meets 261. Stay on 186, travel due east across the Peninsula to Chetumal on the Caribbean coast. At Chetumal, 307 follows the coast northeast to Cancún. From Cancún, take 180 southwest to Mérida.

Another option from Villahermosa is to take 180 following the Gulf coast. This route includes

AIR ROUTES TO CANCUN

NEW YORK
LOS ANGELES
DALLAS
HOUSTON
MIAMI
HAVANA
TO PARIS
GUADALAJARA
MEXICO CITY   CHETUMAL   CANCÚN

© MOON PUBLICATIONS, INC.

several ferryboats (that have frequently interrupted schedules due to rough seas) and takes you through Isla del Carmen, Champotón, and Campeche, and then on to Mérida. With *no* delays, figure the trip from Villahermosa and Champotón to take about 8.5 hours.

Just past Villahermosa, 186 provides the fastest route to Champotón. Take 186 to Escarcega, turn onto 261 and follow it for 85 km to Champotón. Though longer, this is a much faster and less complicated route and avoids several ferries.

Driving Tips

In Mexico, it's recommended that you don't drive outside the cities at night unless it's a necessity. The highways have no streetlights—it's hard to see a black cow on a black road in the black night. Also, pedestrians have no other place to walk; shoulders are nonexistent on the roads. Public phones are few and far between, and

gas stations close when the sun goes down. If you should have a problem while driving during daylight hours on a *main* road, stay with your car. The Green Angels, a government-sponsored tow truck service, cruise the roads several times a day on the lookout for drivers in trouble. They carry gas and small parts and are prepared to fix tires. Each car is equipped with a CB radio and the driver is trained to give first aid, or will call a doctor. If you foolishly travel an isolated road after dark and break down, your best bet is to lock yourself in and stick it out for the night; go for help in the morning. The Mexican people are friendly, especially when they see someone in trouble; sometimes you have more help than you want.

A Word About Toll Roads

Toll roads are springing up all over Mexico. The fees are high and generally the highways are in great shape. In almost all cases, you can still use the old roads to get to your destination (which is what the budget minded locals use). Look for the signs that say *libre* (free); the toll road is the *cuota*. If you can't find the old road, ask a local.

BY PLANE

Today, planes fly to two international airports in Quintana Roo. The newest and most modern is at Cancún. Jets arrive daily, with connections from most countries in the world. It's also possible to fly internationally to the small island of Cozumel. In Quintana Roo there are several small landing strips for private planes and small commuter airlines.

AIRLINES SERVING THE YUCATAN PENINSULA

AIRLINE	TO	FROM
American	Cancún, Cozumel	Dallas, Fort Worth
Aeromexico	Cozumel, Mexico City, Mérida, Chetumal, Monterrey, Cancún	Houston, Los Angeles
Continental	Cancún, Cozumel	Los Angeles, Houston, Denver, San Francisco
Lacsa	Cancún	Guatemala, Costa Rica, New Orleans
Mexicana	Cancún, Cozumel	Miami, Dallas, Philadelphia
United	Cancún	Chicago

BY TRAIN

For many years Mexico has had a fairly efficient railway service, but recent reports say the service is slipping. Traveling by train used to be relaxing and the scenery outstanding. You still can make an entire trip from the States to Mérida by rail (then a 45-minute flight to Cancún). From several stateside cities along the border, buses or trains drop off passengers at Mexican train connections. For information on other departure points along the border plus schedules, prices, etc., deal directly with the railway companies; schedules and prices change frequently. Some travel agents have train information. Government tourist offices can give you schedules and prices for a specific trip, but some of these sources may not be accurate. Note: We have heard reports of robberies on some of the train routes in the Yucatán Peninsula.

BY BUS

Bus service to Quintana Roo is very efficient. Fares will fit the most meager budget, scheduling is frequent, and even the smallest village is accessible from most cities in northern Mexico. From the U.S. it's smart to make reservations with Greyhound or Trailways to your final destination on the Peninsula. The bus driver will take you to the border and then help you make the transfer (including your luggage) to a Mexican bus line. This service saves you a lot of time and confusion when in a strange bus station. When making return reservations, book them for cross-border travel, even if only to the first town on the U.S. side; again you will have an easier time crossing the border and making the connection. When NAFTA matures, transport across the border to Mexican destinations may become less complicated.

Class Choice

You have a choice of super-deluxe, deluxe, first-, second-, and third-class buses. Third-class passengers can bring their animals (and often do); second- and third-class buses are usually older models, with no toilets or a/c. Third-class bus tickets are cheap (as little as a Mexican dinner at Taco Bell in the U.S.). First-class and above

---

LUGGAGE TIP

For those who travel *light*, but don't want to carry a backpack, here's a great soft-sided bag that opens flat because of extra long zippers, allowing efficient packing in separate zippered compartments. It has a shoulder strap, fits under the seat on an airplane, and holds clothes and shoes to sustain the careful traveler for three weeks. Dimensions are 20 by 13 by 10 inches, made of durable puncture-resistant ballistic nylon. This is the way to go. Called the Easy Going carry-on, it is available at Easy Going Travel Shop 1385 Shattuck Ave., Berkeley, CA 94709, tel. (510) 843-3533; and 167 Locust, Walnut Creek, CA 94596, tel. (510) 947-6660. For *super efficiency,* either of these locations offers free packing demonstrations.

---

buses have assigned seats. Deluxe are more comfortable, have fewer seats, and are often triple the price, but are still very moderate compared to U.S. prices. Make reservations in advance. Your ticket will read *asiento* (seat) with a number. Some first-class buses sell food and drinks onboard. If you're traveling a long distance, buy at least first class; the difference in comfort is worth the small added expense. Second- and third-class buses stop for anyone who flags them, and at every small village along the way. First class operates almost exclusively between terminals. This cuts a lot of time off a long journey.

Luggage

If it fits in the overhead rack, almost anything can be carried on. Usual allowance is 25 kilograms, but unless you're ridiculously overloaded, no one ever objects to what you bring aboard. If a driver should refuse your load, you can usually come to an amicable (monetary) agreement. Larger luggage is carried in the cargo hold under the bus where breakables have a short lifespan. Purses and cameras are best kept between your feet on the floor, rather than in the overhead rack—just in case. Luggage should always be labeled, inside and out, with your name, address, and telephone number.

THE ANTHROPOLOGICAL MUSEUM OF MEXICO

Passing through Mexico City? Take at least one day to thoroughly explore the Anthropological Museum in Chapultepec Park. The park covers four square km, with a children's playground, a lake with boating activities, water birds including lovely white and black swans, a botanical garden, a zoo, Chapultepec Castle, and two important museums: Anthropological and Modern Art. The park is the scene of concerts, theater, children's programs, picnics—and much more. People of the city come to enjoy cultural offerings plus lawn, trees, and a feeling of being in the country.

Many flights to the Yucatán Peninsula from the U.S. stop in Mexico City for a change of planes. Though it would take days to really tour the capital city properly, while on your way to Mayaland a highly informative adjunct to your trip would be three days in Chapultepec Park. Devote much of that time to the Anthropological Museum, take in the Museum of Modern Art, and by all means spend a half day at the castle made famous by Maximilian and Carlotta, short-term king and queen from France.

The Anthropological Museum complex was built in 1963-64, beautifully designed by Pedro Ramírez Vásquez. The museum presents a surprisingly harmonious example of contemporary architecture. Incorporated in the roof is an enormous stone umbrella supported on a column 12 meters high, with a curtain of water dropping into a basin below.

As you enter the museum, the shop on the left is well stocked with a great selection of catalogs, brochures, and informative books (in several languages) on many subjects including the Indian cultures of ancient Mexico; the museum guidebook is excellent. Some of the finer reproductions of Maya art are available here at reasonable prices. Unfortunately, the store doesn't ship to the States, so you must either lug your purchases around with you on the rest of your trip or take the time to wrap and ship them yourself.

There are well-informed guides who speak English. For a moderate fee you can join a small group that will give you concentrated information on either the entire museum or the salons you're interested in. Each culture is represented in its own well-laid-out salon. Tickets (small fee) to the museum are sold in the vestibule at the main entrance of the two-story building.

In the Salon of the Maya you'll see some of the finest treasures found on the Yucatán Peninsula. The terra-cotta figures from the Island of Jaina are remarkable images of people, portraying various lifestyles. Reproductions of the colored frescoes found in Bonampak are outstanding, as are the delicate carvings from Chichén Itzá.

A theft during the Christmas season of 1985 saw the tragic loss of some spectacular remnants of Maya history. The fabled jade mask of Pacal found in a tomb in the depths of the Temple of the Inscriptions at Palenque was among the valued pieces stolen. It has since been recovered.

After visiting the museum and seeing the artifacts, you will have gained a greater understanding of the people who created the mysterious structures you visit on the Yucatán Peninsula.

If you plan on staying awhile, the **Presidente Hotel** in Chapultepec Park is within walking distance of all the park attractions and a colorful Mexican hotel. The **Nikko Hotel** is next door, a new Japanese-style hostel, very modern and very large. Mexico City has a plethora of hotels to fit every pocketbook; if you're looking for a luxurious splurge, this is where you'll find sophisticated, beautiful, world-class inns that compete with any in the world.

Budget travelers can find a good selection of hotels all over the large city, plus three youth hostels: **SETEJ**, Cozumel 57, tel. 286-91-53, four blocks south of Metro Sevilla Station (Line 1), which is on Av. Chapultapec, between Zona Rosa and Chapultepec Park. **CREA Hostel** (IYHF), tel. 286-91-53, one block south of Villa Olímpica, on Insurgentes Sur. **International Mexicano Norteamericano de Relaciones Culturales,** Hamburgo 115, between Genova and Amberes, in Zona Rosa (no phone).

Seat Comfort

If you can, choose the shady side of the bus during the day: going south sit on the left side, and going north sit on the right. At night sit on the right, which eliminates the glare of oncoming headlights. The middle of the bus is the best place to be. Steer clear of seats near the bathroom, usually the last few rows. They can be smelly and the aisle traffic and constant door activity can keep you awake. Bring a book and just relax.

BY SHIP

Cruise ships stop over at several ports on Mexico's Caribbean coast. Many lines will take you one way and drop you off either at Cancún, Cozumel, or Playa del Carmen. Check with Princess Lines, Chandris, and Carnival Cruises; your travel agent can give you the names of others that stop along the Yucatán coast. New cruise ships are continually adding the Mexican Caribbean to their ports of call. Cruise passengers have the opportunity to make shore excursions from the Caribbean coast ports to Chichén Itzá, Tulúm, Cobá, and Xelha. Shopping and beach time are also included. For less adventurous travelers, this may be your only chance to visit Maya archaeological zones.

GROUP TRAVEL

Travel agents offer many choices of escorted tours. You pay a little extra, but all arrangements and reservations are made for you to tour by plane, train, ship, or RV caravan. Also, special-interest groups with a guest expert are another attraction. For instance, archaeology buffs can usually find a group through a university that includes a knowledgeable professor to guide them through chosen Maya ruins. Evenings are spent together reviewing the day's investigation and discussing the next day's itinerary. Archaeology laypeople will find many opportunities, including trips offered through Earthwatch, Box 403, Watertown, MA 02172; volunteers can work on a dig under the supervision of professionals; destinations change regularly. *Transitions Abroad,* 18 Hulst Rd., Box 344, Amherst, MA 01004, is a magazine that offers information about study and teaching opportunities around the world. Travel agencies, student publications, and professional organizations can give you more information. It's a good way to mix business with pleasure, and in certain instances the trip is tax deductible.

WHAT TO TAKE

Whatever time of year you travel to Mexico's Caribbean coast, you can expect warm weather, which means you can pack less in your suitcase. Most airlines allow you to check two suitcases, and you can bring another carry-on bag that fits either under your seat or in the overhead rack; this is great if you're planning a one-destination trip to a self-contained resort hotel and want a change of clothes each day. But if you plan on moving around a lot, keep it light.

Experienced travelers pack a small collapsible pocketbook into their compartmented carry-on, which then gives them only one thing to carry while en route. And be sure to include a few overnight necessities in your carry-on in the event your luggage doesn't arrive when you do. Valuables are safest in your carry-on stowed under the seat in front of you rather than in the overhead rack, whether you're on a plane, train, or bus.

Clothing
A swimsuit is a must, and if you're not staying at one of the larger hotels, bring a beach towel. In today's Mexico, *almost* any clothing is acceptable. If traveling during November, December, or January, bring along a light jacket since it can cool off in the evening. The rest of the year you'll probably carry the jacket in your suitcase. For women, a wraparound skirt is a useful item that can quickly cover up shorts when traveling through villages and cities (many small-village residents gawk at women wearing shorts; whatever you do, don't enter a church wearing shorts). The wraparound skirt also makes a good shawl for evenings. Cotton underwear stays cool in the tropics, but nylon is less bulky and dries overnight, cutting down on the number needed. Be sure that you bring broken-in, comfortable walking shoes; blisters can wreck a vacation.

Necessities
If you wear glasses and are planning an extended trip in Mexico, it's a good idea to bring an extra pair or carry the lens prescription. The same goes for medications (make sure the prescription is written in general terms), though many Mexican pharmacies sell prescription drugs over the counter.

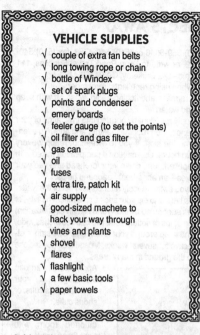

VEHICLE SUPPLIES

√ couple of extra fan belts
√ long towing rope or chain
√ bottle of Windex
√ set of spark plugs
√ points and condenser
√ emery boards
√ feeler gauge (to set the points)
√ oil filter and gas filter
√ gas can
√ oil
√ fuses
√ extra tire, patch kit
√ air supply
√ good-sized machete to hack your way through vines and plants
√ shovel
√ flares
√ flashlight
√ a few basic tools
√ paper towels

Campers

For the purist who vows to cook every meal, here's a list for a handy carried kitchen:

- single-burner stove, two fuel cylinders (fuel not allowed on commercial airlines)
- one large, sharp, machete-type knife; one small, sturdy, sharp knife
- pair of pliers—good hot pot grabber
- plastic pot scrubber
- can opener (with bottle hook)
- hot pad, two if there's room
- two pots that nest, one Silverstone skillet
- wire holder to barbecue fish or meat over open fire
- small sharpening stone
- soap and laundry detergent
- plate, cup, fork, and spoon, plastic or metal
- two large metal cooking spoons
- one long-handled wooden spoon
- one egg spatula
- three fast-drying dish towels (not terry-cloth)
- plastic Ziploc bags, large trash bags
- paper towels or napkins
- two or three plastic containers with tight-fitting lids, nested
- coffee drinkers who don't like instant will want a coffee pot
- several short candles and matches
- flashlight (batteries are usually easy to find)

DOCUMENTS

U.S. and Canadian citizens can obtain a free tourist card with proof of citizenship (birth certificate, passport, voter's registration, or notarized affidavit) good for 180 days. It can be obtained at any Mexican consulate or tourist office, at all border entry points, or from airport ticket offices for those traveling by plane. Hang onto your tourist card for the entire trip. You won't need it after you go through customs until it's time to leave the country. Then you must give it back. If you're visiting Mexico for 72 hours or less, you don't need a tourist card. Ask at the Mexican consulate about extensions for longer periods. If you're a naturalized citizen, carry your naturalization papers or passport. Citizens of the U.S. or Canada are not required

Avid readers in any language besides Spanish should bring a supply of books; English-language reading materials are for sale in limited quantities, mostly in big hotel gift shops and only a few bookstores. Both small and large hotels have book-trading shelves. Ask at the desk to see their collection. Most travelers are delighted to trade books.

Backpackers

If you plan on hitchhiking or using public transportation, don't use a large external-frame pack; it won't fit in most small cars or public lockers. Smaller packs with zippered compartments that will accommodate mini-padlocks are most practical. A strong bike cable and lock secures the pack to a YH bed or a bus or train rack. None of the above will deter the real criminal, but might make it difficult enough to discourage anyone else.

Experienced backpackers travel light with a pack, an additional canvas bag, a small water- and mosquito-proof tent, a hammock, and mosquito netting.

KEEPING THE INSECTS AWAY

There are many insect repellents around, some better than others. Read the labels and ask questions. Some formulas were designed to spray the outdoors, some a room, others your clothes—none of these are for the skin. Some repellents are harmful to plants and animals, some can dissolve watch crystals, and others can damage plastic eyeglass lenses. This can be a particular problem if labels are written in a foreign language that you cannot read. It's best to bring your repellent from home.

Many of the most efficient repellents contain diethyl-toluamide (DEET). Test it out before you leave home; the more concentrated solutions can cause an allergic reaction in some people, and for children a milder mix is recommended. Avoid use on skin with sores and abrasions.

Long Road Travel Supplies has come up with the **Indoor Travel Tent.** This lightweight, portable, net housing is made of ultra-fine mesh netting and fits right on top of the bed. A nylon floor and lightweight poles provide you with a roomy rectangular shape and free-standing protection from both flying and crawling insects that can make sleeping impossible. Convenient with a zipper door, folding flap for extra foot room, and inside pocket for keeping valuables close at hand. Packed in its own carrying bag, and weighing just 2.3 pounds (for single bed), it costs US$79; double weighs 2.8 pounds and costs US$99. Ask about the budget-priced Indoor Tent II, with a drawstring door; single size is US$49 and weighs 1.25 pounds. For more info call

(800) 359-6040 or (510) 540-4763, fax (510) 540-0652, or write to Long Road Travel Supplies, 111 Avenida Dr., Berkeley, CA 94708, USA.

When using repellents, remember:
- If redness and itching begin, wash off with soap and water.
- Apply repellent by pouring into the palms of your hands, then rubbing together and applying evenly to the skin. If you're sweating, reapply every two hours. Use caution if perspiration mixed with repellent runs down your forehead and into your eyes—an absorbent headband helps.
- If you swim, reapply after coming out of the water.
- It's helpful to dip your socks, spray them heavily, or (as suggested by the World Health Organization) dip strips of cotton cloth, two or three inches wide, and wrap around your lower legs. One strip is effective for several weeks. Mosquitoes hover close to the ground in many areas.

- Apply liberally around the edges of your sleeves, pants cuffs, or shorts cuffs.
- Sleeping in an air-conditioned room with tight-fitting windows is one good way to avoid nighttime buzzing attacks; in other situations use a mosquito net over the bed. It helps if the netting has been dipped in repellent, and make sure it's large enough to tuck well under the mattress. A rectangular shape is more efficient than the usual conical, giving you more room to sit up so you'll avoid contact with the critters that might bite through the net.

to obtain certificates of vaccination to enter Mexico; other nationals should check with a local Mexican consulate. Those under 18 without a parent or legal guardian must present a notarized letter from the parents or guardian granting permission to travel alone in Mexico. If a single parent is traveling with a minor, he or she should carry a notarized letter from the other parent granting permission. This is important going in both directions.

Passport
If you have a passport, bring it along even though it's not required (tuck your tourist card inside); it's the simplest ID when cashing traveler's checks, registering at hotels, and going through immigration. If you're visiting an area that has a current health problem and you have a health card with current information, keep that with the passport also. Keep all documents in a waterproof plastic case and in a safe place. Write to the

1. SS *Britanis;* **2.** Midnight buffet, SS *Britanis;* **3.** On the *Britanis* bridge with Captain Fokian Ardavanis and crew; **4.** Enjoying a breezy deck at sea; **5.** Showtime! SS *Britanis*

1. Cancun shoreline; **2.** Calinda Hotel, Cancun

U.S. Secretary of State for the most recent information about isolated areas that might be on the list for immunization. If traveling to such places, you'll need proof of vaccination to get back into the U.S., and perhaps other countries as well.

Driving Procedures

If you're driving, the tourist card serves as a vehicle permit when completed and validated at the border point of entry. Vehicle title or registration and driver's license are required. If you should happen to reach a remote border crossing at night, you may find it unstaffed. *Do not* cross the border with your car until you have obtained the proper papers; if you do, it will cause problems when you exit the country. Mexican vehicle insurance is available at most border towns 24 hours a day.

Pets

If you're traveling with a pet, a veterinarian's certificate verifying good health and a rabies inoculation within the last six months is required. This certificate will be validated by any Mexican consulate for a small fee.

Purchases

When departing by land, air, or sea, you must declare at the point of reentry into your own country all items acquired in Mexico. To facilitate this procedure, it is wise to register any foreign-made possessions with customs officials before entering Mexico and to retain the receipts for purchases made while there. Limitations on the value of imported, duty-free goods vary from country to country and should be checked before traveling. U.S. citizens are allowed to carry through customs US$600 worth of purchases pp duty free and up to US$1000 for 10% tax. However, about 2,700 items are exempt from this limit, most of which are handcrafted or manufactured in Mexico. Consular offices or embassies in Mexico City can supply additional information on exempt items. Plants and certain foods are not allowed into the U.S. Authentic archaeological finds, colonial art, and other original artifacts cannot be exported from Mexico. And, of course, trying to bring marijuana or any other narcotic into or out of Mexico or the U.S. is foolhardy. Jail is one place in Mexico a visitor can miss.

HAZARDS

Security

It's smart to keep passports, traveler's checks, money, and important papers on your person at all times. (It's always a good idea to keep a separate list of document numbers in your luggage and leave a copy with a friend back home. This expedites replacement in case of loss.) The do-it-yourselfer can sew inside pockets into clothes; buy extra-long pants that can be turned up and sewn three-fourths of the way around, the last section closed with a piece of Velcro. Separate shoulder-holster pockets, money belts, and pockets around the neck inside clothing—all made of cotton—are available commercially. If you're going to be backpacking and sloshing in jungle streams, etc., put everything in Ziploc plastic bags before placing them in pockets. Waterproof plastic tubes will hold a limited number of items around your neck while you swim.

Before You Leave Home

Probably the best way to save money is to make sure you don't lose anything along the way. Be practical; leave expensive jewelry at home. Take five minutes to go through your wallet before leaving and remove all credit cards you won't be using and put a good part of your money in traveler's checks. Make two copies of your passport-picture page and any credit cards you carry. Leave one copy of each with someone at home you can reach in case of emergency. After you get your visitor's card, also make a copy of that for your wallet. Keep these copies where you'll have them in the event your wallet and cards are stolen—in another piece of luggage. If your cards should get pinched, the copies will expedite replacement wherever you are in the world. Keep the original visitor's card with your passport in a hotel safe when sightseeing or swimming.

The Hotel Safe

Even the smallest hotels have safe-deposit boxes or some other security system for their guests. Many of the more upscale hotels have in-room safes now, which is very convenient.

Use it for your airline tickets and passports as well as other valuables. Don't leave anything valuable lying around your room. Why create a tempting situation? Most hotel employees are honest (honestly); working in a hotel is a good job, and for the most part that's far more important to the employee than stealing. However (you knew a *however* was coming didn't you?), you might be the unlucky person to draw the unscrupulous thief/maid/bell boy.

A hotel robbery is less common than, say, a setup on the street (a jostle, attention diverted by one person while the other grabs your purse or cuts the strap of a carry bag). Take precautions, act sensibly, be aware of what is going on around you at all times; don't flash large wads of cash, and don't give your room number to strangers. If you're invited to go anywhere with a stranger, suggest meeting him/her there; let someone know where you are going, even if it's the desk clerk.

Pickpockets
Don't forget pickpockets! They love fairs and all celebrations where there are lots of people; it's really easy to jostle people in crowds (that includes buses), so make sure you've got your money where a quick hand can't get to it, like a money belt, or a holster worn over your shoulder under your clothing. Many types are available; check out the trendy travel stores and catalogs. It's a good idea to put everything in a plastic bag before you stash it in your belt/holster; sweat makes ink run.

Legal Help
If after all precautions you still have a problem, contact the 24-hour national hotline of the office of **La Procuradoría de Protección al Turista** (Attorney General for the Protection of Tourists.) Each state has an office. The following number is located in Mexico City; tell the English-speaking operator you have an emergency and she will direct your call; tel. (5) 250-0293, 250-0151, 250-0589.

In the event you should be arrested, contact the nearest American Consul's office. If nothing else, they will visit you and advise you of your rights. Whatever you do, don't get caught with illegal substances; there's little that anyone can do given the current U.S. pressures to stop drug trafficking.

Insurance
Most homeowner's policies cover loss of property while on vacation; check it out before you leave home. *Do* make a police report if you're robbed. It's a long bureaucratic chore, but sometimes your property is recovered as a result. It also helps to have the report in hand when you deal with your insurance back home.

Lastly (yes, this is a repeat), always a make a copy of the front pages of your passport with pictures and all the vital information, numbers, etc., in the event of losing your passport. Then, when you go to your American consul or ambassador, this will expedite getting the passport replaced.

Women Travelers
A solo female traveler is considered very approachable by scammers and con artists. The "May ! Join You?" scam is typical in tourist areas. A seemingly harmless man may ask if he can join you; he orders a drink (or more), and you foot the bill. If you really would like some company, make sure to specify "Cuentos separados por favor" ("Separate checks please") to your waiter.

How you dress depends on where you are. Beach attire is best worn at the beach; it isn't appropriate in urban areas, especially churches. A few beaches may be designated "nude" or "clothing optional," although nude sunbathing in Mexico is almost always inappropriate and unsafe. Gringa or not, one should look to see what the people of the area are wearing and follow their dress codes.

Neither men nor women are advised to hitchhike. When walking at night, find other travelers or trustworthy companions. Let your hotel staff know your plans; they can often provide you with a reliable list of taxi drivers, etc., and look out for your well-being.

Toilets
Many of Mexico's public toilets consist of a hole in the floor. Whether you're in that situation or trekking the jungle, a couple of items make it easier. For women, **Le Funelle** is a scooplike paper funnel with a wide mouth and easy-to-hold handle that enables women to stand up to urinate in comfort and safety. Made of biodegradeable paper, it can be tossed down the toilet when finished. Each Le Funnelle is pack-

aged with a couple of tissues in an envelope about the size of a playing card—comes with instructions. A pack of four is US$2.85, pack of 20 is US$8.99.

This and some other really clever toilet articles and traveling items can be seen in a great little catalog called *Magellan's, Essentials For The Traveler.* Take a look at the anti-bacterial wipes (pre-moistened towelettes with germ killers). A box of 20 costs US$4.85. A disinfectant spray also serves as a good room deodorizer. To receive your own catalog, call (800) 962-4943.

The smaller the town, the more difficulty you'll have in finding a toilet. You can always go into a restaurant, buy a cold drink, and use the facilities. If there are no restaurants in the village, you know you must either stop at the local *tienda* or cantina and ask, *"¿Dónde está el baño?"* ("Where is the bathroom?"), or take a walk into the countryside. There was a time not too many years ago when you could not find facilities at any of the archaeological sites; however, in all of the mid- to large-size sites today, you will find a restroom.

When you see a wastebasket in the stall with toilet paper in it, do not flush paper down the toilet; instead drop the used paper into the wastebasket. Often, the toilet will overflow if you put paper in it.

HEALTH

TURISTA

Some travelers to Mexico worry about getting sick the moment they cross the border. But with a few simple precautions, it's not a foregone conclusion that you'll come down with something in Mexico. The most common illness to strike visitors is turista, Montezuma's Revenge, the trots, or in plain Latin—diarrhea. No fun, it can cause uncomfortable cramping, fever, dehydration, and the need to stay close to a toilet for the duration. It's caused, among other things, by various strains of bacteria in food or water.

Statistics show that most tourists get sick on the third day of their visit. Interested doctors note that this traveler's illness is common in every country. They say that in addition to bacteria, a change in diet is equally to blame and suggest that the visitor slip slowly into the eating habits of Mexico. In other words, don't blast your tummy with the *habanera* or *jalapeño* pepper right off the bat. Work into the fried food, drinks, local specialties, and new spices gradually; take your time changing over to foods that you may never eat while at home, including the large quantities of wonderful tropical fruits that you'll want to eat every morning. Turista can also be blamed on alcohol mixed with longer-than-usual periods of time in the tropical sun.

Water is probably the worst culprit. Many parts of the Yucatán Peninsula (such as Cancún and the newer developments along the Caribbean coast) have modern sewage systems, but the small villages and more isolated areas still have little or none—all waste is redeposited in the earth and can contaminate the natural water supply. While in these places you should take special precautions.

In the backcountry, carry your own water, boil it, or purify it with chemicals, whether the source is the tap or a crystal-clear cenote. That goes for brushing your teeth as well. If you have nothing else, a bottle of beer will make a safe (though maybe not sane) mouth rinse. If using ice, ask where it was made and if it's pure. Think about the water you're swimming in; some small local pools might be better avoided.

The easiest way to purify the water is with purification tablets; Hidroclonozone and Halazone are two, but many brands are available at drugstores in all countries—in Mexico ask at the *farmacia.* Another common method is to carry a small plastic bottle of liquid bleach (use 8-10 drops per quart of water) or iodine (called *yodo,* five to seven drops per quart). Whichever you use, let the water stand for 20 minutes to improve the flavor. If you're not prepared with any of the above, boiling the water for 20-30 minutes will purify it. Even though it takes a heck of a lot of fuel that you'll probably be carrying on your back, don't get lazy in this department. You can get very sick drinking contaminated water and you can't tell by looking at it—unless you travel with a microscope!

When camping on the beach where fresh water is scarce, use seawater to wash dishes and even yourself. If you have access to a sporting goods or marine store, ask for Sea Saver soap. Otherwise, use Castille soap. It only takes a small squirt of the soap to do a good job. (A rub of soap on the backsides of pots and pans before setting them over an open fire makes for easy cleaning after cooking.)

In the larger cities, purified water is generally provided in bottles in each room, or if the hotel is large enough it maintains its own purification plant on the premises. In Cozumel, for example, the Sol Caribe Hotel has a modern purification plant behind glass walls for all to see, and they're proud to show it off and explain how it works. If the tap water is pure, a sign over the spigot will specify this—except in Cancún which, with its modern infrastructure, brags that it's the only Mexican city in which every tap gives purified water. If you're not sure about the water, ask the desk clerk; he'll let you know the status— they prefer healthy guests who will return.

Other Sources Of Bacteria

Handling money can be a source of germs. Wash your hands frequently, don't put your fingers in your mouth, and carry individual foil packets of disinfectant cleansers, like Wash Up (handy and refreshing in the tropic heat). Hepatitis is another bug that can be contracted easily if you're around it.

When in backcountry cafes, remember that fruits and vegetables, especially those with thin, edible skins (like tomatoes), are a possible source of bacteria. If you like to eat food purchased from street vendors (and some should not be missed), use common sense. If you see the food being cooked (killing all the grubby little bacteria) before your eyes, have at it. If it's hanging there already cooked and nibbled on by small flying creatures, pass it by. It may have been there all day, and what was once a nice sterile morsel could easily have gone bad in the heat, or been contaminated by flies. When buying food at the marketplace to cook yourself, use the hints given in "Food."

Treatment

Remember, it's not just the visiting gringo who gets sick because of bacteria. Many Mexicans die each year from the same germs, and the Mexican government is working hard to remedy their sanitation problems. Tremendous improvements have taken place that ultimately will be accomplished all over Mexico, but it's a slow process. In the meantime, many careful visitors come and go each year with nary a touch of turista.

If after all your precautions you still come down with traveler's illness, many medications are available for relief. Most can be bought over the counter in Mexico, but in the States you'll need a prescription from your doctor. Lomotil and Imodium A-D are common, and certainly turn off the faucet after a few hours of dosing; however, each has the side effect of becoming a plug. It does not cure the problem, only the symptoms; if you quit taking it too soon your symptoms reappear and you're back to square one. In its favor, Lomotil probably works faster than any of the other drugs, and if you're about to embark on a 12-hour bus ride across the Yucatán Peninsula you might consider Lomotil a lifesaver. A few other over-the-counter remedies are Kaopectate in the U.S., Imodium and Donamycin in Mexico. If you're concerned, check with your doctor before leaving home. Also ask him or her about some new formulas called Septra and Bactrim. We count on a combination of Imodium (which stops the symptoms fairly quickly) and Septra or Bactrim, which supposedly kills the bug. Don't forget the common Pepto-Bismol. Some swear by it; be aware that it can turn the tongue a dark brownish color—nothing to be alarmed about. Septra and Bactrim must be bought in the U.S. with a prescription; check with your doctor.

For those who prefer natural remedies, lime juice and garlic are both considered good when taken as preventatives. They need to be taken in large quantities. Douse everything with the readily available lime juice (it's delicious on salads and fresh fruit and in drinks). You'll have to figure out your own ways of using garlic (some believers carry garlic capsules, available in most U.S. health-food stores). *Pero té* (dog tea) is used by Mexicans, as well as fresh coconut juice (don't eat the oily flesh, it makes your problem worse!). Plain boiled white rice soothes the tummy. Papaya fruit, juice, and tea all soothe the stomach, as does chamomile tea (*té de manzanillo*). While letting the ailment run its course, stay away from spicy and oily foods and fresh fruits. Don't be surprised if you have chills, nausea, vomiting, stomach cramps, and a fever. This could go on for about three days. If the problem persists, see a doctor.

SUNBURN

Sunburn can spoil a vacation quicker than anything else, so approach the sun cautiously. Expose yourself for short periods the first few days; wear a hat and sunglasses. Use a good sunscreen, and apply it to all exposed areas of the body (don't forget feet, hands, nose, backs of your knees, and forehead—especially if you have a receding hairline). Remember that after each time you go into the water for a swim, sunscreen lotion must be reapplied. Even after a few days of desensitizing your skin, when spending a day snorkeling wear a T-shirt in the water to protect your exposed back, and thoroughly douse the back of your neck with sunscreen lotion. The higher the number on sunscreen bottles, the more protection. Some users are allergic, so try a small patch test before leaving home. If you have a reaction, investigate the new "natural" sunblocks using mica. Ask at your pharmacy.

If, despite precautions, you still get a painful sunburn, do not return to the sun. Cover up with clothes if it's impossible to find protective deep shade (like in the depths of a dark, thick forest). Keep in mind that even in partial shade (such as under a beach umbrella), the reflection of the sun off the sand or water will burn your skin. Reburning the skin can result in painful blisters that easily become infected. Soothing suntan lotions, coconut oil, vinegar, cool tea, and preparations like Solarcaine will help relieve the pain. Drink plenty of liquids (especially water) and take tepid showers. A few days out of the sun is the best medicine.

HEALING

Most small cities in Quintana Roo have a resident doctor. He or she may or may not speak English, but will usually make a house call. When staying in a hotel, get a doctor quickly by asking the hotel manager; in the larger resorts, an English-speaking doctor is on call 24 hours a day. If you need to ask someone to get you a doctor, say, *"¡Necesito doctor, por favor!"* Emergency clinics are found in all but the smallest villages, and a taxi driver can be your quickest way to get there when you're a stranger in town. In small rural villages, if you have a serious problem and no doctor is around, you can usually find a *curandero*. These healers deal with the old natural methods (and maybe just a few chants thrown in for good measure), and can be helpful in a desperate situation away from modern technology.

Self Help

The smart traveler carries a first-aid kit of some kind. If backpacking, carry at least the following:

adhesive tape	hydrogen peroxide
alcohol	insect repellent
antibiotic ointment	iodine
aspirin	Lomotil
baking sodal	pain pills
Band-Aids	sewing needle
cornstarch	sunscreen
gauze	water purification
	tablets

Many of these products are available in Mexico, but certain items, like aspirin and Band-Aids, are sold individually in small shops and are much cheaper in your hometown. Even if not out in the wilderness, you should carry at least a few Band-Aids, aspirin, and an antibiotic ointment or powder or both. Travelers should be aware that in the tropics, with its heavy humidity, a simple scrape can become infected more easily than in a dry climate. So keep cuts and scratches as clean and dry as possible.

Another great addition to your first-aid kit is David Werner's book, *Where There Is No Doctor*. Also published in Spanish, it can be ordered from the Hesperian Foundation, Box 1692, Palo Alto, CA 94302. David Werner drew on his experience living in Mexico's backcountry when creating this informative book.

Shots

Check on your tetanus shot before you leave home, especially if you're backpacking in isolated regions. A gamma globulin shot may also be necessary; ask your physician.

SIMPLE FIRST-AID GUIDE

Acute Allergic Reaction: This, the most serious complication of insect bites, can be fatal. Common symptoms are hives, rash, pallor, nausea, tightness in chest or throat, trouble in speaking or breathing. Be alert for symptoms. If they appear, get prompt medical help. Start CPR if needed and continue until medical help is available.

Animal Bites: Bites, especially on face and neck, need immediate medical attention. If possible, catch and hold the animal for observation, taking care not to be bitten. Wash the wound with soap and water (hold under running water for two to three minutes unless the bleeding is heavy). Do not use iodine or other antiseptics. Bandage. This also applies to bites by human beings. In the case of human bites the danger of infection is high.

Bee Stings: Apply cold compresses quickly. If possible, remove the stinger by gentle scraping with a clean fingernail and continue cold applications till the pain is gone. Be alert for symptoms of acute allergic reaction or infection requiring medical aid.

Bleeding: For severe bleeding apply direct pressure to the wound with a bandage or the heel of the hand. Do not remove cloths when blood-soaked, just add others on top and continue pressure till bleeding stops. Elevate the bleeding part above heart level. If bleeding continues, apply a pressure bandage to arterial points. Do not put on a tourniquet unless advised by a physician. Do not use iodine or other disinfectants. Get medical aid.

Blister On Heel: It is better not to open a blister if you can rest the foot. If you can't, wash the foot with soap and water. Make a small hole at the base of the blister with a needle sterilized in 70% alcohol or in a match flame. Drain the fluid and cover with a strip bandage or moleskin. If a blister breaks on its own, wash with soap and water, bandage, and be alert for signs of infection (redness, festering) that call for medical attention.

Burns: For minor burns (redness, swelling, pain), apply cold water or immerse the burned part in cold water immediately. Use burn medication if necessary. For deeper burns (blisters develop), immerse in cold water (not ice water) or apply cold compresses for one to two hours. Blot dry and protect with a sterile bandage. Do not use antiseptic, ointment, or home remedies. Consult a doctor. For deep burns (skin layers destroyed, skin may be charred), cover with sterile cloth; be alert for breathing difficulties and treat

for shock if necessary. Do not remove clothing stuck to the burn. Do not apply ice. Do not use burn remedies. Get medical help quickly.

Cuts: For small cuts, wash with clean water and soap. Hold the wound under running water. Bandage. Use hydrogen peroxide or another antiseptic. For large wounds, see "Bleeding." If a finger or toe has been cut off, treat the severed end to control bleeding. Put the severed part in clean cloth for the doctor (it may be possible to reattach it by surgery). Treat for shock if necessary. Get medical help at once.

Diving Accident: There may be injury to the cervical spine (such as a broken neck). Call for medical help. (See "Drowning.")

Drowning: Clear the airway and start CPR even before trying to get water out of the lungs. Continue CPR till medical help arrives. In case of vomiting, turn the victim's head to one side to prevent inhalation of vomitus.

Food Poisoning: Symptoms appear a varying number of hours after eating and are generally like those of the flu—headache, diarrhea, vomiting, abdominal cramps, fever, a general sick feeling. See a doctor. A rare form, botulism, has a high fatality rate. Symptoms are double vision, inability to swallow, difficulty in speaking, respiratory paralysis. Get to an emergency facility at once.

Fractures: Until medical help arrives, do not move the victim unless absolutely necessary. Suspected victims of back, neck, or hip injuries should not be moved. Suspected breaks of arms or legs should be splinted to avoid further damage before the victim is moved, if moving is necessary.

Heat Exhaustion: Symptoms are cool moist skin, profuse sweating, headache, fatigue, and drowsiness with essentially normal body temperature. Remove the victim to cool surroundings, raise feet and legs, loosen clothing, and apply cool cloths. Give sips of salt water—one teaspoon of salt to a glass of water—for rehydration. If the victim vomits, stop fluids and take the victim to an emergency facility as soon as possible.

Heatstroke: Rush the victim to a hospital. Heatstroke can be fatal. The victim may be unconscious or severely confused. The skin feels hot and is red and dry, with no perspiration. Body temperature is high. Pulse is rapid. Remove the victim to a cool area, sponge with cool water or rubbing alcohol; use fans or a/c and wrap the victim in wet sheets, but do not over-chill. Massage arms and legs to increase circulation. Do not give large amounts of liquids. Do not give liquids if the victim is unconscious.

Insect Bites: Be alert for an acute allergic reaction that requires quick medical aid. Otherwise, apply cold compresses and soothing lotions. If the bites are scratched and infection starts (fever, swelling, redness), see a doctor.

Jellyfish Stings: Symptom is acute pain and may include feeling of paralysis. Immerse the affected area in ice water from for 5-10 minutes or apply aromatic spirits of ammonia to remove venom from the skin. Be alert for symptoms of acute allergic reaction and/or shock. If this happens, get the victim to a hospital as soon as possible.

Motion Sickness: Get a prescription from your doctor if boat travel is anticipated and this illness is a problem. Many over-the-counter remedies are sold in the U.S.: Bonine and Dramamine are two. If you prefer not to take chemicals or if you get drowsy, the new Sea Band is a cloth band that you place around the pressure point of the wrist. For more information write: Sea Band, 1645 Palm Beach Lake Blvd., Suite 220, W. Palm Beach, FL 33401. Also available by prescription from your doctor is medication administered in adhesive patches behind the ear.

Muscle Cramps: Usually a result of unaccustomed exertion; "working" the muscle or kneading it with the hand relieves cramp. If in water, head for shore (you can swim even with a muscle cramp), or knead the muscle with your hand. Call for help if needed. Do not panic.

Mushroom Poisoning: Even a small ingestion may be serious. Induce vomiting immediately if there is any question of mushroom poisoning. Symptoms—vomiting, diarrhea, difficult breathing— may begin in one to two hours or up to 24 hours. Convulsions and delirium may develop. Go to a doctor or emergency facility at once.

Nosebleed: Press the bleeding nostril closed, or pinch the nostrils together, or pack them with sterile cotton or gauze. Apply a cold cloth or ice to the nose and face. The victim should sit up, leaning forward, or lie down with head and shoulders raised. If bleeding does not stop in 10 minutes, get medical help.

Obstructed Airway: Find out if the victim can talk by asking, "Can you talk?" If he or she can talk, encourage the victim to cough the obstruction out. If he or she can't speak, a trained person must apply the Heimlich maneuver. If you are alone and choking, try to forcefully cough the object out. Or press your fist into your upper abdomen with a quick upward thrust, or lean forward and quickly press your upper abdomen over any firm object with a rounded edge (back of chair, edge of sink, porch railing). Keep trying till the object comes out.

Plant Poisoning: Many plants are poisonous if eaten or chewed. If the leaves of the diffenbachia (common in the Yucatán jungle) are chewed, one of the first symptoms is swelling of the throat. Induce vomiting immediately. Take the victim to an emergency facility for treatment.

Poison Ivy, Oak, or Sumac: After contact, wash the affected area with an alkali-base laundry soap, lathering well. Have a poison-ivy remedy available in case itching and blisters develop.

Puncture Wounds: Usually caused by stepping on a tack or a nail, these often do not bleed, so try to squeeze out some blood. Wash thoroughly with soap and water and apply a sterile bandage. Check with a doctor about tetanus. If pain, heat, throbbing, or redness develops, get medical attention at once.

Rabies: Bites from bats, raccoons, rats, or other wild animals are the most common threat of rabies today. Try to capture the animal, avoiding getting bitten, so it can be observed; do not kill the animal unless necessary and try not to injure the head so the brain can be examined. If the animal can't be found, see a doctor, who may decide to use antirabies immunization. In any case, flush the bite with water and apply a dry dressing; keep the victim quiet and see a doctor as soon as possible.

Scrapes: Sponge with soap and water; dry. Apply antibiotic ointment or powder and cover with a nonstick dressing (or tape on a piece of cellophane). When healing starts, stop the ointment and use an antiseptic powder to help a scab form. Ask a doctor about tetanus.

Shock: Can be a side effect in any kind of injury. Get immediate medical help. Symptoms may be pallor, clammy skin, shallow breathing, fast pulse, weakness, or thirst. Loosen clothing, cover the victim with blanket but do not apply other heat, and place the victim on his or her back with the feet raised. If necessary, start CPR. Do not give water or other fluids.

Snakebite or Lizard Bite: If the reptile is not poisonous, tooth marks usually appear in an even row (an exception, the poisonous gila monster, shows even tooth marks). Wash the bite with soap and water and apply a sterile bandage. See a doctor. If the snake is poisonous, puncture marks (one to six) can usually be seen. Kill the snake for identification if possible, taking care not to be bitten. Keep the victim quiet, immobilize the bitten arm or leg, keeping it on a lower level than the heart. If possible, phone ahead to be sure antivenin is available and get medical treatment as soon as possible. Do not give alcohol in any form. If treatment must be delayed and a snakebite kit is available, use as directed.

Spider Bites: The black widow bite may produce only a light reaction at the place of the bite, but severe pain, a general sick feeling, sweating, abdominal cramps, and breathing and speaking difficulty may develop. The more dangerous brown recluse spider's venom produces a severe reaction at the bite, generally in two to eight hours, plus chills, fever, joint pain, nausea, and vomiting. Apply a cold compress to the bite in either case. Get medical aid quickly.

Sprain: Treat as a fracture till the injured part has been X-rayed. Raise the sprained ankle or other joint and apply cold compresses or immerse in cold water. If the swelling is pronounced, try not to use the injured part till it has been X-rayed. Get prompt medical help.

Sunburn: For skin that is moderately red and slightly swollen, apply wet dressings of gauze dipped in a solution of one tablespoon baking soda and one tablespoon cornstarch to two quarts of cool water. Or take a cool bath with a cup of baking soda to a tub of water. Sunburn remedies are helpful in relieving pain. See a doctor if the burn is severe.

Sunstroke: This is a severe emergency. See "Heatstroke." the skin is hot and dry; body temperature is high. The victim may be delirious or unconscious. Get medical help immediately.

Ticks: Cover ticks with mineral oil or kerosene to exclude air from them, and they will usually drop off or can be lifted off with tweezers in 30 minutes. To avoid infection, take care to remove the whole tick. Wash the area with soap and water. Check with a doctor or health department to see if deadly ticks are in the area.

Wasp Sting: Apply cold compresses to the sting and watch for acute allergic reaction. If such symptoms develop, get the victim to a medical facility immediately.

SERVICES AND INFORMATION

PHOTOGRAPHY

Bring a camera to the Yucatán Peninsula! Nature and the Maya combine to provide unforgettable panoramas, well worth taking home with you on film to savor again at your leisure. Many people bring simple cameras such as Instamatics or disc types, which are easy to carry and are uncomplicated. For boat trips and snorkeling the new disposable waterproof cameras are great. Others prefer 35-mm cameras, which offer higher-quality pictures, are easier than ever to use, and are available in any price range. They can come equipped with built-in light meter, automatic exposure, self-focus, and self-advance—with little more to do than aim and click.

Film

Two reasons to bring film with you: it's cheaper and more readily available in the States. Two reasons *not* to bring lots of film: space may be a problem and heat can affect film quality, both before and after exposure. If you're traveling for more than two weeks in a car or bus a good part of the time, carry film in an insulated case. You can buy a soft-sided insulated bag in most camera shops or order one out of a professional photography magazine. For the average vacation, if your film is kept in your room, there should be no problem. Many varieties of Kodak film are found in camera shops and hotel gift shops on the Yucatán Peninsula. In the smaller towns along the Caribbean coast you may not be able to find slide film.

X-ray Protection

If you carry film with you when traveling by plane, take precautions. Each time film is passed through the security X-ray machine, a little damage is done. It's cumulative, and perhaps one time won't make much difference, but most photographers won't take the chance. Request hand inspection. With today's tight security at airports, some guards insist on passing your film and camera through the X-ray machine. If your film is packed in your checked luggage, it's wise to keep it in protective lead-lined bags, available at camera shops in two

sizes; the larger size holds up to 22 rolls of 35-mm film, the smaller holds eight rolls. If you use fast film, ASA 400 or higher, buy the double lead-lined bag designed to protect more sensitive film. Carry an extra lead-lined bag for your film-loaded camera if you want to drop it into a piece of carry-on luggage. (These bags also protect medications from X-ray damage.)

If you decide to request hand examination (rarely if ever refused at a Mexican airport), make it simple for the security guard. Have the film out of boxes and canisters placed together in one clear plastic bag that you can hand him for quick examination both coming and going. He'll also want to look at the camera; load it with film *after* crossing the border.

Film Processing

For processing film, the traveler has several options. Most people take their film home and have it processed at a familiar lab. Again, if the trip is lengthy and you are shooting lots of photos, it's impractical to carry used rolls around for more than a couple of weeks. Larger cities have one-hour photo labs, but they only handle color prints; color slides must be processed at a lab in Mexico City, which usually takes a week or two. If you'll be passing through the same city on another leg of your trip, the lab is a good cool place to store your slides while you travel. Just tell the lab technician when you think you'll be picking them up. Kodak mailers are another option but most photographers won't let their film out of sight until they reach their own favorite lab.

Camera Protection

Take a few precautions with your camera while traveling. At the beach remember that a combination of wind and sand can really gum up the works and scratch the lens. On 35-mm cameras keep a clear skylight filter on the lens instead of a lens cap so the camera can hang around your neck or in a fanny pack always at the ready for that spectacular shot that comes when least expected. If something is going to get scratched, better a $15 filter than a $300 lens.

It also helps to carry as little equipment as possible. If you want more than candids and you carry a 35-mm camera, basic equipment can be simple. Padded camera cases are good and come in all sizes. A canvas bag is lighter and less conspicuous than a heavy photo bag, but doesn't have the extra protection the padding provides. At the nearest army/military surplus store you can find small military bags and webbed belts with eyelet holes from which to hang canteen pouches and clip holders for extra equipment. It helps to have your hands free while climbing pyramids or on long hikes.

Safety Tips
Keep your camera dry; carrying a couple of big Ziploc bags affords instant protection. Don't *store* cameras in plastic bags for any length of time because the moisture that builds up in the bag can damage a camera as much as leaving it in the rain.

It's always wise to keep cameras out of sight in a car or when camping out. Put your name and address on the camera. Chances are if it gets left behind or stolen it won't matter whether your name is there or not, and don't expect to see it again; however, miracles do happen. (You *can* put a rider on most homeowner's insurance policies for a nominal sum that will cover the cost if a camera is lost or stolen.) It's a nuisance to carry cameras every second when traveling for a long period. During an evening out, you can leave your cameras and equipment (out of sight) in the hotel room—unless it makes you crazy all evening worrying about it! Some hotel safes are large enough to accommodate your equipment.

Cameras can be a help and a hindrance when trying to get to know the people. Traveling in the backcountry, you'll run into folks frightened of having their pictures taken. Keep your camera put away until the right moment. The main thing to remember is to ask permission first and then if someone doesn't want his/her picture taken, accept the refusal with a gracious smile and move on.

Camera Fees
There is an additional charge of US$8-10 to use a video camera at most archaeological sites. There is talk of a similar charge for still cameras as well, though we had no problems using a camera, without tripod, on our last visit. To be sure, check with the tourist office in Mérida before you visit the ruins.

MONEY

New Pesos
Current exchange rate as of July is NP$3.40 to US$1 (give or take a centavo). On 1 Jan. 1993, Mexico's monetary system underwent a cosmetic change. Three zeroes were dropped from the current designations to make the **New Peso.** The value by and large remains the same, although the "change" has in most cases been rounded off to the next largest peso. Instead of 10,999 pesos, it's rounded off to 11,000 pesos, the three zeros dropped, and you have a simple NP$11. Most shops still mark goods with both old pesos and NP, at least for a while. New currency has been issued as well as coins. Paper bills come in 5, 10, 20, 50, and 100 denominations, and peso coins are distributed in 1, 2, 5, and 10 pieces. Coins of smaller value are measured in centavos (10, 20, and 50). All old pesos are supposed to be out of circulation by 1994, though you still may see a few bills in remote areas.

Cashing personal checks in Mexico is not easy; however, it is possible to withdraw money against your credit card in some banks and instant teller machines. Wearing a money belt is always a good idea while traveling—in any country.

Exchange
Usually your best rate of exchange is at the bank, but small shops frequently give a good rate if you're making a purchase. Hotels notoriously give the poorest exchange. Check to see what kind of fee, if any, is charged. You can learn the current exchange rate daily in all banks and most hotels. Try not to run out of money over the weekend because the new rate often is not posted until noon on Monday; you will get the previous Friday's rate of exchange even if the weekend newspaper may be announcing an overwhelming difference in your favor.

Note: According to many foreign travelers in Mexico, it's easier to exchange U.S. dollars for pesos than many other currencies (perhaps with the exception of Canadian dollars). So, foreign travelers might want to come prepared with either U.S. dollars or American traveler's checks. Also, try to spend all your coinage before leaving the country, since most banks or money changers will not buy peso coins with U.S. dollars.

Always go with pesos in hand to the small rural areas of Mexico. And even more convenient, take them in small denominations. In most cases it's a real hassle to cash dollars or traveler's checks.

The Cost Of Traveling?

If we had a crystal ball, we could provide an answer to this question. But, like supply and demand, costs constantly change. A conservative estimate for *real* budget travelers is around **US$20-25** pp, per day. Moderate spenders who want more leeway can expect to spend **US$35-50** pp, per day; and for the luxury seekers, you could hold it down to **US$50-75**. Of course, when it comes to luxury, the sky's the limit in Mexico. Everyone must add more if renting a car, and deduct a little if you're traveling by twos. A lot depends on how you get around; taxis are a lot more expensive than buses, and trekkers get the best bargain of all.

Credit Cards

Major credit cards are accepted at all of the larger hotels, upscale restaurants in big cities, travel agencies, and many shops throughout the Republic. But don't take it for granted; ask. The smaller businesses do not accept them. In some cases you will be asked to pay a fee on top of the charged amount. In Mexico, universally, gas stations *do not* accept credit cards.

Banks And Business Hours

Banks are open Mon.-Fri. 9 a.m.-1:30 p.m. Business offices are open from 8-9 a.m. to 1-4 p.m., then reopen between 2:30-4 p.m. and stay open until 6 p.m. Government offices are usually open until 3 p.m. Stores in cities are generally open 10 a.m.-7 p.m. and close between 1 to 4 p.m. Government offices, banks, and stores are closed on national holidays.

Tipping

If not already included, 10-20% of the bill is standard. Tips for assistance with bags should be equivalent to US$0.50-0.75 per bag. Chambermaids should receive about US$1 per day. It is not necessary to tip taxi drivers unless they have performed a special service. Tour guides should receive US$2-3 for a half-day trip and

US$4-5 per day for longer trips, if they do a good job of course! Gas station attendants are tipped about US$0.30 for pumping gas, cleaning the windshield, checking the oil and water, and providing other standard services. Often tips are the main part of the provider's income.

Moneda

The "$" sign in Mexico means pesos. Shops that accept dollars will often price items with the abbreviation "Dlls." If you see a price that says "m.n.," that indicates pesos, *moneda nacional.* Most large airports have money exchange counters, but the hours generally depend on the flight schedules.

Traveler's Checks

Traveler's checks are the easiest way to carry money. However, certain moneychangers will pay more for cash and some banks charge a fee, so always ask before making a transaction. If you're in a really small town, don't expect the shops or vendors to cash a traveler's check; gas stations deal *only* in pesos—so far. Be prepared. If you need to change money after bank hours, look for a sign that says Casa de Cambio.

The favored credit cards in Mexico are Bancomer (Visa) and Carnet (MasterCard)—way down the list is American Express; in fact most businesses refuse Amex as well as Diners Club. Look for ATMs in the more modern banks. Before leaving home, ask your bank teller if your particular card is authorized for use in Mexico, and, if so, at which branches.

Admission Fees

Admissions to the archaeological sites have taken large leaps in the past few years. INAH (Instituto Nacional De Antropología E Historia) is the arm of the government that directs the museums and archaeological sites of the country. The increase in fees certainly goes hand in hand with the improvements made on the sites. All the larger sites now have or will soon have modern visitor's centers with restrooms, gift shops, snack shops, museums, and auditoriums. Most of the smaller sites will eventually have restrooms. INAH also sets the fees, and at presstime these attractions are rated "A" NP$13, "B" NP$10, "C" NP$7, which roughly computes to US$4.35, US$3.35, and US$2.35. We have in all sections of the handbook rounded off the fees to the nearest fifty cents. There are still one or two sites in way out-of-the-way places that have not added restrooms or visitor's amenities and don't charge at all. Admission to all sites and museums is free on Sunday.

Remember that your video camera will cost more than you do to get into the archaeological grounds, about US$10.

Admission fees do not include the services of a guide; having an English-speaking guide is really worthwhile, but be sure to negotiate your fee (for your entire group), how long the guide will be with you, and where he will take you, before saying yes! A good starting point for negotiations for up to six people is US$25. If he was really good, a tip is fair. By yourself, expect to pay at least US$10 in the larger sites (much cheaper by the dozen) for a half day.

As at the sites, admission to state and national parks is free on Sunday. Fees range US$0.75-5.

Taxes
Note: 10% IVA tax is added to room rates, restaurant and bar tabs, and gift purchases. When checking in or making reservations at a hotel, ask if tax has already been added. And once again, don't forget that when you leave the country or travel from Mexican city to Mexican city, you must pay an **airport departure tax.** National departures, **US$6;** international departures, **US$12.**

Watching Your Pesos
No matter where you travel in the world, it's wise to guard your money. A money belt worn under the clothes is probably the most unobtrusive. They come in a variety of styles, from a shoulder holster to a flat pocket worn around the neck, or even an honest-to-goodness leather belt with a fine flat zipper opening on the inside, where you can insert a few folded bills for an emergency. Using hotel safe facilities is also very practical. In most cases visitors encounter no problems, but take precautions—it only takes one pickpocket to ruin a good vacation.

Bargaining
This is one way a visitor really gets to know the people. Although the influx of many outsiders who don't appreciate the delicate art of bargaining has deteriorated this traditional verbal exchange, it's still a way of life among Mexicans, and it can still build a bridge between the gringo and the Yucatecan. Some Americans accustomed to shopping with plastic money either find bargaining distasteful or go overboard and insult the merchant by offering far too little. It would not be insulting to begin the bargaining at 50% below the asking price; expect to earn about a 20% discount (and new respect) after a lively, often jovial, repartee between buyer and seller.

COMMUNICATION AND UTILITIES

Shipping And Telegraph
Mailing and shipping from Mexico is easy within certain limitations. Packages of less than US$25 in value can be sent to the U.S. The package must be marked "Unsolicited Gift—Under $25" and addressed to someone other than the traveler. Only one package per day may be sent to the same addressee. Major stores will handle shipping arrangements on larger items and duty must be paid; this is in addition to the US$400 carried in person across the border.

Almost every town in Quintana Roo has a post office. If you can't find it by looking, ask—it may be located in someone's front parlor. Airmail postage is recommended for the best delivery. Post offices will hold travelers' mail for one week if it is marked a/c Lista de Correos ("care of General Delivery"). Hotels will extend the same service for mail marked "tourist mail, hold for arrival."

Even the smallest village has a telegraph office. Wires can often be sent direct from the larger hotels.

Area Codes And Zip Codes

Cancún	988	77500
Chetumal	983	77000
Cozumel	987	77600
Isla Mujeres	987	77400
Piste	985	97751
Playa del Carmen	987	77710
Uxmal		97844

Telephone

One of the newest additions to the Yucatán Peninsula as well as other parts of Mexico is the Direct Dial USA telephone booths scattered about. Shiny new touch-tone phones bring you in direct contact with an American operator who will either charge the call to your telephone credit card or make it collect. Look for phones labeled **Ladatel.** Many of these phones use telephone cards available at small markets and pharmacies. The cards are sold in 10, 20, 30, and 50 peso amounts; when you use the card a digital screen shows how much money your call is costing and deducts it from the value of the card. It comes in

very handy when calling ahead to confirm hotel rooms or making other arrangements, and is certainly better than carrying peso coins. The card is quick and efficient and eliminates the language barrier as well as the often-long waits.

However, until the phones are installed in the small towns, expect the same old rules. Hotels (if they have phones) add enormous service charges to direct calls—always ask what it will be first. Calling collect is cheaper, and going to a *larga distancia* office is the most economical. Have the number and name of the city you are calling written down on a piece of paper and give it to the clerk. Another improvement is the installation of phone lines in areas that until recently didn't have telephones, such as the Cancún-Tulúm Corridor.

Note: Fax machines are becoming very common, but can also be expensive. In some smaller towns, one fax services the entire town, so messages can be delayed because the sender must compete with everyone else and encounters a constant busy signal.

TELEPHONE AND EMERGENCY INFORMATION

Information (national)	01
Long-distance operator	02
Time	03
Information (local)	04
Police radio patrol	06
Bilingual emergency information	07
International operator (English)	09

Long-distance direct service:

station to station (national)	91 plus area code and number
person to person (national)	92 plus area code and number

Long-distance direct service:

station to station (international)	95 plus area code and number
person to person (international)	96 plus area code and number

Worldwide:

station to station	98
person to person	99

Radio And Television

AM and FM radio stations, in Spanish, are scattered throughout the Peninsula. Television is becoming more common as well. In the major cities, hotel rooms have TV entertainment. The large resort hotels in Cancún, Cozumel, and Mérida and surroundings have one or more cable stations from the U.S., on which you can expect to see all the major baseball and football games, news, and latest movies.

Time

The states of Yucatán, Quintana Roo, Campeche, Chiapas, and Tabasco are on U.S. Central Standard Time; Mexico is not on Daylight Saving Time.

Electricity

Electric current has been standardized throughout Mexico, using the same 60-cycle, 110-volt AC current common in the U.S. Small travel appliances can be used everywhere; if you have a problem, it will be because there's no electricity at all. In some areas electricity is supplied by small generators and is usually turned off at 10 p.m. The hotels will offer you gas lanterns after the lights go out.

MISCELLANEOUS

Studying In Mexico

In addition to fulfilling the requirements for a tourist card, students must present documents to a Mexican consulate demonstrating that they have been accepted at an educational institution and that they are financially solvent. A number of courses and workshops lasting two to eight weeks are offered throughout Mexico in addition to full-time study programs. Many adults as well as younger folks take part in language programs in which the student lives with a Spanish-speaking family for a period of two to four weeks and attends language classes daily. This total immersion into the language, even for a short time, is quite successful and popular as a cultural experience.

Write to the National Registration Center for Study Abroad (NRCSA), 823 N. Second St., Milwaukee, WI 53203. Request their "Directory of Educational Programs," which describes programs in a number of cities in Mexico.

Churches And Clubs

Mexico is predominantly a Catholic country. However, you'll find a few churches of other denominations in the larger cities (if you find a synagogue, let me know!). Local telephone books and hotel clerks have these listings. Many international organizations like the Lions, Rotary, Shriners, and foreign social groups have branches on the Yucatán Peninsula which welcome visitors.

U.S. Embassies And Consulates

If an American citizen finds him- or herself with a problem of any kind, the nearest consul will provide advice or help. Travel advisories with up-to-the-minute information about traveling in remote areas of Mexico are available.

KATHY ESCOVEDO SANDERS

THE STATE OF QUINTANA ROO

THE LAND AND SEA

The state of Quintana Roo (kin-taw-nuh-ROW) is located on the east coast of Mexico's Yucatán Peninsula, bordered by the state of Yucatán to the northwest, the state of Campeche to the west, and the country of Belize to the south. Quintana Roo occupies 50,350 square km and has a population of more than 600,000 residents. Mostly flat, this long, isolated state is covered with tropical forest and boasts the most beautiful white-sand beaches on the Peninsula. Several islands lie offshore, and the magnificent 250-km-long Belize Reef runs parallel to the Quintana Roo coast from the tip of Isla Mujeres to the Bay of Honduras, whose undersea life provides world-class diving. Chetumal, capital of the state, borders Belize (formerly known as British Honduras).

The east coast of Quintana Roo is lined with Maya ruins, ranging from tiny "watchtowers" in Cancún to the relative grandeur of Tulúm. Although there is evidence of earlier occupation, particularly in Tancah, Xcaret, and Xelha, most structures were built during the Late Post-Classic (A.D. 1200-1530). Some may even post-date the Spanish Conquest. This was the heyday of the Putún Maya traders, who frequented the Gulf and Caribbean coasts of Mesoamerica in large, seagoing canoes (Columbus encountered one off the coast of Honduras on his final voyage). Most of the Late Post-Classic buildings along Quintana Roo's coast were probably built either by the Putún or at their urging to serve as ports, way stations, and lighthouses for their trade.

HISTORY

This stretched-out coastal region was ignored by Mexico longer than the rest of the Peninsula because of its dense jungle and notorious Chan Santa Cruz Indians. When defeated by the Spanish, many Maya took refuge in this coastal territory, keeping would-be intruders easily at

ARCHAEOLOGICAL ZONES OF QUINTANA ROO

Tulúm	Xelha
Cobá	Kohunlich

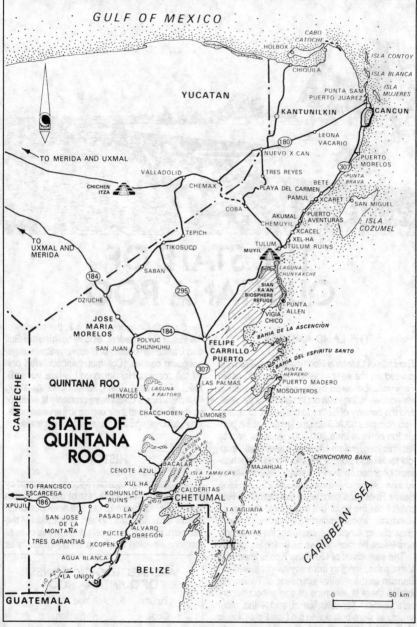

bay until the beginning of the 20th century. The only real Spanish settlement, Bacalar, on the southern end of the state, was destroyed twice, once by pirates and again during the Caste War by rioting Maya. Quintana Roo was held as a territory of the Republic for 73 years, then admitted as the 30th state to the United Mexican States in 1974. Not until the 1970s were highways built, when Mexico finally realized that Quintana Roo possesses all the elements of one of the most beautiful resort areas in the world.

Naming A Territory

For many years, the east coast of the Yucatán Peninsula remained a desolate no-man's land; it had no name because few people ever spoke about it. But when it became a territory, it needed a name. As is often the custom in Mexico, the territory was named for an army general, undoubtedly a sterling soldier who deserved the honor. But sadly the man had not fought a battle in, nor had he ever traveled to, the territory of this Caribbean paradise. His name was Andrés Quintana Roo.

ECONOMY

Until recently the economy of this lost territory amounted to very little. For a few years the chicle boom brought a flurry of activity centered around the harbor of Isla Cozumel. Native hardwood trees have always been in demand; coconuts and fishing were the only other natural resources that added to the economy—but none on a large scale. Today the face of Quintana Roo is changing rapidly. Tourism is its number-one attraction, and Cancún is a multimillion-dollar resort. Building and construction continue south down the Peninsula, bringing new roads that give access to until-now unknown beaches and unseen Maya structures. By 1998 Cancún is expected to have 26,000 hotel rooms.

CANCUN

It's a well-known story: in 1967 a data-crunching computer selected a small, swampy finger of land in an isolated part of the Mexican Caribbean as Mexico's most promising tourist town. And so it happened—Cancún resort was born. Designing Cancún, an island shaped like a seven with bridges at both ends connecting it with the mainland, began from the ground up in 1968: new infrastructure, modern electrical plants, purified tap water, paved tree-lined avenues, and buildings that fit into the landscape (they look similar to Maya temples. When the first hotels opened their doors in 1972, visitors began coming and haven't stopped since.

For some, the name Cancún conjures immediate images of sugar-fine sand, a palette-blue sea, and flashing dollar signs. Absolutely! The beaches *are* stunning and the water *is* enticing, but it can be costly to enjoy Cancún—especially if you just "drop in" at one of the fabulous resorts in the hotel zone. However, with careful shopping for package deals from your travel agent or in the travel pages of your local newspaper, you'll find something to fit your pocketbook.

SIGHTS

Archaeological Zones

Cancún's archaeological zones are minor compared to the big sites spread throughout the Peninsula. But structures built on this narrow strip of land have contributed important information to our knowledge about the people who lived here hundreds of years ago. Remnants of two sites, **Ruinas del Rey** on the south end of the island (at the Westin Golf Resort course) and **Yamil Lu'um** next to the Sheraton Hotel, are both worth a look. Ruinas del Rey are set in the golf course on the lagoon side of the resort, under construction at press time. There will be public access to the ruins once the course is completed. The remains of this Post-Classic structure are made up of a few platforms, two plazas, and a small pyramid. It is said that when the site was originally excavated, a skeleton believed to be a king was uncovered, hence the name del Rey ("of the King"). Yamil Lu'um is on the highest point of mostly flat Cancún. The two small temples (15 meters high) were probably used as watchtowers and lighthouses along

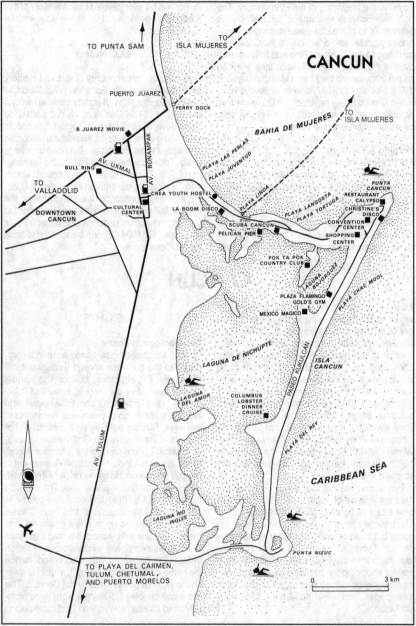

CANCUN

TO PUNTA SAM

TO ISLA MUJERES

PUERTO JUAREZ

FERRY DOCK

BAHIA DE MUJERES

TO ISLA MUJERES

B. JUAREZ MOVIE

AV. BONAMPAK

AV. UXMAL

BULL RING

PLAYA LAS PERLAS

PLAYA JUVENTUD

TO VALLADOLID

CREA YOUTH HOSTEL

PLAYA LINDA

PUNTA CANCUN

RESTAURANT CALYPSO

CULTURAL CENTER

DOWNTOWN CANCUN

LA BOOM DISCO

PLAYA LANGOSTA

PLAYA TORTUGA

CHRISTINE'S DISCO

CONVENTION CENTER

SCUBA CANCUN

PELICAN PIER

SHOPPING CENTER

POK TA POK COUNTRY CLUB

LAGUNA BOJORQUEZ

PLAZA FLAMINGO
GOLD'S GYM

PLAYA CHAC MOOL

MEXICO MAGICO

LAGUNA DE NICHUPTE

ISLA CANCUN

PASEO KUKULCAN

LAGUNA DEL AMOR

COLUMBUS LOBSTER DINNER CRUISE

PLAYA DEL REY

CARIBBEAN SEA

LAGUNA RIO INGLES

TO PLAYA DEL CARMEN, TULUM, CHETUMAL, AND PUERTO MORELOS

AV. TULUM

PUNTA NIZUC

0   3 km

© MOON PUBICATIONS, INC.

this navigational route. Between 400 and 700 years old, they were first noted by two intrepid American explorers, John L. Stephens and Frederick Catherwood, in 1841.

Scenic Spots

All of Cancún is scenic. But the most scenic beaches are on the seaward side of the island, extending 21 km and parallel to Paseo Kukulcán. If you haven't been to Cancún since before Hurricane Gilbert, you will see rearranged beaches. In some areas sand was whisked out to sea; in others the beach was widened with sand deposits. Walking along the coast is rated a five-star activity, and it's free (all beaches in Mexico are public). The panorama is capricious—the color of the sea changes subtly throughout the day from pale aqua at dawn to deep turquoise at noon to cerulean blue under the blazing afternoon sun to pink-splashed purple during the silent sunset.

Nichupté Lagoon

This large lagoon, which parallels Paseo Kukulcán, is a combination of sweet water fed by underground springs and salt water that enters from two openings to the sea. In certain areas where the water is still and swampy, mangroves provide hiding places for the cayman, little brother of large crocodilians found on other parts of the Peninsula. Birdlife is plentiful, with a treasure trove of over 200 cataloged species including herons, egrets, ospreys, screaming parrots, and parakeets; the sooty tern returns here to nest each year. The best way to see the lagoon and its wildlife is by boat. One of the many travel agents or your hotel can arrange a boat and a guide who knows his way around.

Along the north end of the lagoon the marinas bustle with activity, and the trim greens of the Pok Ta Pok golf course extend out over the water. Nichupté is a favorite for water-skiing, sailing (Sunfish and Hobie Cat rentals), riding Wave Runners, and sailboarding. Restaurants from exotic to generic are open all day, with a variety of shopping centers offering something for everybody. The arts and crafts markets offer those who find bargaining stimulating a chance to practice the art. For the more timid who may be used to paying the marked price, try the many Americanized shops. *Almost* all businesses in Cancún accept credit cards.

DRIVING DISTANCES FROM CANCUN

Airport	20 km
Akumal	104 km
Aventuras (playa)	107 km
Bacalar	320 km
Chemuyil	109 km
Chetumal	382 km
Chichén Itzá	192 km
Club Med	25 km
Cobá	167 km
Kohunlich	449 km
Mérida	312 km
Pamul	92 km
Playa del Carmen	65 km
Puerto Juárez	2 km
Puerto Morelos	32 km
Punta Sam	7 km
Tulúm	130 km
Valladolid	152 km
Xcaret	72 km
Xelha	123 km

BEACHES

Note

The water on the ocean side of Cancún can be hazardous. Pay particular attention to warning signs, and if in doubt, don't swim. Each year a few people drown off the beaches of Cancún because of a lack of respect for the power of this beautiful sea.

Bus To The Beach

Cancún is one big beach, or more accurately, a series of breathtaking beaches laid end to end and around corners and curves. It's simple to reach any beach by bus; the route begins in downtown Cancún, making a circuit along Paseo Kukulcán, past the hotel zone shopping malls, and on to the last hotel, whichever that happens to be at the time you're visiting. The buses are modern, comfortable, and inexpensive. Remember that the locals use these buses to get to and from work, so expect them to be crowded during the commute hours. Fare is about US$0.75 anywhere. Bus stops are frequent and marked with blue signs that read "Parada." However, most drivers will stop for a waving arm almost anywhere (if there's room).

Beginning Snorkelers

Cancún's beaches are for relaxing and soaking up the sun. The sandy seafloor along here doesn't provide hiding places for the kind of sealife that prefers cool caves and rocky crevices. (Don't despair; there are a number of reefs in the area with rich marinelife to explore.) But for beginners (including children), this is a great place to learn to snorkel, with sun-loving fish such as tanned beauties and burnt-back beach nappers. Guests at the Camino Real Cancún have access to a calm, man-made lagoon ideal for viewing tropical fish and sea turtles from small to large.

Lifeguards

The hotels on the island all have beaches with various activities; some provide palapa sun shelters, volleyball courts, aerobic classes, bars, restaurants, showers, restrooms, and towels for their guests, and most importantly, lifeguards. Everyone is free to use the 60-foot strip of sand along the sea on any part of Cancún; signs indicating this are prominently posted everywhere by SECTUR, the Ministry of Tourism. Visitors staying in the city have been known to spend their entire vacations (on their own towels) under the eye of a hotel lifeguard.

Public Beaches

Don't expect lifeguards or showers; some have snack stands and good parking areas. **Playa Linda** is close to the city (10 minutes by bus) on Paseo Kukulcán near the Nichupté bridge. Two km past Playa Linda on Paseo Kukulcán is **Playa Tortuga.** The water is clear, calm, and deep; on the beach is a palapa-covered snack bar.

Playa Chac Mool is around the point beyond the Convention Center. This stunning beach displays the vibrant colors that make the Caribbean famous. You can walk out to sea 14 meters in shallow water before it begins to drop off. Check the tide conditions on the sign just south of the beach cafe—the water at times gets rough. **Playa Delfines** at the south end of the hotel zone is a favorite of locals, since this stretch of sand is free of hotels thus far. Sunset watching from the low rise over the beach is particularly fine.

The Surf

There isn't a beach suitable for surfing anywhere on Cancún. Where protected by the reef, the Peninsula is a placid sea ideal for swimming. After you leave the city, the first stretch of beach from the youth hostel to Playa Linda provides calm water and is also protected from strong currents and dangerous surf. The water at the lagoon is usually calm, but not as clear as the sea. Along the lagoonside you'll find many marinas and headquarters for water activities. On the east (the Caribbean or windward) side from Punta Cancún to Punta Nizúc the surf can be as high as three feet, and at certain times you'll encounter an undertow. If you don't see a water-condition sign, ask at the concession stand—or *don't* swim. The calmest and most protected beaches on the windward side face Bahía de Mujeres on the north end of the island.

WATER SPORTS

The Reefs

One of the most popular reefs, despite its shallow depths, is **Chital,** a short distance north of Hotel Presidente on the island. The reef is made up of two sections, both about 20 meters wide. Expect a one-knot current and clear visibility up to 33 meters. **Cuevones Reef,** about three km north of Punta Cancún, is just what its name tells us in Spanish, "Small Caves." Here the body of the reef is comprised of elkhorn, rock, and brain corals. The series of caves varies in size from a five-meter cavern to a two-meter hole, all at a depth of about 10 meters. With an amazing 45-meter visibility, divers find themselves surrounded by large schools of reef fish, groupers, amberjack, and the ever-lurking predators, barracudas. **Manchones Reef** is a shallow reef closer to Isla Mujeres (three km south) than to Cancún (eight km northeast). Its 10-meter depth, 60-meter visibility, lack of current, and abundant sealife make it an ideal learning reef for beginning scuba divers.

Snorkeling

The experienced snorkeler may want to observe the beauty of the reefs, which are mainly made up of a variety of uniquely shaped and textured coral. In the immediate vicinity the most popular snorkeling areas are Chital, Cuevones, and Manchones reefs. They are home to large populations of reef fish, including blue chromis and barracuda. Chital, two km north of the island, has good snorkeling with depths between two and five meters. Cuevones and Manchones reefs are between Cancún and Isla Mujeres, with depths of 10-15 meters. Usually dive boats will take snorkelers along (room permitting) on scuba trips. Tour boats leaving daily for Garrafón Beach on Isla Mujeres carry snorkeling equipment. Garrafón is a logical spot for beginners and intermediates. Nondivers can bring dry bread to feed the little critters. They'll jump from the water and eat out of your hand—watch the fingers! Snorkeling equipment is available for rent at all the marinas and some of the hotels.

Dive Certification

Cancún has a good selection of dive shops; check with the marinas for recommendations. Before a diver can rent equipment, it's necessary to show a certified diver's card. Resort courses (for one dive accompanied by the divemaster) and certification classes are offered. For class info, call **Mundo Marina**, PADI, tel. 83-0554; **Neptune**, NAUI, tel. (98) 83-0722; **Aqua Tours**, tel. 83-0400; fax 83-0403. **Scuba Cancún**, NAUI and PADI, tel. 83-1011.

Scuba Diving

For the experienced scuba diver, Cancún would be second choice; Cozumel is unquestionably *número uno!* For dive spots, however, none of the Caribbean is dull. An abundance of rich sealife surrounds each of the reefs; though around Cancún they're somewhat shallow, the beauty and excitement of the scenery are still dramatic. At **Punta Nizúc** (next to Club Med), divers and snorkelers can explore the starting point of the Belize Barrier Reef that runs parallel to the Quintana Roo coast south 250 km to the Gulf of Honduras. This reef is the fifth-longest in the world after the Great Barrier Reef, Australia (1,600 km); Southwest Barrier Reef, New Caledonia (600 km); Northeast Barrier Reef, New Caledonia (540 km); Great Sea Reef, Fiji Islands (260 km); Belize Reef (250 km). Unfortunately, all the boat activity around Punta Nizúc has heavily impacted the reef, and the coral, for the most part, is dead. Tropical fish still swarm to the area, especially when tour boat crews feed them as snorkelers hit the water. According to local divemasters, serious divers have the best chance of finding living coral and a variety of sealife at Manchones reef.

Windsurfing

For anyone who doesn't know, a Windsurfer (also known as a sailboard) is comprised of a surfboard with a sail on a mast attached to the board by a swivel joint. This is controlled by a standing passenger who manipulates the sail with a wishbone tiller. It's a great wind-powered sport; in a brisk breeze the sail billows and this surfboard-cum-sailboat takes its sailor on an exhilarating ride skimming across the waves at mind-blowing speeds. Lessons are available at most of the marinas or the International Windsurfer Sailing School at Playa Tortuga, tel. (98) 84-2023. Usually six hours of lessons give you a good start. Sailboards are available for rent at many of the hotels and at the marinas.

Sailboats

If your idea of a ride in the wind includes a deck under foot and a tiller in hand, Hobie Cat and Sunfish rentals are available at a few hotels and most of the marinas. These small boats will give you a good fast ride if the wind is up. Negotiate for the fee—sometimes you can get a good daily rate, better than the hourly rate posted.

Water-skiing

Most water-skiers prefer Nichupté Lagoon, although skiers are seen on calm days in Bahía de Mujeres north of the island. Equipment and instruction information are available from the marinas.

Jet Skiing, Wave Runners, And Parasailing

One of the new speed thrills on the lagoon is Jet Skiing, obtained by means of a small motorized sled that will slowly circle around the driver should he or she fall off (rentals available at most marinas). Wave Runners are similar to Jet Skis but have seats for a driver and passenger, and are easier to control.

Parasailing is popular at the busy beaches. The sailor, strapped into a colorful parachute and safety vest, is pulled high over the sand and surf by a speedboat; after about 10 minutes of "flying" he is gently deposited back on land with the help of two catchers. Once in a while the rider is inadvertently dropped in the bay—usually to the guffaws of the beach crowd. Most hotels post signs stating they are not responsible for parasailing accidents and injuries that occur by their beaches. Accidents do happen; watch a few passengers take the trip before you go up, and check the harnesses for wear and tear. Marina Aqua Ray has the newest angle on parasailing with its Skyrider Parasail, a two-seater attached to the parachute, giving the riders an enhanced sense of comfort and safety. Check it out at the marina by Lorenzillo's restaurant on the lagoon, tel. (98) 83-3007. See below for more on equipment rental.

Marinas

Cancún's many marinas provide diving equipment and boats to the best scuba grounds; others have docks for a variety of sports, including a flight on an ultralight, and still other docks are pickup points for organized boat tours.

Marina Aqua Ray is one of the largest operations in Cancún, with a good safety record and a responsible attitude towards Cancún's fragile ecology. They rent Wave Runners, Jet Skis, water-skis, kayaks, and snorkeling and diving gear, and operate several tours to the lagoons and reefs. Their **Aqua Ray Jungle Tour** is a two-and-a-half-hour boat trip through the lagoons, including snorkeling near Punta Nizúc. The **Reef Express** is a 30-minute boat shuttle to Marina Aqua Ray's floating water sports center, where you can hang out on an anchored dock with refreshments and sun deck just off Punta Nizúc, snorkel in the surrounding shallow reefs, and catch a ride on the **SubSea Explorer,** with air-conditioned compartments below deck lined with windows for viewing undersea life. The marina also offers parasailing, sportfishing, diving, and sightseeing tours. It's located at Paseo Kukulcán Km 10.5, on the lagoon at Lorenzillo's restaurant, tel. (98) 83-3007, 83-1773, (800) 833-5402.

Aqua Tours marina offers scuba diving, snorkeling, jungle tours, sportfishing, water-skiing, Isla Mujeres cruises, a floating casino cruise, and a lobster dinner cruise. The marina is at Paseo Kukulcán Km 6.25 by Fat Tuesday's, tel. 83-0400 or 83-1860, fax 83-0403. **Royal Yacht Club** offers all water sports and tours plus canoe rentals, with showers and lockers at the rental area, Paseo Kukulcán Km 16.5 by the Captain's Cove restaurant and Royal Mayan hotel, tel. 85-0391 or 85-2930. **Pelican Pier,** with spectacular flights over Cancún in an ultralight plane, also has a Cessna air taxi

and sportfishing trips, at Paseo Kukulcán Km 5.5, tel. 83-0315. **Mundo Marina,** Paseo Kukulcán Km 5.5, tel. 83-0554, has snorkeling, diving, sportfishing, and cruises. **Marina Playa Langosta** at Paseo Kukulcán at Playa Langosta, tel. 83-2802, has information and reservations for sportfishing trips and cruises.

FISHING

Deep-sea Fishing

Fishermen come to Cancún for what is considered some of the finest game fishing in the world. Charters are available and easily arranged with a day or two advance reservation. For information on half- and full-day trips, call the marinas or check with your hotel. On full-day trips you can cap off the afternoon with a fish barbecue on the beach (ask the captain in advance). One of the most exciting game fish, the sailfish, runs from March to mid-July, bonito and dorado from May to early July, wahoo and kingfish from May to September. Barracuda, red snapper, bluefin, grouper, and mackerel are plentiful all year. Sportfishing trips on 31-foot *Bertram* including gear for up to six passengers run about US$320 for four hours, US$520 for eight hours.

Shore Fishing

Once you find a place to fish from shore, you'll catch plenty. Try fishing in the lagoon off the Nichupté bridge. Perhaps now you're spoiled, used to seeing the crystal-clear water of the Caribbean; well, this water is not as clear, but the fish are down there. Expect needlefish or possibly barracuda, and rumor has it that an occasional shark takes a wrong turn at the bridge and finds itself in the lagoon. Contrary to universal belief, this type of shark is good eating.

ESCORTED TOURS

Organized Boat Trips

Many tour boats are available for a variety of trips, most going to nearby Isla Mujeres: glass-bottom boats slowly drift above flamboyant undersea gardens, or a musical cruise lets you dance your way over to the small island. These tours often include snorkeling, and the necessary equipment is furnished (though there may be an added rental charge). The *Aqua-Quin* is a motorized trimaran going twice daily to Isla Mujeres for snorkeling at Garrafón Beach; it includes a buffet lunch, open bar, music, and fun. Reservations required; check at the Camino Real or Hotel Fiesta Americana Coral Beach marina—fare is about US$45 pp. The **Crucero Tropical Cruiser Morning Express** to Isla Mujeres includes a continental breakfast, snorkeling at Garrafón, time for shopping, lunch at the Pirate's Village on the island, and an open bar. The boat is air-conditioned and departs from the Playa Langosta dock at 10:30 a.m., returning at 4:30 p.m.; fare is US$45 pp, tel. (98) 83-3268.

The *B/M Carnaval Cancún,* a large triple decker that cruises to Isla Mujeres, serves a buffet lunch on board with an open bar, stops for snorkeling, and allows time for shopping in downtown Isla Mujeres. Called the **Caribbean Funday** tour, the boat leaves the Fat Tuesday pier daily; fare is US$50, plus US$5 to rent snorkel gear, tel. 84-3760. The same ship, leaving from the Fat Tuesday pier, is used for the evening Caribbean Carnaval cruise to Isla Mujeres, with a buffet dinner, open bar, and Caribbean floor show; fare is US$60 pp.

The *Nautibus* (referred to as a floating submarine) is a double-keeled boat with transparent panels and individual stools in two air-conditioned compartments. In the submerged keels passengers feel as if they're swimming among the schools of fish that live in Chital Reef. Hundreds of sergeant majors rush alongside the windows, and the boat travels directly over coral formations.

Traveling to the reef on *Nautibus*'s top deck, you get a good view of one of the channels along the mangrove-lined Nichupté Lagoon under the Playa Linda bridge, and a look at the beaches in front of many upscale hotels on the way to the reef. The entire trip takes just under two hours, with six daily departures from Playa Linda Pier in the hotel zone. Fare is about US$35 and includes all the beer and sodas you can drink, tel. 83-3552, 83-2119.

Xcaret

One of the most popular day-trips from Cancún goes to **Xcaret,** a man-made water park a half-hour drive south of Cancún. Wildly decorated air-conditioned buses depart 9-10 a.m. from the Xcaret terminal on Paseo Kukulcán across from Plaza Caracol, next to the Fiesta Americana Coral Beach Hotel, and return in the late afternoon. The tour costs US$30, including transportation and entrance to the park; meals and activities within the park are not included. Tours including the ruins of Tulúm with a stop at Xcaret are also available. Call (98) 83-0654 or 83-0743 for information.

A Tour to Tikal

The Guatemalan airline **Aviateca** has an exciting new tour well worth exploring. Their one-day Tikal Tour takes you by air from Cancún to the spectacular Maya ruins of Tikal in the Guatemalan highlands. The plane departs Cancún at 6 a.m. and lands at Flores, near the ruins. You get five hours to explore the ruins, which many consider to be the most spectacular of the Maya sites. Wildlife is abundant here. Spider monkeys swing from the treetops along heavily wooded paths and parrots fly overhead. Vendors sell Guatemalan crafts and folk art in the ruins parking lot for prices far lower than those at Cancún shops, where Guatemalan crafts have overshadowed those from Mexico. The plane returns to Cancún at 6 p.m. Aviateca also offers extended tours of Guatemala and flights to Guatemala City. For information, contact your hotel tour desk or Aviateca at Plaza Mexico, Av. Tulúm 200, tel. (98) 84-3938 or 87-1386. **Mexicana** airlines also offers Tikal tours, tel. 84-2000.

Self-guided Tours

If you prefer to investigate on your own, a trip to Isla Mujeres is easy and can be cheap. The easiest way to get there is on the **Shuttle Express** from the Playa Linda Pier; the cost is about US$13 RT and the shuttle departs four times a day for the 45-minute trip, tel. 83-3448. If the schedules are inconvenient for your plans, hop a taxi (about US$10 OW) or a bus (marked Ruta 8 from Av. Tulúm) that will take you to either Punta Sam or Puerto Juárez. Punta Sam is where the car ferry docks; it also takes passengers, but Puerto Juárez is the departure and arrival point for the passenger ferries. A small information office at the foot of the dock is sometimes open to answer questions about Isla Mujeres, including the hotels. Two types of boats cover the route. The modern, air-conditioned, enclosed ferries charge about US$3.50 OW and make the crossing in less than 30 minutes. The older open ferries charge about US$1.75 OW and make the trip in 45 minutes. Buy your ticket on board either boat.

One way to make sure you see the sights you want to see without having to follow a group itinerary is to hire an English-speaking taxi driver for an hour or a day. Rates start at US$10 per hour if you stay within the Cancún limits, and get higher the farther you travel. For information, contact the taxi drivers' union, tel. 83-1840 or 83-1844.

Isla Holbox

Locals tell us that one of the best side trips from Cancún for nature lovers is to Isla Holbox off the north coast of the Yucatán Peninsula. A natural preserve and bird refuge, Holbox is but 32 km in landmass (mostly mangrove swamp) and marks the division between the Gulf of Mexico and the Caribbean Sea. Only a few hundred people live on the island, supporting themselves by fishing and hammock weaving. There's a hammock loom in front of nearly every house; this is a great place to see how they're made. The islanders are not accustomed to tourists, and your presence will likely be greeted with curious stares and friendly advances.

To get to Holbox you'll need a rental car and a sense of adventure. Drive west out of Cancún toward Mérida on the old road (not the *autopista*). Near the town of Vicente Guerrero you'll see a road on the right heading north to Kantunilkin. If you miss that, there's another side road heading north near Nuevo X-Can. Your ultimate destination is Chiquila—ask for directions often. The paved road heads north to Kantunilkin past small ranches and pueblos; after about 65 miles you will reach the tiny settlement of Chiquila on the north coast. A fishing community with few residents, and even fewer guests, Chiquila is the departure point for the car ferry to Isla Holbox, which runs only a few days a week, and then only if the demand is high enough. There are a few palapa restaurants on the beach here where you can get cold drinks and a superb lunch of fresh lobster and fish. To reach Holbox you are best off hiring a captain and boat from among the Chiquila fishermen for a tour of the island, which will take about four hours. There are no hotels in Chiquila or on Holbox, but camping is permitted, or you may be able to arrange to stay in a local home. We've had reports that you can also hire a boat in Punta Sam or on Isla Mujeres for a tour around Isla Holbox.

SPORTS

Golf

The **Pok Ta Pok Club de Golf,** Paseo Kukulcán. Km 7.5, tel. (98) 83-1277 or 82-1230, fax 83-3358, has tennis courts and a well-kept 18-hole golf course designed by Robert Trent Jones. The golf club is a great sports center, with a pro shop, swimming pool, marina, restaurant, bar, and even its own small restored Maya ruin near the 12th hole, discovered when the course was built. Temporary club membership allows you to play golf or tennis at the club; arrangements can be made through your hotel. Greens fees are about US$50, with an additional US$30 for golf cart rental. Many of the hotels on the island also have tennis courts, some with night lighting for a fee.

Horseback Riding

Rancho Loma Bonita provides horses for rides along the sea or into the jungle in a wide variety of locations. The ranch is located south of Cancún near Puerto Morelos. Transportation to and from the ranch, drinks, lunch, and a guide are included in the rates. Make arrangements through your hotel tour desk or call the ranch directly, tel. (98) 84-0907.

Working Out

Gold's Gym at the Flamingo Plaza (in the hotel zone) offers new modern machines, aerobics classes, experienced instructors, lockers, and showers. The gym is air-conditioned and open Mon.-Fri. 7 a.m.-9 p.m., Sun. 9 a.m.-9 p.m. Many hotels have state-of-the-art gyms and spas as well, usually available to guests for an added charge.

Bowling

Cancún's first bowling alley opened in Kukulcán Plaza in 1993 and has 20 lanes, a restaurant and video bar, and bowling instruction. It's open 10 a.m.-1:30 a.m., tel. (98) 85-3425.

Spectator Sports

Bullfighting has long been a popular pageant for Latin countries. Cancún's bullring is located on Av. Bonampak at Sayil, tel. (98) 84-5465 or 84-8372. Bullfights are held every Wednesday at 3:30 p.m. and are preceded by a Mexican fi-

Camino Real Hotel offers its own small lagoon with an opening to the sea. There you can see turtles and many tropical fish.

esta with folkloric dance performances at 2:30 p.m. Tickets are available through tour desks or at the bullring.

Jai-alai is Cancún's newest spectator sport, and is played in the enormous purple **Gambling Palace,** on Paseo Kukulcán by Playa Linda, which opened in 1993. Jai-alai games are played nightly 6 p.m.-midnight; dinner is served on the upper level of the viewing area, and betting on the players is encouraged. Also in the palace is the Super Book, where viewers bet on major sporting events and horse races broadcast over satellite television from the United States. Super Book is open daily 1 p.m.-midnight; Jai-alai nightly 6 p.m.-midnight, tel. 83-9000.

ACCOMMODATIONS

With 116 hotels and over 18,000 hotel rooms as of late 1993, Cancún has hotels in all price ranges, though it takes some effort to find budget accommodations. Rates are lowest in the late spring, summer, and fall months, though some hotels raise their rates in August when Mexicans and Europeans typically take long vacations. Rates rise 20-50% around Thanksgiving and again at Christmas, with some hotels actually doubling their rates for the week between Christmas and New Year's Day. The best prices can be found with package rates. As one hotel representative told us, "Nobody books a room at rack rates in Cancún anymore." Packages vary and may include reduced airfare, reduced rates for stays of three or more nights, reduced car rental rates, welcome cocktails, free meals, free use of health clubs, tennis courts, and so on. Have your travel agent check all these options, and keep an eye out for package deals advertised in newspapers and magazines. You can get amazing bargains when occupancy is low, even in the high season. Keep in mind that most prices you'll get do not include the 10% tax.

In Cancún city you'll find new, moderately priced hotels and condos serving up the flavor of Yucatán in the US$30-100-per-night category; they offer easy access to crowded sidewalk cafes (good for meeting people), romantic dinners, hot discos, intimate bistros, cinemas, buses, and a multitude of shops to explore—all within a few kilometers of the beach and lagoon. If you need a shot of luxury, the hotel zone on the "island" has the most modern hostelries on Mexico's Caribbean coast for a first-rate vacation in a sunny tropical setting. There's glamour, excitement, excellent service, great entertainment, lavish rooms, and epicurean delights—to say nothing of the surroundings, which bombard the senses with nature's simple beauty.

Deluxe
Almost every hotel in the island's hotel zone fits into the deluxe category, offering at least one swimming pool (sometimes more) and good beaches; an assortment of restaurants, bars, and nightlife; beach activities and gardens; travel, tour, and car agencies; and laundry and room service. In fact, a few tourists find

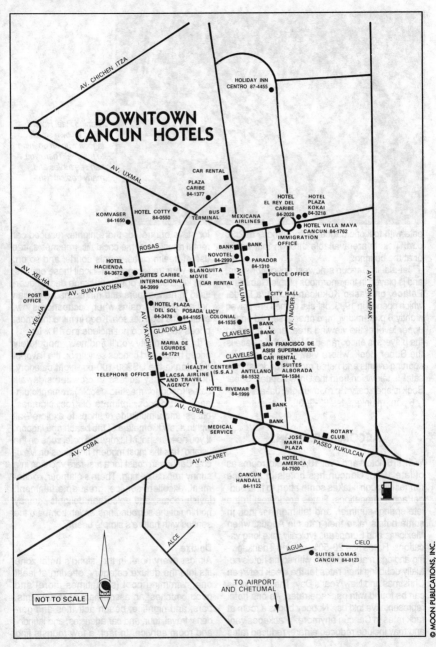

DOWNTOWN
CANCUN HOTELS

HOLIDAY INN
CENTRO 87-4455

AV. CHICHEN ITZA

AV. UXMAL

CAR RENTAL

PLAZA
CARIBE
84-1377

KOMVASER
84-1650

HOTEL COTTY
84-0550

BUS
TERMINAL

MEXICANA
AIRLINES

HOTEL
EL REY DEL
CARIBE
84-2028

HOTEL
PLAZA
KOKAI
84-3218

HOTEL VILLA MAYA
CANCUN 84-1762

ROSAS

BANK

BANK

IMMIGRATION
OFFICE

AV. XEL-HA

HOTEL
HACIENDA
84-3672

SUITES CARIBE
INTERNACIONAL
84-3999

NOVOTEL
84-2999

PARADOR
84-1310

AV. SUNYAXCHEN

BLANQUITA
MOVIE
CAR RENTAL

POLICE OFFICE

POST
OFFICE

CITY HALL

AV. XEL-HA

HOTEL PLAZA
DEL SOL
84-3478

POSADA LUCY
84-4165

COLONIAL
84-1535

AV. NADER

AV. TULUM

AV. BONAMPAK

GLADIOLAS

CLAVELES

AV. YAXCHILAN

MARIA DE
LOURDES
84-1721

BANK

BANK

CLAVELES

SAN FRANCISCO DE
ASISI SUPERMARKET

CAR RENTAL

HEALTH CENTER
(S.S.A.)

SUITES
ALBORADA
84-1584

TELEPHONE OFFICE

LACSA AIRLINE
AND TRAVEL
AGENCY

ANTILLANO
84-1532

HOTEL RIVEMAR
84-1999

BANK

AV. COBA

BANK

MEDICAL
SERVICE

AV. COBA

ROTARY
CLUB

JOSE
MARIA PLAZA

PASEO KUKULCAN

AV. XCARET

HOTEL
AMERICA
84-7500

CANCUN
HANDALL
84-1122

ALCE

NOT TO SCALE

AGUA

CIELO

SUITES LOMAS
CANCUN 84-8123

TO AIRPORT
AND CHETUMAL

© MOON PUBLICATIONS, INC.

everything for a complete vacation under one roof and stay pretty close to the hotel. Rates in the deluxe category start at about US$120 d in the low season, US$150 in the high season, and can get as expensive as you wish; there is a 10% tax on all hotel rooms, usually not included in the quoted rate.

The hotels themselves showcase brilliant architecture, using the lines that would best fit into nature's environment, with a suggestion of the ancient Maya thrown in; add extraordinary comfort and total luxury for an overall description of the majority of the hotels in Cancún's hotel zone. If a rainy afternoon discourages beaching, take a tour of the hotels. It would require a whole book to describe all the hotels in Cancún, so we have chosen a few that are beautiful and comfortable and offer the ultimate in luxury.

The **Hyatt Regency,** tel. (98) 83-0966 or (800) 233-1234, fax 83-1349, has a breathtaking 18-floor-high central atrium that takes in the entire lobby, where afternoon drinks are accompanied by piano music. A bubbling waterfall separates the two swimming pools, where daily games of volleyball keep the actives busy. The views are breathtaking and the services perfect. The rooms are all newly renovated with carpeting replaced by marble floors, ceiling fans and a/c, a modern green-and-gold color scheme with light wood trim, mini-bars, satellite TV, and balconies. The beach was heavily eroded by Hurricane Gilbert; when high tides make sunbathing impossible, guests are invited to use the wider beach at the

adjacent Camino Real. Snorkeling is good at the rocky point right offshore. Both hotels offer their "special hotels within the hotels," called the Regency Club, where services include complimentary breakfast of eggs, fruit, and pastries, and afternoon cocktails and snacks, along with luxury amenities in the rooms.

At the **Hyatt Cancún Caribe,** tel. 83-0044 or (800) 233-1234, fax 83-1514, the Regency Club villas offer lovely sitting areas and share a private pool, whirlpool, and comfortable clubhouse near the pool for complimentary breakfast and afternoon cocktails. The 68 Regency Club rooms and villas and 198 regular rooms have newly remodeled bathrooms. The main pool for all guests is enormous, with a whirlpool big enough for 10 friendly folks, and there is a landscaped jogging track for fitness buffs. The beach is larger than the one at the Hyatt Regency, good for walking in either direction to visit other hotels. If you want to have a really scrumptious dinner New Orleans style, go to the **Blue Bayou** at the Hyatt Cancún Caribe. Fourth- and fifth-time returnees continue to rave about the exquisite food at the Blue Bayou. Not only will you hear great jazz, but authentic Cajun and Creole cuisine are served amid a lush setting of waterfalls and bayou swamp—Louisiana swamps never looked like this!

One of the all-time favorites is the durable **Camino Real Cancún,** tel. 83-0100 or (800) 722-6466, fax 83-2965. You have plenty of space at this place, which is spread out on lovely

a bird's-eye view of the Hyatt Regency Hotel's pool

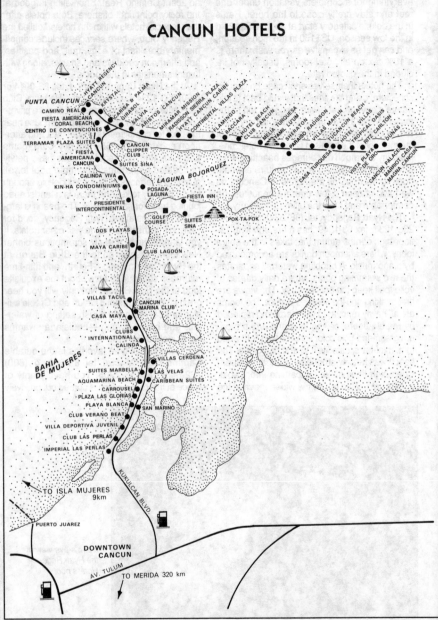

CANCUN HOTELS

HYATT REGENCY
CANCUN
KRISTAL
PUNTA CANCUN
GIRASOL A PALMA
CAMINO REAL
SALVIA
CRISTOS CANCUN
FIESTA AMERICANA
CORAL BEACH
MIRAMAR MISSION
CENTRO DE CONVENCIONES
RADISSON SIERRA PLAZA
HYATT CANCUN CARIBE
CONTINENTAL VILLAS PLAZA
FLAMINGO
BACCARA
HOTEL BEACH
CLUB CANCUN
MELIA TURQUESA
KIMI LUUM
PARAISO RADISSON
SHERATON
VILLAS MARLIN
TUCANCUN BEACH
HOTEL Y VILLAS
TROPICAL OASIS
RITZ CARLTON
CANCUN PALACE CASA
MARRIOTT CASA
MAGNA CANCUN
DUNAS
VISTA PLAYA
DE OHO
CASA TURQUESA
TERRAMAR PLAZA SUITES
CANCUN
CLIPPER
CLUB
FIESTA
AMERICANA
CANCUN
SUITES SINA
CALINDA VIVA
KIN HA CONDOMINIUMS
LAGUNA BOJORQUEZ
POSADA
LAGUNA
FIESTA INN
PRESIDENTE
INTERCONTINENTAL
GOLF
COURSE
SUITES
SINA
POK-TA-POK
DOS PLAYAS
MAYA CARIBE
CLUB LAGOON
VILLAS TACUL
CANCUN
MARINA CLUB
CASA MAYA
CLUBS
INTERNATIONAL
CALINDA
BAHIA
DE MUJERES
VILLAS CERDENA
SUITES MARBELLA
LAS VELAS
AQUAMARINA BEACH
CARIBBEAN SUITES
CARROUSEL
PLAZA LAS GLORIAS
PLAYA BLANCA
SAN MARINO
CLUB VERANO BEAT
VILLA DEPORTIVA JUVENIL
CLUB LAS PERLAS
IMPERIAL LAS PERLAS

KUKULCAN BLVD.

TO ISLA MUJERES
9km

PUERTO JUAREZ

DOWNTOWN
CANCUN

AV. TULUM

TO MERIDA 320 km

© MOON PUBLICATIONS, INC.

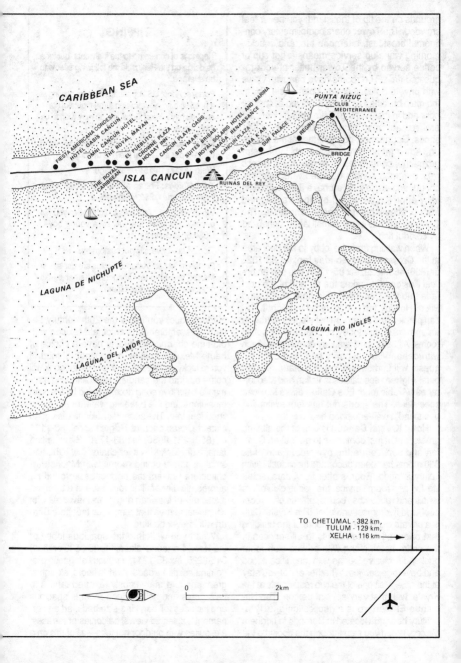

CARIBBEAN SEA

PUNTA NIZUC
CLUB
MEDITERRANEE

FIESTA AMERICANA CONDESA
HOTEL OASIS CANCUN
OMNI CANCUN HOTEL
THE ROYAL MAYAN
EL PUEBLITO
CROWNE PLAZA
HOLIDAY INN
CANCUN PLAYA OASIS
SOLYMAR
SUITES BRISAS
ROYAL SOLARIS HOTEL AND MARINA
RAMADA RENAISSANCE
CANCUN PLAZA
YALMA K'AN
SUN PALACE
REGINA

THE ROYAL
CARIBBEAN

BRIDGE

ISLA CANCUN

RUINAS DEL REY

LAGUNA DE NICHUPTE

LAGUNA RIO INGLES

LAGUNA DEL AMOR

TO CHETUMAL - 382 km,
TULUM - 129 km,
XELHA - 116 km

0   2km

grounds on the tip of the island; you never feel crowded. The **Tower** offers complimentary continental breakfast, afternoon tea, and snacks; morning wake-up service means a hot cup of coffee served by the Tower butler at your requested time. The rooms have beautiful views with private balconies, and color cable TV. In the main building live music is played at cocktail hour and in the evening. Take your pick of several restaurants, including bars and coffee shops. Gourmands, do try dinner at the **Calypso.** A few menu favorites are: chilled lobster gazpacho, *camarones empanizados con coco fresco* (jumbo shrimp breaded with fresh coconut), and apple torta aruba, a flaky crust with juicy apples surrounded by flowers sculpted from peaches, plums, grapes, and kiwis. The Camino Real has its own small lagoon inhabited by colorful fish.

When walking from the lobby to the pool area at the **Crowne Plaza Holiday Inn,** tel. 85-1022 or (800) 465-4329, fax 85-1707, you see an optical illusion that makes the far end of the pool fade into the Caribbean and horizon. Crowne Plaza Holiday Inn is decorated in bright Mexican purples and blues against elegant marble in an immense, airy lobby surrounded by public rooms. All 380 rooms are very comfortable, each with ocean view, security box, and balcony; guests will find several great restaurants and bars. **Alghero** specializes in Italian and Mediterranean/Arabic food; **Los Gallos** offers Mexican specialties. The sports nut has four swimming pools and a well-equipped health club.

Hotel Krystal Cancún is one of the all-time greats, and it just continues to get better. Comfort and service are the bywords. Each of its 330 rooms has been decorated individually, with luxury in mind. Rooms offer servi-bars, satellite TV, and room service; the health club offers tennis and racquetball courts, private club-room pool, and hydromassage pool. The Krystal Club is a private club on the top floors of the building that offers complete access to all services in the entire hotel, along with private club-room pool and exclusive lounge with magnificent food and beverage service. Whether or not you stay at the hotel, visit one of the two restaurants at the Krystal with that very special person. The **Hacienda El Mortero** is a duplication of a 17th-century hacienda located in Durango in northern Mexico. When you step through the door into the

TIPPING

Tipping is of course up to the individual, but for a guideline on the Peninsula the following seems to be average.

Porters: About US$1 per bag. If you're staying at a hotel with no elevator and three flights of stairs and you have lots of luggage, you may wish to be more generous.

Hotel Maids: If staying more than one night, US$1-2 per day left at the end of your stay.

Waitresses: 10-15% is average.

Tour Guides: For an all-day trip, US$5 is appropriate, and US$1 for the driver.

When visiting a ruin, cave, or lighthouse you will usually be shown the way by a young boy—US$0.50 is customary.

Tipping taxi drivers is not customary.

For the most part, American coins are useless in Mexico since moneychangers, whether banks or stores, will not accept them.

outdoor patio, you leave the 20th century behind. The ambience is colonial Mexican with old-time charm, and guests have a choice of haute Mexican cuisine or continental food. If you're lucky, a very old, leathery-faced cook will come out into the candlelit patio and sing a romantic Latin love song accompanied by Mexican musicians and the bubbling water of the plant-lined fountain. The second choice takes you to distant Casablanca at **Bogart's,** tel. 83-1133 or (800) 231-9860, fax 83-1790. Slow ceiling fans, high-backed wicker chairs, low light, and small, intimate dining rooms with Moorish architecture present the perfect background for a romantic dinner. The food here is a treat, an exotic mix of Mexican and Arabic favorites with whimsical names that remind us that here Bogart will forever be king.

When you walk into the spacious lobby of the **Hotel Cancún Palace,** tel. 85-0533 or (800) 346-8225, fax 85-1244, a tranquil elegance predominates: rich woods, marble floors, skylights, greenery, and marvelously textured fabrics in pale grays and beige. Each room is spacious and includes full bar, king-size beds, art and ornaments, splendid views, balconies or terraces, a/c, suites with outdoor hot tubs—all of this on a

492-foot-oceanfront beach with the turquoise sea and sand just a few feet from your hotel. For the ambitious, add tennis and a health spa to the list of swimming, Jet Skiing, fishing, sailing, snorkeling, and scuba diving. For the less ambitious, the pools are lined with chaise lounges near waterfalls, snack bar, pool bar, sunken bar, lobby bar, and gourmet restaurants that offer seafood and international cuisine. Excellent Mexican food is served at **Las Golondrinas,** or have breakfast and lunch by the sea at the enchanting outdoor **Palapas Café las Redes.**

Sheraton, one of the "experienced" hotels, is kept in good condition with frequent remodeling and additions. The 745 rooms and 211 suites are modern and comfortable, with satellite TV, mini-bars, and individually controlled air. The grounds are beautifully kept and include two swimming pools, ample chaise lounges for sun worshippers, and a great shopping arcade; beach lovers have a half mile of white-powder sand and blue sea to frolic in. Archaeology buffs will even find on the grounds a small remnant of the Maya past, **Yamil Lu'um,** one of the few remaining Maya structures in Cancún. Visitors play tennis on one of six lighted courts, visit the fitness center with sauna, steam bath, and whirlpool, or play golf on the mini-course; children enjoy the playground.

The seven-story **Sheraton Towers** is a separate building with 167 rooms, each with a balcony and a spectacular view of the turquoise sea, some suites with terraces and jacuzzis. The Towers offers the private **Towers Lounge,** special concierge, coffee or tea with your morning wake-up call, continental breakfast, daily newspaper, clothes pressing, hors d'oeuvres service each evening, and luxurious amenities in the rooms like hair dryers, safes, alarm clocks, and a special treat from the pastry chef upon retiring.

The Sheraton offers a variety of restaurants and bars: **La Gaviota, La Duna,** and **Yalma Caan Lobby Bar,** which has a lively happy hour with the sea in the background. Call 83-1988 or (800) 325-3535, fax 83-1450.

Located between Nichupté Lagoon and the Caribbean Sea, the **Continental Villas Plaza Hotel** is a unique mix of colonial, Moorish, and Caribbean architecture. A cloud of pink from a distance, the complex includes 636 rooms and suites scattered in 26 villas and one tower. Rooms decorated in pastel colors are cozy and

comfortable, with a/c and views of either the sea or the lagoon. Four pools and 500 yards of white-sand beach encourage guests to hang around. Tennis, squash, and racquetball courts are on the premises along with instructors for all manner of water sports. Five restaurants and three bars cater to every taste. Try **Las Cúpulas,** tel. 83-1022 or (800) 882-6684, fax 83-2270, with its special Italian cuisine.

Fiesta Americana Condesa, tel. 85-1000 or (800) 223-2332, fax 85-2005, is a smashing hotel. Guests enter through a 117-foot-tall palapa at the entrance (with escalator, thank you), the highest palapa roof in Mexico. The Disney people helped with the design of the hotel—and it shows. The magnificent lobby is decorated with stylized marble floors, jewel-toned fabrics, smart, upholstered wicker furniture, and brilliant stained-glass awnings, which extend over the bars. The hotel is reminiscent of a small (upscale) Mexican village with greenery everywhere. Rooms are comfortable, many with spectacular views. Swimming pools are joined by arched bridges, and excellent restaurants offer a variety of ethnic foods to choose from. If you just can't drag yourself out of the pool, try a game of backgammon on a floating table available for the asking. For the health buff, there are three air-conditioned indoor tennis courts and a complete spa and gym.

Fiesta Americana Coral Beach, with 602 suites, is one of the largest hotels in Cancún, with a spectacular atrium lobby covered by a stained-glass dome. A string quartet plays in the lobby in late afternoon—a nice change from the typical happy-hour scene. The spacious suites all have ocean-view balconies and sitting areas a few steps below the bedrooms; master suites have hot tubs. The 660-foot swimming pool flows the length of the property, with several sunning areas separated by waterfalls, bridge, and palms. The **Coral Reef** restaurant, tel. 83-2900 or (800) 223-2332, fax 83-3076, is superb.

The third of the chain's hotels, **Fiesta Americana Cancún,** tel. 83-1400 or (800) 223-2332, fax 83-2502, looks like a small enclosed Mexican village, with buildings painted subdued coral, blue, and gold glowing in the light of the sun, framing a lovely beach. Much smaller than the others with only 280 rooms, this Fiesta Americana has a cozy, friendly feeling, and is, by the way, less expensive.

Presidente Cancún, one of the first hotels on Cancún island, has a loyal clientele who delight in seeing the same faces at the front door and in the restaurant every time they return. Architect Ricardo Legoretta designed the hotel in 1975 using his trademark bold angles and vibrant colors, now overshadowed by a 10-story tower. Private condos and homes sit on either side of the hotel, making the beach less crowded than at other hotels, and the over-sized swimming pool is backed by a waterfall (great for massaging sore shoulders!) and white pyramid. All rooms have comfortable sloping backrests on the beds and include complimentary continental breakfast, afternoon hors d'oeuvres, and late evening pastries and coffee served in a comfortable lounge. The tower's 10th floor was completely remodeled in 1993 into large master suites; view from the both the lagoon and ocean sides of the building are spectacular. The beachfront palapa restaurant **El Caribeño,** tel. 83-0200 or (800) 447-6147, fax 83-2515, has one of the best breakfast buffets in Cancún, and is well worth visiting for any meal.

The **Regina,** tel. 85-0444 or (800) 228-3000, fax 85-0666, opened in 1991 and has a superb location at the southern end of the hotel zone near Punta Nizúc, with pools and lounging areas on the lagoon and the Caribbean. The hotel sits far back from the road and seems somewhat austere at first. But architect Jose Iturbe has taken full advantage of Cancún's natural beauty, designing sweeping hot pink walls that glow with the light of the setting sun, and open windows painted cobalt blue framing the view of the sea. The rooms are extraordinarily user friendly, with both a/c and ceiling fans (so guests can remain cool while listening to the surf crash on shore), sinks over the mini-bars, and shower stall separate from the bathtub. The location is great for those seeking privacy and easy access to the airport and highway heading south down the Cancún-Tulúm Corridor, but not so great if you plan on spending a lot of time at the hotel zone shopping malls and restaurants. The sea gets rough here, but there are pools and whirlpools on both the sea and lagoon sides of the hotel.

Casa Turquesa, a member of the Small Luxury Hotels of the World, has a guard at the front gate to protect the privacy of the guests (both celebrities and just regular folks). Understated elegance is the theme here, with comfort as important as style. The 28 suites have private hot tubs on the balconies (all facing the sea), compact disc players and VCRs (with a long list of CDs and videos available at your request), every kind of toiletry you could possibly need, and comfortable sitting areas. The blue and white color scheme carries through to the peaked awnings covering lounge areas by the pool, designed to appear as if it flows into the sea. With 24-hour gourmet room service, you may never wish to leave the secluded grounds, and with rates running US$350-2000 per night you might as well enjoy your suite. For more information and reservations call 85-2924 or (800) 525-4800, or in Cancún, fax 85-2922.

The **Ritz Carlton,** tel. 85-0808 or (800) 241-3333, fax 85-1015, is the most extravagant hotel in Cancún. The Ritz seems more suited to the ambience of Geneva or Paris than a beach resort. Visitors in sandals and shorts may be intimidated by the white-gloved doorman and awed by the abundance of crystal chandeliers and beveled glass doors—the public spaces inspire a reverential hush common in haughty galleries. The room decor is equally opulent, with televisions and mini-bars hidden in regal armoires and showers surrounded by glass. The private Club Lounge overlooks an atrium, providing a soothing yet formal setting for afternoon tea. The excellent health club facilities, including steam rooms, saunas, and massage, are included in the room rates. The Club Grill has become a favorite hideaway for locals seeking genuine sophistication, and the desserts are as extravagant as the decor. The Ritz isn't for everyone, but it is the ultimate for those seeking unparalleled service and an elegant sense of style.

This is just a sampling of the hotel zone's spectacular resorts. Others in the super-deluxe and most expensive categories (starting at US$150 in the low season) include: **Melía Cancún** (or the five-star **Melía Turquesa**) with its eye-catching steel and glass pyramid roof and black marble entryway, tel. (800) 336-3542; **Oasis Cancún** and **Cancún Playa Oasis,** tel. (800) 446-2747; and **Marriot Casa Magna,** replete with Moorish domes and waterfalls, tel. (800) 228-9290. **Villas Tacul** is a wonderful place to set up housekeeping in beachfront villas with two to five bedrooms, and in studio apartments, all with kitchens. Studios start at

1. Fiesta Americana Condessa, Cancun; **2.** Nichupte Lagoon, Cancun;
3. Cancun Palace Hotel, Cancun; **4.** Crowne Plaza Hotel, Cancun

1. Maya archaeological site, El Castillo, Tulum; **2.** Chichen Itza; **3.** Coba

US$135, two-bedroom villas at US$250 per night; tel. (800) 842-0193.

Moderate (Hotel Zone)

It is possible to stay in the hotel zone without getting a second mortgage on your home. One of the best economically priced places is the **Days Inn El Pueblito,** tel. 85-0797 or (800) 325-2525, fax 85-0731, built on a slight hill above the sea with several low-rise buildings staggered down the hill. Swimming pools flow between the buildings, giving guests plenty of quiet lounging areas away from the largest pool, complete with swim-up bar. A water slide runs down the hill in a separate area—naturally, this is where the kids hang out. El Pueblito is a good choice for families, since the rooms are comfortable rather than fancy and there's plenty of play space on the grounds and beach. Rates start at about US$80 d in the low season.

Other moderately priced Cancún island hotels starting at about US$75 d in the low season (plus 10% tax) are clustered around the Playa Linda area, including: **Playa Blanca,** an older hotel with delightfully overgrown landscaping, tel. 85-1166 or (800) 528-1234, fax 85-0032; **Calinda Beach,** tel. 83-1600 or (800) 221-2222, fax 83-1857; **Plaza las Glorias,** good for package deals, tel. 83-0811 or (800) 882-6684, fax 83-0901; **Verano Beat,** popular with the young, spring-break set, tel. 83-0722, fax 83-0173; **Carrousel,** tel. 83-2312 or (800) 333-1212, fax 83-2312; and **Las Perlas,** which had the lowest rates on the island (US$50) during the low season, tel. 83-2247, fax 83-0106. Closer to the major malls, discos, and restaurants are: **Calinda Viva,** on a nice beach near Plaza Caracol, tel. 83-0800 or (800) 221-2222, fax 83-2087; **Aristos,** popular with families and Mexican tourists, tel. 83-0011 or (800) 527-4786, fax 83-0078; and **Miramar Mission,** popular with tour groups, tel. 83-1755, fax 83-1136.

Moderate (Downtown)

Moderate accommodations are found in bustling downtown Cancún. The biggest drawback to this location is the absence of beach, but blue sea and white sand are accessible in short order by bus every 15 minutes. Some hotels provide free transportation for their guests. Sometimes crowded, these hotels are good bargains. The Yucatecan ambience pervades, and each has a helpful staff willing to answer questions about the city. The hotels have private baths, a/c, hot water, phone in room, swimming pool, bar, and restaurants. The rates run US$30 d to about US$100 in the low season.

The most expensive (and nicest) downtown hotel is the **Holiday Inn Centro,** Av. Nader 1, tel. (98) 87-4455 or (800) HOLIDAY, fax 84-7945, with all the amenities of the beachside hotels, and free transport to get you on the sand. The pretty peach-and-white four-story building sits at the end of Av. Nadir, far from just about everything. The 100 rooms face an inner courtyard and large swimming pool; banquet and meeting facilities are available and it seems this would be a better choice for business travelers than tourists. Rates start at US$90 d in low season, US$100 d in high season.

Hotel Hacienda, Av. Sunyaxchen #39, tel. 84-3672 or (800) 458-6888, fax (714) 494-5088 in the U.S., is a low-key, pleasant hotel with 40 a/c rooms, swimming pool, pool bar, beach club service and transportation, cafe, parking, and travel agency on the premises. Rate in summer is about US$28 s or d, in winter US$38 s or d. **Hotel Plaza del Sol,** Av. Yaxchilán #31, tel. 84-3478, 84-3888, or (800) 221-6509, fax 84-1309, has been around a long time and gets better every year. It's conveniently located in the middle of the city, with scores of cafes and shops within walking distance. Rooms are smallish, with a/c, TV, pool, restaurant, coffee shop, and a free shuttle that takes guests to the beach; towels are provided. The hotel has a pleasant Mexican flavor, decorated with terra-cotta pottery, tile floors, and colorful textiles. Rates in high season from US$72 s to US$78 d, lower during the summer months. **Hotel America,** Av. Tulúm and Calle Brisa, tel. 84-7500 or (800) 262-2656, fax 84-1953, is a large commercial-type hotel with clean rooms, a pool, a/c, and a coffee shop, within walking distance of good food and interesting shops. A free shuttle takes guests to the beach; rate in low season is US$50 s or d, US$70 high season.

Suites Caribe International, Av. Yaxchilán #36, 84-3999 or (800) 223-6510, fax 84-1993, offers both rooms and suites with kitchens. In the heart of downtown Cancún, the multistoried building has a/c, pool, green garden areas, restaurant, bar, and private parking. Twenty-four rooms are junior suites with kitchenettes.

Some suites are large enough for four persons, making them a bargain. The junior suites are US$60 in the low season, US$80 in high season; rooms are US$45 in low season and US$60 in high season.

Another place that gets high marks is the **Parador,** Av. Tulúm #26, tel. 84-1310 or 84-1043, fax 84-9712, located in the center of downtown Cancún next to a favorite budget cafe, Pop. Each of the 66 rooms has a private bath and a/c. Purified drinking water is available in the hall, and a pool and grassy area make sun worshippers happy.

Other place choices in the moderate range are: **Antillano,** Claveles at Tulúm, tel. 84-1532, fax 84-1878, right in the middle of the action, with quieter rooms facing the inner courtyard behind Av. Tulúm; **Cancún Handall,** Tulúm at Cobá, tel. 84-1122, fax 84-9280, popular with tour groups, ask about promotional rates; **Plaza Caribe,** Av. Tulúm at Uxmal, tel. 84-1377, fax 84-6352, run by Best Western, large and dependable, across the street from the bus station (with a decent coffee shop where you may want to hang out while waiting for your bus).

All-inclusive Resorts

The all-inclusive resort is gaining a large foothold in Cancún. For years the only one was **Club Med.** This is still one great place to enjoy the GOs, who really make sure that you enjoy yourself (they remind you of young students in summer stock; they do everything from singing to serving)! The grounds are beautiful on the tip of Point Nizúc, at the end of the hotel zone. The beaches are spread out next to what many consider the most beautiful sea in the world, and the lagoon is also part of the landscape, making it easy to indulge in many water sports. Choose from sailboarding (lessons available), scuba diving (you will be expected to make a check-out dive before they turn you loose), scuba certification course, snorkeling right off the dock, sailing, boat trips to Isla Mujeres for more snorkeling, and water-skiing. The GOs jokingly tell you not to throw your friends into the lagoon or they might have an unexpected meeting with a local crocodile—but it's no joke!

Lessons and rackets are provided at eight tennis courts (four lit for night playing), and there's a volleyball game going on around the clock—or so it seems. This is a place to have

fun; there's music and dancing and games galore. If your idea of fun is to laze around a chaise lounge or swimming pool all day, you've got it. Or would you rather indulge in a beer-drinking contest, talent show, tug-of-war, egg-throwing event, or who knows what else they'll think of by the time you get there?

Dining is buffet style and the choices are endless. There are three different cafes to try, and you can sleep late and still have breakfast. Beer and wine are served gratis with lunch and dinner. For hard liquor and between-meal snacks you must pay with beads.

Club Med, tel. 85-2300 or (800) 258-2633, fax 85-2290, is quite a distance from downtown Cancún, but taxis are always lined up at the gate (for about US$7 OW); however, with just a short walk to the neighboring Regina Hotel, a bus will take you downtown for under US$1. The Club says, please, no topless sunbathing, because it's against Mexican law; however, you always see someone who doesn't read the signs. Wear your bracelets all the time. Security guards are scattered about the property mostly to make sure that intruders haven't wandered in from the beach now that other hotels are getting close to what was once far away from the rest of the world—or at least the Club Med world. Rates in the low season start at about US$860 pp, double occupancy, for a seven-day stay.

Sun Palace, in the hotel zone at Av. Kukulcán Km 20, tel. 85-1555 or (800) 346-8225, fax 85-2040, formerly called Puerto al Sol, is an all-inclusive resort that gives you the feeling you're aboard an intimate (only 150 suites), upscale cruise ship—without the wave action. It offers planned activities, good food, inviting beach, and beautifully decorated suites with shiny marble floors and creamy colors splashed with modern Mexican decor. Each suite also has a whirlpool bath, built-in hair dryer and in-room safe-deposit box, and balcony with a view of the sea. On the grounds, a favorite place to spend time is in the 40-person jacuzzi with its own waterfall to cool you down. Dive students will find a unique aboveground dive tank for scuba diving practice, with a window through which anyone who wishes can observe. Water sports take place on the 550-foot-long white beach that fronts the hotel. The pool is large and inviting. Dinner is served in three separate dining rooms (not buffets): Italian, Mexican, and international, even on those nights when a special theme party is being held. All three meals, snacks, and drinks are included in the price, along with a couple of day-trips as well—even the tips are included in this one. Rate is about US$300 for two persons.

Las Velas, tel. 83-2222 or (800) 223-9815, fax 83-2465, a sprawling resort of 490 rooms, gives you the feeling of staying in a Mexican village: brick-lined streets, bubbling fountains, a cool kiosk, plus the beauty of the Caribbean. Breakfast is served in an open-air beachside restaurant. Guests enjoy fabulous stage shows (some with beautiful Las Vegas-style show girls) and music for every taste. Sportsters have access to all the water sports, including snorkeling, canoes, sailboats, kayaks, and water tricycles; plus aerobics classes, a children's program, handicrafts, dancing, and three pools for swimming and lounging around. Club Las Velas is located on the lagoon, near the center of the hotel zone. There is a minimum three-night stay, with rates starting at US$200. Other all-inclusives are **Beach Palace,** tel. 83-1177 or (800) 346-8225, fax 85-0439; and **Royal Solaris,** tel. 85-0100 or (800) 221-5333, fax 85-0975.

Inns

Of course there are many more luxury hotels to choose from in Cancún, but your choices aren't limited to expensive resorts. Many smaller inns offer an entirely different ambience with charm and grace. **Sina Suites** is a lovely small complex that is a real buy. You have a choice of either one or two beautifully furnished bedrooms, plus two bathrooms, kitchen with all facilities for cooking, and living room. The hotel has two swimming pools, beach towels, maid service, and a terrific little cafe with reasonably priced meals near one of the pools. Both suites have a couch in the living room that converts to a bed. Price in high season is about US$151 per night, but negotiable. For more information contact Carlos Sandoval, Apto. Postal 919, Cancún, Quintana Roo 77500, Mexico, tel. (98) 83-1017, fax 83-2459.

Condominiums

Cancún is sprouting condos everywhere you look. While you wonder when the building will end, they provide some of the best bargains in town for families or small groups. For as low as US$150 a night, a family of five can stay in lovely surroundings near the beach with a pool, cooking facilities, often two bathrooms, and daily maid service included in the price.

Rates can soar much higher or at certain times of the year can even be less. Travel agents can help you find them or you can write directly to the managers. For the daring, good buys come if you just arrive on the scene without reservations, go from condo to condo, and negotiate the price of one that isn't reserved. However, you run a certain risk of not finding what you want, especially during the winter months. **Carisa y Palma** condos are in the heart of the hotel zone near the Convention Center, tel. (98) 83-0211, fax 83-0932. **Vacation Clubs International** also rents condos, tel. 83-0855, fax 83-0206.

Youth Hostel

The best bargain in Cancún is the **CREA Youth Hostel,** tel. (98) 83-1337, on Paseo Kukulcán next to Club Verano Beat. Located in the hotel zone, the YH has a beach (not always in the best condition), swimming pool, bar, inexpensive dining room, and 650 bunk beds in women's and men's dorms. Rate is about US$12 pp, bedding included, plus a US$12 deposit.

Budget

In all honesty, the real *budget* hotel is nonexistent in Cancún. Some of the old-timers have remodeled, added a/c, expanded, and do a thriving business even after raising their prices to the US$50-100 range. The following are about as cheap as you can find (let me know if you find others). **Hotel Tankah,** at Av. Tankah #69, tel. (98) 84-4446, is simple, with 42 rooms, each with a bathroom and fan (a/c extra). Rate is about US$24 s or d. **Hotel Cotty,** Uxmal #44 between Av. Tulúm and Yaxchilán, tel. 84-05509, is still the same spartan hostel, close to the bus station. All 30 rooms have bathrooms and are usually clean (but look before you pay). Rates are US$25-28 s or d; if you want a TV it's extra.

Going up in price, check out **Hotel Rivemar,** at Av. Tulúm #49, tel. 84-1999, with private baths, tile floors, and a/c. It's clean and in a great location downtown. Rates are best in the off-season, US$30 s or d. In a much quieter neighborhood, the **Hotel Villa Maya Cancún,** Av. Uxmal at Av. Rubia, tel. and fax 84-1762, has 16 basic brown rooms with fans and good screens, clean but in need of a paint job, with green tiled bathrooms with showers. The hotel has a small parking lot, and a refrigerator and counter in the lobby stocked with water, sodas, and snacks. The restaurants and shops on Av. Tulúm and Av. Nader are within easy walking distance; rates are US$27-35 s or d.

Hotel el Rey del Caribe, near the corner of Uxmal and Nader, Apto. Postal 417, tel. 84-2028, fax 84-9857, is a pretty blue-and-white inn with more Mexican character than the other downtown hotels. Hammocks hang by the small pool and hot tub, white wrought-iron tables and chairs are set about in the gardens, and Maya statues sit in niches along corridors. Rooms are old but presentable and include kitchenettes, a/c and ceiling fan, and televisions; coffee is served in the lobby; rates US$37-60. **Hotel Plaza Kokai** is downtown on a quiet block of Av. Uxmal near Av. Nader. The four-story hotel has 48 rooms, a/c, lobby bar, swimming pool, jacuzzi, small roof garden, free transportation to the beach, and 12 suites with kitchens. Prices start at around US$50 in the low season, US$63 in the high season, and a continental breakfast is about US$3 at the small dining room in the lobby. For more information and reservations write to Uxmal #26, Cancún, Mexico; or call 84-3218, fax 84-4335. **Novotel,** Av. Tulúm at Av. Uxmal near the bus station, tel. 84-2999, fax 84-3162, has a garden and pool area behind the nicest rooms, which have balconies and fans. Some (but not all) of the 40 rooms have a/c, TV, and phones. The indoor/outdoor restaurant is popular with downtown workers at lunch. Rates start at US$23 s and US$25 for rooms with fans, US$35 s and $US38 d for a/c. Rates with breakfast include about US$4 more. Reservations are necessary in the high season. **Posada Lucy,** at Av. Gladiolas #25, tel. 84-4165, is a longtime favorite with budget travelers; the management and staff are very friendly and helpful, and the location is ideal, between Yaxchilán and Tulúm on a quiet side street. Of the 15 rooms, nine are suites, two with kitchenettes. Rates start at US$36 s and US$42 d in the low season.

FOOD

If you stayed for three or four months, it might be possible to sample each of the fine restaurants in Cancún city and the island. Most budget cafes

---

CAFE DE OLLA
Served at the
Sheraton Towers Breakfast Buffet

Recipe:
1 small earthen pot
3 tbsp. dark roasted coarse ground coffee
1 cinnamon stick
3 cloves
dark brown sugar to taste
1 liter of water

Bring water to boiling in pot, add coffee, cinnamon, and sugar. Bring to boil again, strain, and serve. Optional: Add tequila to taste. Especially good brewed over an open fire!

---

with both American and Mexican cuisine are found in Cancún city near Av. Tulúm and Av. Yaxchilán. For the epicurean explorer, there's Swiss, French, Chinese, Italian, Mexican, Arabic, Polynesian, Texan, Yucatecan, and continental; there's fast food, simple food, fancy food, seafood, homemade, and romantic; don't forget the great Creole food at the Hyatt's Blue Bayou. This is gourmet headquarters for the state of Quintana Roo, and all you have to do is look! Most restaurants accept credit cards.

A curious food fact: Mexico is one of the leading coffee producers of the world, but in spite of this most restaurants in Mexico serve instant coffee. Cancún, however, is the exception. Almost all of its cafes serve good brewed coffee—brewed decaf is available in only a few, like the delicious decaf at La Dolce Vita. On some Cancún menus you can find an old traditional favorite, *café de olla* (coffee cooked and served in a small earthen mug).

Remember, in Mexico it's considered an insult if a waiter submits a bill before it's requested; when you're ready to pay, say, *"La cuenta, por favor"* ("The bill, please"). A recent trend at some hotel zone restaurants is the presence of timeshare representatives pitching their resorts to patrons who are enjoying their meals. If you don't wish to be disturbed, simply say so. If the practice bothers you, mention it to the management.

Mexican
Located in front of a commercial building on Av. Nader, tel. (98) 84-1584, **El Café** has a vast

MEXICAN WINE

It would seem the most natural thing in the world for Mexico to produce good wines, considering the Spanish conquistadors came from a land with a long history of growing rich flavorful grapes and were experts in the field of fermentation. Pre-Hispanics didn't have wine as the Spanish knew it, but did make fermented beverages from such things as corn. It was not long before vine cuttings were brought to the New World and colonists were tending vineyards. By 1524 wine was so successful that Mexican wines were soon competing with Spanish wines. Pressure from vintners at home forced King Felipe II to outlaw its production in Mexico. However, over the years church use continued and no doubt many gallons of the forbidden drink found their way to private cellars. But for all practical purposes and development, the industry was stopped before it had the opportunity to make itself known around the world.

Not until 1939 under then-President Lázaro Cárdenas did Mexican wine-making begin to make a name for itself. Experts from around the world are beginning to recognize the industry in general and several of the wines are considered world-class. Over 125,000 acres of vineyards are under cultivation in the states of Baja California Norte, Aguascalientes, Querétaro, and Zacatecas. It's the vineyards of Baja that produce almost 80% of the country's wines located within the so-called "international wine belt" (between latitudes 30 and 50). Some of the well-known wineries (and their wines) from this area are: **Domecq** (Padre Kino, Calafia,

Los Reyes, and Fray Junipero); **L.A. Cetto** (Don Angel); and **Santo Tomas.**

The wineries, **Cavas de San Juan** (Hidalgo, Edelmann, Carte Blanche, etc.) and **Casa Martell,** are found in Querétaro, some 2,000 miles south of Baja. This was due to the suggestion of a University of California professor of enology who came to the conclusion that the area's 6,100-foot elevation compensated for its located outside the celebrated "wine belt." Zacatecas is the location of the relatively new and promising **Unión Vinícola Zacateca** (Los Pioneros), and Aguascalientes of **La Esplendida** (Armilita) and **Valle Redondo.**

According to Walter Stender of ACA Imports, some Mexican wines are even being imported to the U.S. Please note: Mexican wines don't age well and you need not be impressed by dates. In other words, the whites are ready when released, the reds need "age" no more than 18 months.

If you want champagne, remember to ask for *vino espumoso* or "bubbly wine." A label that reads *methode champenoise* means that the French system for producing sparkling wine was used. Mexico signed an agreement with the French government not to label its sparkling wines *champagne*—along with all other major wine-producing nations of the world except the U.S. Of course there are many imported wines from all over the world available in the fine restaurants of Cancún—many from California—but while in Mexico be adventurous and try the Mexican wine. A personal favorite is L.A. Cetto's white.

---

breakfast menu, including platters of fresh papaya, pineapple, and bananas; baskets of homemade pastries and breads; fresh orange-papaya juice, and bargain-priced *molletes,* rolls split and covered with beans and melted cheese. The *chilaquiles* are the best we've had in Cancún, and *pozole* is prepared daily. A blossoming *flamboyan* tree and green-and-white awning shades the outdoor patio beside the sidewalk; casual. It's obviously a big hit with local office workers and *políticos.* **Perico's,** Av. Yaxchilán #71 downtown, tel. 84-3152, continues to pull in the crowds as other downtown spots close from lack of business. The decor alone is worth a visit. The bar seats are saddles, and a fanciful mural depicting Mexican heroes and Hollywood movie stars covers the wall. The emphasis is on fun, with amiable waiters dressed as ban-

dits pouring tequila quite liberally. The food is dependably good, with generous portions of barbecued ribs and chicken and huge Mexican combination plates. Make sure to tour the whole retaurant, including the restrooms. **La Habichuela,** Margaritas #25 downtown, tel. 84-3158, is another longtime favorite for gourmet Mexican cuisine in a romantic setting, with lush plants and candlelight in a bi-level courtyard and dining room. The owners honored local culture and history by enlisting the talents of artist Wilbert González (see description of his work in the "Ticul" chapter) to create the carvings of Maya gods and rulers set in niches and on platforms in the dining areas. Try the shrimp in a sauce of *huitlacoche,* a black, mushroomlike fungus grown in corn; or go all out with the *cocobichuela,* shrimp and lobster in a curry sauce served in a coconut shell. Reservations suggested; open for lunch and dinner.

With the proliferation of U.S. franchise restaurants, it's hard to find regional cuisine in Cancún. **Los Almendros,** Av. Bonampak at Av. Sayil downtown, tel. 84-0807, is one of the few places where you can get authentic Yucatecan dishes such as *cochinita pibil* and *poc-chuc* served with marinated red onions and *sopa de lima.* Open for lunch and dinner. For a total immersion in local color, visit **Restaurant Río Nizúc** on the edge of the lagoon near Punta Nizúc. Fishermen beach their boats here and supply the restaurant with fresh fish for the house specialty *tikin-xic,* fish covered with *achiote* spice and baked in banana leaves. Locals hang out on the shores and in the lagoon, especially on weekend afternoons, and the fishermen will take you to nearby reefs for snorkeling. Lunch only. The restaurant is just south of the Punta Nizúc bridge, not far from Club Med. Look for a small sign on the side of the road and turn down a dirt road. There's a parking lot at the end of the road.

Flamingo's, near Punta Sam, and **Mandingo's,** right next to the Puerto Juárez ferry pier, serve the freshest fish *tikin-xic* style or grilled with garlic and oil. Covered with huge palapas, these two restaurants are favored by locals who settle in for afternoon-long lunches of seafood cocktails and ceviche, huge platters of fish, and plenty of ice-cold beer.

Italian

The longtime favorite for Italian-food lovers is **La Dolce Vita,** Av. Cobá #87, tel. (98) 84-1384. Why, you say, eat Italian in Mexico? Because it's *soooo* good! From *zuppa* to antipasto to *tutta* pasta to *pesce e frutta del mare* to the hazelnuts in your dessert, the food is scrumptious. If you like fish and you want to be impressed, try *boquinete Dolce Vita,* white snapper stuffed with shrimp and mushrooms, then baked in golden puff pastry (of course shaped like a fish)—*delizioso!* Or pasta lovers will enjoy *gnocchi* served with a delicate sauce of fresh tomatoes, rosemary, and mozzarella chunks. The decaf coffee is fresh brewed and rich. Chocoholics will delight in the rich chocolate truffle dessert—one is plenty for two. A meal with wine averages about US$30-40. Hint: Ask for a table in the back of the restaurant to get away from the traffic noises. Casual atmosphere, open for lunch and dinner, reservations necessary.

Restaurant Rolandi, Av. Cobá #12, tel. 84-4047, just around the corner from La Dolce Vita, might be more familiar to old-timers as Pizzeria Rolandi. No matter the name, the pizzas are still great, with thin, crisp crusts covered with an eclectic selection of toppings. Pastas, calzones, and a great garlicky antipasto round out the menu; save room for the coconut ice cream topped with Kahlúa. Casual, open for lunch and dinner. For a more elegant setting and elevated Swiss-Italian cuisine, try the pizzeria's sister restaurant, **Casa Rolandi,** Plaza Caracol, tel. 83-1817, in the hotel zone. The appetizers alone are worth sampling, and the salad/antipasto bar can be a meal unto itself. Open 1-11:30 p.m.

Rounding out the Italian selections (though there must be a dozen or more pasta and pizza spots these days) are: **Cenacolo,** with outdoor seating at Kukulcán Plaza, tel. 85-3603; **Savios,** an elegant bistro serving northern Italian cuisine, Plaza Caracol, tel. 83-2085; and **Augustus Caesar,** an enduring favorite since 1980 in La Mansión-Costa Blanca, open for lunch and dinner, reservations advised, tel. 83-3384.

100% Natural, at Av. Sunyaxchen #6 downtown, tel. 84-3617, still serves good vegetarian dishes, crispy salads with a good selection of vegies, great healthy shakes—you can really be creative here! Open daily 8 a.m.-midnight, and open 24 hours at Plaza Terramar in the hotel zone, tel. 83-1180.

Multi-ethnic

The following restaurants represent a few more of Cancún's ethnic assortment. At the **Blue Bayou,** try the Cajun menu, great blackened fish, and butter-tender beef fillet. It's located in the Hyatt Cancún Caribe Villas and Resort, tel. (98) 83-0044; reservations recommended. **Gypsy's,** opposite the Continental Villas Plaza Hotel on the lagoon, open 8 a.m.-midnight, tel. 83-2015, brings a little bit of Spain to Mexico with paella and a flamenco show twice nightly; the inexpensive breakfast buffet is a big hit as well. **Cilantro,** upscale and quiet, featuring a Mexican and Italian menu with a weekly salad-and-pasta buffet; and **The Seafood Market,** where shrimp, lobster, and fresh fish are displayed on ice and diners choose their dinner selection, are both at the Hyatt Regency, tel. 83-0966, reservations suggested. Authentic Japanese food is served at **Yamamoto** 1:30-11 p.m. at Av. Uxmal #31 downtown, tel. 87-3366.

For a full night of fine dining, dancing, and entertainment visit **El Mexicano,** La Mansión-Costa Blanca mall, hotel zone, tel. 83-2220. Caribbean and Mexican shows accompany gourmet Mexican dishes, many flambéed tableside. The setting is elegant, and though tour groups tend to congregate here, even solo diners receive impeccable service and attention.

At **The Mine Co.** there's an ongoing party, Av. Kukulcán next to Verano Beat, tel. 83-0670. **The Captain's Cove** provides a tropical dining experience, with excellent seafood. It's on Paseo Kukulcán across from the Royal Mayan, Omni, and Oasis Cancún hotels; a second location is near Playa Linda. **Lorenzillo's,** Paseo Kukulcán across from the Continental Villas Plaza, tel. 83-1254, is one of the few restaurants right on the lagoon, great for sunset watching; don't miss the crocodile that hangs out by the pier at the restaurant; expensive. Upscale, expensive, and elegant, **Grimond's Mansión,** Calle Pez Volador off Paseo Kukulcán, next to the Casa Maya hotel, tel. 83-0704, serves excellent gourmet French and Mexican cuisine in a French-country setting; reservations required.

El Pescador, Tulipanes #26 downtown, tel. 84-2673, is a homey Mexican restaurant with outstanding seafood; be prepared to wait in line for a table. Open for lunch and dinner, closed Monday. Their second restaurant, **La Mesa del Pescador,** is located in Kukulcán Plaza in the hotel zone. **Iguana Wana,** in Plaza Caracol, tel. 83-0829, has something for everyone on its enormous menu, with such unusual finds as conch fritters, vegetarian fajitas, fried bananas, and chicken with *chipotle* sauce; frozen yogurt, and a dazzling pastry tray as well. Enjoy a straightforward, no-nonsense, American-style breakfast, lunch, and dinner at **Pop,** open daily 8 a.m.-11 p.m., Av. Tulúm #26 (next to city hall), tel. 84-1991.

American

It is impossible to ignore the proliferation of U.S.-based restaurants and fast-food chains throughout Cancún city and the hotel zone—you certainly can't miss the Domino pizza delivery mopeds zooming to the hotels. It seems that many travelers prefer the familiarity of names they've come to trust at home, judging from the full tables at McDonald's, Burger King, Wendy's, Subway, and Kentucky Fried Chicken. **T.G.I. Friday's**

was one of the first franchises in Cancún (even the locals have come to love their burgers), and has an enviable location across the street from the Convention Center, tel. (98) 83-3542. **Tony Roma's** serves dependably good barbecued ribs and steaks at its huge dining room in the Continental Villas Plaza Hotel, tel. 83-0084. **Planet Hollywood,** Plaza Flamingo, tel. 85-0723, said to be owned by a group of Hollywood stars, serves California cuisine in a raucous setting with music videos and movies on four screens and a boutique selling gear bearing the Planet Hollywood logo. Open 11 a.m.-2 a.m. Locals line up at the Dunkin' Donuts stands on Av. Sayil, downtown, and in Plaza Kukulcán.

Groceries

The *mercado municipal,* six blocks north of the bus station on Av. Tulúm, is well supplied; come early for the best selection of fresh produce and meat. Traffic is dreadful here, and the market a bit of a disappointment. **Javier Rojo Gómez,** behind the post office on Sunyaxchen, is a smaller version of the *mercado municipal.* Old favorite **San Francisco de Asis Super Market** on Tulúm now has a new location in the hotel zone. These are modern, well-stocked markets designed for one-stop shopping (somewhat novel to much of Yucatán): butcher case, bakery counter, row upon row of groceries, liquor, electric appliances, even clothes. **Comercial Mexicana** at the *glorieta* (traffic circle) and intersection with Av. Uxmal is an enormous grocery and department store, a good place to stock up on supplies (from coolers to sneakers) if you are driving around the Peninsula. **Super Deli** is the current favorite for imported cheeses, cookies, crackers, even frozen Sara Lee pastries and Haagen Dazs ice cream, and has a good bakery and deli section. Both locations, on Av. Uxmal, downtown, and Plaza Nautilus in the hotel zone, have cafes serving great sandwiches and full meals, and are open 24 hours. The **Super Gourmet Deli** in Plaza Kukulcán has a similar selection, but the prices are outrageously high.

Bakeries

Indulge yourself in fine Mexican and French pastries and crusty *bolillos* at **La Francesca Panadería** on Av. Uxmal at Av. Nader. A smaller bakery is **Los Globos** on Tulipanes just west of Av. Tulúm. **Super Deli** on Av. Tulúm and in Plaza Nautilus has a great selection of breakfast pastries and breads. At **Ciao,** Av. Cobá #30 by La Dolce Vita, cappuccino and espresso are served with sublime pastries, Danish, cakes, and pies. The prices are high, but so is the quality, and there's nothing like a strong cup of coffee and a sticky pecan roll to lift flagging spirits.

ENTERTAINMENT

Cancún has a marvelous choice of nighttime entertainment. It's easy to dance the night away at any one of a number of inviting places. Most of the hotels on the island have discos in motion until the early morning hours. Some cantinas offer live bands ranging from jazz to popular marimba to reggae, and several hotels offer Mexican "fiestas" weekly, including *típico* dinners, traditional dances, and colorful costumes.

Music And Dancing
The casual **Mexican Fiesta** at the Hyatt Regency, tel. (98) 83-0966, has been running nightly for years, packing in newcomers and return guests for a full-on party with a lavish buffet and folkloric dance performances. **Ballet Folklórico de México** performs nightly at 7 p.m. during a Mexican buffet at the Continental Villas Plaza Hotel, tel. 85-1444.

Cancún has some of the most upscale, modern discos in Mexico, with all the newest effects to make for the best entertainment. Many discos don't even open until 10 p.m., and get wild after midnight. Dress codes are enforced; most of the fancier discos do not allow tank tops, sandals, or other casual wear. Men can get by with a nice T-shirt or polo shirt and dressy shorts (some don't allow shorts at all) or long pants. Women tend to wear sundresses. Expect cover charges of US$5 or more and high drink prices. Check out: **Christine's Disco,** superb sound and light show, dressy, next to Hotel Krystal, tel. 83-1133; **La Boom,** very high-tech with fog and wind machines and a sound system that reflects the disco's name, Av. Kukulcán Km 3.5, tel. 83-1372; **Dady'O,** known for its bikini contests and boisterous young crowd, tel. 83-3333; and **Up & Down,** a super-extravagant disco and restaurant with dining and mellow music upstairs and full-scale disco downstairs, in front of the Oasis Cancún, tel. 85-2909.

Fiesta night at the Hyatt Regency Hotel offers excellent típico food and dancers.

Tropical music isn't as common as you would think; your best bet is **Azúcar,** a classy club with a tropical garden decor and live salsa bands, next to the Camino Real, tel. 83-0100. **Batacha,** by the Miramar Mission Hotel, is more casual, and attracts couples of all ages who love the Latin beat, tel. 83-1755. **Cat's Reggae Bar** on Av. Yaxchilán, downtown, is the best spot for Caribbean music; no phone. Rock 'n' roll oldies also get dancers on the floor at **Hard Rock,** tel. 83-1266, and at **Planet Hollywood,** tel. 85-0723, on Paseo Kukulcán.

Bars And Nightclubs
More subdued settings are harder to find; your best bets are in the hotels. Classy spots for music and conversation are: **Lobby Bar,** elegant, classy, casual-nice, Hyatt Regency, tel. (98) 83-0966; **Tropical Oasis Piano Bar,** casual, Hotel and Villas Tropical Oasis; **Reflejos,** upbeat and lively, casual-nice, Hyatt Regency, tel. 83-0966; **Oasis Bar,** with live jazz and dancing, Hyatt Cancún Caribe Villas and Resort, tel. 83-0044; and the **Club Grill,** an elegant restaurant with a cozy

lounge where well-dressed couples dance to romantic music, Ritz Carlton Hotel, tel. 85-0808.

For zany fun with wild and comedic waiters as well as exceptionally good food (try the Mexican combination plate with *carne asada*), you can't beat **Carlos N' Charlie's**, and **Señor Frog's**, on Paseo Kukulcán. Similar in ambience and decor, but with a more authentically Mexican flair, is **Perico's** on Av. Yaxchilán downtown. And for a serene, romantic spot to begin or end an evening, watch Cancún's sensational sunset or glittering stars in **La Palapa**, a mellow bar in a thatch-roof pavilion on the end of its own pier over the lagoon at Hotel Club Lagoon Caribe, Paseo Kukulcán. La Palapa serves snacks and exotic drinks, and has live music and dancing 9 p.m.-1:30 a.m.

Dinner Cruises

The **Columbus Lobster Dinner Cruise** leaves the Royal Mayan Marina dock (hotel zone) daily at 4 p.m and 7:30 p.m. The *Columbus*, tel. (98) 83-3268 or 83-3271, is a 62-foot motor-sailing vessel that cruises for three hours during the sunset or under the starry sky while guests enjoy an open bar and dine on delicious broiled lobster or steak. Dress is casual, reservations necessary. On the **Pirate's Night Adventure**, tel. 83-3268 or 83-3283, diners cruise on the *Crucero Tropical Cruiser* to Treasure Island (actually a beach on Isla Mujeres facing Cancún). Once onshore, passengers feast on a buffet dinner and free drinks while watching a floor show with lively games and lots of audience participation. Departs nightly (except Sunday) from the Playa Langosta Pier at 6 p.m. and returns at 11 p.m.

Mexico Mágico

That massive, cobalt-blue hulk with the six-foot-high plaster piñata out front is Mexico Mágico, a theme park that opened in 1993 on the landfill shores of Laguna Bojórquez, open nightly 5:30 p.m.-12:30 a.m. The park aims to captivate adults with entertainment, dining, drinking, and shopping in several areas fancifully designed to suggest various parts of the world. The entrance fee of just under US$20 allows guests to attend several music and dance revues, including a cabaret show and a mock bullfight. For an additional US$15 you can attend several dinner shows with lavish buffets and imaginative floor shows. Theme-decorated bars and food stands are scattered throughout the com-

---

TO GET MARRIED IN CANCUN

Call (98) 4-1311, ext. 129, to make an appointment with Señor Pedro Solis Rodríguez, official of the Civil Registry. When you go to the Civil Registry Office at the city hall located downtown on Av. Tulúm, bride and groom should have:

√ Tourist cards
√ Birth certificates
√ Blood tests
√ Passports or driver's licenses
√ Final divorce decrees if applicable
√ The names, addresses, ages, nationalities, and tourist card numbers of four witnesses
√ Pay fee to the cashier at the city hall, about US$35.
√ Fill out the application you will be given by the judge.
√ Very important: these things must be done at *least* two days before the wedding.

---

plex, which is built on a grander-than-grand scale, filled with sky-high murals of Picasso, Matisse, and Frida Kahlo paintings. An abundance of shops displays items from England, France, India, and even Mexico. A second phase of the park will include a display on the Maya, which may put the place into context.

Convention Center

Cancún's smashing **Centro Convenciones Cancún** offers 108,000 square feet of convention space with the latest high-tech audiovisual equipment. The adjacent Sky Tower and 129,000-square-foot shopping center are not scheduled to open until 1994. The center is located in the heart of the Cancún hotel zone, Paseo Kukulcán Km 9, nine miles from the international airport, five minutes' walking distance to 4,000 upscale hotel rooms. For more information contact PS Enterprises, (800) 538-0424, in the U.S. tel. (202) 797-1222.

Cinema

Unlike in most Peninsula cities, the majority of films shown in Cancún are usually American-made with Spanish subtitles. Expect the bill to change every three or four days. However, **Cines Cancún**, Av. Xcaret #112, tel. 84-1646, and **Cine Royal**, Av. Tulúm, offer Mexican films that provide a cultural experience. Some of the larger hotels have their own movie theaters and large-screen TVs. The theaters at Plaza Kukulcán show first-run movies from the U.S.

SHOPPING

Shopping Centers

La Mansión-Costa Blanca, a small, exclusive mall painted hot pink (some sections have returned to the original white), features unique boutiques, several of the city's top restaurants, a money exchange, and a bank. **El Parian** shops are constructed around a small garden off to one side of the Convention Center. **Las Velas,** though small, includes a pizza parlor, liquor store, art gallery, fancy-dress boutique, and more. **Mayfair Gallery** is located opposite the Fiesta Americana Hotel and contains a wide variety of boutiques and restaurants in a lovely atrium-roofed, two-story building. **Plaza Caracol,** one of Cancún's biggest and most contemporary shopping centers, is conveniently located in the hub of the hotel zone, fully air-conditioned, and elaborately finished with marble floors and lots of windows. This two-story mall consists of over 200 shops and boutiques, including signature stores of the world's most famous labels: Gucci, Fiorucci, Christian Dior, Benetton, and more.

Plaza Flamingo, a one-story center with Maya-inspired architecture, beautiful marble floors, and high-tech lighting, seemed to be suffering for lack of tenants last time we checked, but still has a few fairly good souvenir shops, a great sporting goods store, and several restaurants, including a **Denny's** that serves good enchiladas (true, true!), and a fully equipped **Gold's Gym. Plaza la Fiesta** is actually a huge one-floor department store featuring all the fabulous crafts of Mexico; they offer a particularly fine selection in gold and silver jewelry.

Plaza Lagunas, at the center of the hotel zone, features all manner of sportswear, including those of famous designers. Various small restaurants, a snack bar, and an ice cream parlor are set among the shops. **Plaza Nautilus,** a modern, two-story plaza, is suffering from the competition but still has some good restaurants. **Terramar,** located opposite the Fiesta Americana Hotel, is a city block of shops, eateries, real estate offices, a pharmacy, and a small

hotel. **Kukulcán Plaza,** opened in 1993 near Casa Turquesa, brings shops and restaurants within walking distance of the newer hotels. The two-story, air-conditioned plaza has Cancún's first bowling alley, plus movie theaters, several restaurants, and plenty of boutiques and shops.

Downtown, **Plaza America** is located on Av. Kukulcán just as you leave town going south, and houses mainly offices. **Plaza Bonita** is housed in a large hacienda-style structure replete with hand-painted Mexican tiles and a collection of boutiques, restaurants, and the family-oriented **Fun Place** filled with video, pinball, and mechanical games.

Plaza México on Av. Tulúm is an air-conditioned mall that specializes in Mexican crafts, among them Maya textiles, leather goods, woodcarvings, stoneware, and sportswear. **Plaza Safa,** a lovely arcade that fronts Av. Tulúm, houses a snack bar, a series of shops, and a money exchange. **Tropical Plaza** has shops selling everything from jewelry to designer clothing; there's also a bank, travel agency, and real estate office. It's next door to Plaza México.

Crafts Markets

In the hotel zone, **Coral Negro,** located next to the Convention Center, is a collection of approximately 50 stalls selling handicrafts from all parts of Mexico. Located downtown on Av. Tulúm, **Ki Huic** is Cancún's main crafts market, with over 100 different vendors and just about every kind of craft and souvenir you can imagine. **Plaza Garibaldi,** also downtown at the intersection of Av. Tulúm and Uxmal, contains several stalls of serapes, tablecloths, traditional clothing, onyx, and other handcrafted items.

Photo Supplies

At all locations of **Omega Photo**—Av. Uxmal #45, tel. (98) 84-1679; Av. Tulúm #103, tel. 84-3860; Kukulcán Plaza, tel. 85-2198—you will find film, batteries, and other accessories, as well as one-hour film processing. Hours are Mon.-Sat. 9 a.m.-9 p.m., Sundays 1-9 p.m.

SERVICES AND INFORMATION

Laundromat

A large, pleasant laundromat is located downtown at 5 Av. Nader. Either you can do it yourself or pay extra to have it done for you—laundry and dry cleaning are tremendously cheaper here than at the hotels. A shady patio offers chairs for waiting.

Medical Information
Most hotels in Cancún can provide the name of a doctor who speaks English. For simple first aid downtown, stop at **Cruz Roja** at Av. Labná #2, tel. (98) 84-1616. If the problem is more serious, there is a small walk-in 24-hour emergency hospital, **Total Assist Hospital**, Claveles #5 and Av. Tulúm, tel. 84-1092 or 84-8116, geared more to tourists than to locals, and they usually have an English-speaking doctor on call. For other questions call the American Consulate, tel. 84-2411.

Pharmaceuticals and Souvenirs: Pharmacies are tourist-oriented, and someone there can usually speak a little English. Hotel delivery service is available, open daily at the Caracol Plaza in the hotel zone, 9 a.m.-10 p.m., tel. 83-1894 or 83-2827.

Post Office And Telegrams
The post office, tel. (98) 84-1418, is west of Av. Tulúm on Av. Sunyaxchen at Av. Xel-Ha; open Mon.-Fri. 8 a.m.-7 p.m., Sat. 9 a.m.-noon. The telegraph office can be reached at 84-1529.

Consulate Representatives
The **U.S. Consular Office,** tel. (98) 84-2411 or 84-6399, keeps hours Mon.-Fri. 9 a.m.-2 p.m. and 3-6 p.m., at Av. Nader 40, near La Dolce Vita restaurant. In Mérida, you can reach the American Consulate by calling (99) 25-5011 or (99) 25-5409. For the **Canadian Consulate** go to Plaza México #312, second floor, Mon.-Fri. 11 a.m.-2 p.m. For emergencies outside business hours call the Canadian Embassy in Mexico City at (915) 724-7900. The **French Consulate** is at Instituto Internacional de Idiomas, Av. Xel-Ha #113, open Mon.-Fri. 8 a.m.-11 a.m., 5-7 p.m., tel. 84-6078. The consular representative of **Spain** is in the Oasis Building on Paseo Kukulcán, open Mon.-Fri. 10 a.m.-1 p.m., tel. 83-2466. The **Italian Consulate** is in La Mansión-Costa Blanca Mall, open 9 a.m.-2 p.m., tel. 83-2184.

Tourist Information
The **state tourist office** is on Av. Tulúm at the Plaza Municipal Benito Juárez, next to the Multi-

banco Comermex, open Mon.-Sat. 9 a.m.-5 p.m., tel. (98) 84-8073. *Cancún Tips* is a helpful, free tourist information booklet available in hotels and shops; the publishers also operate tourist information offices in Plaza Caracol, Plaza Kukulcán, the Convention Center, and Playa Langosta Pier. The chamber of commerce, tel. 84-4315, is also a good source of information. Booths with tourist information signs abound along Av. Tulúm and Paseo Kukulcán; most are operated by time-share companies offering free tours and meals in exchange for your presence at a timeshare presentation.

CANCUN EMERGENCY NUMBERS

Police	84-1913
Fire	84-1202
Red Cross	84-1616
Air-Vac Medical Life	
Service (Houston, Texas)	(713) 961-4050

Immigration
Remember that you must turn in your Mexican visitor's card when you leave the country. If you should lose it, need an extension, or have any questions, call Mexican Immigration, tel. (98) 84-1749; at the airport, tel. 84-2992. Your tourist card is normally good for 30 days or less; if you should need an extension (*before* your card expires), go to the main immigration downtown office at Av. Nader #1, tel. 84-1749, fax 84-0918, open Mon.-Fri. 8:30 a.m.-noon. You will be asked to leave your card and pick it up the following day.

Travel Agencies
With the advent of the tour guide's union, tours around the area are supposed to be the same price at all agencies; however, we are hearing that's not always the case. So, try bargaining the price. All the larger hotels in Cancún have travel agencies available to help you with your travel needs locally and internationally. Many more are scattered about the city as well. Remember that most offices close between 1 p.m. and 3 p.m., then reopen till 7 p.m. or 8 p.m. **Turismo Aviomar,** Av. Yaxchilán downtown, tel. (98) 84-8831, fax 84-5385, offers many tours of the area from Cancún through the entire area in modern air-conditioned buses. The agency

will make reservations for party boats to Isla Mujeres, and can arrange most of your vacation plans. The **American Express** office is located at Av. Tulúm #208 at Calle Agua, downtown, tel. 84-1999. A few other good firms are **Intermar Caribe,** Av. Bonampak and Calle Cereza, tel. 84-4266, fax 84-1652; **PTT Travel,** Av. Cobá #12-20, tel. 84-8831; **Viaje Bojórquez,** Calle Alcatraces 12, tel. 87-1156, fax 84-1652.

Mayaland Tours
With an office downtown, the Mayaland Tours company, tel. (98) 87-5411 or 87-2450, offers many day-trips and packages (some great packages include hotels and autos, a real bargain) that begin in Cancún and continue on to Chichén Itzá, Uxmal, Palenque, Mérida, and more. Modern air-conditioned double-decker buses have friendly, knowledgeable guides and attendants on board. The Mayaland office is at the Hotel America on Av. Tulúm; most travel agencies and tour desks have information and can make reservations for Mayaland Tours. In Mérida call (99) 25-2122 or 25-2521, fax (99) 25-7022.

Bookstores
Most of the island's hotel gift shops sell American magazines as well as a supply of paperback novels, Spanish-English dictionaries, and several English-language newspapers: the *News* (published in Mexico City), *Miami Herald, New York Times Weekly Review,* and *USA Today.*

Fama, tel. (98) 84-6586, is a good source of English-language newspapers, magazines, and books. The shop is located on Av. Tulúm between Tulipanes and Claveles. Or trade reading material with other travelers. Many hotels have maintained the trade shelf as well. If you don't see it, ask the desk clerk.

Radio Time
An English-language radio station is now available in Cancún; if you want to catch international news, dial 105.1 on your radio for the latest financial reports, weather, sports, and music, 24 hours a day.

GETTING THERE AND AROUND

By Air
Quintana Roo's busiest airport is Cancún's international airport, 20 km south of Cancún.

Along with everything else around this infant city, the airport is new and shiny and continues to grow and add to its facilities each season. It now has two runways. There are no storage lockers at the airport; however, most hotels are willing to check your tagged luggage for you. *Colectivos* are available to take you directly to your hotel when you arrive. Buy your ticket near the baggage pickup for US$10 pp. These vans are cheaper than taxis and they *will* be filled to capacity. It's always a good idea to watch each person removing their luggage on the way to your hotel, just to avoid a mix-up. When you depart from Cancún, you will have to take a taxi since the *colectivos* only run one-way. Depending on the number of people in the cab, it will cost US$10-15 from downtown hotels, and from the hotel zone about US$20. Be sure you have saved US$12 for departure tax to be paid at the airport.

Visitors from many cities in the U.S. arrive daily on: **Mexicana,** Av. Cobá #39 downtown, tel. (98) 87-4444, airport tel. 86-0120; **Aeromexico,** Av. Cobá #80 downtown, tel. 84-3571, airport tel. 86-0018; **United,** airport tel. 86-0158; **Continental,** airport tel. 86-0040; **Lacsa,** Av. Bonampak and Av. Cobá downtown, tel. 87-3101, airport tel. 86-0014; **Northwest,** airport tel. 86-0044; **Taesa,** Av. Yaxchilán downtown, tel. 87-4314, airport tel. 86-0206; and **Aviacsa,** Av. Cobá downtown, tel. 87-4214 or 87-4211. **Aerocaribe** and **Aerocozumel,** Av. Tulúm #29 downtown, tel. 84-2000, airport tel. 86-0083, bring passengers on daily flights from Isla Cozumel. **Aviateca** airport, tel. 86-0155, flies to Guatemala. Car rentals and taxis are available at the airport. Remember to reconfirm your flight 24 hours in advance and to be at the airport one hour before local flights or two hours before international flights. Several airlines run charter flights to Cancún from major U.S. gateways at reduced fares. Ask your travel agent to check out this option.

By Bus
From Mérida and Chetumal, buses make frequent trips daily, linking smaller villages to Cancún en route. The bus terminal is located in downtown Cancún on Av. Tulúm. Call or go to the terminal for complete schedules—they change frequently. You will find both first- (**ADO**) and second-class (**Autotransportes del Caribe**) bus

stations across from the Hotel Plaza Caribe at the intersection of Avenidas Tulúm and Uxmal (next door to each other) and at Av. Pino, a small side street off Uxmal. These buses run frequently; fares are very cheap. Try to buy your ticket well ahead of your departure since the traffic is heavy. **Playa Express** has air-conditioned mini-bus and regular bus service between Cancún, Playa del Carmen, Tulúm, Felipe Carillo Puerto, and Chetumal. The mini-buses do not have luggage compartments. The office is on Av. Pino. Right across the street, **Interplaya** has mini-bus service every half-hour 5 a.m.-10 p.m., with stops at all the beach areas between Cancún and Playa del Carmen. **InterCaribe** has first-class, nonstop service to Mérida and Chetumal.

A luxury service for longer trips, the **Caribe Express,** runs between Cancún, Chetumal, Campeche, and Mérida. These first-class buses are air-conditioned, have an attendant who will serve you drinks and cookies, and feature earphones, TV, music, and bathrooms. These are the 747s of the road. They make trips to surrounding areas easy. To reserve tickets, call (98) 87-4174. Caribe Express has an air-conditioned waiting room on Av. Pino, around the corner from ADO. **Expresso de Oriente** has direct nonstop deluxe service between Cancún and Mérida, with 11 trips daily, and deluxe service between Cancún and Mérida with stops in Playa del Carmen, Tulúm, and Valladolid. Reserve tickets by calling 84-5542 or 84-4804; reservations must be confirmed two hours before departure or they will be canceled. Their air-conditioned waiting room is on Av. Uxmal.

Car Rentals

Car rentals are available from Mexican and American agencies at Cancún airport and many hotels. Remember there is a hefty drop-off fee in a city other than the origination point. Most companies rent jeeps, sedans, and Volkswagen bugs, and accept credit cards. You may find that you get the best rates by reserving your car in advance through U.S.-based agencies, though some of the small local agencies offer great deals when business is down.

The 320-km, four-hour drive from Mérida to Cancún is on a good highway (Hwy. 180) through henequen-dotted countryside, historic villages, and archaeological ruins. The new *autopista* toll highway cuts 30-60 minutes off the drive on a straight, high-speed, somewhat monotonous eight-lane road. The tolls from Cancún to Mérida were about US$30 when the highway was completed in 1993; complaints from locals may bring the price down. There are reports of new toll roads in the planning stages for the Cancún-Tulúm Corridor, and between Playa del Carmen on the coast to Nuevo X-Can in the interior, though thus far no new construction has begun. From Chetumal (Hwy. 307) it's 343 km (four hours) along a well-maintained highway through thick tropical brush parallel to the Caribbean coast.

Car rentals in Cancún can be found at: **Avis,** Mayfair Plaza, tel. (98) 83-0803, airport tel. 86-0222; **Budget,** 15 Av. Tulúm #214 downtown, tel. 84-4101; **Caribbean Rent,** Av. Uxmal #20 downtown, tel. 87-6671; **Dollar Rent-A-Car,** Av. Tulúm #77-80 downtown, tel. 84-0708, airport tel. 86-0165; **EconoRent,** Av. Tulipanes #16 downtown, tel. 84-1826 or 84-1435, Hotel Casa Maya in hotel zone tel. 83-0555; **Hertz,** Calle Reno #35 downtown, tel. 87-6604; **National,** Av. Uxmal #12 downtown, tel. 84-0097, airport tel. 86-0153, Fiesta Americana Condesa tel. 85-1000.

LOUISE FOOTE

ISLA DE COZUMEL

Cozumel ("Land of the Swallow") is a Caribbean island surrounded by water the color of imperial jade. Edged with stretches of white sand and craggy castles of black limestone and coral, its shoreline is continuously washed by an inquisitive, restless sea. The island rose from the sea in the Pleistocene epoch to its maximum height of 45 feet above sea level. At 47 km long and 15 km wide, it's the largest of the three islands off the east coast of Quintana Roo—and the largest island in the Republic of Mexico. The other islands lying off the Quintana Roo coast are Isla Mujeres and Contoy. Cuba is 153 km north and Cancún is 48 km northwest. Across a 3,000-foot-deep channel that's 19 km offshore, Cozumel was a sacred mecca for Maya noblewomen who traveled in large dugout canoes to worship Ixchel, the goddess of fertility.

A calm sea on the lee (west) side of the island makes it ideal for swimming, diving, water-skiing, sailboarding, beachcombing, or relaxing in the sun. It's also the developed side, where clusters of buildings in the (only) town of San Miguel de Cozumel house 50,000 residents and visitors. Offices, shops, banks, markets, hotels, restaurants, and two docks are all concentrated in this small seaside town. The east coast is another world, with few people and little activity but dotted with isolated coves and bays, some with placid water, others with spectacular surf crashing on the beach and spraying mist on passing windshields. Clear water and the proximity of at least 20 live reefs make snorkeling a must, even for the neophyte. Exploring the Maya ruins in the overgrown interior of the island is an adventure by motorcycle, bike, car, or foot. The people of Cozumel, in their quiet way, are accepting and friendly to the growing number of visitors who come each year. Although Cozumel, with its lively discos and steady influx of divers and cruise ships, is more upbeat than Isla Mujeres, it still lacks the jet-set feeling of Cancún—perhaps because it's a real town where fishing and diving flourished long before outsiders arrived.

Climate

The climate is warm year-round (average 27° C). The heaviest rains begin in June and last through October. It's possible for rain to fall almost every day during that time, but the usual afternoon shower is brief and the ground absorbs moisture quickly. In most cases any travel interruption is minimal, though there are the exceptions. The rainy season occasionally opens up and lets loose torrents. During wet months,

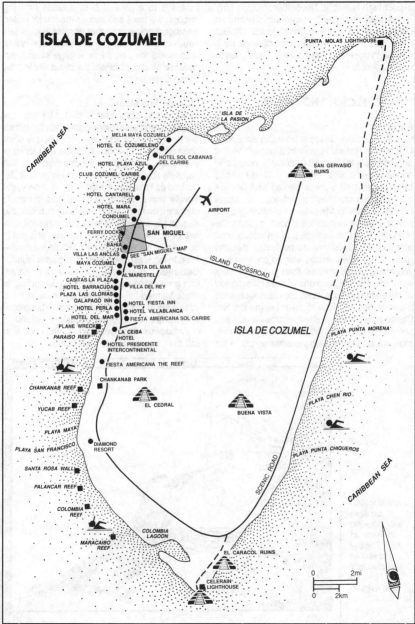

ISLA DE COZUMEL

PUNTA MOLAS LIGHTHOUSE

CARIBBEAN SEA

ISLA DE LA PASION

MELIA MAYA COZUMEL
HOTEL EL COZUMELEÑO
HOTEL SOL CABANAS DEL CARIBE
HOTEL PLAYA AZUL
CLUB COZUMEL CARIBE

SAN GERVASIO RUINS

HOTEL CANTARELL
HOTEL MARA
CONDUMEL
FERRY DOCK

AIRPORT

SAN MIGUEL

BAHIA
VILLA LAS ANCLAS
MAYA COZUMEL
CASITAS LA PLAZA
HOTEL BARRACUDA
PLAZA LAS GLORIAS
GALAPAGO INN
HOTEL PERLA
HOTEL DEL MAR
PLANE WRECK
PARAISO REEF

SEE "SAN MIGUEL" MAP

VISTA DEL MAR
AL'MARESTEL
VILLA DEL REY

ISLAND CROSSROAD

HOTEL FIESTA INN
HOTEL VILLABLANCA
FIESTA AMERICANA SOL CARIBE

LA CEIBA HOTEL
HOTEL PRESIDENTE INTERCONTINENTAL

FIESTA AMERICANA THE REEF

CHANKANAB PARK

CHANKANAB REEF

YUCAB REEF

EL CEDRAL

ISLA DE COZUMEL

PLAYA PUNTA MORENA

BUENA VISTA

PLAYA CHEN RIO

PLAYA MAYA

PLAYA SAN FRANCISCO

DIAMOND RESORT

PLAYA PUNTA CHIQUEROS

SANTA ROSA WALL

PALANCAR REEF

SCENIC ROAD

CARIBBEAN SEA

COLOMBIA REEF

MARACAIBO REEF

COLOMBIA LAGOON

EL CARACOL RUINS

CELERAIN LIGHTHOUSE

0   2mi

0   2km

© MOON PUBLICATIONS, INC.

expect high humidity. November through May is generally balmy, with lower humidity and an occasional cool evening (average 25° C). But remember, tropical climes can change from mellow to miserable very quickly—and then to mellow again.

FLORA AND FAUNA

Birds

In 1925, Ludlow Griscom from the American Museum of Natural History was one of the first ornithologists to discover Cozumel's varied and concentrated birdlife. Since then, Cozumel has been considered a prime birding site; outside of town, civilization has not intruded into natural habitat. Except for the network of aboveground plastic water lines paralleling graded roads, the tangled brush, tall trees, and an occasional abandoned hut all ensure protected nesting grounds for these exotic winged creatures. If you enjoy watching birds, then getting up very early and trekking into one of several swampy areas on the island is worth the effort. One such place is located close to town behind the Sol Caribe Hotel. Here, at dawn, you're likely to see flocks of small multihued parrots, blue warblers, macaws, and spindly-legged white egrets, while listening to a glee club of sounds echoing through the trees and across the murky water. Another marshy area that attracts fowl is just south of the junction where the cross-island road meets the east shore. A large swamp, accessible by car, parallels the coast behind the Punta Celerain Lighthouse.

Iguanas And More

Iguanas and other lizards skitter through the jungles. The iguana, more visible than the others because of its size and large population, is often seen sunning atop rocks along the east shore or even in the middle of the warm paved road that parallels the beach. Though the iguana is described as timid and is said to move slowly, the traveler with a camera has to be lightning fast to capture it on film. Once it spots an outsider, the iguana slips quickly into its underground burrow or up the nearest tree. The secret is not to be seen by the wary creature. (Photographers—keep trying, it can be done!) The iguana found in Cozumel is commonly shades of dark green, can grow up to two meters long, including its black-banded tail, and has a comblike crest of scales down the middle of its back. Varicolored species are found on the Yucatán mainland.

Armadillos, deer, small foxes, and coati also call the Cozumel jungle their home.

Hummingbirds are seen everywhere in the Yucatán bush. The tiny bird was an important part of Maya art and religion.

DIANA LASICH HARPER

Plantlife

Cozumel has never been known for its agriculture, partly because of the shortage of water. However, during the early 1900s chicle sap was gathered from numerous zapote trees, which grow wild in the interior. Evidence of abandoned huts can be seen now and then where farmers once tried to eke a living from the thin, rocky soil. Coconut palms grew thick near the sea (before the devastating "yellowing" disease destroyed many trees), and it's still not unusual to see a sprouted coconut bobbing up and down in the surf. Many coconut trees take root that way, but if grown too close to the sea, they produce poor-tasting fruit. Take a stroll through the cool botanical garden at **Chankanab National Park,** where hundreds of tropical plants found on the island have been planted and labeled. An entry fee (US$3.50) gives access for the day to the lagoon and beach.

Marinelife

Brilliantly colored fish—from tiny, two-inch, silver bait fish traveling in cloudlike schools, to the grim, thick-lipped grouper—lurk in and around graceful, asymmetrical formations of coral with names like: cabbage, fan, and elk. You'll see rainbow-hued parrot fish, yellow-and-black-striped sergeant majors, French angelfish, yellow-tailed damselfish, and shy silver-pink squirrel fish with their big, sensitive-looking eyes. In shallow coves, daring Bermuda grubs come up out of the water to eat from your hand; watch the teeth!

HISTORY

Earliest Maya And Spanish

Cozumel's history alternates with bursts of unique activity and years of obscurity. During the Post-Classic period, Cozumel was not only a sacred island but an important trading center. Artifacts, especially pottery remnants of the female figure made in distant parts of Mesoamerica, were left by women who traveled from all over Quintana Roo to worship Ixchel at shrines scattered throughout the jungle. At one time during the Caste War, the Talking Cross cult was active on the island. After that era the island existed undisturbed until 1517, when it was briefly visited by Juan de Grijalva, who traveled from Cuba on a slave-hunting expedition.

He was soon followed by Spaniard Hernán Cortés, who embarked on his history-changing course in 1518. Cortés used Cozumel as a staging area for his ships when he launched his successful assault on mainland Indians. It was here that Cortés first heard of Geronimo de Aguilar, a Spanish shipwreck survivor of several years before. Aguilar had been living as a slave with his Indian captors. One story claims that when he heard of Cortés's arrival, he swam 19 km from the mainland to meet him. Because of Aguilar's fluency in the Maya tongue, he became a valuable accomplice in Cortés's takeover of the Indians. Francisco de Montejo also used Cozumel as a base in his war on the mainland. With the influx of Spaniards and accompanying diseases, the Maya all but disappeared. By 1570 the population had dropped to less than 300.

Pirates

The sparsely inhabited island led a placid existence until the late 1600s, when it became a refuge for bandits of the sea. Pirates such as Jean Lafitte and Henry Morgan favored the safe harbors of Cozumel, especially during violent storms. The buccaneers frequently filled their water casks at Chankanab Lagoon and created general havoc with their heavy drinking and violent fights, disrupting life within the small population of Indians and Spanish. By 1843 the island of Cozumel had been totally abandoned. Then refugees from the Caste War began to resettle it.

Chicle

Cozumel again became a center of activity when the chewing gum industry began to grow in the U.S. For centuries, the Maya had been satisfying their thirst by chewing raw sap from the zapote tree, which grows on Cozumel and throughout most of Central America. In the early 1900s, the developed world was introduced to this new sweet, bringing an economic boom to the Quintana Roo coast. New shipping routes included Cozumel, one of the best harbors along the coast suitable for large ships. Several big companies made fortunes on the nickel pack of chewing gum, while the Indians who cut their way through the rugged jungle to tap the trees managed only subsistence. Because of these gum companies, however, obscure but magnificent jungle-covered ruins hidden deep in the forests were discovered, fascinating the urban explorers. This was the beginning of a large-scale interest in the Maya ruins by outsiders that continues into the present. At one time the only route to Cozumel was by ship from the Gulf of Mexico port of Progreso. Cozumel's shipping income dwindled gradually as airstrips and air freight became common on the Peninsula. In addition, synthetics replaced hard-to-get chicle and are now used almost exclusively in the manufacture of chewing gum.

WW II And Cousteau
In 1942, as part of their defense network guarding the American continent, the U.S. government made an agreement to protect the coastline of Mexico. The American Army Corps of Engineers built an airstrip on Cozumel where the Allies also maintained a submarine base. After the war, the island returned to relative obscurity until 1961, when a TV documentary produced by oceanographer Jacques Cousteau introduced the magnificent underwater world that exists in and around its live reefs. Since statehood in 1974, Quintana Roo (including Cozumel) has enjoyed (or suffered) a rebirth into the world of tourism.

The Mexican government is making progress developing its beautiful Caribbean coast. For years it was believed that Cozumel itself would always maintain its pleasant small-town ambience, with just a smattering of tourism to add spice to the small island, and would never grow into a high-rise city; the water supply cannot support an enormous increase of people, and goods must be shipped from the mainland. But now the word is out, and the historical "Land of the Swallow" has a new desalinization plant and several new hotels.

SAN MIGUEL DE COZUMEL

Cozumel has only one city: San Miguel. Though it's no longer a sleepy fishing village, it still has a relaxed, unhurried atmosphere, a good selection of restaurants from budget to gourmet, and hotels in every price range. Grocery stores, curio shops, banks, a post office, telegraph office, dive shops, and anything else you might need are available. The main street, known either as the *malecón* ("seawall") or Av. Melgar, depending on which map you're studying, extends 14 blocks along the waterfront. The main

dock is at the foot of Av. Juárez, in the center of town. Plaza del Sol, the large central plaza, boasts modern civic buildings and an imposing statue of the late Mexican president Benito Juárez and a great general named András Quintana Roo. The surrounding streets are closed to vehicular traffic, making it a pleasant place to stroll, shop, and enjoy the tranquility of Cozumel. In spring, masses of orange *flamboyán* (poinciana) flowers bloom on the surrounding shade trees under which local townspeople gather for festivals, religious celebrations, or friendly chats. Cafes and gift shops surround the plaza.

ACCOMMODATIONS

San Miguel de Cozumel offers a good selection of hotels from budget to upscale and a lot in between. Always look at your room before accepting it. Many of the newer hotels have water purification systems, but always ask. Most of the prices quoted here do not include 10% tax. Don't hesitate to try to get a cheaper price at any of the hotels. The off-season is especially a good time to negotiate price. Often there will be a promotional price lurking in the depths of the computer; ask even when making reservations in advance from the states. A few time periods are very busy and you can expect to pay top dollar. Make advance reservations during 15 Dec.-2 Jan.; Carnival; Easter week; and August. Note: Cozumel is a favorite place for honeymoon couples; be sure to ask about special honeymoon packages that often save money or give a few extras that make them good deals.

Budget
Hotels in the center of San Miguel are often less expensive and within walking distance of cafes, discos, shops, and the seafront promenade. A wide variety of rooms is available: some small and sparsely furnished, others expansive with heavy colonial decor, central courtyards, restaurants, and comfortable gathering places to meet fellow travelers. Some hotels offer an economical junior suite with cooking facilities and private bath, a great bargain for families or small groups. Most have ceiling fans; some have a/c. With few exceptions, higher winter rates prevail from the middle of December through Easter week, and reser-

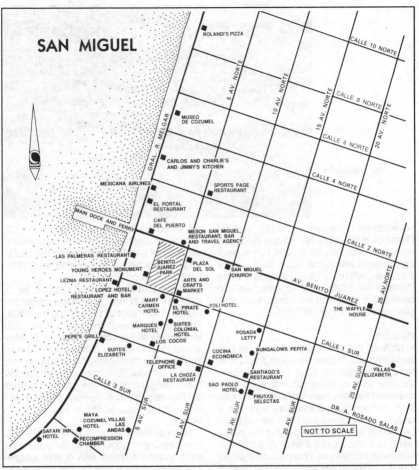

SAN MIGUEL

ROLANDI'S PIZZA

CALLE 10 NORTE

5 AV. NORTE

10 AV. NORTE

15 AV. NORTE

20 AV. NORTE

CALLE 8 NORTE

MUSEO
DE COZUMEL

CALLE 6 NORTE

CARLOS AND CHARLIE'S
AND JIMMY'S KITCHEN

CALLE 4 NORTE

MEXICANA AIRLINES

SPORTS PAGE
RESTAURANT

GRAL. R. MELGAR

MAIN DOCK AND FERRY

EL PORTAL
RESTAURANT

CAFE
DEL PUERTO

MESON SAN MIGUEL,
RESTAURANT, BAR
AND TRAVEL AGENCY

CALLE 2 NORTE

LAS PALMERAS RESTAURANT

BENITO
JUAREZ
PARK

PLAZA
DEL SOL

SAN MIGUEL
CHURCH

AV. BENITO JUAREZ

25 AV. NORTE

YOUNG HEROES MONUMENT

LEZMA RESTAURANT

ARTS AND
CRAFTS
MARKET

LOPEZ HOTEL,
RESTAURANT AND BAR

MARY
CARMEN
HOTEL

EL PIRATE
HOTEL

YOLI HOTEL

THE WAFFLE
HOUSE

MARQUES
HOTEL

SUITES
COLONIAL
HOTEL

POSADA
LETTY

PEPE'S GRILL

LOS COCOS

SUITES
ELIZABETH

TELEPHONE
OFFICE

COCINA
ECONOMICA

BUNGALOWS PEPITA

CALLE 1 SUR

VILLAS
ELIZABETH

CALLE 3 SUR

5 AV. SUR

10 AV. SUR

LA CHOZA
RESTAURANT

15 AV. SUR

SANTIAGO'S
RESTAURANT

SAO PAOLO
HOTEL

FRUTAS
SELECTAS

25 AV. SUR

DR. A. ROSADO SALAS

MAYA
COZUMEL
HOTEL

VILLAS
LAS
ANDAS

NOT TO SCALE

SAFARI INN
HOTEL

RECOMPRESSION
CHAMBER

© MOON PUBLICATIONS, INC.

vations are recommended. Double-check prices upon arrival if reservations aren't made in advance. There are no youth hostels on the island.

Take a look at the **Hotel Mary Carmen,** tel. (987) 2-0581, 5 Av. Sur #4; this small, pleasant, though simple hotel is just a stone's throw from the plaza, discos, restaurants, shops, and all other downtown activities. The 28 rooms are clean and surround a nicely cared-for garden. Rate is about US$40 d.

Yoli Hotel, at Calle 1 Sur #164, tel. 2-0024, is still around after who knows how many budget travelers have stayed in the 10 rooms over the years. Always clean, painted vivid colors, it has basic, spartan rooms, all with bath and fan. Rates are US$11 s and US$15 d.

Hotel Posada Cozumel, Calle 4 Norte #3, tel. 2-0314, is another basic hostel for those looking for low-cost accommodations. All rooms are doubles with bathroom and hot water, some with a/c, others with a fan. The simple, clean hotel has a swimming pool. Room rates start at US$17 d (with fan).

Check out **Al' Marestel,** a small bargain. Its 25 rooms are located at Av. 25 and Calle 10, tel. 2-0822. Not exactly in the middle of everything,

Plaza las Glorias

but worth the money. Rate is US$30 d. **Hotel Flamingo** is on Calle 6 Norte about five blocks north of the *malecón,* tel. 2-1264. Large, clean rooms, some with balconies; a good deal for the money, starting at US$20 d. Located **Hotel Flores** at Salas #25, tel. 2-1429, fax 2-2475, is close to the plaza and waterfront, with clean basic rooms starting at US$20 d.

Moderate

At **Club del Sol,** you stay across the road from the waterfront for a good price. This simple hotel has a great ambience. Enjoy a swimming pool, a/c, dive shop, open-air cafe with good food, and rooms that are simply furnished, and across the road there's a small snorkeling area. This is really a special place if you like a low-key Mexican feeling with few frills. Many of the guests return annually, staying a week or a month in rooms with kitchenettes. There is even a garden area planted by guests, and hammocks hanging about the heavily landscaped property. Rates begin at US$45 d in low season, US$65 in high season. For more information call (800) 228-6112 or (987) 2-3777, fax 2-2329.

Hotel Barracuda, another old standby, is a favorite with divers, right on the beach. It has 50 simple rooms with balconies, a restaurant, and a dive shop, and is only a half mile from town. Rates start at US$45 d in low season, US$65 d in high season; for more information write to Apto. 163; tel. 2-0002, fax 2-0884.

Take a look at **Villa del Rey** at Calle 11 Sur. It's simple, clean, and located downtown, and of-

fers 43 rooms at US$60; tel. 2-1600, fax 2-1692.

Another small (seven rooms), moderately priced hotel with fully furnished apartments is **Villas las Anclas** at 5 Av. Sur #325, tel. 2-1955, fax 2-1403. Room rate is US$60.

Mesón San Miguel, Av. Juárez 2B, tel. 2-0233, fax 2-1820, one of the "experienced" hotels, is in the heart of town facing the plaza. From here it's convenient to shop 'til you drop and sample all the cafés in town; on Sunday evening you'll hear the often-loud music from the plaza. The hotel is simple and clean, with a/c and a small pool. Some rooms have balconies overlooking the plaza. The usually crowded outdoor cafe draws a laid-back group of visitors. Rate is about US$58 d, less in the off-season.

Hotel el Marqués, tel. 2-0677, fax 2-0537, near Los Cocos restaurant on Av. 5 Sur, is a great downtown option, with eclectic furnishings and good views from the third-floor rooms; rates start at US$25 d in low season, US$30 d in high season. **Hotel Caribe,** tel. 2-0325, fax 2-1913, opened in 1992 on Calle 2 Norte about four blocks inland. The bright pink buildings frame a green lawn and small pool; rooms are decorated with cheery floral prints. Rates start at US$45 d. **Maya Cozumel,** tel. 2-0011, fax 2-0781, is a nice find on Calle 5 Sur three blocks south of the plaza. Rooms and grounds are filled with Maya statues and paintings; rates start at US$38 d in low season. **Suites Bazar Colonial,** tel. 2-0506, fax 2-1387, is a longtime favorite on the pedestrian walkway on Av. 5

Sur, with studio and one-bedroom apartments, and some rooms with kitchenettes, all starting at US$45 in low season.

Hotels For Divers

Some hotels go out of their way to accommodate divers. One such hotel is the 12-room **Safari Inn** located above Aqua Safari Dive Shop downtown on Av. Melgar across from the Safari boat dock. The hotel is modern but simple and clean, has a/c, and is very convenient for diving expeditions. The rates are US$36-45 s or d. Write to Safari Inn, Box 41, Cozumel, Quintana Roo 77600, Mexico, for package information; tel. (987) 2-0101, fax 2-0661. Other hotels offering dive packages include: **Galápago Inn,** a dedicated-dive hotel with a great dive shop, hammocks hanging by the beach, and a very good restaurant (stop by even if you're not staying here); often full with groups from U.S. dive shops. For information on dive packages contact Aqua-Sub Tours, tel. (800) 847-5708, or the hotel, tel. 2-0663. **La Ceiba Hotel** has a sunken airplane in the sea in front of the hotel, popular for shore dives, as well as an on-site dive shop, tel. 2-0844, fax 2-0064.

South Of San Miguel

One of the most convenient hotels, **Plaza las Glorias,** is on the Chankanab road at Km 1.5. For more information and reservations call (800) 882-6684 in the U.S.; in Cozumel tel. (987) 2-2200, fax 2-1937. The pretty pink upscale hotel is right on the beach, and features in-house diving through **Aqua Safari.** It's a convenient walking distance to downtown and offers 163 a/c rooms, outdoor pool, ocean swimming, restaurant, swim-up bar, music, Mexican fiesta night, and dancing, all with spectacular ocean views. Junior suites offer roomy sitting areas, refrigerators, wet bars, and balconies. Room rates start at US$100 in the low season, US$135 in high season; good package deals are often available.

Fiesta Inn Cozumel Hotel, on the Chankanab road at Km 1.7, with 180 rooms across the street from the beach, offers guests white sand, the sea, and a beach palapa for drinks and snacks. The rooms are well decorated and arranged around a large pool away from the road. Room service is available until 11 p.m., and **Los Arcos** dining room serves a breakfast buffet for US$9 and a dinner buffet for US$12. Room rates start at US$75 in low season, US$100 in high season; tel. (800) FIESTA1 or 2-2899, fax 2-2154.

Fiesta Americana Sol Caribe Cozumel offers 350 a/c rooms; those on the upper floors have lovely views of the bay. Everyone should take a look at its extraordinary Maya-style entry with an enormous peaked palapa roof. The hotel imparts a comfortable upscale atmosphere with a pool area that meanders through the garden and includes a well-patronized swim-up bar, a large palapa outdoor cafe, outdoor music, and an intimate dining room with piano melodies in the evening. The beach club across the road offers diving services as well as a small beach. Ask about the Fiesta Mexicana, where great entertainment is served up with an immense Mexican buffet. Room rates begin at US$110 in the low season, US$125 in high season. Located on the Chankanab road at Km 3.5. For more information contact Fiesta Americana, tel. (800) 223-2332 or 2-0700, fax 2-1301.

Fiesta Americana The Reef, tel. (800) 223-2332 or 2-2622, fax 2-2666, one of the newer hotels on the island, is located just south of town on the Chankanab road at Km 7.5. Though the hotel sits on the landward side of the street, beach access is simple with a pedestrian bridge from the hotel over the road to a beach club, with a pool, ocean, restaurant, dive shop, and boat dock. The 164-room hotel is modern with tile and marble rooms (all but those on the first floor have ocean views), two double or king beds, no smoking and handicap rooms available, two lit tennis courts, and another pool and dining room in the main building. Room rates start at US$110 in the low season, US$125 in high season.

Hotel Presidente Intercontinental is on one of the best beaches on the San Miguel side of the island. Visitors find a friendly atmosphere, 260 a/c rooms, beautiful grounds and public rooms, and several dining rooms that serve delicious meals with music. Be sure you try the open-air palapa near the sea. Rooms are all pretty much the same, well decorated in pastel colors but priced according to their locations. Some are upstairs with a "partial" view of the sea, others have a full view, some have private balconies, and some (the most expensive) open onto the beach with private patios. All sea sports are available, as well as car rentals and taxi service. Rates start at US$110 in the low season, US$170 in the high season. For more information call (800) 447-6147; in Cozumel tel. 2-0322, fax 2-1360.

Located on San Francisco Beach, the **Diamond Resort** is presently the hotel farthest south. Guests stay in modern, two-story, palapa-roofed villas, each with eight rooms. Everything is included in the daily price—meals, drinks, gratuities, tennis—and since it's located on the edge of the sea, the major focus is on water sports. Dive packages are available at the dive shop, and the best dive spots are just minutes from shore. Guests enjoy all the splash-sports, plus Sunfish sailers, pedal boats, and one free scuba lesson in the pool. Daytime and nighttime activities include aerobics, cocktail parties, and theme nights. Car, moped, and bicycle rentals are available at the hotel, and you can easily bike to nearby beaches and Chankanab park. Town is a US$10 cab ride away. The hotel is often filled with tour groups; book your reservations early. Rates for high season start at US$160 pp based on double occupancy; in the low season prices drop to US$100 pp. For more information, call (800) 858-2258 or 2-3433, fax 2-4508.

North Of San Miguel

Club Cozumel Caribe, around for some time under various guises, has been developed by the Barbachano family into an all-inclusive resort with good prices, especially for scuba divers. Prices include meals, drinks, sports activities, and a kids' club that provides great activities and supervision. Activities for guests include a trivia tournament by the pool, a Mexican buffet with folkloric show in the dining room, a movie in the disco, aerobics, beach volleyball, tennis, Spanish lessons, Mexican cooking classes, kayak races, Windsurfing, starlight cruises, plus a lot more. The food is fair, but it is all you can eat, and dinners are sometimes served outside by the pool. Rooms are spacious, each with private balcony, a/c, and old-fashioned Mexican decor; those in the low-rise building by the pool are in far better condition than those in the tower. The hotel has several boats, including the 100-foot, seven-stateroom MV *Oceanus*, where guests travel to Palancar Reef on an overnight scuba diving trip (extra US$40 pp). Rates begin

at US$99-119 pp, double occupancy. Horseback riding is available next door at **Chaka Stables** at a discount for Club Cozumel Caribe guests. For more information call (800) 327-2254 or 2-0100, fax (800) FAX-MAYA.

Melía Mayan is another five-star hotel, with marble tile floors, pastel decorated rooms, private balconies, 24-hour room service, direct-dial phone service, a/c, satellite color television, minibar, tennis, two pools, and a dive shop. Dining is exquisite, with a choice of continental haute cuisine or typical Yucatecan specialties. The Melía is located at the far north end of the leeward side of the island, about a 15-minute drive to town. Room rates vary widely according to season, beginning at US$115 d in the low season, US$152 in high season. For more information, call (800) 336-3542 or 2-0412, fax 2-1599.

El Cozumeleño, Playa Sta. Pilar, tel. (800) 437-3923 or 2-0344, fax 2-0381, is a multistoried hotel right on the sand, with the blue Caribbean at your feet. The rooms are nicely decorated, with private balconies and a/c. Keeping cool is easy with the sea, two pools, and water sports that include sailing and Jet Skis; deep-sea fishing nearby is arranged in-house. Dining is a delight on the terrace with a beautiful view of the sea. Rates begin at US$98-120 d, depending on the season. Ask about their "free nights" program every month except July and August.

Sol Cabañas del Caribe, Carretera San Juan, Km 4.5, tel. (800) 336-3542 or 2-0411, fax 2-1599, has a good location on the Caribbean just south of El Cozumeleño Hotel. It has nine simple little cabanas in addition to the regular hotel rooms. Certainly not glitzy, but the price puts them into the upper end of the scale. Each has a/c, simple furnishings, and comfortable beds, and there's a pool. The cabanas are a little smaller, a little homier, and available on a first-come, first-served basis. The windsurfing shop at the hotel is operated by one of Mexico's top windsurfing champions and is a great place to learn; kayaks are available for rent as well. Prices start at US$90 d.

Hotel Mara is an older hotel and the rooms all have double beds, a/c, and TV; each has an ocean view, most have balconies. There's a snorkel shop and a circular pool on a raised deck, as well as a seawall beach. A minimum three-night stay is required; rates begin at US$60 d per night; tel. (800) 221-6509 or 2-

0300, fax 2-0105. Other hotels on the north side are: the budget-priced **Cantarell,** tel. 2-1779, fax 2-2809; the **Coral Princess Resort,** with fully equipped condos overlooking the beach, tel. (800) 253-2702 or 2-3200, fax 2-2800; and the family-oriented **Playa Azul,** tel. 2-0043, fax 2-0110.

Condominiums

Condos have not taken over the Cozumel shoreline—yet! A few are popping up here and there, and one of the older but finest to rent is the small, intimate, well-laid-out **Condumel,** a 20-minute walk or a five-minute cab ride north of town. Condumel has its own beach and swimming dock where iguanas sunbathe with the visitors. The condos each have one bedroom with a king-size bed, living room, roomy modern marble bathroom with tub and shower, and well-equipped kitchen ready for the cook. A few basic food items, including beer and purified water, are chilling in the fridge in case you don't want to go shopping right away. Fans and the offshore breezes usually keep your rooms cool, but there's also a/c if you want it cooler. Maid service is included in the price, and laundry service is available. Just ask, and you can borrow fins, mask, and snorkel to use while there. Rates for two people start at US$90 per night 16 Dec.-31 May; US$70 per night 1 June-15 December. For reservations write to Condumel, attn. Sara, P.O. Box 142, Cozumel, Quintana Roo 77600, Mexico; or call (800) 262-4500 or (987) 2-0892, fax 2-0661. Owner Bill Horn also manages Aqua Safari dive shop and will arrange diving trips and equipment.

If you don't need to be on the waterfront, look for a cluster of white stucco townhouses with red-tile roofs about 10 blocks from the plaza. Each townhouse has tile floors, three bedrooms, and a/c; there's also a swimming pool, daily maid service, and a good storage area for scuba equipment. Total cost per night is US$154. For more information on condo, townhouse, and house rentals contact **Cancún Yucatán Adventures,** tel. (800) 6CANCUN, fax (707) 765-1723 in California. Other agencies representing rental condos, apartments, and homes are **Casa Cozumel Vacation Villas and Condos,** tel. 2-2259, fax 2-2348; **Agencia Quintana Roo,** tel. 2-1376, fax 2-3191; **Cozumel Vacation Homes,** in the U.S. tel. (918) 742-7070, fax (918) 742-3353; and **At Home in Cozumel,** in the U.S. tel. (800) 833-5971 or (212) 254-5623, in Cozumel fax (987) 2-1865.

Island Camping

Cozumel has no campgrounds with facilities. However, hidden coves and isolated beaches on the east side of the island let the outdoorsperson enjoy roughing it. Bring everything needed to camp, including water. Don't expect even a tiny *tienda* at which to buy forgotten items. If you ask the tourist office about beach camping, they'll tell you to get permission from the navy, which occupies the large building south of town, on the ocean side across from the Costa Brava cafe and hotel. Check for camping permission at **Mescalitos Bar, Balneario Popular,** and **Paradise Cafe** (formerly the Naked Turtle), all on the back side of the island. None of these places have camping facilities of any kind, but they might let you stay on their property.

FOOD

San Miguel has a variety of ways to spotlight mealtime. Fast-food stands and restaurants abound and fit all budgets. Seafood is exquisite and fresh. Yucatecan specialties simply must be tasted! *Camarones con ajo* (shrimp with garlic), *caracol* (conch), and tangy ceviche (fish or conch marinated in lime, vinegar, chopped onions, tomatoes, and cilantro) are all tasty treats. *Huachinango Veracruz* (red snapper cooked with tomatoes, green pepper, onions, and spices) is popular, and snapper is caught off the reef year-round; eat it a few hours after it's caught. Fresh seafood at its best is sold in most cafes.

Moderate Cafes

Budget-class **La Cocina Económica Mi Chabelita,** two blocks from the plaza heading inland on Calle 1 Sur to Av. 10 Sur, gives ample servings of *pescado frito* (fried fish) and *carne asada* (grilled meat) for about US$4. **Casa Denis,** the yellow house just up Av. Juárez from the plaza, has a few tables set out by the street and more in a back garden. Have a cold beer and *empanadas* stuffed with fish for a light lunch or snack for under US$4. **Comida Casera Toñita,** on Calle Salas at Calle 10, is a great find for its *comida corrida,* the fixed-price after-

The best food show in town is at Morgan's, where waiters make a tasty flaming dessert.

noon meal that covers both lunch and dinner and fills you up for about US$6. A bit over the low-budget class but well worth every peso is **Los Moros** on Av. Sur between Calle 3 and Morelos, with great Mexican and Yucatecan specialities. Prowl around on the back streets away from the sea toward the middle of the island—more and more small cafes are opening up, and prices are usually cheaper than at those near the ocean. **Las Tortugas,** Av. 10 Norte #82, serves good tacos.

Pepe's, a half block south of the plaza on Av. 5 Sur, noted for its relaxed atmosphere and sunset view from the nautical-style second-story dining room, has been popular for 20 years. Open for dinner only, with main courses running US$10 and up. **El Portal,** an open cafe facing the waterfront, serves tasty family-style food. A sturdy breakfast of bacon, eggs, beans, and toast costs about US$5. Open for breakfast, lunch, and dinner.

Las Palmeras at the foot of the pier in the center of town has been serving good food for many years and is always busy. Have dinner and a drink at **Costa Brava,** on Av. Melgar across from the navy buildings on the waterfront. The food and prices are very good. A simple breakfast begins at about US$3, set lunch starts at US$5, and you can indulge in normally high-priced shrimp, crab, or lobster dinners at reasonable prices. If the chef has had a good night, he treats his customers to an after-dinner glass of Xtabentun, spicy liqueur made in Yucatán.

Italian

For a special (expensive) dinner, try **Donatello Ristorante,** Av. Melgar Sur #131. They serve traditional classic Italian seafood such as scampi along with delicious veal and pasta dishes. The decor is very pink with a feel of the Italian Renaissance. On the *malecón* facing the sea, dinner is served every evening 5-11 p.m., reservations suggested, tel. (987) 2-0090. If you're ready for something different, try the Swiss-Italian specialties at **Pizza Rolandi,** on Av. Melgar #22. Good pizza, lasagna, calzone, and salads, plus beer and great sangria. The outdoor patio/dining room is a pleasant place to be on a balmy Caribbean evening; indoor dining is available in case of rain. **Karen's Pizza** is another place for fun and good food. Try the *taaaaallll* glass of beer, served in a wooden holder, in their large outdoor patio located on the closed-to-vehicles section of downtown.

Mexican And American Entrees

Once you discover **Los Coco's,** on Av. 5 Sur one block from the plaza, open for breakfast and lunch, you'll probably return frequently. The breakfasts are great, from the spicy, flavorful coffee to the hash browns and cream cheese muffins. **La Misión,** at Av. Juárez #23, is beloved by hungry divers who devour huge portions of fresh fish, *carne asada,* and fajitas prepared in the open kitchen by the front door. **Mr. Papa's,** on Av. Melgar at Calle 8, is another favorite for hearty eaters, especially on the nights they offer the all-you-can-eat barbecued chicken dinners. For the zany crowd, **Carlos and Charlie and Jimmy's Kitchen,** north of the plaza on Av. Melgar, tel. (987) 2-01-91, is a lively restaurant that specializes in fun. Respectable beer drinkers owe it to themselves to witness the beer-drinking contests held nightly. Sound like a place to drink and not eat?

Well, the food isn't as good as it once was; stick to the lower-priced dishes. Open nightly. **El Capi Navegante,** located on Av. 10 Sur, tel. 2-1730, serves good seafood, and you can usually find a coupon for a free margarita in the tourist brochures. Yearning for an American hamburger and a football game? Go to the **Sports Page,** a video bar/restaurant (usually a good money exchange also) on the corner of Calle 2 and Av. 5, tel. 2-1199. Try a taste of "Americana" with hamburgers, steaks, or sandwiches; if you happen to be in Cozumel in January, rest easy, you'll be able to watch the Super Bowl right here.

Calling all Mexican food lovers, don't miss **La Choza,** on the corner of Av. 10 Sur and Adolfo Rosado Salas, tel. 2-0958. The simple little corner cafe with oilcloth on the tables, painted cement floor, and Mexican wood furniture is always crowded with those aficionados who come back year after year! This is a friendly, family-operated restaurant, owned by Jorge, food cooked by mother Doña Elisa with the assistance of her daughter. The kitchen is open so all may watch the magic as it takes place. Start out with one of their *huge* margaritas, then on to scrumptious dishes such as *chiles rellenos* stuffed with shrimp, or a huge chicken breast covered with a green pepper sauce, or an aluminum-foil package filled with shrimp in sweet mustard sauce. If you like it simple, try the savory chicken kabobs cooked on the grill, or *mole* dishes. Even the dessert is original: have you ever had avocado pie? I prefer the great chocolate cake and the flan—you can also expect good brewed coffee here. Open 8 a.m.-11 p.m.

At **Pancho's Backyard,** Rafael Melgar #27, tel. 2-2142, in another old building on the waterfront, you'll find vintage Mexico in a lovely restaurant designed to remind you of gracious colonial days. The tableware is *típico* pottery, but guaranteed to be lead-free. The *carne asada* is tasty here, as is the shrimp brochette served on its unique charbroiler at the table. The jicama salad is served with a delicious orange-and-coriander dressing, refreshing on a hot summer night. Take a look at the store **Los Cinco Soles** in the same building, where you can buy handsome tableware and glassware, and **Galería del Sol,** displaying original art and sculpture.

More Expensive
Lobster, lobster, and more lobster is what you'll find at **La Cabaña del Pescador,** north of town near Club Cozumel Caribe. Diners choose their lobster at the front counter; then it is weighed and the meal priced accordingly—about US$15-20 for a hefty lobster tail served with bread, potato, and vegetables. There's nothing else on the menu except drinks, and the place is packed in the high season. Open for dinner only, no reservations, tel. (987) 2-3917. The **Acuario Restaurant,** a half km south of town on Av. Melgar at Av. 11 (open noon-midnight), serves elegant fish and lobster dinners with cocktail service. Walls are uniquely lined with huge aquariums filled with tropical fish, including a few brightly colored eels. Open tanks outside have even larger denizens of the sea (sharks and giant turtles) on display. If you happen to be in the neighborhood around 2 p.m., stop by for a drink and watch the handler feed the fish. It's a bit scary seeing sharp shark teeth in action!

Morgan's, on the north side of the plaza, is an elegant/casual restaurant serving a continental menu along with typical fish and Mexican entrees. You can spend a little or a lot. A special treat is crepes suzette with a spectacular flaming show (and they taste terrific!). Music starts about 6 p.m. For two people expect to pay anywhere from US$15 to as much as US$40 for a good dinner including crepes, a drink, tax, tip, and entertainment—worth it. Reservations suggested; open for lunch 11 a.m.-3 p.m., dinner 6:30-11 p.m.; tel. 2-0584.

Hotel Restaurants
The **Plaza las Glorias** and **Fiesta Americana Sol Caribe** hotels present a Mexican buffet and folkloric entertainment (about US$25), offering literally dozens of tasty dishes, fun, and good music and dancing at least one night a week. Reservations can be made through most hotels.

Sweets And Stuff
The Waffle House, on Av. Juárez at Av. 25 Norte, five blocks inland from the *malecón,* is a special place well worth walking a few blocks out of your way. The owner is one of the best pastry chefs on the island. Check out the refrigerated case for an irresistible display of chocolate cakes, lime pies, brownies, and cookies, and if there's a birthday party happening that night,

you're likely to see an elaborate cake as well. The made-to-order waffles are a real treat, filled with fruit or nuts, covered with syrup, or even replacing tortillas as the base for the savory *huevos rancheros*. Other breakfast options include eggs, hash browns, and homemade whole wheat toast. When we last checked, a lunch menu was in the planning stages.

Blue Bell ice cream, Calle 4 Norte, is now available in Cozumel. Just like in the States, you can get low-fat ice cream and frozen yogurt in a large variety of yummy flavors. Open 9 a.m.-10 p.m. Or if you want a pastry and a cup of coffee or superb cappuccino, try **Cafe Caribe.** The aromatic coffee fragrance will lead you right to the door, but just in case, write this down: Av. 10 Sur #215, open 8 a.m.-noon and 5-9 p.m. **Miss Italia** serves superb gelato in tropical flavors, across the street from the church.

Street Vendors And Markets

During spring and summer, street vendors offer mangos on a stick, peeled and artistically carved to resemble flowers, for US$0.50 each with your choice of lime or chile powder garnish, or both! A good selection of grocery stores, fruit vendors, and two bakeries makes it easy to eat on the run. Nothing tastes better than a crusty hot *bolillo* (hard roll) fresh from the **Panificadora Cozumel,** a bargain at US$0.25 each. **Bakery Zermatt** is on the corner of Calle 4 Norte and Av. 5. Great Mexican pastry, bread, and even pizza by the slice. Other bakeries (one is a block north of the main plaza at Calle 2 Norte and the other on the corner of Calle 3 and Av. 10 Sur) sell a variety of pastries and cookies. The *tortillería* makes corn tortillas all day; buy a kilo for only US$0.50 hot off the *tomal* (griddle).

The **Centro Comercial** on Av. Juárez facing the plaza and **Comercial Caribe** on Av. Juárez closer to the waterfront are grocery stores that stock a wide variety of canned goods, fresh produce, notions, and alcoholic drinks. Expect American-made products to cost more. Looking for plain Mexican ground coffee in Cozumel markets is frustrating; instant coffee and coffee grounds with sugar added are often all you can find. Cafe Caribe now sells its fresh roasted coffee in some markets and at its coffeehouse restaurant on Av. 10 Sur. American brands are available (at inflated prices) at **Pama** on Av. Melgar.

ENTERTAINMENT

Discos are popular in Cozumel. At night the town jumps with lively music, as energetic people meet and mingle. Dancing continues till morning at **Neptuno,** Av. Melgar/Calle 11, and **Scaramouche,** Av. Melgar at Salas. The **Presidente, Fiesta Americana Sol Caribe, Plaza las Glorias, La Ceiba,** and **Melía** hotels have music at cocktail hour and often during dinner. **Joe's Lobster Pub,** Av. 10 Sur 229, has live salsa and reggae after 8 p.m.

Special Events

The **Billfish Tournament** is held every year in May, bringing fishing enthusiasts from all over, especially boaters from the U.S. who cross the Gulf of Mexico to take part in the popular event. **Carnival,** a movable fiesta usually held in February, is a great party with street parades, dancing, and costumes—all with a tropical flavor. Another popular event is the celebration of the patron saint of San Miguel, held the last week of September.

Cinemas

Cinema Cozumel is on Av. Melgar (the *malecón*) at Calle 4 Norte; **Cine Cecilio Borgues** is at Av. Juárez and Av. 35; showtime 9 p.m. at both. Sometimes U.S. films are shown with original soundtrack and Spanish subtitles, but most are Spanish-language films.

The Museum

The **Museo de la Isla de Cozumel** is located on the waterfront north of the plaza in an old building that once housed a turn-of-the-century hotel. It has lovely informative exhibits of the wildlife, reefs, and corals surrounding the island, and artifacts of historic Cozumel. This small non-profit museum is definitely worth seeing (small admission) and offers a bookstore, library, and meeting room; on the second floor there's a pleasant outdoor cafe overlooking the sea. The museum is closed on Saturdays. Anyone interested in joining the **Group of Friends of the Museum,** write to Av. Melgar and Calle 6 Norte, Cozumel, Quintana Roo 77600, Mexico; tel. (987) 2-0841 or 2-1557.

*Cozumel's new museum
is conveniently located
on the oceanfront.*

Bullfights

For those into the traditional attractions of Mexico, a bullfight is scheduled on Wednesday mornings at 9:30 a.m. during the high season. Check with your hotel for price and reservations.

The Plaza

On Sunday evenings local citizens and tourists meet in the central plaza. Only a few women still wear the lovely white *huipiles*. Men in their best white hats look crisp and cool in the typical *guayabera* with its open collar and tailored pleats. Families (sometimes three generations) gather in the plaza to hear Latin rhythms and the tunes of the day presented by local musicians. The charming white gazebo takes on a modern look with the addition of powerful speakers placed around the park. Children, dressed as miniatures of their parents, run, play, and chatter in front of the live band. It's hard to say who does the best business—the balloon man or the cotton-candy vendor. This is a nice place to spend an evening under the stars, meeting the friendly folk of Cozumel.

SHOPPING

You can buy almost anything you want in Cozumel. Gift shops are scattered all over town. You'll see black coral jewelry, pottery of all kinds, and typical Mexican clothing and shoes. A few trendy fashion houses carry the latest sportswear, T-shirts, and elegant jewelry. One of the nicer gift shops, **La Concha,** Av. Rafael Melgar at Calle 2 Norte, displays traditional folk art from all over Mesoamerica, including beautiful Guatemalan weavings in flamboyant colors.

Talavera has gorgeous hand-painted dishes at Av. 5 Sur #141 near the plaza. A small shop that sells a conglomeration of unique souvenirs and artwork is **The Flea Market** (formerly Antiques and Artifacts) on Av. 5 Norte between Calle 2 Norte and Calle 4 Norte, on the west side of the street: you'll find Cuban cigars, old coins, weird sculpture, Xtabentun (you can tastetest this Yucatecan liqueur), artwork from strange to talented, and good English-language books.

Farther down the street, at the corner of Av. 5 Norte and Calle 4 Norte, is the home of Manuel Azueta, who weaves gorgeous multihued hammocks on his front porch. The prices are higher than in the souvenir shops, but the quality is far better. The gift shops of some hotels also carry a limited selection of English-language reading material. **La Belle Ondine,** on Melgar at Calle 4 Norte, has an unpredictable selection and also sells maps of the coastal area. Several excellent jewelry shops line Av. Melgar, with a stunning selection of precious and semiprecious gems at **Casablanca** and **Van Cleef.**

SERVICES

The four banks in town—**Bancomer, Banpaís, Banco del Atlántico,** and **Banco Serfín**—are all near the main plaza: exchange dollars or traveler's checks 10 a.m.-12:30 p.m. Since the advent of the cruise ships, almost everyone in town will accept dollars, but be sure you know the daily rate. There have been complaints that cruise-ship passengers often are taken advantage of with the exchange; know your rates and count your money. The **long-distance phone office** is on Calle 1 on the south side of the plaza, open 8 a.m.-1 p.m. and 4-9 p.m. There are several new Ladatel phone booths in town near the plaza; dial 09 to place collect calls with an international operator for free. Long-distance calls can be made from many hotels as well. Calling collect will save a good part of the added tax. The **post office** is on Melgar close to Calle 7, open Mon.-Fri. 9 a.m.-1 p.m. and 3-6 p.m.; the **telegraph office** in the same building is open Mon.-Fri. 9 a.m.-8:30 p.m., Sat. and Sun. 9 a.m.-1 p.m., tel. (987) 2-0106l or 2-0056.

The **tourist office** has moved to Av. Juárez between Avenidas 5 and 10 Norte, tel. 2-0972, open Mon.-Friday. An information booth in the plaza is an on-again, off-again affair. When open it's a font of information, usually staffed by someone who speaks English. A complete list of hotels in every price bracket is available, along with maps of the island and any general info you might need; tel. 2-1498.

For **taxi** service it's usually a matter of standing on the sidewalk and waving your arm, or waiting on Av. Melgar at the foot of the downtown dock—taxis queue along the sidewalk on the waterfront. The taxi office is on Calle 2 Norte, tel. 2-0236 or 2-0041, and any hotel will call a taxi. The closest **U.S. Consular Office** is in Cancún, tel. (98) 84-2411. Cozumel has one **gas station,** five blocks from downtown at Av. Juárez and Av. 30, open daily 7 a.m.-midnight. Cozumel has government-sponsored **Green Angel** motorist assistance. If your car should break down on the coastal highway, stay with it until they come by with gas, parts, or whatever help you need to get you on your way. The Green Angels cruise only on paved roads during daylight hours.

Lavandería Mañana, Av. 11 #101, charges by the kilo; open Mon.-Sat. 7 a.m.-8 p.m., usually one-day service. Pickup service on request, tel. 2-0630. A self-serve laundry, **Margarita Laun-**

SAN MIGUEL DE COZUMEL EMERGENCY NUMBERS

Police	2-0092
Fire Department	2-0800
Hospital	2-0140
Red Cross	2-1058
Ambulance	2-0639
Clinic (24 hours)	2-1081

---

dromat, is at Av. 20 #285, tel. 2-2865. **Express Laundry** on Av. Salas between Avenidas 5 and 10 Sur has self-service machines and dry-cleaning service, tel. 2-2932.

Camera Shops

Several camera stores in town sell film, rent underwater cameras, and have one-hour color-print processing service. Most of your photo needs can be satisfied at **Foto Omega** at Av. 5 Norte #7, tel. (987) 2-0471.

Medical Services And Pharmacies

In the event of a medical emergency, contact your hotel receptionist for an English-speaking doctor. **Hospital y Centro de Salud,** a small clinic with a doctor on duty, is open 24 hours a day, Av. Circunvalación, tel. (987) 2-1081. **The Medical Specialties Center of Cozumel** has a 24-hour clinic and access to air ambulance services, Av. 20 Norte #425, tel. 2-1419. One pharmacy, **Los Portales,** is located on Calle 11 Sur, tel. 2-0741. Another is in Centro Comercial on the north side of the plaza. **Farmacia Joaquín** is on the plaza in front of the clock tower; open 9 a.m.-1 p.m. and 5-9 p.m., tel. 2-0125. If still in need of help, call the U.S. Consular Office in Cancún, tel. (98) 84-2411. Three dentists are listed in Cozumel's Blue Guide: Z. Mariles, tel. 2-0507; T. Hernández, tel. 2-0656; and Escartín, tel. 2-0385.

Troubleshooter

Every once in a while, tourists encounter a problem that needs a little extra unraveling. If so, contact **American Consultation.** Ask for Bryan Wilson, tel. (987) 2-0654, on call 24 hours a day. Bryan is a transplanted American who has lived on Cozumel for years, and in the past has been very active with tourism. He knows everyone on the island and can advise you on just about any problem you come up with.

GETTING THERE

By Boat

Passenger ferries come and go to Playa del Carmen from the downtown dock in San Miguel. Two types travel between Playa del Carmen and Cozumel. The faster MV Mexico is air-conditioned and makes the trip in about 30 minutes; fare is about US$6 pp OW. The slower open-air boats take about 45 minutes; fare is about US$3. Between the two, there is a ferry departing just about every hour 6:30 a.m.-8 p.m. Check the schedules posted at the ferry pier. Car ferries use the **International Pier** across from the Fiesta Americana Sol Caribe Hotel, where cruise ships dock. Arrive a few hours early and be prepared with exact change and your car license number when you approach the ticket window—or you may lose your place in line and possibly on the often-crowded ferry. The car ferry departs once a day for Puerto Morelos on the mainland. Check the schedule at the International Pier or call (987) 2-1824.

By Air

Air travel from various points on the Yucatán Peninsula is becoming more common. Close by there are flights from Mérida and Cancún to Cozumel (Aerocaribe). It may be possible to fly between Cozumel and Playa del Carmen when you visit; the service is inconsistent. Check with your hotel tour desk. International flights arrive from the States via several airlines. Remember that schedules change with the season. Airlines serving Cozumel include: **Aerocaribe/Aerocozumel,** tel. (987) 2-3456; **Continental,** tel. 2-0847; **Mexicana,** tel. 2-2945; **Taesa,** tel. 2-4220; and **United,** tel. 2-0468. Charter flights are available from major U.S. gateways in the high season; ask your travel agent for information.

Travel Information In The States

For a knowledgeable travel agent, call **Four Seasons Travel** from anywhere in the States, (800) 552-4550. They specialize in Mexico's Caribbean coast and will work with you to create a vacation that best suits your needs, whether it's to Cozumel, Cancún, Isla Mujeres, or low-key resorts along the entire Quintana Roo coast.

Cozumel International Airport

The airport is approximately three km from downtown San Miguel. Taxis and mini-buses meet incoming planes. Taxi fare to town is US$3-5 pp in a collective taxi (a van) that will take you to your hotel; it's more for the return trip in a private taxi. When departing, an airport-use tax (about US$12) is collected. This tax applies to all international Mexican airports, so hang onto US$12 for each international airport city where you plan to stay 24 hours or more. Although there's a *casa de cambio* (moneychanger) at the airport, change your money in town, as banks and some shops (when you're making a purchase) give the best exchange rates, with hotels notoriously giving the worst. Cozumel airport has many small duty-free shops with a good selection of gifts. Reading materials, especially English-language pictorial books about the area, are found here and there. The airport has a dining room upstairs, and on the ground level a snack bar, but they're usually not open before the earliest flight departs.

GETTING AROUND

Getting around on the island is easy; it's flat and the roads are maintained. It's easiest in the city of San Miguel. The roads are laid out in a grid pattern with the even-numbered *calles* to the north of the town plaza, odd-numbered *calles* to the south; numbered *avenidas* run parallel to the coast. There is now a public bus running along Av. Melgar and to the hotels north and south of town on the leeward side. The schedule was erratic on our last visit; ask about it at your hotel. All of downtown San Miguel is easily reached on foot.

Several transport options exist for exploring the outlying areas of the island on your own—which everyone should do! Escorted tours around the island are available through any travel agency or your hotel. Avenida Juárez begins in downtown San Miguel at the dock and cuts across the middle of the island (16 km), then circles the south end. The road around the north end of the island isn't paved. Walking the flat terrain is easy, but distances are long. The 70 km of paved island roads are easily explored by bike (available for about US$15 per day at most hotels and at **Ciclissimo,** tel. (987) 2-1593. Mopeds and 125cc motorcycles are the most popular vehicles on the island, but some risks are involved. Helmets are now required by law on the island, a definite improvement that helps prevent serious injury. Be conscious of the vehicles around and behind you when on a motorbike, and get out of the way of impatient taxi drivers. Mopeds and motorcycles are available at most hotels and at rental shops all over town, and rent for US$25-30 daily. Remember to bargain; at certain times of the year you'll get a discount—supply and demand.

Taxis will take you anywhere on the island and are available by the day; agree on a price before your tour begins. Traveling with a local cabbie is often a real bonus since drivers know the island and its hidden corners better than most guidebooks (other than this one of course!). Remember, when the cruise ships arrive, many of the taxis are busy with cruise passengers at the ferry pier and the International Pier, leaving the rest of the visitors high and dry. Ask at your hotel for ship times if possible and plan your movements around it. The same goes for the larger shopping centers: they are jammed when the ships are in port.

Another option for seeing Cozumel is renting a car, which means total freedom to explore. Car rentals run approximately US$40-50 daily. Cars and motorcycles are available at: **Auto-Rent,** at La Ceiba Hotel, tel. 2-0844; **Budget** at the airport, tel. 2-0903; **Hertz** at the airport, tel. 2-1009; **Rentador Cozumel,** Av. 10 Sur, tel. 2-1120; and **National Inter Rent,** Av. Juárez #10, tel. 2-1515.

ARCHAEOLOGICAL SITES

Cozumel was one of the most important ports-of-trade for the Post-Classic Putún Maya seafarers. The island was a major producer of honey and contained the most important pilgrimage destination on the Peninsula's east coast. Women from throughout Mesoamerica traveled to Cozumel to worship at the shrine of the Ix Chel, "She of the Rainbow," the goddess of childbirth and medicine. Twenty-four sites have been discovered on the island, which was occupied from A.D. 0 on. It grew significantly after A.D. 800 and reached its peak in 1400. During the Post-Classic, the Putún built inland warehouses on raised platforms that were connected to the water by *sacbeob* (raised causeways). Many Maya structures were destroyed by the U.S.

Army Corps of Engineers when they built Cozumel's airport during WW II.

Three building groups are visible at San Gervasio; these are connected by trails that are built along the old Maya causeways. The structures are mainly small temples and shrines built on platforms around a plaza. In the middle of one causeway you come to the Temple of Ix Chel, a small but well-preserved building that was probably a shrine, although the connection to the goddess is not certain. Archaeologists at San Gervasio have recently found a grave containing 50 skeletons as well as some Spanish beads, leading them to believe that these were victims of a European disease brought by the conquistadors.

Most ruins on the island are of the "oratorio" type: small square buildings, low to the ground, with short doors that led early Spaniards to believe the places were once inhabited by dwarfs (a myth no longer believed). **El Cedral** is the exception; though the temple is small, major ceremonies were probably held on this site. The story goes that a Maya site was destroyed when the U.S. Army Corps of Engineers built an airstrip in dense jungle (now the location of the new Cozumel airport). The **Cozumel Archaeological Park** opened in 1993 a few blocks inland from the International Pier on Av. 65 Sur. The landscaped park contains reproductions of Mexico's most famous archaeological finds, and an exhibit of a typical Mayan home. The park is open daily 8 a.m.-6 p.m., admission US$3.

El Cedral

Several of the ruins are easily reached by car or motorbike. Just beyond San Francisco Beach on the main highway leaving town, a paved road takes off to the left and ends in 3.5 km at El Cedral. Small and not enormously impressive, this is the oldest Maya structure on the island. Amazingly, it still bears a few traces of the paint and stucco applied by the original Maya artist. But the deterioration indicates that hundreds of years have passed it by. A tree grows from the roof, with thick, exposed roots interminably tangled in and around stones of the ancient structure. Fat iguanas with bold black stripes tracing their midsections guard the deserted, mold-covered rock structure; sounds of cows blend with the songs of countless birds and the resonant buzz of unseen insects. Located in what is now a small farm settlement, El Cedral was once used as a jail in the 1800s. Right next to it is a rustic, modern-era stucco church painted vivid green. Go inside and take a look at two crosses draped with finely embroidered lace mantles—a typical mixture of Christianity and ancient belief, which some believe is associated with the Talking Cross cult.

Aguada Grande

Aguada Grande is more difficult to reach. After crossing the island (via Av. Juárez) to the beach, turn left on the dirt road and travel 21 km to another dirt road going inland; it's about a 1.5-km hike to the site. This is 0.75 km from the northern tip of the island, the **Punta Molas** lighthouse, and **El Real** (30.5 km from San Miguel). The beach along here is difficult because of a rocky shoreline—you make better time on the dirt road. At about Km 12, prepare for one of the most beautiful beaches on the island.

San Gervasio

San Gervasio is a well-preserved and recently reconstructed group of structures. Travel east on Av. Juárez, then left (north) on a dirt road (look for the San Gervasio sign) for approximately 10 km until it dead-ends at the entrance to the site. The silence of these antiquities looming in the midst of dense brush, with only birds singing in the tall trees, overwhelms the visitor with an image of what it must have been like centuries ago when only the Maya visited. San Gervasio has a snack bar for cold drinks and is open 8

a.m.-5 p.m., US$3.50 entry fee. Be prepared; guides will offer their services for about US$10 for two people, a bit pricey when you can do just as well in this small area by getting solid information at Cozumel's museum (downtown) first and then buying the green map, usually available at La Concha.

WEST SHORE BEACHES

Chankanab Lagoon

Chankanab, nine km south of San Miguel, is a national park. A small, crystal-clear natural aquarium is surrounded by a botanical garden of 352 species of tropical and subtropical plants from 22 countries, as well as those endemic to Cozumel. The lagoon contains more than 60 species of fish, crustaceans, turtles, and intricately designed coral formations. This is a wonderful, shady park in which to spend hours watching underwater activity. The lagoon is shallow, and until recently swimmers could go from the lagoon to Chankanab Bay (on the sea) through underwater tunnels; the tunnels have collapsed and no longer assure safe passage. Now there's *no swimming*. Don't bring your crumbs and stale tortillas: caretakers frown on anyone feeding fish in Chankanab Lagoon. Without the tunnels opening to the sea, scientists must work at protecting life in the small area. Save food offerings for your short walk from the lagoon to the bay, where hundreds of fish will churn water along the shore to get a scrap of anything.

Chankanab Lagoon

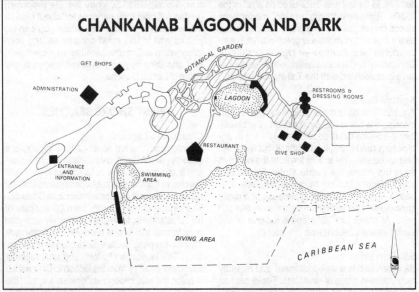

CHANKANAB LAGOON AND PARK

BOTANICAL GARDEN

GIFT SHOPS

ADMINISTRATION

LAGOON

RESTROOMS & DRESSING ROOMS

RESTAURANT

DIVE SHOP

ENTRANCE AND INFORMATION

SWIMMING AREA

DIVING AREA

CARIBBEAN SEA

© MOON PUBLICATIONS, INC.

Chankanab Bay

This is a popular beach for sunbathers, swimmers, divers, and snorkelers who want to explore limestone shoreline caves. Showy sea creatures have no fear of humans invading their domain. For adventurous scuba divers, the coral reef close offshore is 2-16 meters deep. A sunken boat, rusty anchors, coral-crusted cannons, and an antiquated religious statue all make for eerie sightseeing among the fish. A well-equipped dive shop is located here for rentals, air, sales, and certification instruction. Several gift shops, a snack stand, and La Laguna restaurant are conveniently located near the beach where shade palapas, freshwater showers, dressing rooms, and lockers are included in the small entrance fee of US$3.50. The national park is open daily 9 a.m.-5 p.m.

San Francisco Beach

Following the main road past Chankanab (14 km from town), you'll come to Playa San Francisco on the right. This 3.5 km of busy beach has two open-air restaurants, dressing rooms, bar, gift shops, volleyball net, wooden chaise lounges, and snorkeling equipment rental (US$5 per day). During the week it's relatively quiet, but during busy seasons and on weekends it's inundated with tourists, many brought by bus from cruise ships that anchor in the downtown harbor. San Francisco is also a popular Sunday destination for local citizens. Fresh fish and Mexican specialties are served to the accompaniment of loud music, live music, romping kids, and chattering adults. The bay is usually filled with dive boats attracted to nearby San Francisco Reef. The new Diamond Resort is just up the road.

Beach Clubs

On the main road from town going south toward San Francisco Beach, a small *balneario* called **Paloma Beach Club** is a pleasant place to spend an afternoon: good fresh fish and cold *cerveza* served at the outdoor cafe, white-sand beach, and good swimming and snorkeling. More and more of these little beach clubs are popping up along this area. Another one, **Playa Maya,** four km south of Chankanab, offers a small, calm swimming area on a narrow strip of sand. A snack stand is open daily, and you'll find beach facilities, dressing rooms, and a bar.

1. Cancun parasailing; **2.** Snorkeling at Garrafon Beach, Isla Mujeres;
3. Pool games at the Hyatt Regency, Cancun; **4.** Enjoying the sun and the sea, Cancun

1. street snacks, Quintana Roo; 2. Young Yucatecans vacationing at Don Armando's Bungalows close to Tulum; 3. Fiesta dancers at the Hotel Sol Caribe, Isla Cozumel; 4. German Mendez from Caribbean Argonauts Divers; 5. Celebrating the first day of spring, Chetumal

Isla De Pasión

This tiny island in **Abrigo Bay** has secluded beaches and a rocky shoreline good for underwater exploring (no cafes, restrooms, or any other facilities). Formerly the destination of Robinson Crusoe picnic trips, it is now a state reserve.

WINDWARD BEACHES

South To North

From **San Francisco Beach** around the southern end of the island are many beaches. Some are good for swimming; some are dangerous for swimming but great for beachcombing. Add sunning, camping, and birdwatching to provide more than enough reason to visit this shoreline, which stretches from **Punta Molas** at the north tip to **Punta Sur** at the south. To visit beaches on the east shore north of the island-crossing highway, take either a motorcycle or 4WD for the unpaved sandy road. If you rent a jeep for this trip, make sure that the 4WD hasn't been disengaged by the rental agency. Because of its condition, the 24.5-km road is seldom used, and few people see these beautiful beaches. If you decide to hike along this coast, you'll make better time in many areas on the road than on the rocky portions in between sandy beaches.

The first two beaches, **Santa Cecilia** and **Playa Bonita,** are good beachcombing spots, and Playa Bonita is a good camping beach (no facilities). For the real adventurer, the *Brown Map of Cozumel* shows trails from this dirt road to various little-known Maya ruins, abandoned cenotes, and caves. This kind of jungle trek requires carrying all essentials. From the Maya site at **Castillo Real** to the north, there are no more sandy beaches before the lighthouse on Punta Molas. Many ships have sunk along this violent shore: cannons and anchors are occasionally found to prove the legends.

Chen Río

At the end of the cross-island highway is tiny **Mescalitos Cafe.** Turn right (south) to Chen Río (Km 42). Space for tent campers and a few camping vehicles is on a broad flat area next to the beach. From here the beach becomes **Playa de San Martín** and after that, **Punta Chiquiero,** with a protected cove for swimming

in crystalline water. A small restaurant, formerly the Naked Turtle, now called the **Paradise Cafe,** sits on the edge of a lovely crescent bay with white sand. A bar serves ceviche, snacks, and hard and soft drinks; next door is the dining room. You can camp on the beach—with a tent or a vehicle—but there are no facilities. If driving an RV, check with the restaurant owners before you park.

Isolated Beaches

Along the highway from here to Punta Celerain is access to many beaches and the remains of a few small ruins. A dirt road meandering parallel to the coast behind sand dunes leads to **Punta Celerain Lighthouse.** All along this road you'll find paths turning out to the left, all leading to beautiful isolated beaches. Along the dirt road, a small, conch-shaped structure was restored. One of the docents at the museum in town explains how the small openings at the top were used as a warning—the wind blowing through creates a foghorn effect. According to archaeologists, it was built A.D. 1200-1400 as a ceremonial center and navigational guide using smoke and flames tended by the Maya keeper. Behind this small building, a dirt path over a sand dune goes to another beach great for swimming, sunbathing, and beachcombing.

Punta Celerain

This lighthouse is four km from the main road. From a distance it appears white, tall, and regal; up close it needs a paint job. Next to the lighthouse is a small army base with soldiers on guard. An exciting spot, it's well worth the detour to wander around the point, where a strong surf crashes over the irregular black limestone shore in great clouds of misty surf, spraying tall geysers through jagged blowholes. The family at the lighthouse is friendly, and usually you'll run into them on the grounds either doing their laundry or cooking. Ask to climb to the top for a spectacular 360-degree view of the island (a tip wouldn't hurt); don't forget your camera and wear comfortable walking shoes. The view one way is a long strip of white sand with a lacy scalloped edge of turquoise waves; in the opposite direction you'll see red marshy swamps in the middle of green scrub jungle; beyond it all—unending sea. On Sundays the

Cozumel's reefs make it a favorite divers' destination.

lighthouse keeper sells cold drinks and fried fish. The soldiers nearby often hike back to the barracks carrying several iguana ready to be prepared for lunch, much like their ancient ancestors did.

Back on the paved road just as it rounds the curve and turns north, a large sign warns of the consequences of taking turtle eggs. There's a stiff fine for this, since the turtle is a protected species; they come to shore here in large numbers during the summer to lay their eggs. You'll often find a soldier (with tent) standing guard over the sign. This coastal watch keeps tabs on the boating activity between Cozumel and the Yucatán coast; boatloads of illegal drugs are frequently picked up along here. A return to the paved highway takes you through the hotel zone and into downtown San Miguel.

WATER SPORTS

Snorkeling

Snorkeling and diving are the most popular outdoor activities on Cozumel. If you can swim but haven't tried snorkeling, Cozumel is the finest place to begin. For those who don't know, snorkeling is floating along the surface of the water with your face (in a mask) underwater while you breathe through a plastic tube called a snorkel. The little glass window on your mask

gives you heady visions of the colorful underwater world found nowhere else. For beginners, it's easy to find a fascinating marine environment close to shore without swimming or boating; in many cases you need only step from your hotel. Along the lee side of the island almost all beaches are ideal sites. If it's your first time, practice with a snorkel and mask while sitting in shallow, calm surf with your face underwater, breathing through the snorkel that protrudes above the surface. (Or use your bathtub to learn before leaving home.) Once you're accustomed to breathing with the tube, the rest is simple. Wear fins, which make it easier to maneuver in the water. A few easy-to-reach snorkeling sites include: Chankanab Bay and San Francisco Beach, Presidente Cozumel beach, Club Cozumel Caribe beach, and La Ceiba Hotel beach (where there's an underwater plane wreck). Rental equipment is available at hotels and dive shops. For the pros, check with a dive shop and you'll find many trips that motor groups to a suitable reef daily.

Scuba Diving

If you've always wanted to learn to scuba dive, here's the place to do it. A multitude of dive shops and instructors offer certification, or instruction sufficient for one dive, so use a lot of common sense finding a *qualified* instructor.

Look at his qualifications, ask if he's ever had an accident while in charge, ask about him around town (try the harbormaster). It's your life you're placing in his hands. Thousands of people come to Cozumel because of the surrounding reefs, and there are occasional accidents! Fairly simple dives for the neophyte are on offshore fringing reefs. Caves and crevices line the shore, and coral heads rise to within three meters of the surface. Some experienced divers prefer wall diving, while others find night diving more exciting. Certain reefs are for only the most expert diver. Boat reservations must be made in advance. Diving is an exciting sport, and the clear waters around Cozumel allow outstanding photographs; underwater camera rentals are available at some dive shops. **Note:** All divers should be aware that even touching the delicate coral reef kills it. Take care not to scrape your equipment or push off from the coral with your feet. These delicate creations of nature take millions of years to build.

Dive Spots

Plane Wreck: The average nondiver wouldn't think of a wrecked plane as a reef. However, if it sits on the bottom of the sea it serves as a reef by affording schools of fish shady hiding places on the white sandy bottom. A 40-passenger Convair airliner (engines removed) reposes upside down after being purposely sunk in 1977 for the Mexican movie production of *Survive II*. The water's clarity allows a clear view of the submerged wreck, located 100 meters off the La Ceiba Hotel pier. Beyond the wreck are huge coral heads in 14 meters of water. At the plane wreck, a 120-meter trail has been marked with underwater signs pointing out the various types of marinelife on La Ceiba reef. The visibility is up to 30 meters, and the average depth is 9-17 meters. A pillar of coral is an impressive sight and multicolored sponges are outstanding here.

Paraíso Reef: About 200 meters off the beach just south of the International Dock (between the Presidente and the dock), North Paraíso Reef can be reached either by boat or from the beach. It averages 9-17 meters deep and is a site of impressive star and brain corals and sea fans. The south end of the reef, farther offshore and located south of the International Dock, is alive with churning reeflife. This is a good spot for night diving.

Chankanab Caves and Reef: For easy-access diving, go to Chankanab Lagoon. A series of three caves on the shoreline provides a unique experience. Along the shore, steps are carved from coral for easy entry into water that surges into large underground caverns. Within seconds, you're in the first cave filled with hundreds of fish of all varieties. Striped grunt, snapper, sergeant majors, and butterfly fish are found in all three caves. Dives average 5-12 meters.

A boat is needed to dive Chankanab Reef, several hundred meters offshore south of Chankanab Lagoon (sometimes referred to as Outer Chankanab Reef). There's good night diving here in depths of 8-15, meters where basket starfish hang out with octopi and jail-striped morays. At the drop-off, stunning coral heads are at a maximum depth of 10 meters; in some spots coral is within three meters of the surface. Coral heads are covered with gorgonians and sea fans; striped grunt and mahogany snapper slowly cruise around the base. This is a good location for snorkelers and beginning divers.

Tormentos Reef: This is a medium-depth reef with innumerable coral heads in 8-12 meters of water above a sandy bottom. The heads are decorated with fans, gorgonians, and sponges. With little current, you can get excellent photos. Along the sandy bottom are great numbers of invertebrates: flamingo tongue shell, arrow crab, black crinoid, coral shrimp, and sea cucumber. When the current is going north, the farthest section of the reef drops to 21.5 meters, where you'll see deep-sea fans, lobsters, and immense groupers.

Yucab Reef: One km south of Punta Tormentos, Yucab Reef is fairly close to shore, shallow (good for beginners), and alive with such beauties as queen angelfish, star and brain corals, sponge, and sea whip. The coral reef is about 120 meters long, with an average depth of nine meters, and coral heads about three meters from the floor. When there's a current it can be two or three knots.

Tunich Reef: A half km south of Yucab—directly out from Punta Tunich—this deeper reef (15-24 meters) has about a 1.5-knot current or more, and when it's stronger you could be swept right along to Cuba! The reef is loaded with intricately textured corals, and the water activity attracts manta rays, jewfish, and barracuda; a good reef to spot shy moray eels.

San Francisco Reef: Another popular reef is located one km off San Francisco Beach. The abbreviated (half-km) coral runs parallel to shore; this is a boat dive into a site teeming with reef fish of many varieties and brilliant colors. Depths average 17-19 meters.

Santa Rosa Wall: This sensational drop-off, which begins at 22 meters and just keeps going to the black bottom of the Caribbean, really gives you a feeling for the ocean's depth. Strong currents make this a drift-dive, a site for experienced divers only (watch your depth gauge). You'll discover tunnels and caves; translucent sponge; stony overhangs; queen, French, and gray angelfish; white trigger fish; and many big groupers.

Paso del Cedral: This flat reef with 22-meter, gardenlike valleys is a good wall dive. In some places the top of the reef begins 15.5 meters from the surface. Sealife includes angelfish, lobster, and thick-lipped grouper.

Palancar Reef: The reef most associated with Cozumel Island is actually a five-km series of varying coral formations about 1.5 km offshore. Each of these formations offers a different thrill. Some slope and some drop off dramatically into winding ravines, deep canyons, passageways, or archways and tunnels with formations 15 meters tall—all teeming with reef-life. Startling coral pinnacles rise to 25 meters from the sloping wall. Much deeper at the south end, the top of the reef begins at 27 meters. **Horseshoe,** considered by some to be the best

diving in the Caribbean, is a series of coral heads that forms a horseshoe curve at the top of the drop-off. The visibility of 66-86 meters, plus a solid bronze, four-meter-tall, submerged modernistic sculpture of Christ, make this a dramatic photo area. The statue, created especially for the sea, was sunk on 3 May 1985, with great pomp and ceremony and the presence of Ramón Bravo, well-known TV reporter and Mexican diver. The much-discussed reef lives up to its good press.

Colombia Reef: Several kilometers south of Palancar, Colombia Reef is a deep-dive area, with the top of the reef climbing 25-30 meters. This is the same environment as Palancar, with canyons and ravines; here the diver may encounter giant turtles and huge groupers hiding beneath deep overhangs of coral. Seasonally, when the water cools down, you'll see spotted eagle rays (water temperature averages 23° C in winter and 27° C in summer). This reef is best for experienced divers, as there's usually a current; visibility is 50-66 meters.

Maracaibo Reef: At the southern tip of the island, this reef is an exhilarating experience. For the experienced only, Maracaibo is considered by most to be the ultimate challenge of all the reefs mentioned. At the deepest section, the top of the wall begins at 37 meters; at the shallow area, 23 meters. Unlike at many other reefs, coral formations here are immense. Be prepared for strong currents and for who-knows-

Aqua Safari Dive Shop

COZUMEL DIVE SHOPS

Aqua Safari, south of the plaza, on Malecón at 5 Calle Sur, tel. (987) 2-0101 or 2-0661; for more info (including hotel reservations): Box 41, Cozumel, Quintana Roo 77600, Mexico.

Aventuras Tropicales, on Malecón north of the plaza, tel. 2-03-93.

Blue Angel Scuba School, Villablanca Hotel, tel. 2-0730.

Bonanza Boat Trips, north of the plaza on 2 Calle Norte, tel. 2-0563.

Caribbean Divers, Hotel Cantarell, Mayan Plaza, and Cabaña del Caribe.

Deportes Acuáticos, four blocks north of the plaza on Calle 8, a short distance from Malecón, tel. 2-0640. Underwater cameras available.

Discover Cozumel, south of the plaza on Malecón; also at Chankanab Lagoon, tel. 2-0280.

Fantasía Marina, south of town, in front of Hotel Sol Caribe, tel. 2-0725.

La Ceiba, south of town, at Hotel La Ceiba, tel. 2-0379.

SCUBA Cozumel, south of the plaza on Malecón, tel. 2-0627; also at the Galapagos Inn, two km south of town, tel. 2-0853.

Sociedad Cooperativa, tel. 2-0080.

Viajes y Deportes del Caribe, south of town, at the Hotel El Presidente, tel. 2-0322.

what pelagic species, including shark. Dive boats do not stop here on their regular trips and advance reservations are required for this dive.

Other Good Diving Areas: Not shown on most maps are **Cardona Reef, La Francesa Reef, Barracuda Reef,** and parallel to Barracuda, **San Juan,** for *experienced divers only*—currents can be as much as six knots. In that kind of current a face mask could be ripped off with the wrong move. The faster the current, the clearer the water and the more oxygen, definitely a specialty dive (somewhat like a roller coaster!). Check with Aqua Safari for more information, including length of time to reach these reefs: three hours in a slow boat, an hour in Aqua Safari's fast boats. Reservations are necessary. A handy scaled map-guide with water depths around the island (and other reef information), *Chart of the Reefs of Cozumel Mexico,* is put out by Ric Hajovsky; it's available at most dive shops.

Dive Trips
Note: Many package dive trips originate in the U.S., with airfare, hotel, and diving included. Unless you have your own boat, many of the reef dives mentioned may be arranged through one of the many dive shops in town, through the boatmen's co-op, or by some of the hotels that have their own equipment and divemaster.

All equipment is provided and sometimes lunch and drinks. Prices vary, so shop around. For beginners, scuba lessons for certification or a resort course for one-day dives are available at most of the same shops. Be sure to check the qualifications and track record of the dive shop and divemaster you choose. A few are outstanding; most are good.

Also, shop around for your needs and level of diving. **Aqua Safari** has an excellent reputation for safety, experience, good equipment, and happy divers who return year after year. Aqua owns several large fiberglass boats geared for 16-18 divers each, with platforms for easy entry and exit, and fast boats for up to six divers, which reach the reefs more quickly but do not have shade. Two-tank morning and one-tank afternoon dives are available, as well as evening dives. The morning boats leave from in front of the dive shop at about 8:30 a.m. and stop at the shop's second location at the Plaza las Glorias hotel and other hotel docks along the way; they operate daily except Sunday, Christmas, and New Year's Day.

A typical morning dive day with Aqua Safari consists of two dives, on different reefs. The first dive is usually about 19-25 meters, the second dive about 13 meters. The exact locations are determined by the divemaster on each boat according to the weather conditions, currents, and divers' requests and experience. Afternoon dive boats depart at about 1 p.m. and visit one reef. The fee is about US$45 plus 10% tax (check; these prices change often). This includes two tanks, weights and belt, dive guide, and soft drinks. Additional gear may be rented: regulator with pressure gauge, B.C., tanks for beach diving (includes weights, belt, and backpack), mask, snorkel, and fins. They have a few lights available for night diving but suggest that you bring your own. During the winter months water temperature drops slightly and it's suggested you bring a wetsuit top. Aqua Safari Dive Shop hours are 8 a.m.-1 p.m. and 4-6:30 p.m. It's located on Av. Melgar at Av. 5 Norte, tel. 2-0101; and in the Plaza las Glorias hotel, tel. (987) 2-3362.

Other reputable Cozumel dive shops include: **Blue Bubble Divers,** tel. 2-1865; **Caribbean Divers,** tel. 2-1080; **Del Mar Aquatics,** tel. 2-1833; **Scuba Du,** tel. 2-1379; **Dive Paradise,** tel. 2-0017; and **Fantasia Divers,** tel. 2-2840.

New on the dive scene is **Tony Tate's Cozumel Underwater Video Service.** Tate accompanies divers on their dives and shoots a video of their underwater adventure for a great souvenir. You may run across him on your dive, or if you wish to get a customized video, contact him at tel. 2-1444, fax 2-1850. Underwater cameras are available for rent at **Island Foto-Video Center,** at La Ceiba Hotel, tel. 2-0379.

Notice To Divers

Since 1980, a refuge has protected marine flora and fauna on the west coast of Cozumel from the shore up to and including the Drop-Off (El Cantil). It is illegal to fish or to remove any marine artifacts, including coral, from the area. So, scuba divers and snorkelers, take only pictures. No one wants this product of millions of years to be damaged; on the contrary, it must be protected and saved for future generations of divers to enjoy.

Dive Safety

Because of the growing influx of divers to Cozumel from all over the world, the small island continues to increase safety services. All shops require divers to show their certification card and state the date of their last dive. Some shops require divers who haven't been in the water for a while to go through a checkout dive so divemasters can ascertain their ability. The **SSS**

(Servicios de Seguridad Sub-Acuática) is available for US$1 per dive day (at affiliated dive shops). This entitles the distressed diver to the use of Cozumel's hyperbaric chamber, marine ambulance, and fully trained round-the-clock personnel (each facility offers 24-hour service). All divers are welcome to use these services; however, nonparticipants pay regular commercial rates, so check with the dive shop before you choose. The recompression chamber is on Calle 5 Sur near Av. Melgar, tel. (987) 2-2387.

Boat Tours

For the nondiver, glass-bottom boats provide a close-up view of Cozumel's flamboyant underwater society. Small boats cruise along the lee side of the coast, and bigger motorized launches travel farther out to the larger reefs. Prices vary accordingly. Ask at your hotel, one of the dive shops, or Fiesta Cozumel, tel. (987) 2-0831. The **Nautilus IV** is the island's newest tour boat. Called a floating submarine, the boat actually has a glass-enclosed area below deck for viewing shallow reefs; contact Fiesta Cozumel at 2-0831.

Charter Boats

Customized boat trips can be arranged through Bill Horn at **Aqua Safari,** tel. (987) 2-0101, for crossing the channel to Tulúm for a day of sightseeing at the Maya ruins; return trip at your leisure. Trips to Cancún and Isla Mujeres or some other mainland destinations can also be arranged.

Off-island Excursions

Trips to Cancún, Isla Mujeres, Playa del Carmen, or a number of other mainland destinations can be arranged. Boat/plane/bus excursions to the Maya ceremonial centers are offered through your hotel or travel agency. Tulúm is close by boat or plane and too good to miss. Xelha, a natural aquarium harboring thousands of tropical fish, is also a pleasant stopover when going to the ruins at Cobá or Tulúm.

Fishing

Cozumel boasts good deep-sea fishing year-round. Red snapper, tuna, barracuda, dolphin, wahoo, bonito, king mackerel, and tarpon are especially plentiful March through July, also the high season for marlin and sailfish. Hire a

Aqua Safari boats wait for passengers for an all-day dive trip.

boat and guide for the day at the downtown dock or at Club Naútico de Cozumel. Small to large boats, including tackle, bait, and guide, cost US$125-825, half and full day, depending on size of boat, number of people, and season. Arrangements can be made at the boatmen's co-op, tel. (987) 2-0080, or by contacting Club Naútico de Cozumel at Marina Puerto de Abrigo Banco Playa, Box 341, Cozumel, Quintana Roo 77600, Mexico; tel. 2-0118. One of the best ways to choose a fishing boat is to visit the marina in the mid-afternoon when the boats are returning from the day's fishing trips. You can talk with boat captains and their customers

and negotiate the fee. The main marina is just north of town, and there is a smaller marina by the Presidente Cozumel hotel.

Other Activities

Several hotels north and south of town have tennis courts, and for a small fee nonguests can use them. **Sea Horse Ranch** offers horseback expeditions into the Cozumel bush, where you will see off-the-beaten-track Maya ruins and even the **Red Cenote.** English-speaking guides explain the flora and fauna of the island. Regular tours leave daily Mon.-Sat., reservations necessary, tel. (987) 2-1958.

KATHY ESCOVEDO SANDERS

ISLA MUJERES AND VICINITY

Isla Mujeres is just 13 km across the bay from Cancún via several transportation options. Many visitors return year after year, hop the ferry, and spend a few hedonistic days relaxing or diving on the outlying reefs of Isla Mujeres. This finger-shaped island lying off the east coast of the Yucatán Peninsula is eight km long and 400 meters at its widest point. While exploring the small island, take a walk through Hacienda Mundaca, snorkel along the coast, visit the lighthouse, and see the marine biology station—devoted to the study of the large turtle. Visitors are not encouraged, but if you're a science buff and can speak the language, give it a try.

Though the overflow of tourists from Cancún and Cozumel is very noticeable, the island is relatively quiet, especially if you choose to visit during the off-season—June and September are great! For some adventurers, Isla Mujeres is a favorite even though it's "growing up," with more visitors than ever. Everyone should snorkel at least once at teeming Garrafón Beach (it's teeming with fish *and* tourists!). The easygoing populace is getting used to all the people; the small town still smiles at backpackers. Travelers from budget to (almost) deluxe can easily find

suitable lodging, though in the budget category it's getting harder.

Isla Mujeres has a large naval base, with many ships in its harbor. By the way—the Mexican Navy doesn't like people photographing the base, ships, or crewmen on duty. If you're struck with the urge to photograph *everything,* ask someone in charge first. Before tourism, fishing was the prime industry on the island, with turtle, lobster, and shark the local specialties. Today the turtle is protected; they may *not* be hunted during any time of the year. The eggs are *never* to be taken and stiff fines are given to those who break this law.

History

One legend tells us that the name Isla Mujeres ("Island of Women") comes from the buccaneers who stowed their female captives here while conducting their nefarious business on the high seas. Another more prosaic (and probably correct) version refers to the large number of female-shaped clay idols found on the island when the Spaniards arrived. Archaeologists presume the island was a stopover for the Maya Indians on their pilgrimages to Cozumel to worship

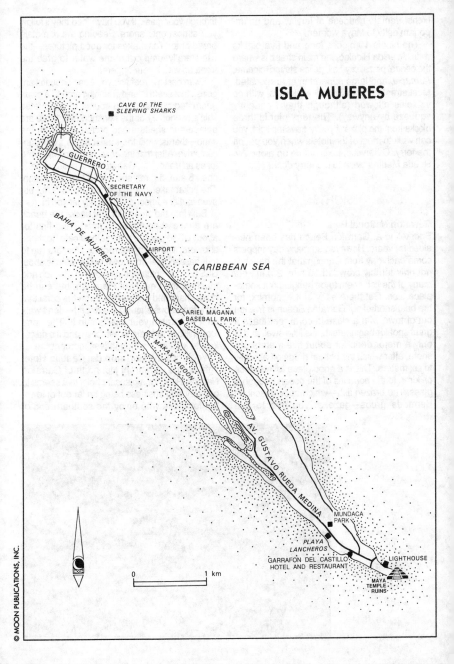

ISLA MUJERES

CAVE OF THE
SLEEPING SHARKS

AV. GUERRERO

SECRETARY
OF THE NAVY

BAHIA DE MUJERES

AIRPORT

CARIBBEAN SEA

ARIEL MAGANA
BASEBALL PARK

MAKAX LAGOON

AV. GUSTAVO RUEDA MEDINA

MUNDACA
PARK

PLAYA
LANCHEROS

GARRAFON DEL CASTILLO
HOTEL AND RESTAURANT

LIGHTHOUSE

MAYA
TEMPLE
RUINS

0   1 km

© MOON PUBLICATIONS, INC.

Ixchel, female goddess of fertility and an important deity to Maya women.

The city is 10 blocks long and five blocks wide. Avenida Hidalgo, the main street, is where the central plaza, city hall, police station, cinema, *farmacia,* and large supermarket are located. Most streets are really only walkways, with no vehicles allowed (although they frequently squeeze by anyway). The ferry pier is three blocks from the plaza; if you're traveling light, you can walk to most of the hotels when you get off the ferry. Otherwise, taxis queue up along Av. Rueda Medina close to the ferry dock.

SIGHTS

Garrafón National Park

Snorkeling at Garrafón Beach has been heralded for years. However, so many day-trippers come each day from Cancún that the beach is not only terribly crowded 10 a.m.-2 p.m., but many of the fish seem to be hanging out someplace else. Get there early in the morning for the best snorkeling! Garrafón Beach is five km out of town with a close-in coral reef that's a great spot for beginners. It has little swell and is only a meter deep for about five meters offshore, after which the bottom drops off abruptly to six meters. This is a good place to introduce children to the beauties of the ocean through a glass. The brazen fish—which aptly describes Bermuda grubs—gaze at you eye to eye

through your mask; if you have food they'll follow you almost onto shore. Feeding the fish stale bread or tortillas makes for good pictures—the fish literally jump out of the water to grab the treat, so watch your fingers!

Swim past the reef and you'll see beautiful angelfish that seem to enjoy hanging around a coral-encrusted anchor and a couple of antiquated ship's cannons. For the nonsnorkeler, there are palapa sun shelters and beach chairs on the sand—that is, until the tourist boats from Cancún arrive. After that the beach gets crowded and loses its tranquility. Garrafón is a national park, open 8 a.m.-5 p.m.; about US$2 pp admission. The ticket taker doesn't arrive until 8 a.m., but even earlier someone will usually let you in.

Built into the steep cliff that backs the beach are a dive shop (snorkel, mask, and fins for about US$6 per day), a seafood cafe, lockers, showers, and changing rooms. Taxi fare (up to four passengers) from town to Garrafón is about US$4. Coral outcroppings along this beach add much to the beauty of Garrafón, but can be razor sharp and dangerous. Even the coral that isn't dangerous should be avoided—don't walk on it or scratch your initials into it. The coral took millions of years to establish and it's ridiculous to kill it in one thoughtless moment.

You'll find the **Garrafón del Castillo Hotel** right on the waterfront just north of Garrafón National Park. It's a pleasant hotel that seems to get very little business being so far out of town, but for those who enjoy the southern end of

Garrafón Beach is popular with tourists and residents.

the island and quiet nights, it's located at Km 6 Carretera Punta Sur, tel. (987) 7-0019 or 7-0107, fax 7-0508. The three-story buildings facing the sea have 12 rooms with a/c and fan, large tile showers, refrigerators, and balconies. A restaurant, two souvenir shops, and a dive shop with snorkeling gear rentals sit above the sea, and the snorkeling is nearly as good as at Garrafón next door. Admission to the park is free to guests of the hotel. Moped rentals are available at the hotel, making it easy to get to town. Rates start at US$50 s or d in the summer, US$60 s or d in winter.

Maya Ruins

A short distance past Garrafón, at the southern tip of the island on a cliff overlooking the sea, is the reconstructed ancient Maya temple used as a coastal observation post. It was little more than a pile of stones after Hurricane Gilbert's devastation. It's still a beautiful lookout point if you happen to be in the "neighborhood." To get there, continue on the main road from Garrafón until you can see the lighthouse road going off to the right. Park your car, moped, or bicycle in the small clearing near the lighthouse, and follow the dirt path from the lighthouse to the ruins. These ruins were first seen and described by Francisco Hernández de Córdoba in 1517. In addition to being a temple of worship to Ixchel, goddess of fertility, the temple had narrow slits in its walls facing the four cardinal points, which were used for sophisticated astronomical observations—part of Maya daily life.

Today, the lighthouse keeper, Juan Martín Jiménez, looks after what's left, sells fresh fish ceviche, and makes colorful hammocks and black coral jewelry. A friendly guy, he's more than happy to let you try out the hammocks, will answer all questions (if asked in Spanish), and loves to pose for the camera (especially for a tip). Ask Señor Martínez if you can go up in the lighthouse; it's 10 meters high and worth the climb for the vista. Yes, it is polite to tip the caretaker. Sometimes you have to call for him, since he might be behind his house on the side of the hill hoeing his garden of tomatoes, peppers, and watermelons. This is a magnificent spot to see both the open sea on the windward side of the island and peaceful Mujeres Bay on the protected side.

If traveling by taxi, ask the driver to wait while you look around. Or let him go—you can walk back to Garrafón Beach and catch a taxi to town (till 5 p.m.). The walk to town is long and sweaty—figure about two hours.

Hacienda Mundaca

To make a visit to Hacienda Mundaca meaningful, dwell on a touching local legend from the mid-1800s. It tells of a swashbuckling, slave-trading pirate, Fermín Mundaca de Marechaja, who fell in love with a young woman on Isla Mujeres, Prisca Gómez, also called *Trigueña* ("Brunette"). In some versions she was a visitor from Spain, in others she was from the island. After 10 years of plying the seas and buying and selling slaves, he retired to the land to court her, unsuccessfully. Coincidentally, pirates were slowly being put out of business by the British Navy right about then. Mundaca built a lavish estate to woo her further, but to no avail. She married another Mujeres man and ultimately moved to Mérida and the high life, leaving the heartsick slave-trader behind to live alone in the big house with only his memories of the past. If you're a romantic, you'll feel a haunting melancholy while strolling in the once-gracious gardens of this deserted, almost destroyed estate. Mundaca lived the remainder of his lonely life on the island and left behind this inscription on his tombstone—*"Como tu eres yo fui; como soy, tu serás"* ("Like you are I was; like I am you will be"). Fate can be fickle—and perhaps just.

Rumor has it that the government is going to restore Mundaca and make it into a park, which would be nice since it is literally rotting away now. To get to Hacienda Mundaca from downtown, follow the main highway going toward the southern end of the island until you see a sign (Mundaca), and turn left off the road. Finally we see hints of restoration at the old site, but so far the only reconstruction is a lovely archway at the entrance. Mundaca is approximately 4.5 km south of downtown.

Just before the Mundaca turnoff, there's a dirt road to the right (at four km) that takes you to the small center for marine biology studies. Again, this is not officially open to the public; however, visitors have been known to gain entrance simply by knocking on the door and asking.

Beaches

The closest beach to downtown is **Playa Norte,** also called Coco Beach and Nautibeach (perhaps because of the topless women?), on the north edge of town, the lee side of the island. Here you can relax in the sun and swim in a blue sea that's as calm as a lake. In this shallow water you can wade for 35 meters and still be only waist deep. At the west end of the beach are palapa cafes, with both soft and hard beverages. If you see a rugged-looking, sun-tanned muscle man, it's probably the local beach character named Tarzan. He runs the equipment rental in front of **Las Palapas de Chimbo** beach cafe. You have a choice of renting sailboards, water skis, or three-wheeled "bikes" that float. Tarzan is a PADI-trained diver and offers scuba lessons (*always* check out a dive instructor's credentials for yourself). He is always open for bargaining and is flexible with prices, especially during the quiet season.

Four km south toward Garrafón on the main road out of town is **Playa Lancheros.** Playa Lancheros and Playa Paraíso are both quiet beaches where people formerly swam and rode the backs of giant sea turtles. No more (or so the rules say)! President Salinas let everyone know that the animals of Mexico were going to be protected. Today, the area is another place to enjoy the sun, sand, and sea; an open palapa restaurant specializes in seafood. A bus from town travels as far as Playa Lancheros about every half-hour; fare is about US$0.50. Very close by is a much nicer beach near the **Hacienda Gomar** restaurant, which features a bountiful buffet lunch and live marimba music.

WATER SPORTS

Snorkeling And Scuba Diving

The snorkeler has many choice locations to choose from, and the common-sense approach is to snorkel with a companion. **Garrafón** is good, and the east end of **Playa Norte** has visibility up to 33 meters near the wooden pier, though on occasion the sea gets choppy here, clouding the water. The windward side of the island is good for snorkeling if the sea is calm; don't snorkel or even swim on the windward side on a rough day and risk being hurled against the sharp rocks. An open wound caused by coral laceration often becomes infected in this humid climate.

The Yucatecan boatmen keep a sharp watch for the reef between Isla Mujeres and Isla Contoy. Hundreds of ships over the past 400 years have been wrecked on the reef that runs parallel to the coast from Quintana Roo to the Bay of Honduras.

The dive shops on the island sponsor trips to nearby reefs for snorkeling and scuba diving. A lot of press has been devoted to Isla Mujeres's **Sleeping Shark Caves.** Ask at the dive shop for detailed information. Although some divemasters will take you in among the sluggish though dangerous fish, others feel that it isn't a smart dive. Bill Horn, experienced diver/owner of Aqua Safari Dive Shop on Isla Cozumel, warns that there's always danger when you put yourself into a small area with a wild creature. In a cave, even if a large fish isn't trying to attack, the swish of a powerful tail could easily send you crashing against the wall. Reasons given for the shark's somnambulant state vary with the teller: salinity of the water or low carbon dioxide. Divers must dive to 150 feet deep or more to see the sharks, who may or may not be around. Local divemasters say that divers have a 30% chance of spotting the sharks. Between Cancún and Isla Mujeres, experienced divers will find excitement diving **Chital, Cuevones, La Bandera,** and **Manchones** reefs.

Scuba diving and snorkeling trips or rental equipment can be arranged at **Carnavalito Dive Shop** (to the left of the ferry on Av. Rueda Medina, tel. 987-7-0118), **Mexico Divers** (to the left of the dock on Av. Rueda Medina, tel. 7-0131), and **La Bahía Dive Shop** (across the street from the car ferry, Medina #166, tel. 7-0340). These dive shops are qualified and reliable, and give excellent service. Remember, always check out the divemaster's certification and consider what kind of a divemaster it is who doesn't ask to see yours.

Fishing
Deep-sea fishing trips can be arranged through any of the marinas. Spring is the best time to catch the big ones: dorado, marlin, and sailfish. The rest of the year you can bring in good strings of grouper, barracuda, tuna, and red snapper. **Mexico Divers** (Av. Rueda Medina) just left of the boat dock offers a day-long deep-sea fishing trip that includes bait, tackle, and lunch. The **Boatmen's Cooperative** on the waterfront just north of the ferry pier (tel. 987-7-0036) and the Club de Yates (Av. Rueda Medina next to the Pemex station, tel. 7-0211 or 7-0086) arrange deep-sea fishing trips and boat rentals.

Boat Regattas
Sailors from the southern U.S. have the opportunity to take part in sailing regattas each year. Organized by the Club de Yates of Isla Mujeres and started in 1968 from St. Petersburg, this event, scheduled for either the last week in April or the first week in May, draws many participants. Every two years in the spring, groups sail to the island from Galveston, Texas, and from New Orleans. This is a challenging trip for the adventurous navigator.

This is also a great time for a party. The town opens its homes and hearts to people who have in many cases been returning for years and have become friends. The boaters reciprocate and open their vessels to the islanders. The kids of Isla Mujeres work all year long learning dances, and the women make the costumes for cultural entertainment. An annual basketball game takes place between the "Bad Boys" of the island and visiting boaters, and no matter how they try, the boaters always lose. The name "Bad Boys" indicates these are the worst players on Isla Mujeres!

During Regatta Amigos, which occurs several times a year, everyone has a good time. In 1989, almost the entire population of 182 local children was aboard a single boat, attacking with water balloons the adults on another—the two boats head to head. The town provides food, tequila, and bands; with music everywhere, there's dancing in the streets, and a queen is chosen by the commodore of the regatta. During religious holidays, visitors will find the same kind of good times. For more info and dates, contact Club de Yates de Isla Mujeres, Av. Rueda Medina, tel. (987) 7-0211 or 7-0086.

Dock Facilities
The marinas in Isla Mujeres are getting more sophisticated, with many services available. **Pemex Marina** in the bay offers electricity, water, diesel, and gasoline. At the navy base dock you'll find a mechanic, tel. (987) 7-0196. **Laguna Makax** offers only docking facilities. For boating emergencies call either by radio, using the word "Neptuno" for the Coast Guard, or on VHF channel 16 or band 2182. Use channel 88 to get clearance to enter the country. Gasoline for cars and boats is at Av. Rueda Medina. Your best source for information on supplies and repairs is the Club de Yates, tel. 7-0211 or 7-0086.

ACCOMMODATIONS

You'll find a surprising number of hotels on this miniscule island. Most of them are small, simple, family-run inns downtown near the oceanfront. None can really be considered luxury class, but some offer more services than others. Since most are clustered downtown, it's simple to shop (on foot) until you find the one that suits you.

First-class
Posada del Mar is an older, multistoried building with your choice of bungalows or hotel. This is a happy place with many return customers each year, always a good sign! If they suspect

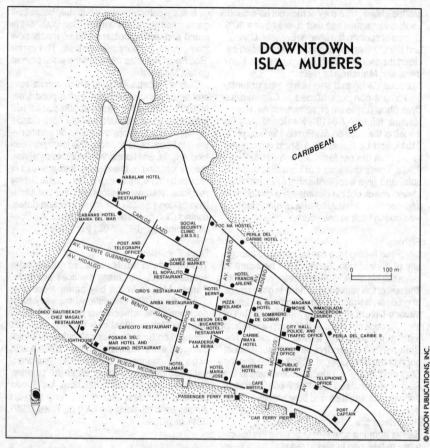

DOWNTOWN ISLA MUJERES

CARIBBEAN SEA

NABALAM HOTEL

BUHO RESTAURANT

CABANAS HOTEL MARIA DEL MAR

CARLOS LAZO

SOCIAL SECURITY CLINIC (I.M.S.S.)

POC NA HOSTEL

PERLA DEL CARIBE HOTEL

POST AND TELEGRAPH OFFICE

AV. VICENTE GUERRERO

AV. HIDALGO

JAVIER ROJO GOMEZ MARKET

EL NOPALITO RESTAURANT

AV. ABASOLO

HOTEL FRANCIS ARLENE

CIRO'S RESTAURANT

HOTEL BERNY

MADERO

AV. BENITO

ARIBA RESTAURANT

PIZZA ROLANDI

EL ISLEÑO HOTEL

MAGANA MOVIE

INMACULADA CONCEPCION CHURCH

EL SOMBRERO DE GOMAR

CONDO NAUTIBEACH CHEZ MAGALY RESTAURANT

AV. MATEOS

JUAREZ

CAFECITO RESTAURANT

EL MESON DEL BUCANERO HOTEL RESTAURANT

CITY HALL, POLICE, AND TRAFFIC OFFICE

PERLA DEL CARIBE II

LIGHTHOUSE

POSADA DEL MAR HOTEL AND PINGUINO RESTAURANT

AV. MATAMOROS

PANADERIA LA REINA

CARIBE MAYA HOTEL

TOURIST OFFICE

AV. MORELOS

AV. GUSTAVO RUEDA MEDINA

HOTEL VISTALAMAR

HOTEL MARIA JOSE

MARTINEZ HOTEL

PUBLIC LIBRARY

AV. BRAVO

TELEPHONE OFFICE

CAFE MIRTITA

PASSENGER FERRY PIER

CAR FERRY PIER

PORT CAPTAIN

0   100 m

© MOON PUBLICATIONS, INC.

---

it's your birthday, anniversary, or engagement—look out. Guests who stay for a week usually have a surprise in store—maybe a Maya Sacrifice (a flaming drink served with pomp and ceremony). Rooms overlook the waterfront with swimming in either the sea or the hotel's own lovely pool, where a stone, colonial-style aqueduct brings splashing water into the pool. A low-key palapa bar, where swings substitute for barstools and hammocks hang in the shade, sits next to the pool. Bar manager Miguel is known throughout the island for his creative concoctions. Try the Pinguino, diva, or excellent margarita. The restaurant Pinguino, Av. Rueda Medina #15A, tel. (987) 7-0212, fax 7-

0266, which opened in 1993, is at the front of the property with tables overlooking the sidewalk and beach and a big bar at the back of the room. Live bands perform during the high season, when Pinguino's becomes the hottest dance spot in town. The hotel rooms are air-conditioned and very comfortable, though the furnishings have seen better days. At the ferry dock turn left (north) and walk four blocks. Rates are about US$50 s, US$60 d; ask about good discounts given in the low season, and about special weekly rates.

Facing the windward side of the island, **Hotel Perla del Caribe I** offers pleasant rooms with private bathrooms, a/c or fan (ask for your choice), snack bar, and pool. Rooms have terraces and balconies, so be sure to ask for one facing the sea (great view of the coast). The hotel's (rough-water) beach is good for sunbathing and walking; swim only when the sea is calm. The concrete *malecón* walkway along the backside of the island is conveniently close to La Perla. The staff is very friendly; we looked at four rooms before we found the one we wanted, and they were still smiling in the end when they brought our luggage. Credit cards are okay; rates are about US$60 s or d with a/c and an ocean view, or US$45 s or d with fan and town view during the high season, but prices drop considerably during the low season; three suites with kitchens are available. For reservations, write to Av. Francisco I. Madero #2, tel. 2-0444 or (800) 258-6454, fax 7-0011.

The **Hotel Perla del Caribe II** has opened in the old Hotel Rocamar, Av. Nicolás Bravo, tel. 7-0587 or (800) 258-6454, fax 7-0011, a three-story hotel with balconies directly over the often-wild sea. The hotel provides lounge chairs for sunning on the beach (remember, swimming is usually treacherous here), small pool, clean rooms, hot and cold water, ceiling fans, bar, restaurant serving good food, and friendly staff. From the boat dock it's one block to the right and three blocks to the back side of the island. Rates are about US$55 d with town view and US$70 d with ocean view in the high season.

Cabañas María del Mar, on Playa Cocos at Av. Carlos Lazos No. 1, tel. 7-0213 or 7-0179, fax 7-0173, began providing visitors with simple bungalows many years ago. It has grown and modernized until it now has one of the nicest complexes on the island. You have a choice of simple or upscale, and continental breakfast is part of the tariff on all rooms. Check out the bungalows if you're looking for simplicity and something a little less expensive; they start at US$30 s or d in the low season, and go up to US$40 s or d in the winter. Then there's the Tower section and the Castle section, which start at US$45, up to US$85. Most of the rooms have two double beds, ceiling fans, a/c, terraces, refrigerators, and purified water, and are right on the beach. Facilities include a pool, restaurant, bar, video, and play room.

The nicest rooms on Playa Cocos are at **Nabalam** on Calle Zazil at Playa Cocos, tel. and fax 7-0436, just up the road from Cabañas María del

Mar. Two-story white stucco buildings face the sea, and all rooms are junior suites with sitting areas, dining tables, a/c and fans, and patios or balconies. Folk art and photographs from Chiapas and Maya carvings decorate the rooms and public spaces; landscaped trails lead to the restaurant and beach. Hammocks hang under the palms beside comfortable lounge chairs in a small garden facing the beach. The restaurant Zacil Ha is one of the best on the island, and the palapa bar is a popular happy hour hangout for local expats. Rates are about US$70 d in the high season, US$50 d in low season. Located on Calle Zazil (the road to the Del Prado), tel. 7-0279, fax 7-0446.

For the visitor who plans to stay a week or two, two-bedroom apartments are available on the beach at **Condo Nautibeach,** the large pink structure at the end of Av. Rueda Medina. The condos have full kitchens and eclectic decor chosen by the individual owners, who rent out their places to tourists. The pool is particularly attractive, backed by the sea, with a palapa bar at one end. The restaurant Chez Magaly is the fanciest on the island. Rates are US$100-120.

On the northernmost tip of the island, the old Hotel del Prado (formerly El Presidente) has yet to be reopened, though rumors about its future have abounded since the hotel closed after the 1988 hurricane. For now, the site is abandoned and continues to deteriorate, marring one of the loveliest settings on the island.

Out-of-downtown Hotels

Looking for a great beach, good pool, modern facilities with a fully equipped kitchen thrown in? Then check out the **Cristalmar Resort and Beach Club,** tel. and fax 7-0007, south of town on the Cancún side of the island. These apartment suites have one or two bedrooms. Each is air-conditioned and comfortable, and has lots of tile and a color TV. Continental breakfast and lunch are served by the pool near the palapa bar. Taxis to town are about US$5. You can snorkel, sun, and swim; fishing and scuba diving can be arranged through the front desk. Hacienda Gomar is right next door and the tranquility can be a little disturbed when day-trippers arrive for lunch. (Under Gomar's dock is a great place to see large groups of colorful fish enjoying the shade.) Rates are US$100 for one bedroom (maximum four people), and US$110 for two bedrooms (maximum six people). Prices go down in the low season. Ask about their get-away resort at Punta Allen if you want a real wilderness vacation. In the same neighborhood, between Laguna Makax and Bahía de Mujeres, **Villas Hi-Na-Ha,** tel. (98) 84-7074, has two-bedroom and three-bathroom villas with full kitchens overlooking the sea.

For something intimate, not fancy but away from town, check out **María's Kan Kin Restaurant Française,** tel. 7-0015, fax 7-0333, near Garrafón Beach. It has just a few rooms available and is a little bit pricey for what you get. Rates are US$40 s and US$55 d.

A Little Better Than Moderate

These hotels are clean, with pleasant staffs and pleasant surroundings. **El Mesón del Bucanero,** Av. Hidalgo #11, tel. (987) 7-0210, fax 7-0126, is a small hotel, located above the Bucanero restaurant. The recently constructed rooms are pleasant and clean, with private bathrooms and hot water, though the location above a busy restaurant is a drawback; US$23 s and US$50 d, year-round. Right across the street is the **Hotel Belmar,** Av. Hidalgo, tel. 7-0430, fax 7-0429, above Pizza Rolandi. The 10 rooms are nicely decorated with a/c, tiled floors, and satellite TV; the master suite even has its own hot tub and kitchenette. Rates start at US$27 s and US$32 d in the low season, US$35 s and US$40 d in high season; the master suite is US$75.

According to one reader, the **Hotel Gomar,** Av. Rueda Medina #150, tel. 7-0142, is "better than average." Opened in early 1990, the hotel is conveniently located across from the ferry in a long, narrow, four-story building. The hotel is colorfully decorated, clean, with comfortable beds (with Simmons mattresses), private bathrooms, fans, and a friendly staff. Rate is around US$45 d. **Hotel Francis Arlene,** on Av. Guerrero near the Casa de la Cultura, tel. and fax 7-0310, is in the budget category when it comes to price, yet meets the standards of the more expensive hotels. The owners keep a close eye on the condition of the immaculately clean rooms, which have a/c or fan, tiled baths, and good mattresses. Some rooms have refrigerators, toasters, and coffee makers, and some have stoves. Rates begin at US$18 s, US$20 d in the low season; and US$24 s, US$30 d in high season.

Budget

As you will discover, low-priced hotels are no longer as easy to find as they once were. Please look at budget hotel rooms carefully before paying your money—they change from day to day. What can be clean and friendly one day can be dirty the next. Hot water can be an elusive, unreliable item. If these things are more important than your pocketbook, don't look at budget hotels.

The youth hostel **Poc Na,** at Av. Matamoros #91, tel. (987) 7-0090, fax 7-0059, is a good choice for the backpacker. The hostel offers clean, dormitory-style rooms with fans, communal baths and toilets, and either mattresses or hammocks. The cafeteria is simple with few choices, but its food is adequate and inexpensive. Rates start at US$5 for mattress and sheet, US$2.50 for a hammock, and US$1 for a towel, with a US$7 deposit required for all rentals. Walk from the oceanfront to the end of Calle Matamoros.

For another peso saver, take a look at the simple, multistoried **Caribe Maya,** Av. Madero #9, tel. 7-0190. It's old but clean with 20 rooms, each with private bath and thrift-store furnishings, some with a/c, the rest with fans; the air circulation is better on the upper floors. Rates US$20 s or d, less in the low season. From the ferry dock, walk left for one block, turn right, and go 1.5 blocks.

Another old-timer where guests come each year is the **Hotel Martínez,** Av. Madero 14, tel. 7-0154. The 14 rooms are dependably clean, and all have fans and bathrooms. About US$18 s or d, less in low season. From the ferry dock, walk left for one block, turn right to the hotel. The **Hotel López** offers simple, usually clean, rooms for about US$15 d, located at Av. Juárez #29A Norte.

On the oceanfront, the **Hotel Vistalmar,** Av. Rueda Medina s/n, between Abasolo and Matamoros, tel. 7-0209, fax 7-0096, is really spartan, but guests enjoy the friendly ambience. Rooms have ceiling fans, private bathrooms, hot water, and a terrace overlooking the bay, and they are clean. A small restaurant overlooks the sea and serves tasty, but simple, meals. Rates for high season are US$18 s and US$24 d, in low season US$11 s and US$15 d. **El Isleño,** Calle Vicente Guerrero at Madero, tel. 7-0302, shouldn't be your first choice for budget accommodations, since cleanliness is not its hallmark, but if the other places mentioned are full, check here; a double room with shared bath runs about US$15, and with private bath US$20. **Hotel María José** on Av. Madero at Av. Rueda Medina, tel. 7-0130, is another good choice, with street-facing balconies in some rooms.

FOOD

As always, seafood is the highlight of most restaurant menus on Isla Mujeres; the fish is caught right in the front yard. Around town are dozens of indoor and outdoor cafes, simple and informal, plus a number of small fast-food places selling *tortas*, tacos, and fried fish.

Arriba

Vegetarians and health-food fans are in luck at this great second-story restaurant on Hidalgo. The salads of fresh vegies and cucumber dill dressing are worth celebrating, as are the vegetable kabobs and tempura served with wasabi and soy sauce. Fish and poultry dishes are prepared with a minimum of oil; potatoes are sautéed with jicama, onions, and herbs; and the Caribbean rice with ginger, vegetables, and egg is a meal in itself. Try the watermelon margarita and avocado pie for a real change of pace. Look for the blue-and-white trim and narrow stairway on Hidalgo between Abasalo and Matamoros. Open for lunch and dinner.

Cafecito

As the name implies, Cafecito, on Calle Juárez at Matamoros, serves great cappuccino and espresso, along with wonderful crepes filled with fresh fruit and ice cream. Breakfast choices include fresh waffles, fruit plates, and eggs, and at dinner the chef goes all out with specialties that include a sublime shrimp curry. Open 8 a.m.-noon and 6-10 p.m., closed Thursday and Sunday nights. Glass-topped tables cover pretty arrangements of sand and shells, and soothing soft jazz plays in the background. You may find yourself starting every day here!

Pinguino

Sunset watching is superb from the porch tables looking out to sea at the Posada del Mar's restaurant on Av. Rueda Medina, tel. 7-0300.

The chef does marvelous things with lobster here; if you're going to splurge, this is the place to do it. Plan on spending the evening and start with an appetizer of nachos or a seafood cocktail, then move on to the feast. Bands perform inside Pinguino during the high season, and at times it seems like everyone in town partakes in the party. Pinguino is also good for huge breakfasts of *huevos rancheros,* yogurt and granola, and toasted homemade whole wheat bread.

El Mesón Del Bucanero

On Hidalgo, this large outdoor cafe serves good seafood and Yucatecan specialties for breakfast, lunch, and dinner. Prices are reasonable—a breakfast of bacon, eggs, beans, and toast runs about US$3.50. Good fried fish and *chilaquiles.*

Miramar Restaurant

It's always nice to discover a cafe with good food, good service, and a nice ambience, and what makes it even nicer is to get letters from readers who tell me it's still great! That's the Miramar. Not to be considered a fancy cafe, but open-sided, it's located on the ocean side of the *malecón,* where you have a great view of the harbor. You can see the ferries come and go and watch the fishermen cleaning their catch and tossing scraps to the waiting pelicans, and on top of that find good food and friendly waiters. Whole fried fish is good and the price is about US$7.

Pizza Rolandi

This small cafe, on Av. Hidalgo between Madero and Abasolo, tel. (987) 7-0430, has good food and a usually efficient staff. In March 1988, Isla Mujeres was caught in a tremendous tropical storm. It wasn't raining buckets—it was raining truckfuls. The early lunch crowd would ordinarily be emptying out and a new crowd coming in, but no one was moving. The water had risen knee-deep in front of the cafe and no one was too anxious to get out into it except the kids paddle-boarding up the street. Rolandi played host to the entire crowd for hours, making space under the dry-roofed part of the patio for everyone. The coffee kept coming all afternoon. There was lots of laughing; visitors got acquainted with each other as well as with the waiters and management. Be sure to try their garlic bread;

it's great with beer. The cafe serves beef, great fish, pastas, calzone, and pizza.

Ciro's

On Matamoros and Guerrero, this is still an old favorite with glass-topped tables; in the evening, light reflects from old-fashioned glass lamps mounted on the walls. The clean, modern, fan-cooled, open-sided dining room serves good food all day. Moderate prices, well-stocked bar, and choice seafood, including excellent shrimp in garlic, as well as lobster. Good bargain breakfast: bacon and eggs with toast and black beans for about US$3.50. Special omelettes with ham, bacon, and cheese are just a little more. Ask when their trio will be playing—good entertainment includes a singer who occasionally croons in Mayan.

María's Kan Kin Restaurant Française

If your palate yearns for something continental, get a taxi and have an elegant lunch at **María's** (close to Garrafón Beach). She serves food in a palapa dining room overlooking the Caribbean. A small seawater tank holds live lobsters from which you can take your pick. The sophisticated menu offers curries, snails, and rabbit, and her prices are accordingly more expensive. Closed Sunday. A good meal for two with a cocktail can average US$20-35; tel. (987) 7-0015.

Chez Magaly

Head for the pink buildings on Nautibeach at Av. Rueda Medina Playa Norte, tel. and fax (987) 7-0436 (closed Monday). Sit by the sea and enjoy Caribbean food with a European flavor. The steaks are tender, shrimp and lobster superb, Caesar salad authentic, and service special. Sipping a tequila sunrise while watching the sunset is the *only* way to end a tropical day—or to begin a romantic candlelight dinner. This is where you'll find the Nautibeach Condominiums; it's hard to say whether Chez Magaly is in the Nautibeach Condominiums, or the condos are at the restaurant.

Others

Restaurante El Sombrero de Gomar, on the corner of Hidalgo and Madero, tel. (987) 7-0142, gives visitors an ice cream parlor on the street floor and a colorful Mexican patio ambience on the second floor. The food is good,

especially the barbecued meats. Everyone, even the waiter, seems to be having a good time, a real Mexican party; it's a little pricey but worth it; open 7 a.m-11 p.m. **La Peña Pizza** is another good restaurant at Calle Guerrero #5. It's a pretty place with a candlelight ambience in the evening. Dining can be either on the landward side overlooking the plaza, or on the seaward side looking out to sea. The pizza is tasty, as are a variety of other dishes. Open for breakfast, lunch, and dinner.

On Playa Norte, try **Las Palapas Chimbo** open-air beach cafe. Simple, but good fish dishes. **Café Mirtita** on Av. Rueda Medina across from the sea serves great (brewed) coffee and all-around simple good food. A small fan mounted at each table ensures your comfort. This old standby consistently puts out good hotcakes, egg dishes, sandwiches, and hamburgers with all the trimmings (US$4), plus friendly, quick service; very clean and reasonable.

Check out the **Plaza Las Flores,** Benito Juárez #32, not too far from the city cemetery, a simple cafe with a backyard dining area that serves really tender steaks, spicy fajitas, and excellent ceviche. Open daily noon-10 p.m. When we last visited, Las Flores was serving a bountiful buffet lunch for tour groups from Cancún. And one of the fun hangouts on the island is **Cocos Fríos,** where you can get good chicken and pork tacos, fried fresh fish, or a quarter of a roasted chicken. The quality of the food isn't as good as at other restaurants, but Cocos remains a popular meeting spot for locals and travelers; located at Hidalgo #4.

Anyone who likes crepes with mushrooms and hollandaise sauce better check out **El Nopalito,** across from Ciros at Av. Guerrero #70 near Matamoros, tel. 7-0555, a small cafe attached to the folk art shop, El Nopal. You'll find homemade bread, yogurt, muesli, and lots of good sandwiches. The cafe is run by Anneliese Warren, who speaks English, German, and Spanish and who loves to talk about her island. The cafe is open daily for breakfast, and Mon.-Fri. for dinner.

Robert's is a pretty pink and blue Caribbean-style house right on the main square, a good spot for lunch and people-watching, tel. 7-0451. **Estrellita Marinera** is one of the cheapest places to eat on Hidalgo, and also a good people-watching spot from the streetside tables.

Buho at Cabañas María del Mar is a popular spot for breakfast and lunch near Playa Cocos.

Off The Beaten Path

For an unbeatable eating adventure, go *inside* the *mercado* and to your left; look for the sign on the wall that says *Don Nacho Beh, rey del taco* (Don really is the "king of the taco" makers). Early Sunday mornings he prepares his prize recipe, *tacos de cochinita pibil.*

Be sure you try the *licuados* (liquefied fruit in sweetened water and ice) and ice cream at **La Flor de Michoacana** across from the playground.

ENTERTAINMENT AND SHOPPING

Gambling

That's right, legal gambling has found its way to Isla Mujeres at **La Peña,** a fine little cafe where the food is good and reasonably priced. In the back of the room, those interested in games of chance can make bets on just about anything at the **Caliente Racetrack, Race & Sports Books.** La Peña also has dancing to live music on weekend nights, on Calle Guerrero.

Markets

If you prefer to cook your own, there are several places to buy groceries. The *mercado municipal* opens every morning till around noon; it has a fair selection, considering that everything must come from the mainland. Two well-stocked supermarkets have liquor and toiletries: **Mirtita** (Juárez #14, tel. 987-2-0127) is open 6 a.m.-noon and 4-6 p.m; the larger **Super Betino** (Morelos #5, tel. 7-0127) is on the plaza, open 7 a.m.-9 p.m. **La Melosita,** Av. Hidalgo #17 and Abasolo, tel. 7-0445, is a mini-supermarket open 10 a.m.-midnight, with candies, piñatas, film, sundries, cigarettes, gifts, and snacks. **Panadería La Reina,** on Av. Madero, makes great *pan dulce,* open 6 a.m.-noon and 5-8 p.m. Fresh pastries appear on the shelves at 5 p.m.

Nightlife

Travelers complain there's little to do in the evening on little Isla Mujeres. It is true. Those who need to be "entertained" by the hour will not find the clubs, shows, fireworks, and other glitzy coddling that is everywhere in Cancún.

ISLA MUJERES SHOPPING HINTS

Artesanías Prisma; Garrafón Park; souvenirs and crafts

Bazar Pepe's; Av. Hidalgo #4; clothing and souvenirs

Caribbean Queen Handicrafts; Madero Norte #25; wool rugs, Mexican curios, gifts

Caribbean Tropic Boutique; Av. Juárez #3; souvenirs and crafts

El Nopal; Guerrero and Av. Matamoros; authentic clothing and crafts

Gomer Restaurant and Boutique; Hidalgo and Av. Madero; clothing

Isleño T-shirt & Shell Shop; Av. Guerrero 3-A Norte

La Loma; Av. Guerrero #6; arts, crafts, collector's masks

La Melosita; Av. Hidalgo #17; piñatas, mini-super

Mariola Boutique; Garrafón Park; souvenirs

Mari-Tona; Garrafón Park; clothing and souvenirs

Paulita; Morelos and Av. Hidalgo; imports

Rachat & Rome; in front of main pier; fine jewelry

Vamily; Av. Hidalgo and Parque; clothing and souvenirs

The **Calypso,** a favorite for locals, is on Rueda Medina at Playa Norte, tel. (987) 7-0157. **Tequila Video** attracts mostly teens (15-19) and is good, noisy fun for an evening. Some nightlife spills over from Cancún on party boats that bring crowds of people for **Caribbean Carnaval and Pirate Night.** If you're already in Isla Mujeres and you care to join in, it's easy to get to these beach locations by taxi. Make arrangements at your hotel or a travel agency, such as the **Intermar Caribe Travel Agency.**

Other evening activities include: Spanish-language movies (theater on Morelos near the plaza), local ball games in the plaza (visitors are always welcome to join in), an occasional boxing match, dancing in the plaza during special fiestas, and listening to the military band that occasionally comes to the navy base. You might check out the **Casa de la Cultura** on Av. Guerrero, where they offer classes in a variety of things, folk dancing, aerobics, and drawing, and there's a library with a book exchange. But the reason many folks come back to Isla Mujeres is to stroll around the plaza, watch the moon reflect off the water, buy hot *elote* (corn) and sweets from the vendors, and watch families at play, observing the respectful relationships between the very young and old. This is the real Mexico.

Shopping

There are several excellent folk-art shops on Isla Mujeres. **La Loma** on Av. Guerrero is the best, with carved wooden masks from Guerrero, wooden animals from Oaxaca, lacquered boxes and trays, textiles from Guatemala, and a huge display of handcrafted jewelry. **El Nopal,** at the El Nopalito restaurant, has some beautiful embroidered dresses and shirts. Several shops along Av. Hidalgo were filled with Guatemalan bags, vests, and jackets when we last looked, with a great selection at **The Flea Market** and **Isla Ixchel.** Batiked T-shirts bearing the images of Maya gods are featured by the hundreds at **Casa del Arte México** on Av. Hidalgo; check out the fine limestone carvings as well. Gorgeous jewelry and precious gems are displayed at **Van Cleef & Arpels** and **Rachat & Rome,** both near the ferry pier.

Special Event

The **Isla Mujeres International Music Festival** takes place the second weekend in October and lasts for 12 days. The island rocks with bands and dancers from everywhere. Reservations are a must.

SERVICES

A well-stocked **drugstore** is at Av. Juárez #2. **Farmacia Lily** is on Av. Francisco Madero and Hidalgo. A limited selection of **newspapers** and **magazines** can be found on the corner of Juárez and Bravo. Check at **Foto Imagen** in the new Plaza Isla Mujeres on Av. Hidalgo near the cemetery for film and batteries. Two banks in town will change money Mon.-Fri. 10 a.m.-noon: **Bank Atlántico** (Rueda Medina, tel. 987-7-0005) and **Banco Serfín** (Av. Juárez #3). The **post office** (Av. Guerrero #15) is open Mon.-Fri.

ISLA MUJERES EMERGENCY NUMBERS

city hall	7-0098
police station	7-0082
customs office	7-0189
chamber of commerce	7-0132
office of tourism	7-0188

---

8 a.m.-8 p.m., Sat. half-day, and is closed Sun. and holidays. General delivery will accept your mail and hold it for 10 days before returning it. Addresses should read: your name, Lista de Correos, Isla Mujeres, Quintana Roo, Mexico. The **telegraph office** next to the post office (Av. Guerrero #13) is open weekdays 9 a.m.-9 p.m., and Sat., Sun., and holidays 9 a.m.-noon. Money orders and telegrams will be held for 10 days only. Address to your name, Lista de Telégrafos, Isla Mujeres, Quintana Roo, Mexico.

Telephone Service

Great things are happening with telephones in Mexico, even in Isla Mujeres. Remember, a heavy-duty service charge is placed on all long-distance calls from a hotel, even on collect calls. Look for the Ladatel public phone booths scattered about. There is direct-dial U.S.A. service in several locations, one on the northwest corner of the plaza. Within a few seconds you are in contact with an American operator. Ask about the phones, and any other questions you may have about the island, at the **state tourist office** at Hidalgo St. #6, open 8 a.m.-2 p.m. and 5-8 p.m, tel. (987) 7-0188.

Travel Agencies

While on Isla Mujeres, for all of your travel needs contact **Club de Yates de Isla Mujeres.** They can fix you up with side trips to the mainland or fishing trips from Isla Mujeres. Even if you don't want a ticket but have a problem while you're on the island, stop in and ask for help—they'll do their best. To get to Club de Yates coming off the dock, turn left and walk about 150 meters; their office is on the left; tel. (987) 7-0086 or 7-0211.

In the States, for good guidance in choosing a hotel or purchasing airline tickets, and for local transport information, call Isla Mujeres specialists **Four Seasons Travel,** tel. (800) 552-4550 or (608) 297-2332, fax (608) 297-2272.

Another interesting contact is an American woman who spends half the year in Isla Mujeres and helps visitors in a rather unusual way. Arlene Coates, in the U.S. tel. (608) 244-4341, finds good deals in hotels and tours. She sends a map of the island to her clients, will meet visitors at the ferry dock if asked, changes dollars into pesos, and is right there to answer any and all questions that might come up. For this service she charges US$10 pp, a bargain!

Medical

In the event of a medical emergency, you have several options on Isla Mujeres. Ask your hotel manager to recommend a doctor. If that's not possible, the following medical contacts might be helpful. **Centro de Salud** (health center) is located at Av. Guerrero #5 on the plaza. Emergency service 24 hours daily, open for regular visits 8 a.m.-8 p.m.; tel. 7-0217. An English-speaking doctor, Dr. Antonio Salas, has an office open daily 11 a.m.-2 p.m. and 5-9 p.m.; tel. 7-0195 or 7-0477.

GETTING THERE

Many hotels and travel agencies arrange escorted day tours to Isla Mujeres. Independent travelers may be confused by the boat schedule; more than one boat goes to the island from more than one departure point. For those traveling the Peninsula by bus, it's easier to make ongoing connections in Puerto Juárez than in Punta Sam. One is a car ferry (also takes walk-on passengers) and the others are passenger boats.

Two types of passenger boats travel from Puerto Juárez to Isla Mujeres. The modern, air-conditioned, enclosed ferries charge about US$3.50 OW and make the crossing in less than 30 minutes. The older open ferries charge about US$1.75 OW and make the trip in 45 minutes. Buy your ticket on board for either boat. At least one boat leaves every hour from Puerto Juárez to Isla Mujeres 6 a.m.-8 p.m., and from Isla Mujeres to Puerto Juárez 5 a.m.-6 p.m. At the foot of the dock in Puerto Juárez you'll find a tourist information center sponsored by the municipal government, with bilingual employees and a restroom (small fee). The office is open sporadically.

A car ferry leaves Punta Sam (five km north of Puerto Juárez) daily and carries passengers and cars. You really need a good reason to bring a car to this short island with narrow, one-way streets. RVs can travel on the ferry, but there are very few places to park and no hook-ups. The trip on the ferry from Punta Sam is slightly longer than from Puerto Juárez. If driving, arrive at the ferry dock an hour before departure time to secure a place in line; tickets go on sale 30 minutes in advance. The car ferry departs from Punta Sam six times daily 7 a.m.-8 p.m., and six times daily from Isla Mujeres 6 a.m.-7 p.m. **Note:** Be aware of the time that the last passenger boat leaves Isla Mujeres. If you haven't got a hotel reservation you might have to sleep on the beach, and it can rain any time of the year.

GETTING AROUND

Mujeres is a small and mostly flat island, and in town you can walk everywhere. The eight-km length is a fairly easy trek for the experienced hiker. Other options include taxi, bicycle, rental car, golf cart, motorcycle, and municipal bus. A tour around the island in a taxi (three passengers) and back to your hotel costs US$15 and takes about an hour, including stops to watch the lighthouse keeper making hammocks and inspect the Maya temple on the south tip.

Cars, Carts, Mopeds And Bicycles

If you want to see the outer limits of the island, bicycles and mopeds are the most popular ways to go. The newest trend in transportation is the golf cart, which travels at a top speed of about 10 miles per hour. The carts are safer than the mopeds and provide more shelter from the sun. Rental cars are beginning to appear on the island as well. Most hotels can arrange rentals, or you can check with the shops scattered all over downtown. Rental cars cost about US$50 per day, golf carts and motorcycles are about US$20 for eight hours or US$35 for 24 hours, and bikes go for about US$7 for eight hours.

By Taxi

Taxis are many, are easy to get, and have reasonable fares. To go anyplace downtown the fare is about US$3. The main taxi stand is on Av. Rueda Medina next to the ferry dock; service 24 hours, tel. (987) 7-0066.

La Vikinga *travels to Isla Mujeres from Cancún in eight minutes.*

By Bus
The municipal bus operates daily 6 a.m.-9 p.m.; about US$0.75. It runs from Posada del Mar on Av. Rueda Medina to Playa Lancheros. Ask for the schedule and stopping points at the state tourist office at Av. Hidalgo #6.

CONTOY

Contoy is an island 24 km north of Mujeres: the small bit of land (2.5 by one-half km) is a national bird sanctuary. Outside of wayward flamingos, herons, brown pelicans, the magnificent frigate bird, olivaceous cormorants, and a couple of humans at the biology station, you'll find a lush, isolated island—the kind of place around which fantasies are spun. From a tall viewing tower (about three stories of steps) open to the public, you can see most of the island. Under a shady arcade there's an information display with lighted photos of numerous birds, including full details of each specimen. A white-sand beach close by provides a refreshing swim with delicate tropical fish. Often you'll swim amid large schools of young trumpetfish, almost transparent as they glide through the water sucking up small fish and shrimp. Tiny flying fish in groups of 10-30 or more skim the surface as they flee large predators.

Isla Contoy was closed to tourists in August 1993, when officials feared the island's ecology was being harmed by its popularity. At press time, biologists and government officials were considering changing Contoy's status from a bird sanctuary to a biosphere reserve, giving it many of the same protections as the Sian Ka'an reserve on the mainland. Once the island's status is secured, tourists may be able to visit once again, but on a much more limited basis. Check with the tourist office at Av. Hidalgo #6 or with the Boatmen's Cooperative next to the ferry pier for information on possible tours to Contoy.

Getting There
Contoy's transportation carriers have a high rate of turnover. For the *real* birdwatcher, Ricardo Gaitan's overnight-trip 10-meter sailboat, the *Estrella del Sur,* is the best way to see the birds, both at dusk and at dawn. The two-day trip is well worth the time, which includes all meals (mostly fresh-caught fish, liquor extra), snorkeling equipment, a cruise around the island, and time for hiking and exploring. Bring your own sleeping bag for the beach (an inflatable mattress makes the beach or deck more comfortable), and don't forget sunscreen, bug repellent, and mosquito netting. The boat anchors close to shore near some excellent birdwatching sites (bring your camera and Fielding's *Mexico Bird Guide*). Rick can be contacted at the Boatmen's Cooperative in town, tel. (987) 7-0036, or write to him directly: Apto. Postal 42.

Other boatmen offer one-day trips departing 8 a.m. and returning 7:30 p.m. These cruises typically include a stop at the reef to snorkel (equipment provided), fishing off the end of the boat en route (if you wish), a light breakfast snack of *pan dulce* and fresh fruit, and a delicious lunch of *tikin chik* (fresh fish caught along the way and barbecued at Contoy) along with Spanish rice and green salad. Soda and beer are extra. The captain often treats his passengers to a lime/salt/tequila drink on the return trip. Many of the boats are motor/sailers, usually motoring north to Contoy and raising the sail for the trip back to Isla Mujeres. Many are neither luxurious nor too comfortable (wooden benches), but you can look forward to meeting people from various parts of the world. Check at the marinas or at Dive Mexico for Contoy trips. If passenger boats still travel to the island, you'll see signs giving full information all over town; or contact the Boatmen's Cooperative, tel. 7-0036.

LOUISE FOOTE

PUERTO MORELOS

Puerto Morelos, on the northern Caribbean coast, is 17 km south of Cancún. It has limited accommodations and few attractions to detain most people. At one time its only claim to fame was the vehicle ferry to Cozumel. But more and more people are beginning to notice Puerto Morelos's peaceful mood, lack of tourists, and easy access to the sea. As with some of the other towns on the Caribbean coast, divers are bringing low-key attention to this small town, using it as a base to explore the rich coastline. Until Hurricane Gilbert, Puerto Morelos had been the coastal headquarters of CIQRO (Centro de Investigaciones de Quintana Roo), an ecological-study organization sponsored by the Mexican government, the U.N., and environmental groups dedicated to maintaining the ecosystem of the Quintana Roo coast. The building was thrashed, so ask one of the locals for the most current information and CIQRO's present location.

Canoe Harbor
In pre-Hispanic times this was a departure point for Maya women making pilgrimages in large dugout canoes to the sacred island of Cozumel

to worship Ixchel, goddess of fertility. Remnants of Maya structures are located near the coast and throughout the jungle. Though small, the ruins are not considered insignificant, but as usual there's a shortage of money to investigate and restore them. The descendants of Indians in these parts occasionally find artifacts dating to pre-Columbian times, which sadly are often sold to private collectors, and their archaeological value is never measured. If caught with the genuine article—whether a pottery shard you picked up at one of the ruins or a piece bought from a local—you will be fined and your treasure taken from you. *Caveat emptor!*

SIGHTS

A short walk through town reveals a central plaza, shops, a cantina, and nearby military base. Puerto Morelos's most spectacular attraction is its reef, which begins 20 km north of town. Directly in front of Puerto Morelos, 550 meters offshore, the reef takes on gargantuan dimensions—between 20 and 30 meters wide. For the scuba diver and snorkeler this reef is a dream come true, with dozens of caverns alive with coral and fish.

Jardín Botánico
Just south of Puerto Morelos, this is a lovely area (150 acres and three km of trails) through which to wander under the trees and learn about the plants and flowers of the Peninsula. The exhibits are marked in English, Spanish, and Latin. Habitats range from semi-evergreen tropical forest to mangrove swamp. This is also a study center and a tree nursery. Look for the epiphyte area, with a variety of orchids, tillandsias, and bromeliads. As you wander around you'll find a re-creation of a *chiclero* camp showing how chicle is harvested to be used in chewing gum. Some small ruins from the Post-Classic period are on the premises, as well as a contemporary Maya hut that illustrates day-to-day life, from cooking facilities to hammocks. Wear good walking shoes. This is well worth the price, US$2 pp (you'll get a map of the area); if you wish to have a guide, add US$5. Open daily 9 a.m.-5 p.m.

ACTIVITIES

Snorkeling
Snorkeling is best done on the inland side of the reef where the depth is about three meters. Snorkelers can expect water clarity up to 25 meters along the reef.

Scuba Diving
The reef has been a menace to ships for centuries. Early records date losses from the 16th century. Many wrecks have become curiosities for today's divers, who come from great distances to explore the Quintana Roo coast. Puerto Morelos can provide the most experienced diver with exciting destinations, including a wrecked Spanish galleon with coral-crusted cannons—clearly visible from the surface five meters above. Looking for another kind of excitement? **Sleeping Sharks Caves** are eight km east of Puerto Morelos. Intriguing, yes, but the sharks still claim proprietorship.

Sub Aqua Explorers, operated by Shedor Palma Muñoz (PADI Instructor #29934), offers good diving service. He can be contacted at the Cabañas Playa Ojo de Agua, or write to Apto. Postal 113, Puerto Morelos.

Fishing
A never-ending variety of fish provides good hunting for sportspeople. Onshore fishing is only fair off the pier, but if you're interested in deep-sea fishing, ask around the plaza or make arrangements at the hotel **Posada Amor.**

ACCOMMODATIONS

Budget
No one minds if campers spread their sleeping bags north and south of the lighthouse away from town, houses, and hotels. Choose a high spot (so you'll stay dry). It can get gritty if the wind freshens, and if it's very still be prepared for mosquitoes. Remember, the beach is free and this is a relatively safe, peaceful town. The area code is 987.

The **Posada Amor** is a simple, 20-room, friendly, family-run hotel with ceiling fans, shared baths (some private), and hot water. The decor is mosquito-netting tropical and lighthearted, with a little patio on which to meet other independent travelers. Rates begin at about US$30 for a room that will accommodate four people (shared bathroom). A room for one or two people with private bath and double bed costs US$25 d; shared bathroom US$20. A very simple palapa, shared bathroom for one person, costs US$18. If you just want to stop by and take a hot shower, it costs US$3. You can call to make reservations (telephones will soon be available down the coast!), tel. (987) 1-0083. The family-run restaurant is in the front; even little Mariana is there to greet guests!

Hulking **Motel Eden** offers 20 clean rooms each with private bathroom, hot water, refrigerator, and one double and one single bed. The whole place looks rather dismal, but the price is good when the town is filled up: US$20 s, US$25 d. When you get into town (from the highway), turn left on Av. Niños Héroes until you get to Villas Shanti, turn left again and you'll see Motel Eden across the street. They offer a good restaurant with a continental breakfast for about US$3, fried chicken US$4.50; tel. 1-0015.

CANCUN-TULUM CORRIDOR

Once upon a time the adventure traveler could escape south along the coast from the upscale world of Cancún to the wilderness of palm plantations, low jungle, seldom-seen animals and birds, isolated beaches, crystalline coves containing flashing fish, and little more than palapa-hut accommodations—just a few hours away. Today this area is called the Cancún-Tulúm Corridor. Often unpronounceable names like Morelos, Tulúm, Akumal, Xcalacoco, Xcacel are now travel-agent jargon. The corridor is developing rapidly and has been on the tourism drawing board since Cancún was conceived in the early '70s.

When you fly over this coastal area you'll see miles of white beach edged on one side by the jungle and on the other by blue sea, with nary a human artifact in view. But much has happened over the years. In another five years maybe none of us lovers of Mexico's Caribbean coast will recognize it. For now, hurry up and leave your footprints; you can still find an isolated beach and a happy palapa resort owner—even if he has only 10 clients a night, or week. Right on Hwy. 307 you will find attractions that are fun and more attuned to the nature of the country—designed for the tourist, of course. On the following pages you will find an overview of the cities growing the quickest.

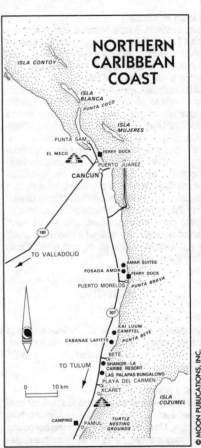

Acuario Palancar

About 20 km south of Cancún, look on the left for a biggish sign advertising a smallish aquarium. Don't expect Marine World; however, this does have about 20 tanks showing off the marinelife you would see if you were to go snorkeling or scuba diving in the waters just offshore. With classical music in the background, take a look at parrot fish, angelfish, colorful eels, crustaceans, and—piranha? This is a small exhibit and won't take more than 15 or 20 minutes to observe. Admission (a little pricey for what you get) about US$3 pp; open 8 a.m.-7 p.m.

Croco Cun

Anyone fascinated by crocodiles will be intrigued by a wander through this breeding station next door to the aquarium. A path leads around separate walled ponds where you can spend as long as you wish studying these long-snouted, ugly beasts, some found only in Mexico. About 300 reptiles are on display, including Morelet's crocodiles, Central American caymans, and American crocodiles. Eggs are removed from the dirt mounds, after all of mama's trouble, and then monitored in temperature-controlled rooms, a practice said to determine the sex of the offspring. Heed the signs, and watch your children. On the premises, you will find a snack bar and a small gift shop. Open daily 8 a.m.-6 p.m., admission is about US$3.50 pp. Located right next door to the aquarium.

To Boca Paila

Quintana Roo's Caribbean coast from just below Cancún to Boca Paila is a 153-km stretch with dozens of fine beaches, some with camping facilities, several with modest cabanas, and a few with more deluxe accommodations. Others offer nothing but nature's gifts: the sun, white sand, and blue sea—free! Often the only way to spot the entrance to these beaches is by noting the kilometer count on small highway signs that begin at Chetumal and end at Cancún (360 km). To get to some of them you must leave Hwy. 307 at the Tulúm turnoff and continue on the uneven, potholed road that parallels the sea, officially called Boca Paila Road. This road ends at Punta Allen, an isolated bit of paradise with little more than a lobstering village and a lighthouse—but what a place to forget about civilization for a while!

Hurricane Gilbert hit this Quintana Roo coastal area in September 1988. This was one of the most devastated areas. The small town of Puerto Morelos suffered tremendous damage but is just about put back together. Docks, homes, hotels, and other structures are slowly being rebuilt.

This tranquil dock offers good fishing.

Moderate

New on the scene in 1993, the **Hacienda Morelos** overlooks the beach south of the town square. The rooms in the second story of the brick building are especially nice, with a great view of the sea, cooling ocean breezes, mini-refrigerators, immaculate white decor, and bathtubs as well as showers—a rarity in these parts. A small pool and sunbathing area sit right above the beach and an enclosed parking lot in front. The main entrance is at the Muelle 8 restaurant, one of the best in town (see "Food, Shopping, and Services," below). Rates start at US$50 d. To get there, turn south at the waterfront; the hotel is one block south of the plaza, tel. (987) 1-0015.

Los Arrecifes is a great windswept spot north of town right on the beach with eight nicely furnished apartments, all with separate bedrooms and full kitchens. Owner Vicki Sharp keeps a close eye on the place, and also operates a beautiful guesthouse closer to town called **Casa Miguel**. Sharp knows about all sorts of rental properties in the area. Contact her by writing to Box 986, Cancún, Quintana Roo 77500, Mexico, or call 1-0112; fax (98) 83-2244 in Cancún. **Villa Latinas** has seven furnished apartments for weekly and monthly rentals, tel. 1-0075.

Since Hurricane Gilbert, **Hotel Playa Ojo de Agua** has been rebuilt with 12 modern rooms including kitchen, ceiling fans, dive shop, and pool. This beautiful beach just north of town center is as lovely as ever. Write for information: Ernesto Muñoz, Calle 12 #96, Colonia Yucatán, Mérida, Yucatán 97000, Mexico; tel. (99) 25-0293; in Puerto Morelos tel. (987) 1-0015.

Deluxe

A fine resort in Puerto Morelos is south of the ferry dock on an isolated stretch of white-sand

QUEEN CONCH

A popular, easy-to-catch food beautifully packaged—that's the *problem* with the queen conch (conk). For generations inhabitants of the Caribbean nations have been capturing the conch for their sustenance. The land available for farming on some islands is scant, and the people (who are poor) have depended on the sea—especially the conch—to feed their families. Even Columbus was impressed with the beauty of the peach-colored shell, taking one back to Europe with him on his return voyage.

The locals discovered a new means of making cash in the 1970s—exporting conch meat to the U.S. The shell is also a cash by-product sold to throngs of tourists looking for local souvenirs. An easy way to make money—except for one thing: soon there will be no more conch! In recent years the first signs of overfishing have become evident: smaller-sized conch are being taken, and fishermen are finding it necessary to go farther afield to get a profitable catch.

It takes three to five years for this sea snail to grow from larvae stage to market size. It also takes about that long for planktonic conch larvae carried into fished-out areas by the currents to replenish themselves. What's worse, the conch is easy to catch; large (shell lengths get up to 390 cm) and heavy (about three kilograms), the mollusk moves slowly and lives in shallow, crystalline water where it's easy to spot. All of these attributes are contributing to its demise.

Biologists working with various governments are trying to impose new restrictions that include closed seasons, minimum size of capture, a limit on total numbers taken by the entire fishing industry each year, limited numbers per fisherman, restrictions on the types of gear that can be used, and most important—the cessation of exportation. Along with these legal limitations, technology is lending a hand. Research has begun, and several mariculture centers are now experimenting with the queen conch,

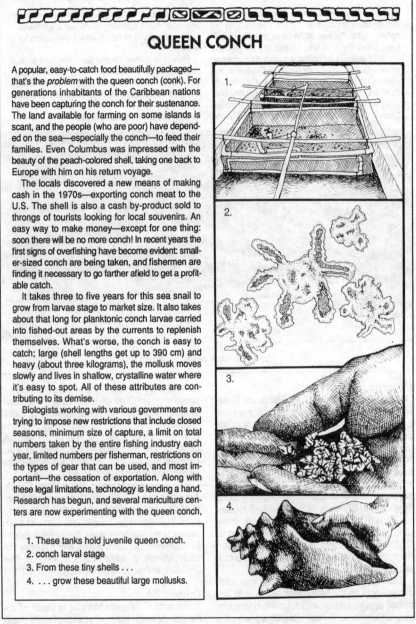

1. These tanks hold juvenile queen conch.
2. conch larval stage
3. From these tiny shells . . .
4. . . . grow these beautiful large mollusks.

DIANA LASICH HARPER

raising animals in a protected environment until they're large enough for market or grown to juvenile size to be released into the wild.

A new research center at Puerto Morelos is in operation and recently released its first group of juvenile conchs to supplement wild stock. This is not always successful. Sometimes one group of larvae will survive, and the next 10 will not—for no clear-cut reason. In the wild, not only does the conch have humans to contend with, it also has underwater predators: lobsters, crabs, sharks, turtles, and the ray.

The conch is not an endangered species yet—but it must be protected for the people who depend on it for life.

beach. The **Caribbean Reef Club at Villa Marina** is three floors of white-stucco construction. Twenty-one spacious rooms and suites (one-bedroom or studio) have fans and a/c, cool tile floors, cozy living area and terraces, even kitchen facilities with microwave ovens. Guests will find satellite TV, a pool, a friendly bar, and a beachfront restaurant where you get not only great fresh seafood, but the best downhome Texas ribs since Dallas Mom's. All diving equipment is available on the premises, along with free use of Windsurfers, Sunfish sailboats, tennis courts (rackets and balls), and more! This is a great getaway spot just a few minutes' walk from "a European-style beach." Ask about the cheapest way to get to Puerto Morelos from Cancún airport. Rooms for two (without kitchens) are US$70 low season, US$100 high season; studios for two with kitchens are US$90 low season and US$125 high season; one-bedroom suites (four people with kitchen) are US$90 low season, $100 high season; and villas (four people with kitchen) are US$130 low season, US$175 high season. For more information call (987) 4-2932 or (800) 3-CANCUN, in the U.S. (404) 257-2424; in the U.S. fax (404) 257-0808.

Bed And Breakfast
Amar Suites is a rambling house on the beach with four nice rooms in the main house with private bathrooms and fan; rate is US$40 d. On the landward side of the house are five small cabanas that sleep two to four people. Each has a loft bedroom, simple cooking facilities, toilet and shower, fan, TV, and small sitting area. These are very spartan accommodations close to the sea; rates are US$30. For more information write to Apto. Postal 136A, Cancún, Quintana Roo 77500, Mexico, tel. (98) 81-0026.

Yoga Retreat
Villa Shanti guests are treated to something special—yoga classes and shiatsu therapy! Owners Jack and Jean Loew have created a secluded, comfortable retreat in their eight-apartment villa just a block from the beach. Each apartment has a bedroom, modern bathroom, kitchen, a/c, and fan; outside there's a barbecue area, swiming pool, and large palapa strung with hammocks. Jean Loew offers yoga classes twice a week and week-long yoga retreats in the high season. The Villa is also used by other groups for health-oriented yoga, rebirthing, channeling, and healing retreats. The apartments rent for US$575 d plus tax for a week 15 Dec.-30 April; US$350 d plus tax 1 May-14 December. For information on reservations and upcoming retreats, contact the Loews 1 May-30 Nov. at P.O. Box 464, Glen, New Hampshire 03838-0464, tel. (603) 383-6501; 1 Dec.-30 April at PO Box 789, Cancún, Quintana Roo 77500, Mexico, tel. (987) 1-0040, fax (987) 1-0041.

Rental Properties
Puerto Morelos is popular for stays of a week or more, and there are several rental houses and apartments available. Most are located on the north side of town; drive the street that parallels the beach and you'll see signs for rental properties. Along this street, Bill and Connie Bucher have two properties for rent. **Cabañas Puerto Morelos** includes three one-bedroom units with sitting areas and kitchens, renting for US$450 a week for two persons. **Villa Amigos** is a two-bedroom, two-bath house (the master bathroom has a bathtub, rare in these parts) with a full kitchen and outside patio. It rents for US$750 a week for four persons. For information and reservations in the U.S., call (612) 441-7630 (phone and fax); in Puerto Morelos tel. and fax (987) 1-0004.

Villas Clarita is a two-story, Spanish-style building five blocks from town with four one-bedroom apartments with kitchens and a balcony or patio. Separate one and two bedroom cabanas are set around a swimming pool. For rates and information call (508) 535-4869 in the U.S. or (987) 1-0042 in Puerto Morelos.

FOOD, SHOPPING, AND SERVICES

Restaurants
Several good small budget cafes serving typical Mexican food and good seafood circle the main plaza. The **Posada Amor Restaurant** can be depended on for outstanding *mole poblano* and other regional dishes at moderate prices. **Los Pelicanos** serves good hamburgers. And the waterfront **Restaurant las Palmeras** can be counted on to serve excellent fresh seafood in a pleasant atmosphere; *pulpo Mexicano* (octopus) is delicious, as is conch in garlic sauce. **Palapa Pizzeria** is a popular hangout by the plaza. **Muelle 8,** on the beach south of the plaza at the Hacienda Morelos hotel, is the fanciest in-town restaurant, with a large brick dining room facing the sea, complete with fountains and folk art. The seafood is excellent, as are the Mexican dishes, and the staff is most accommodating. For all-out feasting, the best restaurant in town is at the **Caribbean Reef Club**, where steaks, ribs, and burgers are imported from the U.S.

Shopping
Puerto Morelos has a great new supermarket called **Autoservicio Marino.** Look for a red-brick front and a big sign with Popeye and Olive Oyl next to the Posada Amor. They carry *almost* everything in a shopping-cart atmosphere. Stop at **Arte Maya** to see some unique artwork,

and watch them create it. The finished product is cut-out metal painted in bright enamels—bracelets, wall hangings, etc., in a great variety of sizes and designs. Started some 17 years ago by Armando Fernández in his home, his shop now has a staff of craftspeople. You'll see his work in upscale shopping centers in Cancún. (The prices are better here!)

Services
Puerto Morelos has one of the best gas station rest areas along this route. Though gas availability has become more reliable and the stations are placed reasonably close to each other (also at Tulúm, Playa del Carmen, and Puerto Felipe Carrillo), be advised to top off your tank whenever you find a gas station. Stations still run out of gas when the demand is high, so get it wherever and whenever possible. If you run out near the coast and can find a dive shop, they're usually willing to help out with a couple of gallons of outboard motor gasoline. Though laced with oil, it might get you to a gas station without doing irreversible damage to your car. Also, many rural towns have a supply of gas in five-gallon drums even though you don't see a sign or a gas pump. Ask at the local store.

At the Puerto Morelos station you'll also find two markets, a public Ladatel phone, restrooms, and a restaurant. Other long-distance telephone service is found just south of the military camp, open daily 8 a.m.-1 p.m. and 4-7:30 p.m., and at the public phone near the plaza and pier. The **bank** is open to cash traveler's checks Mon.-Fri. 9:30 a.m.-1 p.m.

Look around; the little town offers most services. You'll find a liquor store, pharmacy, and even car repair, almost all within walking distance of downtown. Ask at the pharmacy about the laundromat; last we checked it was a few km away, near UNAM.

TRANSPORT

Getting There
Buses from north and south stop at Puerto Morelos frequently. From Cancún it's about a 40-minute drive, from Chetumal about five hours. Hitching is reasonably easy from the larger towns (Chetumal, Cancún, Puerto Felipe Carrillo, Playa del Car-

men); try Hwy. 307 where the service roads enter the towns.

Vehicle Ferry
The vehicle ferry to Cozumel departs Puerto Morelos daily beginning at 6 a.m. Check the schedule the night before, in case it changes. Be at the dock two or three hours early to get in the passenger-car line. It also expedites things to have correct change and the car's license number. The ticket office is open 5 a.m.-6 p.m. The trip takes two hours and can be a rough crossing, so put on your elastic cuffs if you tend to get seasick (see "Health" in the "Introduction"). For those with sea legs (and stomachs), light snacks are sold on the passenger deck.

PUNTA BETE

Punta Bete, a four-km stretch of beach, is a complete tropical fantasy—swaying palms hover along the edge of pure white sand, with gentle blue crystal waves running across the shore. Getting in and out of the water here can be hazardous to your feet, with rocks and coral scattered on the sea floor. Shoes or sandals help. The rocky bottom makes a perfect snorkeling area 10-20 meters offshore. As recently as 1965, no tourists visited this part of the coast. At that time Quintana Roo was only a federal territory. There wasn't even a road to this fine white-powdered beach. Family groups, mostly descendants of the Chan Santa Cruz Indians, tended their small, self-sufficient *cocales* (miniature coconut plantations). Together, a family harvested enough coconuts each year to earn spending money from the resulting copra. The custom continues today (although a coconut blight begun in Miami in 1980 has spread south to the Quintana Roo coast, in some areas decimating the coconut palms). Palm groves are looking healthier as a new disease-resistant variety of palms is being planted.

Note!
Before shedding your shoes to stroll along the southern part of Punta Bete beach, look it over. Sharp little bits of coral hide in the sand—in fact, be careful along the entire beach front. When swimming, beware of the sharp limestone in the shallow places; if you have diving booties, use them.

ACCOMMODATIONS AND FOOD

Along the four-km stretch are several resorts in a variety of price ranges. Each of them (depending on your travel style) is ideal. Rumor has it that Kai Luum is scheduled to move a few km south of Lafitte sometime in 1994—but believe it when you see it! From the look of the plans, the unique resort will be better than ever, but with the same great ambience everyone has learned to love over the past 20 years.

Kai Luum Camptel
For the traveler who wants to avoid the glitz of the high rise but doesn't want the work of setting up a campsite, Kai Luum is the lazy person's campout. In the tradition of the British safari, it's camping with a touch of class. Though there's no electricity, Kai Luum offers modern tents on the beach with large comfortable beds, communal hot and cold showers, clean toilets close by, and daily maid service. Each tent is shaded by a shaggy palapa roof and strung with two hammocks facing the sea for lazy afternoons.

The restaurant is one of the great attractions at Kai Luum—the food is outstanding. Prepared by Maya cooks, the menu is overseen by owner Arnold Bilgore, who happens to have a gourmet touch and plans something new and unusual (often continental) every day. The dining room is a large palapa structure on the sand, where a sumptuous buffet breakfast always includes tropical fruits, fresh juice, sweet rolls, hot coffee, tea, chocolate, and a different hot dish each day. Dinner is served under the sparkling light of hundreds of candles. Arnold jokes that next to the church, Kai Luum is the biggest buyer of candles in Mexico. The bar is at one end of the dining room: each person makes and keeps track of his or her own drinks with a numbered pegboard. The whole feeling of the resort is much like the honor system at the bar—relaxed, intimate, friendly. If you have a problem, see Mino, Arnold's son who grew up on the beach and is now the manager of the operation. The

Kai Luum divemasters, Cassie and Richard

restaurant attracts travelers from other area resorts as well. There are no telephones, so if you aren't staying at Kai Luum and would like to eat at the restaurant, you must drop by and make arrangements in advance.

Everyone enjoys browsing in Kai Luum's boutique, called the "xop" (pronounced "shop"), where the discerning shopper can purchase unique treasures from throughout Latin America, including handwoven fabrics and colorful clothing from Guatemala. You have a choice of water sports at the dive shop. They've got a personable, highly skilled and trained staff, including a registered PADI dive instructor, Richard. Boats and state-of-the-art equipment are available for rent. Other activities include snorkeling trips, beach picnics, and fishing trips as well as scuba instruction, PADI certification, check-out dives, and a short "resort course," which entitles you to dive for the length of your holiday.

Ask at the dive shop about **Vagabonder** daytrip suggestions to various sights close by, including appropriate travel tips and maps. If you've always wanted to see Belize, ask about extended Vagabonder trips that include both the Punta Bete coast and Belize.

Rate at Kai Luum is US$40 pp, double occupancy (surcharge for holiday periods), and includes breakfast, dinner, and 10% government tax. Three persons maximum in each tent, no children under 16. An airport transfer service is now availabe at extra cost; you must reserve it 30 days in advance of your arrival. No credit cards or personal checks; traveler's checks are okay. For accommodation reservations write to Turquoise Reef Group, Box 2664, Evergreen, CO 80439; in Colorado tel. (303) 674-9615, from anywhere else tel. (800) 538-6802, fax (303) 674-8735.

Deluxe

Cabañas Capitán Lafitte, around for many years, is as well-known for its charming managers, Jorge Fuentes and family, as it is for its fine service, wonderful beach location, good food, swimming pool, and pleasant game room. All provide a serene backdrop for welcome camaraderie among the people who return year after year from distant parts of the globe. Note a few new cabanas on Laffite's southern perimeter. The restaurant has been expanded, and you can now have coffee delivered to your room in early morning. Everything else will be the same in this popular resort. The stucco oceanfront cabanas have double- and king-sized beds, hot water, ceiling fans, and private bath. Along with daily maid service, each room is provided with a handmade reed broom to help keep the sand out.

A full dive shop on the premises has a good selection of rental equipment, including sailboards. The management provides transport by skiff to nearby Lafitte Reef, an exciting snorkeling destination. Here, a lazy day of floating on the clear sea will bring you face-to-face with blue chromis, angelfish, rock beauties, and often the ugly grouper—a great place to use your underwater camera. Fishing is another satisfying sport—you'll always come away with a tasty treat that the restaurant chef will be happy to prepare for your dinner. Hands off the large, handsome turtles you may see, and don't expect to find turtle soup or conch ceviche on the menu. The management makes it clear that they support the preservation of these endangered species. And, speaking of species, every after-

dive boat, Isla Mujeres

1. Snorkeling off the tip of the Camino Real Hotel, Cancun; **2.** Isla Mujeres harbor; **3.** From Isla Mujeres you can see the tall towers of Cancun; **4.** Isla Mujeres; **5.** Isla Mujeres, north end

Shangri La cabanas, Punta Bete

noon between 5 and 6 p.m. a flock of small, colorful parrots flies over the swimming pool, unmistakable with their awkward wing movements and peculiar squawk.

Each week the hotel staff and guests get together and have a *fiesta*—not the impersonal version that you see at the big clubs, but the type of good time that a family has at a Mexican birthday party, where everyone takes part. The waiters demonstrate rhythmic dance skills, balancing filled glasses on their heads, then teach anyone else who wants to give it a try—it's not easy! A zesty smorgasbord of *típico* food is served. It's a downhome party, Maya style.

During high season it's best to have reservations. Rates include breakfast and dinner, US$70-75 pp double occupancy, ages 7-12 US$30 per night, ages 13 and over full rate; there's an extra US$10 charge per room for a/c, and a US$20 per room surcharge on holidays. Ask about Casa Olé and El Cofre, large two-story beachfront duplexes for families. No credit cards or personal checks; cash and traveler's checks only. Car rentals are now available at Lafitte. For more information and reservations write to: Turquoise Reef Group, Box 2664, Evergreen, CO 80439; tel. (800) 538-6802, in Colorado tel. (303) 674-9615, fax (303) 674-8735.

Shangri-La Caribe Resort

Just 62 km south of Cancún is a village resort of exotic stucco and palapa bungalows; *almost* luxurious! A perfect place to kick back; comfortable beds, private bath, fans, tile floors, hot water, balconies or patios with hammocks, swimming pool, and pool bar; car rentals available on-site. Beachfront bungalows are just steps from the sea. A large, circular palapa serves as a gathering place during the cocktail hour; a great place to meet fellow travelers. Next door is a gift shop, and near the pool guests can have grilled hamburgers and drinks all day. A dive shop on the property, **Cyan Ha,** is open seven days a week, offers rentals and lessons, and has a PADI-certified divemaster. Beginners, ask about trips to the shallow reefs of Chenzubul, a perfect place to enjoy a secure but exciting introduction to the myriad colors of the Caribbean underwater world and its exotic inhabitants. All swimmers will enjoy exploring the cenote Jabali, close to Shangri-La. Visitors enjoy the proximity to Playa del Carmen and its shops, cafes, and departure docks to Isla Cozumel. Shangri-La rates include breakfast, dinner, taxes, and tips; US$150-180 d depending on proximity to the beach, children under six free in same room with parents, ages 7-12 US$30. No credit cards. For reservations, contact Turquoise Reef Group, tel. (800) 538-6802, in Colorado tel. (303) 674-9615, fax (303) 674-8735.

Las Palapas Cabanas

Just south of Shangri-La Caribe, lovely **Las Palapas Cabañas Resort** is nearly idyllic, with 50 units in two-story palapa-roofed buildings. Hammocks hang on the front porches and small desks face the windows looking out to landscaped walkways or the beach. The rooms are comfortable, clean, and upscale. The large pool is great for swimming laps, while the white-sand beach seems to go on forever—in fact, you can easily walk to Playa del Carmen along the shore. Gourmet meals are served in the large palapa-covered dining room, and often feature German dishes for the frequent German tour groups that stay here. The management and staff go out of their way to make your stay comfortable; many guests stay put for a week or more! Rates include breakfast and dinner, tax, and tip, and begin at US$120-180, depending on time of year and location. Call 2-2977 or (800) 527-0022, in California, fax (619) 438-8201.

Budget

You have a choice of campgrounds, trailer park, simple palapas, or cabanas, all on a lovely beach just steps away from the sea. Cabana rooms are clean, have private bathrooms with hot and cold water—some with double beds, others with kings. No electricity, but a very romantic ambience with candles and lanterns. Good food at the restaurant/bar on the grounds. This is one of the really pretty beaches along Punta Bete. Cabanas rent for about US$40, palapas for about US$4 per person. Write well in advance for reservations to Ricardo or Rosa

Novelo, Apdo Postal #176, Playa del Carmen, Quintana Roo, 77710 Mexico, no phone.

If you plan on camping don't forget your bug repellent and mosquito netting; to camp on the beach is about US$4. Follow Hwy. 307 until you see the Punta Bete sign where you turn on a white single track road; go 2.2 km and you will arrive at the beautiful Caribbean and Xcalacoco.

TRANSPORT

Getting There

If you arrive by plane in Cancún, taxis are available; arrange your price before you get in the cab. Figure approximately US$45-55 (up to four passengers). From Playa del Carmen (a ferry arrival point from Cozumel), taxi fare is less. Car rentals are available at Cancún airport, which is a straight shot north on Hwy. 307; look for the large sign on the left side of the road that says Capitán Lafitte; here you'll find both Lafitte and Kai Luum. From Capitán Lafitte it is approximately eight km farther to Shangri-La and Las Palapas.

A couple of good mini-buses run from Cancún to the resorts along the Tulúm Corridor, leaving from the ADO bus station. Ask for directions when making reservations.

BOB RACE

PLAYA DEL CARMEN

For years there was but one reason to go to the then-small village of Playa del Carmen—the Cozumel Island ferry dock. And though thousands of people pass through here each year on their way to or from Cozumel (a popular island 19.2 km off the Quintana Roo coast), many now come just to enjoy the laid-back pleasures of Playa del Carmen. Playa offers the latest water transportation to Cozumel—conventional boat and fast water jets, and sporadic airport service. Playa's proximity to attractions such as Tulúm, Xelha, Cancún, and coastal Hwy. 307 makes it a convenient stopover.

The town is taking on a personality of its own and adds to its modest beginnings each year. In fact, Playa del Carmen is currently the fastest-growing area in Quintana Roo, with population increasing nearly 20% annually. The town is sprawling farther north as more and more visitors return for a permanent stay. Nature did its part by endowing the small town with a broad, beautiful beach, one of the finest in Quintana Roo. The waterfront has been greatly improved with a walkers-only *malecón*, lined with neat bricks and a low wall, perfect to sit on in the evening for either people-watching or star-gazing. The walkway reaches from the entrance to the dock in front of the Hotel Las Molcas all the way past the plaza to Av. Principal (also called Av. Juárez), the street that runs along the north side of the plaza through the central business district to the highway. Av. 5, the main street running parallel one block up from the beach, has also been turned into a pedestrian walkway, and new cafes and shops are opening (and some closing) at an amazing rate.

One of the busy, though entertaining, times to visit is during the **Navy Day** fishing tournament on 1 June. Trophies are given out, there are lots of beach activities, and you don't have to be a fisherman to have a good time. For those who love morning walks along the water, the long beach is perfect to stroll for hours, sometimes without seeing another soul—almost a thing of the past.

Traffic Note

The road going to the dock is now closed to all vehicle traffic; watch the signs and follow the traffic to the parking lot north of the new brick *malecón* and the plaza. All the streets in town were dug up in 1993 for a new sewer and water system, completed in 1994. Av. 5, the first street parallel to the waterfront, has been turned into a

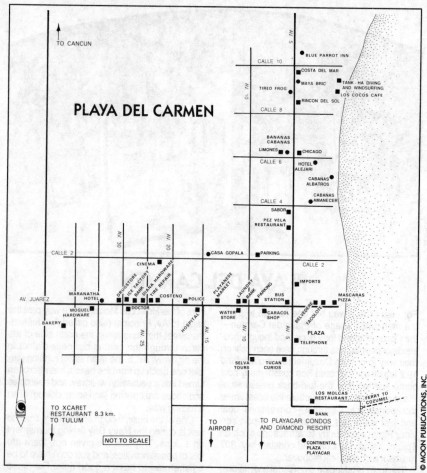

PLAYA DEL CARMEN

TO CANCUN

AV 5

BLUE PARROT INN

CALLE 10

COSTA DEL MAR

MAYA BRIC

AV 10

TIRED FROG

TANK-HA DIVING AND WINDSURFING

LOS COCOS CAFE

RINCON DEL SOL

CALLE 8

BANANAS CABANAS

LIMONES

CHICAGO

CALLE 6

HOTEL ALEJARI

CABANAS ALBATROS

CABANAS AMANECER

CALLE 4

SABOR

PEZ VELA RESTAURANT

AV 30

AV 20

CALLE 2

CASA GOPALA

PARKING

CINEMA

CALLE 2

IMPORTS

DRUGSTORE

ICE FACTORY

BANK

OAXA HARDWARE

FIRE REPAIR

PLAYANESE MARKET

LAUNDRY

BANK

PARKING

MASCARAS PIZZA

AV. JUAREZ

MARANATHA HOTEL

COSTENO

POLICE

BUS STATION

BELVEDERE

TACOLOTE

MOGUEL HARDWARE

DOCTOR

WATER STORE

CARACOL SHOP

PLAZA

TELEPHONE

BAKERY

AV 25

HOSPITAL

AV 15

AV 10

SELVA TOURS

TUCAN CURIOS

AV 5

TO XCARET
RESTAURANT 8.3 km.
TO TULUM

TO AIRPORT

LOS MOLCAS RESTAURANT

FERRY TO COZUMEL

BANK

TO PLAYACAR CONDOS AND DIAMOND RESORT

CONTINENTAL PLAZA PLAYACAR

NOT TO SCALE

© MOON PUBLICATIONS, INC.

pedestrian walkway, and traffic is prohibited to Calle 10. Most other streets are now one-way in a confusing system designated by one-way signs. Parking is severely limited. There are public (for a fee) lots on Av. Juárez (Principal) by the bus station and on Calle 2 between Avenidas 5 and 10. Street signs are beginning to appear, but most locals give directions by using landmarks. In short, park wherever you can and rely on your feet to get you around town. If you're headed to the hotels north of the ferry pier, turn off from the main highway before you reach the Faisán y Venado restaurant—this helps you

avoid some of the traffic congestion. Another highway turnoff south of the main Playa del Carmen exit takes you to the Playacar development and resorts.

SIGHTS

By far the nicest thing to do in Playa del Carmen is to enjoy the people and the sparkling Caribbean. Take a walk through the village. Only five or six years ago you would have been escorted by children, dogs, little black pigs, and incredibly ugly turkeys. Nowadays it's mostly tourists crowding the streets—everywhere. Once you're off the main paved entry road into town, you'll find the streets still bumpy, but they improve a little each year. Playa's lack of sophistication and topsy-turvy growth is appealing. Alas, the milkman no longer delivers milk from large cans strapped to his donkey's back; pleasant mini-supermarkets, with modern refrigeration, are scattered about town. The number of small curio shops, cafes, and cantinas increases daily, and there's a movie theater. Yes, Playa del Carmen has become a "tourist resort," and the increase in prices reflects this metamorphosis. However, it's still a bargain compared to Cancún or Cozumel.

The cool early hours are best for walking along the beach. Warm afternoons are perfect for swimming and snorkeling, snoozing on the sand, or watching the magnificent man-o-war frigate bird make silent circles above you, hoping to rob another bird of its catch. Ferries from Cozumel come and go all day; in addition, luxury cruise ships anchor close by in the bay, and tenders bring to shore tourists who then crowd into all the gift shops. The ships' passengers have a choice of lounging on the beach, or of being escorted immediately to large modern buses and whisked off to the more famous sights of Xelha and Tulúm. You can count on Playa del Carmen's beach being filled with jet-setters when ships are in port; the rest of the time it plays host to a mixed conglomeration of young and old, archaeology buffs, students of the Maya culture, backpackers, adventure seekers, sun-lovers who prefer the ambience of Playa del Carmen over Cancún, and independent travelers from many parts of Europe.

ACCOMMODATIONS

Though it's still uncluttered by *real* high rises, large, upscale new hotels are spreading along the beach south of the dock: Continental Plaza Playacar and the Diamond All-inclusive Resort (see below); several more are on the drawing board. Condominiums are spreading out in the same area. If you haven't been to Playa del Carmen for a while, you'll also be surprised by the many *simple* hotels popping up everywhere. The same funky campground still holds its space near the beachfront. There's an efficient laundry service in the heart of town as well as a real estate office.

Continental Plaza Playacar

Some of the newest and most luxurious lodgings in Playa del Carmen are located on the beach on the south side of the boat dock, which is referred to as the Playacar development. Ultimately it will house about five hotels, many shops, cafes, condominiums, and a golf course. The first hotel of the group is the Continental Plaza Playacar, the big pink structure a few steps south of the dock. The hotel faces the

Continental Plaza Playacar

sea and is pretty high for Playa, with five floors, 188 rooms, and 16 suites. All have a/c, satellite color TV, private terraces overlooking the Caribbean, tile bathrooms and floors, and comfy beds. The hotel offers a beautiful pool and lounging area, several dining rooms, bars, and a spacious, attractive lobby (as you walk in look to the right and note the striking painting of the birds and animals of Quintana Roo). Stroll the grounds of the hotel and take a look at the many maintained Maya ruins that were carefully saved while the hotel was being built. If you want luxury, this is the place to stop. Reservations are a must, since the hotel is often filled with large tour groups, which has left some rooms a bit the worse for the wear. Rates begin at US$130 d; for reservations call from Canada or the U.S., (800) 882-6684. Ask about good package deals. In Mexico, call (987) 3-0100, or fax 3-0105.

Diamond All-inclusive Resort

This resort is part of the Diamond chain, with another location just across the sea at Isla Cozumel. Rooms are upscale, with lovely decor, a/c, modern bathrooms, and comfortable beds. Rates include almost everything: meals, snacks, drinks, taxes, tips, and most activities, including diving, snorkeling, tennis, volleyball, scuba lessons, bikes, and aerobics. It's one big party with theme nights, live entertainment, and excellent food. Rates begin at US$150 pp, double occupancy, depending on the season. Ask about the child's discount and special senior rates; suites are available for an extra charge. For more information, call (800) 858-2258 or (987) 3-0341, fax 3-0348.

Condominiums

Located close to the Continental Plaza Playacar, these are individually owned and rented when not in use by their owners. They are beautifully designed in a convenient location either right on the beach or a short walk away. A five-minute stroll from town, each has one to three bedrooms, a fully equipped kitchen, washer and dryer, and living room; some have balconies, and there's a swimming pool. These are great for families or small groups, or for those who prefer to do their own cooking. Prices begin at US$80 for a one-bedroom condo, depending on time of year. For more information write to Box 396, Cancún, Quintana Roo 77500, Mexico.

Almost Luxury Class

Los Molcas Hotel is one of the older hotels in town, in the upper price range of moderate hotels. The look is colonial Mexico, with white stucco and arched doorways, and dark woods. It's very close to the foot of the ferry dock and the beach. Rooms are spacious and nicely decorated with a/c and private bath; plus there's a swimming pool, dining room, terrace dining, and three bars. A lovely new palapa restaurant fronts the hotel at the edge of the sea near the dock. The hotel offers tours (Chichén Itzá, Tulúm, and Cobá), diving equipment, and laundry service. Rates start at about US$85 d, considerably less during the summer/fall season. For reservations write to Las Molcas Hotel, Calle 1 Sur, Apto. 77; tel. (987) 3-0134, fax 3-0105.

Suites Quintas, tel. 3-0341, fax 3-0348, is a pleasant hotel; if it were on the beach it would be rated "luxury," but it's located on the main street into town about halfway to the highway. The suites are about US$75 d. The complex is clean, modern, and nicely furnished, with a/c and nice decor—except for one thing; no toilet seats! I have a feeling this will change if many Americans stay here.

Moderate Hotels

Albatros Royale, three blocks north of the plaza at Calle 6 and Av. 5, is one of the nicest hotels along the beach north of the plaza, where the competition increases annually. Owner Sam Beard, an American who's put down roots in Playa, knows how to offer his guests comfort without exorbitant rates. The Royale's two-story buildings face each other across a landscaped pathway leading to the beach. Hammocks are strung by the front door or on the balcony of each room, and guests tend to congregate on patios for card games and conversation. Tile floors and fans keep the 31 rooms cool and comfortable. Call (800) 538-6802 (Turquoise Reef Resorts) or (987) 3-0001 for reservations.

Beard's brother owns the **Cabañas Albatros,** just south of the Royale, a longtime favorite of budget travelers. Another beachfront hotel with a dedicated following, the **Maya Bric,** on Av. 5 between calles 8 and 10, tel. and fax 3-0011, is enclosed by a gate (locked at night), giving guests an added sense of privacy and security. The 24 rooms are in two-story buildings surrounding the pool and gardens; some rooms have ocean views and some have a/c. The on-site dive shop Tank Ha arranges trips to the reefs. Rates start at US$30 s or d in the low season, US$40 in high season.

The **Hotel Costa del Mar** complex, on Calle 10 at the beach, tel. 3-0058, sits on the beach-front next to the Blue Parrot. It features spacious tiled bathrooms, hot water, and a small pool, plus an indoor-and-beach restaurant (prime rib advertised for US$18). Choice of rooms or bungalows; rates start at US$22-44 (less in low season). The **Maranatha Hotel**, tel. 3-0143, is on the north side of the main street, Av. Juárez (Principal), coming into town. It offers a swimming pool, dining room, bar, tile floors, fans, private bathrooms, double beds, and some rooms with kitchenettes. They take MasterCard and Visa.

A Robinson Crusoe-type hotel is the **Blue Parrot Inn** on the beach north of town. It's a whimsical stucco tower structure with palapa roof, tile floors, clean bathrooms, lots of hot water, and one or two double beds in each room. Some rooms have a/c, and more are getting it as the hotel is renovated. Future plans include more luxurious units, giving guests the options of complete comfort or of roughing it. For a midnight swim, you need only step out your front door. Each room has a view of the water, and just a short walk north on the white sand takes you to where you can watch fishermen throw their nets or return in their open launches with the morning catch. Videos are shown in the second-story bar/lounge, complete with bean-bag chairs for comfortable viewing. The Blue Parrot offers 30 rooms, from simple thatch-roof rooms on the sand to spacious two-story stucco cabanas with fantastic views. A beachside club/cafe offers shady palapas, tables in the sand, a volleyball court (at 4:30 p.m. most afternoons you can find a hot game), and an occasional fiesta or barbecue. The restaurant serves breakfast, lunch, and dinner. Try the pecan shrimp—good stuff! Nice place for cold drinks and light snacks in the middle of the day.

Room rates begin at US$55-75 during the high season and US$30-75 during the low season. For more information and reservations write to 655 W. Wisconsin Ave., Orange City, FL 32763, tel. (904) 775-6660, toll-free (800) 634-3547. Or write the inn directly at Box 64, Playa del Carmen, Quintana Roo 77710, Mexico; tel. 3-0083, fax 3-0046.

Cabañas Nuevo Amanecer, at Calle 4 Norte #3, Box 59, is a neat palapa hideaway with private baths, double beds and hammock, mosquito netting, and the use of a hot tub and billiard table on the property for US$30-38 s or d, year-round. Clean and pleasant.

Hotel Alejari on Calle 6 is another little hidden gem in Playa del Carmen. These duplexes and studios are very clean and simple, with a/c or fan, tile floors, hot water, and private bathrooms; some have kitchenettes. It's set in a garden environment; take a look. Beach access is available through the back gate. Rates are US$35-60 d, depending on the room and the season. For more information write to Box 166, or call 3-0374, fax 3-0005. There's a public phone in the reception office.

Apartments
Quinta Mija, behind the Blue Parrot Inn, offers three one-bedroom fully furnished apartments with living room, kitchen, bathroom, and small pool for US$75 per night for two persons, US$10 for each additional person. **Casa Jacques** apartments have two bedrooms and two baths and will accommodate one to four people for US$125; extra bedroom/bath US$50. For a family, **Bal Na Kah** is a fully furnished two-bedroom, two-bath house about two blocks from the beach; one to four people US$200 per night, and US$25 for each additional person (up to six total). For information and reservations contact Turquoise Reef Resorts, Box 2664, Evergreen, CO 80439; tel. (800) 538-6802, in Colorado tel. (303) 674-9615, fax (303) 674-8735.

Budget Hotels
Playa del Carmen has a CREA youth hostel. You can't miss the sign as you come into town. Good value—too bad it's not closer to the beach. Follow the signs from the main street into town about one km. Fairly new, clean, single-sex dorms cost US$5 per night, and simple cabanas rent for US$17 per night. There's a dining room with reasonably priced food, a basketball court, and an auditorium. It's well worth the effort: figure a 15-minute walk to the bus station.

Casa de Gopala, at Calle 2 Norte two blocks from the beach, and near downtown activities, tel. and fax (987) 3-0054, has 10 large rooms and a pool that's been under construction for a while (should be finished when you have this

This relaxed family enjoys living out of their camper on the beach for several months each year.

book). Each room has two double beds, tiled bathroom, hot water, closet, ceiling fan, and large windows, which make for good air circulation. The property is three floors, white stucco, and surrounded by a white stucco wall enclosing a lovely garden—lots of flowers and trees on a quiet street. If you have a problem just look for Steve and Gabriela Telander. Rate is US$30 d in high season.

The **Tucan** is a good buy for a simple hotel. Follow the signs; it's about two blocks beyond the Blue Parrot turnoff. The rooms have overhead fans, hot water, group refrigerator, mosquito netting, peace and quiet (usually), and friendly staff. It's one of the best structures on Av. 5 Norte; rate is about US$20 s or d, much less in low season.

Another whimsically named cabana resort is the **Tired Frog**, located five blocks north of the bus station; follow the signs (past Bananas Cabanas). This is a relaxed palapa-roofed setting with double beds, private bathrooms with hot water, and a laid-back patio. The transplanted American owners are great. Rates are around US$18-30 s or d, and prices drop drastically in the summer. For reservations write Apto. Postal 149.

Posada Rosa Mirador on Calle 12 off Av. 5, about a 10-minute walk from the ferry pier, is a great choice for budget travelers, with nine simple rooms with bath and good screens, near the Blue Parrot. Rates are US$15 s, US$20 d; friendly manager.

True recluses on the lowest of budgets who don't mind truly roughing it might want to check out **Hotel Agua Azul Profundo,** the hotel farthest north in Playa. For US$12 s or d you get a private room with thin mattresses, and private bath, but no toilet seat. The owners are talking about renovations. The hotel is on the beach about a 20-minute walk from the ferry. There's no phone, so you'll probably have to take a cab to check it out.

Close to the bus station on Juárez (Principal), between avenidas 5 and 10, the **Hotel del Carmen** is good for travelers just passing through town; it's basic but clean, and within walking distance of everything you need. No phone.

Camping
The only *official* campground in Playa del Carmen, **Las Ruinas Camping,** has changed its image a little. It *might* be a place to bring your children now; check it out first. Prices for tent space are US$2.50-4, trailer spaces US$4-6 (not large enough for anything but smallish trailers), and there are a few small, simple rooms for US$6-8; community showers and toilets. No matter what your choice, everyone is charged a refundable US$8.50 deposit. For reservations call (987) 2-1474 in Cozumel.

FOOD

New restaurants are springing up even faster than hotels in Playa del Carmen. Around the central plaza several small cafes serve a variety of good inexpensive Mexican, Italian, and seafood. **Los Molcas Hotel** serves good food, but it's hard to spend less than US$20 here for a meal. If you want to stick with typical Yucatecan food at moderate prices or are looking for good fresh seafood, try **Pez Vela,** open 8 a.m.-11 p.m., located on Av. 5 near Calle 2. Buffet dinners served at the **Continental Plaza Playacar** are different each night (we had a great Asian dinner that was worth the money, US$17). The hotel has an outdoor palapa dining area overlooking the pool and dock serving good sandwiches in a nice breezy atmosphere; a little more costly than downtown, but good.

Belvedere is located on Av. Principal (Juárez) across from the main square and serves great pastas and other Italian specialties taken from recipes straight from Roma. Eat either in the upstairs dining room or in the small, simple patio (which can be very noisy). Pasqual, the cook, is from Italy. If you like Italian seafood and pasta mixtures, try the fettucine Alfredo with shrimp (for something a little different ask for half pesto and half tomato sauce, really good!). Prices are moderate. Check out the Italian wines. Right next door try **Tacolote,** beloved for its many varieties of tacos and heaping platters of fajitas, and modeled after a cafe of the same name in Cancún (but not the same owners). It gets very noisy, especially when all the restaurants along that road decide to turn up their music to outdo each other.

Pollo Caribe, on Av. 10, prepares tasty barbecued chicken, in a simple but pleasant palapa restaurant; inexpensive!

At Av. Juárez #170, you can buy ripe sweet fruit at **Frutería La Merced,** open 7 a.m-2 p.m and 5-11 p.m. Go next door to **Rikis Cafetería** and have a taco or *torta,* and then go next door to **Panadería Burgos,** one of the *best* bakeries in Playa del Carmen. Fruit markets line the north end of Av. 5 as well, and bakeries are multiplying all over. The best of them all is **Sabor,** where you can sit outside and watch the crowds while devouring carrot cake, nut pie, chocolate brownies, or, for the more health conscious, fruit salads and soy burgers. If you need a dose of ice cream, check out **Holanda,** Av. Juárez (Principal) next to the telephone, for a great variety of flavors, plus tasty hamburgers. For a good, budget *torta* (sandwich) or a full Mexican meal, head for **El Tortón,** on Av. Juárez (Principal), across the street from the bank.

Another good Italian restaurant, **Máscaras,** is on the first block off the beach across from the plaza. Their pizza and pasta are excellent. Try the spinach cannelloni—marvelous! Be sure to take a close look at the brick, wood-burning oven where most everything is baked. Máscaras makes good fresh limeade, served in bulbous glasses with lots of purified ice. You can also get *big* margaritas and cold Yucatecan León Negra *cervezas.* A sure hit for a big night out is **Limones** on Av. 5

at Calle 6. The owners, who also have the Albatros Royale and Cabañas Albatros, have created a pretty, peaceful setting with lots of plants and candlelight. They serve great pastas (you can choose small or large portions, and even have your fettucine topped with shrimp) and fish, topped off with flaming crepes and coffee drinks. **Chicago** is just across from Limones and is a great hangout for anyone interested in seeing CNN news breaks or sporting events, or who happens to like great spareribs, hamburgers, a variety of Mexican platters, and imported steaks. Happy hour is 4-7 p.m., two-for-one drinks and complimentary *bocaditas* (literally translated, it means small bites or, as Americans put it, appetizers).

Nuestra Señorita Carmen on Av. 5 was one of the most popular budget spots when we lasted visited, with grilled fish and Yucatecan meals priced under $5. **Karen's Pizza** has a huge courtyard dining area on Av. 5 that gets absolutely packed at dinner. New in 1993, **Papas Tapas** is a small gourmet delight across from the Albatros Royale. Just north of the Hwy. 307/Playa del Carmen intersection, note the **Faisán y Venado** restaurant, one of the few places around for Yucatecan cuisine, clean, with good food and friendly service. Check out **Deep Blue,** located just north of the Blue Parrot. Right on the beach, it's run bu Annette, an American from Georgia, serving good soup, fish, and chicken.

Groceries

Super Turquesa, on Av. Juárez (Principal), is an American-style supermarket where you can buy a little of everything, including groceries. Lots of small shops around town sell fruit and vegetables. A good variety of meat is available at the butcher shop, and several open-air *rosticerías* around town have chickens turning brown and crispy on a barbecue. Some offer a few tables; others expect you to carry it away.

Several shops sell purified ice, and you'll find a drugstore and many bakeries. Liquor is sold across from Los Molcas Hotel and in several other locations in town.

SHOPPING

Shops selling carved masks, T-shirts, Guatemalan textiles, and resortwear are located in the colonial-style **Rincón del Sol** center on Av. 5 at

Calle 8. **La Catrina** is filled with shells, figurines, and *papeles picados,* the tissue-paper cutouts Mexicans string up for fiestas. **Luna Maya** has one-of-a-kind jewelry from Guadalajara. **El Vuelo de los Niños Pájaros** carries handcrafted papers made from bark, and a good selection of Latin American CDs and casette tapes. But best of all is **Xop** (pronounced "shop" in Maya), carrying terrific arts and crafts items from all over Mexico. Included are colorful woven cloth, antique *huipiles,* impressive wooden masks, and whimsical folk art like you see in Oaxaca. Owner Joan Bilgore has befriended some of the most talented jewelers from throughout Mexico, and her selection of handcrafted jewelry is exceptional: dangling earrings and necklaces made of deer horn, boa constrictor ribs, crocodile and wild boar teeth, and the most impressive display of amber you'll see on the coast.

The plaza is truly a pretty spot, with a tree-filled courtyard that will likely house a restaurant by the time you arrive. **Turquoise Reef Realty** has an office upstairs where you can check on everything from hotel reservations to home purchases. **La Playense,** on Av. Juárez (Principal), offers gifts of all kinds—check out the woodcarvings. Get your photo supplies at **Omega** on Av. Juárez (Principal) across from the bank. If you need to send a fax, go to **Computel** on Av. Juárez (Principal) at Av. 5, for copies and long-distance phone service as well.

SERVICES

Banco del Atlántico, three blocks from the ferry dock, at avenidas Juárez (Principal) and 10; and **Bancomer** at avenidas Juárez (Principal) and 25, cash traveler's checks (fee charged) Mon.-Fri. 10 a.m.-12:30 p.m. *Larga-distancia* phone service is located across from the bank next to the ice cream shop, Holanda, open daily 8 a.m.-1 p.m. and 3-8 p.m, as well as at many hotels and at the Ladatel phone on the plaza. Two **hardware stores** will help you out with twine, a gas can, or a knife blade. There's a **doctor** *and* a **dentist** in town (ask at your hotel). Playa del Carmen has postal service at a small building between the police station and the mayor's office on Av. Juárez.

No matter how well you plan, it seems most folks run out of clothes and need a laundry. At **La Palma** on Av. 5 you can either do it yourself, or have it done for you. To do it yourself you must wait until after 6 p.m. Laundry service is provided all day, and usually takes three to four hours. Another laundry at the Hotel del Carmen on Av. Juárez is open Mon.-Sat. 8 a.m.-8 p.m., Sun. 7 a.m.-noon.

Buying A Piece Of Playa Del Carmen

More and more people are falling in love with this low-key resort town. Playa has a beautiful white beach and blue sea, close enough to the bright lights of Cancún to enjoy its international airport and the growth it has brought into the area, but far enough away to know the benefits of a more moderate lifestyle. It's easier than ever to invest in Mexico, whether you're looking for a lot to develop a business, or a small cabana to retire in. For all your questions, check with Mino Tomacelli Alexander or Jorge Fuentes at **Turquoise Reef Realty.** Both men have been in Playa del Carmen since before it grew up. The office is located on Av. 5 at Calle 10 in the Rincón del Sol plaza. In Playa call (987) 3-1001, fax 3-0050; in the States call (800) 538-6802; or write Box 2664, Evergreen, CO 80439.

TRANSPORTATION

By Taxi

Taxis at Cancún International Airport will bring you to Playa del Carmen. If there are several passengers, you can make a good deal—bargain with the driver before you start your journey. Expect the trip from Cancún to Playa to cost about US$40-50. Nonmetered taxis meet the incoming ferry at Playa del Carmen and are available for long or short hauls; again, make your deal in advance. A trip from Carmen to Tulúm (with three passengers) can be about US$25-30 RT, depending on supply and demand and the time of year. If you're interested in a good diving spot, tell the cabbie. He may share with you his favorite cove that you'd never find on your own, and in fact he might join you for a swim.

If taking the ferry to Isla Cozumel for the day, park your car at the public parking lot by the bus station; fees are posted. (The newest rumor is that the car ferry will soon be moving from its home port at Puerto Morelos to a new dock just south of Playa del Carmen.)

By Ferry
Because of the ferry traffic, this is a good place to try hitchhiking north or south. Two types of passenger ferries travel between Playa del Carmen and Cozumel. The faster MV *Mexico* is air-conditioned and makes the trip in about 30 minutes; fare is about US$6 pp OW. The slower open-air boats take about 45 minutes; fare is about US$3. Between the two, there is a ferry departing just about every hour 6:30 a.m.-8 p.m. You can request a specific ferry, but invariably you will get a ticket on the next boat out. (This is a way to keep all the ferries in business, including the older ones.)

The ferry crossing is usually a breeze. However, the calm sea does flex its muscles once in a while, making it difficult to berth the boat snugly against the dock. When this happens, hefty crewmen literally swing each passenger over the side into the capable hands of two other strong-armed receivers—quickly followed by the individual's luggage. This adds a bit of adventure to the voyage. But if it isn't your forte, delay your departure till the next day—the sea seldom stays angry for long. Young boys with imaginative homemade pushcarts or three-wheel *triciclos* meet incoming ferries at the dock to carry luggage for a small fee.

By Bus
Three bus lines provide this small town with the best bus transportation on the coast. Buses going north to Cancún's bright life travel the 65 km in 50 minutes. **Autotransportes del Caribe** is trying out a new service, bringing passengers from Cancún in a small bus that makes six daily trips to Playa del Carmen with reserved seats. Ask about this one; buy your ticket a half hour in advance. ADO bus company offers one first-class reserved Playa bus to Cancún that leaves at 12:30 p.m. **Playa Express** mini-buses run throughout the day to Cancún nonstop, with minimal room for luggage. Check at the bus station for the current bus schedule from Playa del Carmen to Cancún.

From Mérida via Cancún (a five-hour trip), three first-class buses and seven second-class buses arrive daily. **ADO** has three luxury express buses with a/c, bathrooms, and refreshments, to Mérida daily. Buses arrive frequently from Chetumal and other points south as well. Playa del Carmen is an ideal base for many attractions along the Quintana Roo coast.If sightseeing on the bus south to Chetumal, just a word to the driver and he'll drop you off at the turnoff to Tulúm, Xelha Lagoon National Park entry road, or one of the small beaches south along the coast. Ask what time his schedule brings him back, since you must be on the highway waiting to return to Carmen.

XCARET TO PUERTO AVENTURAS

XCARET

If you haven't been to Xcaret for a few years you are in for a big shock! Almost everything about the place has been changed. It has been expanded, examined, and exhumed (no bodies yet, just more Maya structures). I have received a lot of mail about Xcaret, both pro and con. The most vehement letters claim the lovely little inlet has been destroyed by development, and that it shouldn't even be mentioned in my book. On the other hand, there are those who rave about it. The travelers who enjoy a more commercial attraction say "It is a lot like Disney World—everything you want in an idyllic setting, and absolutely jammed with people.

The river float was like being packed in a sardine can. Still, it was worth it; we would recommend it to anyone who has been to and liked Disney World." Succinct and to the point. Those who think it has been destroyed should really just stay away.

The Future
Some compare this park to Disneyland. Miguel Quintana, the developer, says it's much more. Eventually he hopes this will be a testing station under the auspices of scientists of CIQRO, where the turtles, manatees, and bats will be studied. A nocturnal village is also in the planning stages, where the light will be reversed and scientists (and tourists) can watch bat activity in the daytime. There will also be a study

center for students involved with geology, archaeology, and marine biology.

Xcaret Ecoarchaeological Park

Xcaret is about an hour's drive south of Cancún and one km off the highway toward the sea. The small port, called Pole during the Post-Classic period (A.D. 1200-1500), was an important trading center as well as a ceremonial center and jumping-off point for the Maya making pilgrimages to Isla Cozumel to worship the goddess Ixchel. It is said the Maya were frightened of the sea and would always spend several days in religious ceremonies praying for a safe crossing before boarding their wooden canoes.

Archaeology

Archaeologists, under the direction of the Instituto Nacional de Antropología de Historia, continue excavating this area, which is rich with hidden history. They are convinced they'll eventually find traces of a *sacbe* beginning at Cobá and ending at Xcaret. Several ruins have been restored, and there are the remains of an old chapel from the colonial era. The ruins you see in the developed area of the park are, according to archaeologist Tony Andrews, only some of dozens more structures scattered throughout the bush in the area; so far 60 buildings and remnants of hundreds of platforms have been found. The work will probably take another six or seven years to complete. This was an eminent location for the ancient Maya's navigational lookouts.

Underground River

Tree-lined paths meander throughout this large park, and what used to be an underground river has been made into a "floating adventure." Openings were made in the earthen ceiling of this underground cavern to let in light and circulate air. People are given life jackets and, starting at the entrance of what was once considered a sacred cenote, they spend 20 or 30 minutes floating along the underground river admiring coralline deposits and unusual little fish until they reach the other end, 1,000 feet south. Many visitors say the "float" alone is worth the admission, US$20.

Dolphins

The admission gives entry to the museum, picnic areas, good snorkeling spots, and a lovely sandy beach adjacent to placid aqua water. Wandering about, you'll find many trees covered with orchids, a large variety of tropical plants, and ferns from all over southern Mexico. A stroll along the breakwater gives you a view of the regal dolphins, with whom you can swim for an extra fee.

Activities

A dive shop offers equipment rental and lessons. There's a restaurant, a gift shop, clean restrooms, and some fine rental horses for those who would like to ride through the jungle surrounding the beach. Large, informative plaques placed about the park explain just about everything. The gift shop sells postcards, cold drinks,

It's fun to spend an entire day at Xcaret.

Float for 20-30 minutes on the surface of an underground river at Xcaret.

and souvenirs. Under construction is a model Maya village, where a living museum is planned.

Snorkeling
At the small, landmark *caleta* (small bay) at Xcaret, beginning snorkelers, especially children, will find a perfect learning spot. The water is shallow and there's little current, though to enter the water you must either climb over the rocks or jump off the small wooden platform. But it's not necessary to go much beyond the limestone shoreline to discover colorful denizens of the sea; resident schools of parrot fish and blue and French angelfish almost always put in an appearance. One problem is fighting off the tourists who have discovered the lovely small *caleta*. Come early in the day and you might have the small bay almost to yourself.

Getting There
The park is open 9 a.m.-5 p.m. Oct.-March, and 9 a.m.-6 p.m. April-September. If driving, look for the only high hill on Hwy. 307 and you will find the entrance to the park, at Km 72, six km beyond the Playa del Carmen turnoff. There are bus tours to Xcaret from Cancún (see "Cancún"). For more information, call Cancún, tel. (98) 83-0654 or 83-0743.

PAMUL

Another small beach that deserves exploring is Pamul. Beachcomb here for shells, coral, and interesting jetsam. This is not one of the wide, white-sand beaches so common along the coast; in some places Pamul is steep and rocky, in others narrow and flat. The water is crystal clear, allowing you to examine the fascinating life within the shallow tidepools cradled by rocks and limestone. Snorkeling is better the closer you get to the reef 120 meters offshore. On the way the sea bottom drops off to about eight meters, and its colorful underwater life can absorb you for hours.

The Quintana Roo coast offers miles and miles of pristine dive spots, and the waters near Pamul are especially ideal for scuba diving. The south end of Pamul's beach is sandy, but the shallow water along here harbors the prickly sea urchin—look before you step, or wear shoes while you're wading. Fishermen and divers along this coast are a jovial group always ready for a potluck beach party when fishing is good—especially during lobster season (15 July-15 March).

Turtles
If it's a bright moonlit night in July or August, you may be treated to the unique sight of large turtles lumbering ashore to lay eggs in the sand. If you're here 50 days later it's even more exciting to watch the tiny (about eight cm in diameter) hatchlings make their way down the beach to begin life in the sea. Much has been written about protecting the turtles of the Caribbean from humans, but nature in the form of egg-eating animals provides its own threat to this endangered species. On the beach of Pamul, more than half the eggs are scratched up from the sand and eaten by small animals that live in the adjacent jungle.

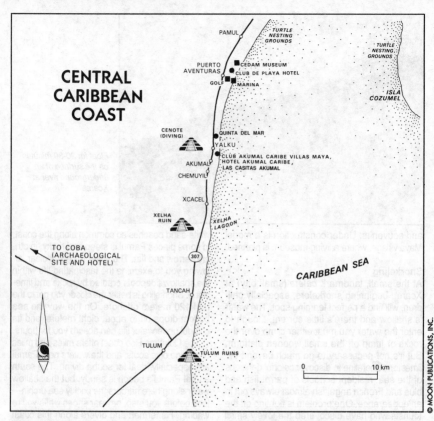

CENTRAL CARIBBEAN COAST

PAMUL
TURTLE NESTING GROUNDS
TURTLE NESTING GROUNDS
PUERTO AVENTURAS
CEDAM MUSEUM
CLUB DE PLAYA HOTEL
GOLF
MARINA
ISLA COZUMEL
CENOTE (DIVING)
QUINTA DEL MAR
YALKU
CLUB AKUMAL CARIBE VILLAS MAYA, HOTEL AKUMAL CARIBE, LAS CASITAS AKUMAL
AKUMAL
CHEMUYIL
XCACEL
XELHA RUIN
XELHA LAGOON
TO COBA (ARCHAEOLOGICAL SITE AND HOTEL)
CARIBBEAN SEA
TANCAH
TULUM
TULUM RUINS
0   10 km

© MOON PUBLICATIONS, INC.

Practicalities

You have a choice of two lodgings in the area, **Cabañas Pamul,** a small hotel on the beach, or the campground at the south end of the hotel. The hotel is considered spartan, but it's usually clean and does have electricity between sunset and 10 p.m., hot and cold water, and shared bathrooms. It's a little pricey for what you get—about US$34 d for a cabana. The campground has room for 15 RVs. All spots have electricity and water; eight are large pads with sewer hookups (US$8), and seven will accommodate small trailers (US$5). You can use the showers and toilets in the hotel. Camping fee is about US$3.50 pp, which includes bathroom privileges. The small cafe next to the hotel is run by the family that owns the hotel and usually offers fresh-caught seafood plus other typical

dishes at reasonable prices, open 8 a.m.-8 p.m. A small cenote nearby provides water for Pamul; boil it before drinking. Otherwise, bottled water can be bought from the hotel manager. Mailing address is Apto. Postal 1681, Cancún, Quintana Roo 77500, Mexico.

PUERTO AVENTURAS

The corridor south of Cancún buzzes with the growth of new resorts, both large and small. One of the most ambitious developments is an enormous marina (advertised as the largest in the Caribbean), located just a few minutes south of Akumal. Some of these waterways are left from the days of the Maya, simply improved and opened to the sea. In other cases they are

GIANT TURTLES

At one time the giant turtle was plentiful and an important addition to the Indian diet. The turtle was captured by turning it over (no easy matter at 90-100 kilos) when it came on shore to lay its eggs. Any eggs already deposited in a sandy nest on the beach were gathered, and then the entire family took part in processing this nourishing game. First, the parchmentlike bag of unlaid eggs was removed from the body, then the undeveloped eggs (looking like small, hard-boiled egg yolks). After that, the meat of the turtle was cut into strips to be dried in the sun. The orange-colored fat was put in calabash containers and saved for soups and stews, adding rich nutrients and considered an important medicine. The Indians wasted nothing.

Today CIQRO, a protective organization, along with the government, keep a sharp lookout along the coast for egg poachers during the laying season. Turtle-egg farms are being developed to ensure the survival of this ancient mariner. Sadly, the poacher of the '90s travels the entire coast, and each beach is hit night after night. The turtle can lay as many as 200 eggs in an individual nest or "clutch." One beach may be the instinctual home for hundreds of turtles (at one time thousands) that return to the site of their own hatching each year.

Turtles can live to be a hundred years old, which means they can lay a lot of eggs in their lifetime. But as the poachers steal the eggs on a wholesale basis, the species could eventually be wiped out entirely. If caught, poachers are fined, and can be jailed—though the damage has been done. When released they usually return to their lucrative habits. In most Mexican

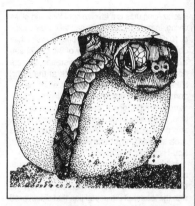

marketplaces a ready market for these eggs exists among superstitious men who believe the eggs are an aphrodisiac.

The survival of the giant sea turtle lies within the education of the people—locals and visitors alike. Shoppers will see many sea turtle products offered for sale: turtle oil, tortoise-shell combs, bracelets, rings, buttons, carvings, and veneer inlaid on furniture and jewelry boxes, plus small stuffed, polished hatchling paperweights. **Note:** It is against the law to bring these products into the U.S. and other countries. If discovered they will be confiscated. Sadly, many travelers are not even aware of the law, and often the products get by the inspectors. If tourists refused to purchase these products, the market would dry up—a big step toward preserving these gentle lumbering beasts.

---

totally man-made and can moor almost 300 boats up to 120 feet in length with a draft of 10 feet. The marina is located at **Puerto Aventuras,** a massive mega-development with residential housing, time shares, hotels and all sorts of resort amenities. It's well worth a look around, but keep in mind that real estate and timeshare salespersons aggressively pursue anyone who enters the front gate, starting at the information booth by the highway. If you want to explore

without enduring sales pitches, just say you're going to the museum or restaurants.

Boating
At the marina, yachtspersons will find everything you need: gas and diesel, a spare-parts store, minor maintenance shop, purified water and ice, bait, 24-hour radio station and medical service, restrooms and showers, car rentals, travel agencies, shopping center, hotels, yacht

MIKE MADDEN'S DIVE CENTER

Puerto Aventuras is a favorite spot for world-class diving. In just minutes divers can take their choice of 10 different dive sites. Everyone knows (if they don't, they should) the beauty of the Caribbean along this coast. The water is crystalline, and curious marine creatures look back at the diver. Mike Madden's Dive Center offers all of the opportunities for water sports, including scuba instruction, night dives, daily reef dives, cavern trips, snorkeling, jungle adventures, cenote diving, and deep-sea fishing. Visit almost secret dive spots such as Canyonland Reef, Chanyuym Reef, Xpu-Ha, Xaac, and Xaac Chico.

Madden has been involved in some unusual adventures which have placed his name in the *Guinness Book of World Records*. In 1987 he was the leader of the expedition that discovered and surveyed what is the longest underwater cave system in the world, Nohoch Cave. A permanent guide line has been placed along 43,600 feet of passageways to ensure that divers will be able to find their way out of the cave, as well as to provide a baseline for surveying the cave. Some of these vast chambers are as much as 1,000 feet wide. In the Maya language, Nohoch means "huge" or "giant." But what makes Nohoch even more unique is its majestic beauty, sparkling columns, rimstone pools, stalagmites, stalactites, cave pearls of pristine white limestone, and blue passageways channeling off in all directions. One room has six feet of airspace overhead, allowing even beginning snorkelers to view the breathtaking visions of this marine wonder.

Cavern diving is very dangerous and different from open-sea diving. It requires highly specialized training. The danger of getting lost within this subterranean and subaquatic world is very real; hundreds of untrained divers have lost their lives in underwater caves over the years. Open-sea divers should always remain within sight of a source of natural light.

Mike Madden's CEDAM Dive Center also offers a trip called an Indiana Jones Adventure, which goes to Nohoch Nah Chich ("Giant House of the Birds"), named for the bats that lived in the cave. Part of the giant cave system can safely be reached from a cenote on the property of a local farm family. A jeep takes you within three km of the cenote; from there you hike in. Trekkers have a chance to visit with the family; they still get their water from the cenote. There's about a 15-minute guided tour of the cenote for snorkelers (after which snorkelers can go back in and spend as much time as they wish). This is a fascinating trip for snorkelers since you have the opportunity to see some of the sparkling wonders of the underwater caves, usually accessible only to scuba divers. The group departs at 9:30 a.m. and returns at 2:30 p.m.; cost is about US$38; no children under 10. You can find a short article and photo on one of the caves in the September 1990 issue of *National Geographic* magazine.

Madden has another CEDAM dive center at the Diamond resort in Playacar and at Club Aventuras Akumal. For more information, write Box 117, Playa del Carmen, Quintana Roo 77710; tel. (987) 3-5129.

---

club, and restaurants. Boat access into the marina is through a carefully planned channel, well marked for navigation and ready with an escort service through the reef 24 hours a day.

Golf, Tennis, And Diving
Puerto Aventuras has an 18-hole golf course, destined to be the scene of world-class golf tournaments. Eventually, condos will be spaced around the golf course with an upscale hotel in the center of the fairways. Golf carts are already available for rent.

Several tennis courts are available, and work is in progress on more. One of the big attractions is expected to be the University of the Sea, a five-star PADI institution for diving instruction where divers will not only learn about diving but can take continuing courses on the preservation of the Belize Reef.

CEDAM Museum
Artifacts brought from the sunken ship *Mantanceros* can be seen at the CEDAM Museum located along the waterfront. There's a small col-

lection of belt buckles, cannons, coins, guns, tableware, and various clay relics from Maya ruins along the Quintana Roo coast. The *Mantanceros* ("Our Lady of the Miracles"), a Spanish merchant ship that left Cadiz, Spain, in 1741, headed for the New World loaded with trade goods; it foundered and sank on the reef two km north of Akumal. No one knows for certain why the *Mantanceros* sank, since there were no survivors. However, the CEDAM organization spent several years salvaging it, beginning in 1958. Research suggests the ship probably engaged in a violent battle with a British vessel and then drifted onto the treacherous reef now known as Punta Mantanceros. For more detailed information on the finds of the *Mantanceros*, read *The Treasure of the Great Reef* by Arthur C. Clarke.

Hotels

Club de Playa, tel. (987) 3-5100 or (800) 446-2747, Puerto Aventuras's first hotel, celebrated its grand opening with the Miss Universe entrants as the first visitors in June 1989. The Club de Playa is a small, intimate hotel with 30 rooms. It faces the marina on one side and a shimmering white beach and the translucent water of the Caribbean on the other. The hotel has a swimming pool, pool bar, lobby bar, dining room with a Swiss-trained chef, health spa called Body And Sol, and juice bar. All types of watersports equipment are available. The rooms are spacious, with marina and ocean views, tile floors, king-size beds, game room, and first-class room amenities.

Oasis Hotel, tel. 3-5051 or (800) 446-2747, has 72 rooms equipped with kitchen facilities, including a microwave. The rooms are well furnished and spacious, with marble floors, luxurious bathrooms, a/c, and all first-class amenities. At the hotel, guests have access to pool, pool bar, convenience store, restaurants, and lobby bar; a shuttle makes regular trips to the golf course, tennis courts, and marina. Rate is US$160 d during high season, less in the low season. Ask your travel agent about special packages at this hotel.

Food

A series of cafes serves a remarkable selection of food. **Mama Mia's** makes good Italian, including pizza. **Carlos 'N' Charlie's** is just what you have come to expect, crazy but with good Mexican food; the Mexican platter is delicious, about US$7. Of course you can get good coffee at **Café Olé** along with fresh-made yogurt and great breakfast items; and **Gringa's** serves the best (imported) beef steaks and brochettes around. On the side of the building facing the kiosk, stop at **Potatoes R Us** for ice cream!— and of course good baked taters with a large selection of toppings.

Papaya Republic is another desert island-type restaurant, far from the madding crowd on a beach a short distance from the central part of Puerto Aventuras. After you turn off Hwy. 307 onto the main entry road, take the right arm through the golf course and start looking for the signs. You want to wend your way to the beach. It's well worth it, whether you lunch on the chilled fresh gazpacho, shrimp in wine sauce, *dorado almendrado,* or quesadillas and cold beer. This is gourmet heaven on a little bit of sand with a palapa roof and the gorgeous sea at its front door. Of course there's no phone or address; this is a desert island! Stop by here even if you're on your way farther south. It's only five minutes off the highway.

Fitness Center

There is a state-of-the-art fitness center near the dive shop by the Oasis Hotel, open to anyone for a fee. You'll find good equipment and great staff here.

Shopping

For such a small village, you'll find several pretty good shops. Check out the **Marina Boutique,** the **Pharmacy And Tobacco Shop, Sports And Sorts Boutique,** and **Van's Handicrafts.** The gift shop at the Oasis Hotel has an excellent selection of Mexican folk art, better than any south of Playa del Carmen.

Services

You'll find most everything you need here. There's a laundromat; also several markets that carry sundries as well as groceries, ice, and drinks. And what would the kids do without video games for a week? You need never find out; take them to **Videorama.** You can rent a car for a day at your hotel; also ask about bike rentals. There's a small medical service for emergency first aid, a beauty parlor, a travel agency, and a taxi stand.

KATHY ESCOVEDO SANDERS

AKUMAL AND VICINITY

About 100 km south of Cancún, Akumal Bay is a crescent of intensely white sand along the blue Caribbean. This quiet beach is home to an ever-growing resort that survives nicely without telephones, TVs (well, one or two have shown up—with satellite dishes), or bustling activity. The traveler desiring the tropical essence of Yucatán *and* a dash of the good life will appreciate Akumal. Compared to Cancún, it could not be described as luxury class but is more luxurious than many of the small resorts along the coast. It offers a good range of hotel rooms, dining, and activities.

The barrier reef that runs parallel to the Quintana Roo coast protects Akumal Bay from the open sea and makes for great swimming and snorkeling. Proximity to the reef and easy access to the unspoiled treasures of the Caribbean make it a gathering place for divers from all over the world. For the archaeology buff, Akumal is 10 km north of Tulúm, one of the few walled Maya sites located on the edge of the sea. From Tulúm, it's five km north to Xelha, a natural saltwater aquarium where divers (even amateurs) snorkel or scuba among surrealistic limestone formations that give the eerie impression of an ancient sunken city. In Mayan, Akumal means "Place of the Turtle," and from prehistoric times the giant green turtle has come ashore in summer to lay its eggs in the warm sands of the Caribbean.

History

Akumal was a small part of a sprawling working coconut plantation until 1925, when a *New York Times*-sponsored expedition along the then-unknown Quintana Roo coast stumbled on this tranquil bay; it was another 33 years before the rest of the outside world intruded on its pristine beauty. In 1958, Pablo Bush formed the nucleus of CEDAM, a renowned diver's club, and introduced Akumal to world-class divers. Soon the word was out. The first visitors (divers) began making their way to the unknown wilderness. At that time, the only access to Akumal was by boat from Cozumel. A road was built in the 1960s. Since then, Akumal has continued to grow in fame and size each year, but it was Bush who introduced this part of Mexico as the "diving capital of the world." Though many people come here, it still remains a beautiful, tranquil place to study the sea and stars.

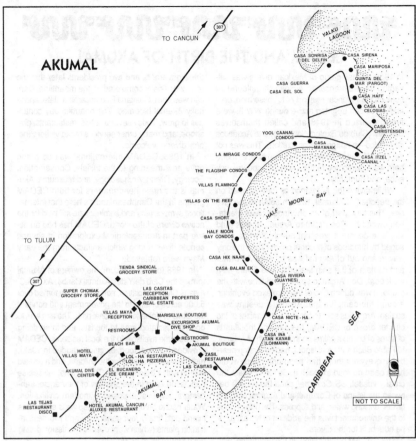

AKUMAL

TO CANCUN

307

YALKU LAGOON

CASA SONRISA DEL DELFIN

CASA SIRENA

CASA MARIPOSA

QUINTA DEL MAR (PARGOT)

CASA GUERRA

CASA DEL SOL

CASA HAFF

CASA LAS CELOSIAS

CASA CHRISTENSEN

YOOL CAANAL CONDOS

CASA MAYANAK

CASA ITZEL CAANAL

LA MIRAGE CONDOS

THE FLAGSHIP CONDOS

VILLAS FLAMINGO

HALF MOON BAY

VILLAS ON THE REEF

CASA SHORT

HALF MOON BAY CONDOS

CASA HIX NAAH

CASA BALAM EK

CASA RIVIERA (GUAYNES)

CASA ENSUEÑO

CARIBBEAN SEA

CASA NICTE-HA

TO TULUM

307

TIENDA SINDICAL GROCERY STORE

SUPER CHOMAK GROCERY STORE

LAS CASITAS RECEPTION
CARIBBEAN PROPERTIES REAL ESTATE

VILLAS MAYA RECEPTION

MARISELVA BOUTIQUE

EXCURSIONS AKUMAL DIVE SHOP

RESTROOMS

RESTROOMS

AKUMAL BOUTIQUE

BEACH BAR

CASA INA (TAN KANAB (LOHMANN))

HOTEL VILLAS MAYA

LOL-HA RESTAURANT

LOL-HA PIZZERIA

ZASIL RESTAURANT

CONDOS

AKUMAL DIVE CENTER

EL BUCANERO ICE CREAM

LAS CASITAS

AKUMAL BAY

LAS TEJAS RESTAURANT DISCO

HOTEL AKUMAL CANCUN / ALUXES RESTAURANT

NOT TO SCALE

© MOON PUBLICATIONS, INC.

Flora

Akumal is surrounded by jungle. In March, bright red bromeliads bloom high in the trees, reaching for a sun that's rapidly hidden by fast-growing vines and leaves. These "guest" plants that find homes in established trees are epiphytes rather than parasites: they don't drain the sap of the host tree, but instead sustain themselves with rain, dew, and humidity; their leaves absorb moisture and organic requirements from airborne dust, insect matter, and visiting birds. The bromeliad family encompasses a wide variety of plants, including pineapple and Spanish moss. The genus seen close to Akumal is the tillandsia, and the flame-red flower that blooms on the

tops of so many of the trees here is only one variety of this remarkable epiphyte. While searching for bromeliads, you undoubtedly will see another epiphyte, the orchid.

The Beach

The porous sand of Quintana Roo never gets hot enough to burn. The white shores are ripe for beachcombing, with lots to investigate: conch shells, lacy red seaweed, an occasional coconut that has sprouted after soaking in the sea for months, and the ever-present crabs, all sizes and colors, popping in and out of their sandy holes. Take a walk at dawn. The sun bursts from the sea, spotlighting leaping

CEDAM AND THE BIRTH OF AKUMAL

In 1958 a small group of Mexican divers was salvaging the *Mantanceros,* a Spanish galleon that sunk off the Palencar reef in 1741. These men, originally Mexican frogmen active during WW II, were first organized in 1948 and called themselves CEDAM (Club de Exploración y Deporte Acuáticos de Mexico—a nonprofit organization). This was not the typical fun-and-games type of dive club; its members were dedicated to the service of country, science, and humanity.

While diving the *Mantanceros* they camped on the beaches of Akumal, two km south of the dive site. This bay, part of an enormous copra plantation owned by Don Argimiro Arguelles, was (and still is) a deserted crescent beach of white sand edged by hundreds of coconut palms. Then the only way in and out of Akumal was by ship. As owner and captain of the ship leased by the divers as a work boat, Don Argimiro spent much time with the group. It was during one of those relaxed evenings around the campfire that Akumal's destiny was sealed. Arguelles sold Pablo Bush (organizer of the charter group of CEDAM) the bay and thousands of acres of coconut palms north and south of Akumal.

Pablo Bush's tropical lagoon had no airstrip nearby, and even if there had been one, there would have been no road to reach it. So for 12 years the creaky vessel, SS *Cozumel,* plied the waters between the island of Cozumel and Akumal carrying divers, drinking water, and supplies. The only change to the environment was the addition of typical palapa huts built for the divers.

The CEDAM organization, in the meantime, was gaining fame and introducing Cozumel and the Yucatán to the diving world. Visiting snorkelers and scuba divers were entranced, and the word soon spread about the exotic Mexican Caribbean coast.

In 1960 the idea of promoting tourism began to circulate; but Quintana Roo was still a territory. Pablo Bush and other movers and shakers began talking road and airport. The government began listening. But governments move slowly, and it was

three governors and two presidents later that the road was finally completed. In the meantime, Cancún was born, Quintana Roo became a state, and finally Akumal bloomed. The beautiful bay continues to grow. Today several hotels, restaurants, dive shops, and many other services make visitors (not only divers) welcome.

In 1966, CEDAM International was born and gave new meaning to the initials: Conservation, Ecology, Diving, Archaeology, and Museums. Akumal is the main headquarters for both CEDAM groups in the Caribbean and it's here that international symposiums and seminars are still held for the active divers of the world. CEDAM has had an active part in archaeological exploration in several cenote dives during which artifacts from the early Maya were retrieved.

In 1968 (before Cancún), the owners of Akumal formed the Club de Yates Akumal Caribe, A.C. (A.C. means Civil Association, nonprofit). They turned over 5,000 acres of land to the government and donated the Cove of Xelha for a national park. The aim was to open the isolated area to tourists, and in so doing jobs became available to the local residents. CEDAM provided housing, food, electricity (added in 1982), running water, a school for the children, and a first-aid station with a trained nurse. Till this time, the sparse population lived in the shadow of their ancient ancestors, few ever exposed to modern civilization. Water had to be brought from deep wells eight miles inland until finally four generators and two desalinization plants (which went out of commission during each storm) were brought in.

In 1977 a fire destroyed one of the original large palapa structures built on the beach; the closest fire protection then was in Cancún. The only communication even today is by shortwave radio. Although it's still rather primitive (who knows for how long), all who visit Akumal fall in love with its slow, rustic way of life and tropical beauty. Houses are springing up, and though many more visitors come today, the wide beaches are still never *too* crowded.

fish as they jump at winged breakfast-bugs hovering just above the surface of the water. When the sun rises higher, late sleepers stake out spots on the beach and create a colorful patchwork of beach towels on the sand. For-

tunately, the beach is so large that it never gets crowded—only coveted spots under shady palms become scarce. A palapa bar, open until 6 p.m., serves beer, cocolocos, piña coladas, and more. This is a friendly place to

Akumal beach

meet other travelers and swap adventure stories and great snacks.

WATER ACTIVITIES

Two dive shops on the beach rent equipment, including boats and motors, for scuba divers and snorkelers. Many divers come for the excitement of exploring the wreck *Mantanceros,* sunk in 1741. Although it was completely salvaged, a job that took CEDAM several years, the sea still yields an occasional coin or bead from this ancient Spanish merchant ship. A good collection of memorabilia from the *Mantanceros* is on display at the CEDAM Museum at Puerto Aventuras (just a few kilometers north), open daily 8 a.m.-5 p.m., with a small entry fee. A multitude of dive spots are hidden in the reefs about 130 meters offshore.

Dive Shops
Akumal's dive shops have excellent equipment for rent, and they offer a good selection for sale. Rental fees vary slightly between both shops. Akumal was born because of divers so it's natural that there should be some of the best around. **Akumal Dive Shop,** owned by Dick Blanchard and Gonzalo Arcila, has been taking divers from Akumal to pristine dive spots like La Tortuga and The Nets for more than 15 years; dive lessons are available. For information and reservations call (800) 777-8294, in Mexico tel. (987) 2-2453; or write to Apto. Postal #1,

Playa del Carmen, Quintana Roo 77710. The **Akumal Dive Center** offers a three-day dive certification course. If you just want to make one dive on the reef, instructors give a four-hour "resort course," providing equipment, transportation, and one escorted dive. If you decide to take a resort course from any dive shop, check to make sure that you'll be making the dive one-on-one with a divemaster. The Akumal Dive Center is fully PADI certified. Contact the Center for advance dive information: Akutrame Inc., P.O. Box 13326, El Paso, TX 79913; in Texas tel. (915) 584-3552, outside of Texas tel. (800) 351-1622, in Canada tel. (800) 343-1440. Rentals include kayaks and sailboards.

Snorkeling
Akumal Reef not only protects the bay from the open sea but also provides calm swimming areas ideal for snorkeling. A good spot within wading distance is the rocky area on the north end of the bay. Floating along the surface of the water and looking through your private window into the unique world below can be habit-forming along this coast. Take it slow and easy, and you won't miss anything. Search the rocks and crevices that you'll drift over, even the sandy bottom—what may look like a rocky bulge on the floor of the sea may eventually twitch an eye and turn out to be a stonefish hiding in the sand; hands off, it's deadly. You'll even see a new crop of sea urchins growing once again. Most of the urchins disappeared after the El Niño current passed through several years ago.

Quinta del Mar is a beautiful villa on Half Moon Bay.

Fishing

World-class fishing is farther out to sea, where piscatorial game, including marlin, sailfish, and bonito, grow to enormous size. The **Akumal Dive Center** and **Akumal Dive Shop** will arrange outings with all gear provided; make reservations in advance if possible.

Yalku Lagoon

Within walking distance of Akumal, this secluded tiny replica of Xelha Lagoon is worth a snorkel for the many fish you'll see in a quiet hideaway. Parrot fish gather here in numbers and make a multicolored glow just below the surface. A current of fresh water flows into this small lagoon, which is at most three meters deep; the visibility is about five meters. This is just a stony little pond—no rooms, no cafes, no toilets, no tourists, just fish and you. On the ocean side of the Yalku, lovely villas are springing up on private property. From Akumal it's about a half-mile stroll north on the road that runs past Half Moon Bay.

ACCOMMODATIONS

There are good accommodations at Akumal. During the off-season you'll have little difficulty finding a room. However, if you travel 1 Dec.-15 April, make reservations. No camping is permitted at Akumal, but just a few kilometers south, good beaches with camping facilities are available at Xcacel (sha-SELL) and Chemuyil (shem-

oo-YEEL). The hotels at Akumal are all on the beach, close to the sea—perfect for a tropical vacation. A few villas and condos are available for rent on Half Moon Bay, just a short distance north of Akumal Bay. (See below.)

Hotels

While Akumal cannot be considered a budget resort area, the most economical choice is **Club Akumal Caribe Villas Maya,** the original cottages built for the CEDAM diving club. The owners replaced the elderly thatch roofs with Western-style coverings years ago. These roomy cabanas on the beach are clean, with private bath, tile floors, and a/c; even the lighting has been improved for readers. There are plenty of water sports, but if you prefer land sports, check out their tennis and basketball courts. Bungalow rates start at about US$77 d, including tax. Villas Maya also offers three lovely condos on a separate beach around the point north of Akumal Bay. Each has two bedrooms, two bathrooms, fully equipped kitchen, and living room with two sofa beds. These rent for US$115 per night for up to four adults; two children could also be squeezed in. For something special, ask about the Cannon House Suite and Cannon House Studio.

One of the newest facilities on Akumal Bay is the beachfront hotel (still part of Villas Maya), offering 21 rooms on three floors, with lovely views of the Caribbean and the garden area, which includes a swimming pool and a pool bar. The rooms each have full bath, compact refrigerator, and small porch or balcony. Winter rate is

US$90 d, including tax. These rooms are just a few steps from the sea, Lol Ha restaurant, and all the other facilities of Akumal. Note: Many of these prices drop drastically during low season.

Villas Flamingo, part of Club Akumal, four smashing villas built on Half Moon Bay (the next bay north), is close enough to Akumal for guests to enjoy its restaurants and other facilities, as well as luxury living. Each villa has an enormous living room, an ocean view, tasteful furnishings, fully equipped kitchen, dining room, upstairs bedroom (or two), large terrace with barbecue grill, daily maid service, laundry facilities, and a/c; a swimming pool is shared by the four individual villas. Prices range from around US$145-300, depending on size of villa, number of people, and season. For reservations and information on all of Club Akumal's facilities, including dive packages with a room and some meals, contact Akutrame Inc., P.O. Box 13326, El Paso, TX 79913, in Texas tel. (915) 584-3552, outside Texas tel. (800) 351-1622, in Canada tel. (800) 343-1440.

Las Casitas Akumal, at the north end of the beach with the bay at your front door, has airy, furnished condominiums with two bedrooms, two baths, living room, kitchen, and patio; daily maid service included. Walking distance to restaurants, grocery store, snack stand, dive shop, sandy beach, and beach bar. Up to five persons, US$135 plus tax; for reservations and information write Box 527, Hackensack, NJ 07602.

Another fine hotel is located on the south end of Akumal Bay. In a two-story structure, **Hotel Akumal Cancún's** 110 rooms are simple but pleasant, with private bath and terrace and distinctive Mexican decor. Also available are 10 apartments and 10 suites. The Hotel Akumal Cancún has a/c throughout, plus a nice pool, tennis courts, disco, and two restaurants. Rates begin at US$75 d. For reservations, call (987) 2-2567 or 2-2453; in Mexico City call (5) 520-0053.

Located on Yalku Lagoon, **Quinta del Mar** is another striking villa that faces the sea and can accommodate over six people. The beautiful white stucco structure is set in a garden with cooling breezes, and is decorated with weavings, paintings, and pottery showing off the colorful touches of Mexico. Daily maid service is provided by Mercedes and her husband, Alejandro, caretakers who live in a small cottage on the property. If you wish, Mercedes and Alejan-

dro will prepare meals (extra fee); there's a notebook/menu available for your choice. The villa has three bedrooms, 3.5 baths, living room, dining room, fully equipped kitchen, red-tile floors, and lots of windows to bring in the luxuriant outdoors. Terraces on both floors offer stunning views of the Caribbean. Though having transportation is much more convenient, Quinta del Mar is within walking distance (one km) from the dining rooms and activities of Akumal Beach. It's also a short walk to Yalku Lagoon and a swim in your own private aquarium. Weekly rates: summer US$1400, winter US$1700, holidays US$2200. For more information contact Arlene Pargot, 850 Washington Ave., Martensville, NJ 08836, tel. (908) 469-6932. This area is a residential park with building lots for sale.

Condo Resort

This small, secluded resort, **Villas on the Reef** and **La Joya,** is right on the sandy beach of Half Moon Bay. Each condo has a view of the sea and includes one or two bedrooms, fully equipped kitchen, one or two bathrooms, living room, and dining room; all are fully screened, fan cooled, and nicely decorated with art and weavings from the Yucatán and Guatemala. Maid service is provided daily; local cook available to hire on request. Ask about the beach-level suite offering **handicap access.** These attractive and comfortable accommodations are a short distance from the restaurants, dive facilities, and shops on Akumal Bay (about one-km walk; a car is very convenient). Divers, check out good-value dive packages. Other seagoing day-trips are available. Condo rates are US$100 for one bedroom, one bath (two people maximum); US$132 for two bedrooms, two baths (five people maximum). Rates are lower in the off-season and slightly higher during holidays. For information and reservations contact Akumal Vacations, Box 575, Conroe, TX 77305, tel. (800) 448-7137.

FOOD

Next door to the dive shop on the beach, **Lol Ha** serves excellent food. At breakfast and dinner you can expect tasty food, especially wonderful fresh fish, and a friendly staff. Prices are not cheap (though much cheaper than in Cancún), but the food is worth it. When you sit down for

*the entrance to Hotel-
Club Akumal Caribe*

breakfast, a basket of homemade sweet rolls is brought to your table immediately. If you should happen to be here on Thanksgiving, the cook prepares a turkey dinner American-style (almost), and all gringos in the area come and party well into the night, using the Pilgrims as a good excuse. Adjacent to Lol Ha is a snack bar serving lunch noon-5:30 p.m., and **Pizzas Lol Ha** serves food 1-9 p.m. The beach bar is open for drinks 11 a.m.-11 p.m.; between 4 p.m. and 5 p.m., happy hour means half-price drinks.

The largest of several restaurants in Akumal is **Zasil,** open for breakfast, lunch, and dinner. On the north end of the beach next to Las Casitas, it's housed under an enormous traditional palapa roof with a garish, obtrusive sign that for a minute makes you forget you're in paradise. Several times a week, a busload of tourists is brought in from cruise ships that anchor off Cozumel, Cancún, and Playa del Carmen—don't eat here then! Another large palapa restaurant, **Aluxes** (with a 35-foot center pole), is at the south end of the beach, part of the Hotel Akumal Cancún complex. The food is good, specializing in Mexican rather than Yucatecan entrees. Continental breakfast is served with a large platter of fresh tropical fruit; prices are just a shade more than at the other restaurants on the beach, but worth it.

A bit harder to find but worth the search is **La Luna Chueca,** located at Half Moon Bay in the Hacienda de la Tortuga condos. Expats living in the condos and throughout the Akumal area gather here for breakfasts of orange-flavored French toast and dinners of fresh lobster. To get there, turn left just after the entrance to Club Akumal Caribe and follow the road past several condo complexes to Tortuga. Open for breakfast and dinner.

Kids can discover great ice-cream cones at **El Bucanero Ice Cream Parlor.** Just before the main entrance/arch to Akumal, a small general/grocery store called **Super Chomak** sells a good selection of groceries, cold drinks, liquor, beer, ice, sundries, fresh fruit, vegetables, meat, frozen chicken, and fresh-baked *pan dulce* (get here early in the morning for the baked breads). Attached to the store is a small fast-food window selling tacos and *tortas.* Open 7 a.m.-9 p.m.; really good!

ENTERTAINMENT

You can usually find a disco open. High season or not, there's an appreciative audience; music continues into the wee hours. A small **theater group** (they don't have a name) presents plays like *Our Town* in one of the Bush palapas on the beach. Ask at Lol Ha or Super Chomak for perfomance dates.

SHOPPING

Two gift shops, one next to Zasil and a larger one called **Mariselva Boutique** farther down the beach, sell a little of everything: typical Maya clothing, leather sandals, shawls, postcards, pottery, original Maya art and reproductions, black coral and silver jewelry, and a good selection of informative books (in English, French, and German) about the Peninsula and the Maya.

Original Paintings

In Akumal, you won't find the best art in a gallery. Instead, the small pink building (turn right after the entrance arch) that was a real estate office is now a gift shop. Here you'll find Bill Guynes and his lovely paintings of highland Mexico and of many beautiful faces from Chiapas. Guynes lives in the area at Casa Riviera on Half Moon Bay; ask around if you want to see more of his work.

SERVICES

Laundry service is available around the corner from Super Chomak—leave clothes before 9 a.m. for next-day pickup. The closest **bank** is 36 km north at Playa del Carmen. A convenient **gas station** is at the junction of Hwy. 307 and the Tulúm ruins road, 24 km south. Stations are located in Playa del Carmen and Puerto Morelos. Remember, the gas stations are just that, with no mechanics. However, there's a good **mechanic** in the village of Tulúm on Hwy. 307. He doesn't have a sign but is easy to find (on the left side of the road going south) by the many cars parked under a large metal awning; prices are reasonable.

Stamps are sold at the Villas Maya lobby, and mail is taken from there to the post office every day except weekends and holidays.

TRANSPORT

By Taxi

Taxis will bring you to Akumal from Cancún or from the ferry docks at Playa del Carmen. Arrange the price before you start. The average fare from Cancún to Akumal is around US$45-55 (up to four passengers; they say this price is controlled by a taxi drivers' union); from Playa del Carmen it's approximately half that.

By Car

Traveling by car is the most convenient way to get up and down the coast. From Cancún, it's

an 80-km, one-hour drive south on Hwy. 307 to Akumal. From Mérida take Hwy. 180 east to Cancún and turn south on 307 (both good two-lane highways), which passes the entrance road to Akumal. Car rentals are available in Cancún and Mérida. If you're using public transportation but want to explore some of the dirt roads and off-the-beaten-track beaches south of Akumal for only a day, car rentals are available at **Capitán Lafitte, Shangri-La Resorts,** and **Puerto Aventuras,** resorts all fairly close to Akumal. Check with the manager for details (rentals are priced just about the same as those in Cancún). Highway 307 is good, and the side roads (though rough and pot-holed) are drivable.

By Bus

Local buses frequently pass the Akumal turnoff, going both north and south throughout the day. Ask the driver to drop you off (it's not a regular stop); from here walk about one km toward the sea. A new trial service from Cancún runs a mini-bus five or six times daily; check at the Autotransportes office in Cancún. The bus from Playa del Carmen to Tulúm makes the trip several times each day. Ask the driver what time you must be on the highway to be picked up.

Tours

Mayaland Tours is now offering tours from the Akumal area to Chichén Itzá. Tour buses pick you up at your hotel and transport you to and from the ruins. Lunch is provided at the Mayaland hotel, where you can also use the swimming pool. Free beer, wine, and soft drinks are served on the bus back to your hotel. The tours run on Monday, Wednesday, and Friday and cost US$66 pp. For information contact Mayaland's Cancún office at tel. 87-2450, fax 87-2438, or from the U.S. call (800) 235-4079.

AVENTURAS AKUMAL

Nearly isolated but also upscale, Aventuras Akumal is a breathtaking bay of turquoise water. Another white-sand beach, it's close enough to Akumal to get a dose of civilization if you wish. Not too far away from this great walking beach is a small Maya structure mostly hidden by jungle growth. However, the beach isn't occupied only by gulls and crabs; modern, comfortable villas, condos, and a hotel with pools and bars are perched along the water's edge. The condos are privately owned but can be rented from absentee owners. The area is isolated and 60 miles from Cancún, so a car is really the best way to go; if you buy a package tour, you have pickup and delivery to the Cancún airport.

Club Oasis

This upscale, Club-Med-type resort offers a beautiful beach, swimming pool, daily events, movies, satellite TV, organized activities, sailboarding and sailing, lighted tennis courts, dive instruction, and other water sports, including snorkeling, pedal boats, canoes, and kayaks. The all-inclusive price includes: transfers between airport and hotel, hotel accommodations, all meals, domestic drinks, water sports, daily and nightly entertainment, an introductory scuba diving course, and all gratuities at the hotel. Prices fluctuate depending on the time of year and room location; figure about US$200-240 pp in high season. For reservations and information phone (800) 446-2747.

Don't expect to just drop in and have an enchilada and a *cerveza* at one of Club Oasis's lovely dining rooms—you must buy a food package even if it's for one meal. These packages include either lunch or dinner or a complete meal plan and a specific number of drinks. If driving by, do stop and take a look.

De Rosa Villa

This is a great spot to spend a really laid-back vacation or an Indiana Jones holiday. Accommodations are either condos or villas with one and two bedrooms, all lovely, right on white sand with the sea just steps away. You can snorkel, literally, in your front yard. The accommodations are really upscale and comfortable, with spacious living quarters and modern amenities including one sauna, a rooftop bar, and in most units a fully equipped kitchen. There isn't a regular restaurant at De Rosa's, but they have a unique way of feeding everyone. Of course, guests are welcome to eat at the Club Oasis just down the beach (buy a meal package), or you can bring your own food to cook, or you can buy a food package from Nancy and Tony. The food package includes a do-it-yourself

breakfast; they bring you all the makings—eggs, bacon, milk, coffee, juice, cereals, bread, pancake mix, syrup, etc.—and you fix it when you wish. For lunch they either have a buffet on-site with sandwiches, salads, and drinks, or they will pack it for you to take elsewhere. Dinner is special, a gourmet dining treat in your own villa/condo. You choose from a menu of delicious Yucatecan treats that include appetizers, entrees, dessert, and drinks (nonalcoholic) served at the table with the "caterers" right there to clean up afterwards.

De Rosa Villa will rent you villas or condos by the night or by the week. Prices vary according to the season; high season starts at US$85 per night for a studio, US$50 per night for a double hotel room, US$90 per night for a one-bedroom apartment (this is behind the villas and not on the beach), on up to a three-bedroom beachfront villa at US$190 per night, and other options in between. These are high-season prices; summer months are somewhat lower.

Tony De Rosa, an avid diver, works closely with Mike Madden from Puerto Aventuras Dive Center. He offers packages that include an Indiana Jones adventure trip to the Nohoch caverns, or diving, or snorkeling, or a combination adventure/diving package. All include accommodations. For more information, phone or fax (987) 4-1271.

Condo rentals are also available through **Villas las Palmas.** Dan Mincey and Karen Jenkins manage several properties in the Aventuras area, from basic studio condos to luxurious villas. For information, write to them at Box 124, Playa del Carmen, Qunitana Roo 77710, Mexico, tel. and fax (987) 4-1886.

CHEMUYIL

Chemuyil (shem-oo-YEEL) is a tranquil beach with natural attributes of powder-fine sand, a turquoise sea, and crowds of shady coconut palms. The water is calm, thanks to the reef, and snorkeling and fishing attract many day visitors.

The entrance fee (US$3) is paid at the front gate after you turn off Hwy. 307 at the sign directing you to Chemuyil. Pay fees and get information at the circular palapa refreshment stand near the parking lot entrance.

The "Chemuyil Special," devised by an international clientele and Eduardo on a rainy day at the bar, is a refreshing drink served in a coconut-shell bowl with straws. It has strong overtones of Kahlúa but slips down as easily as a chocolate ice-cream soda. **Warning!** It tends to sneak up on the unwary. No wonder this bar becomes a fiesta every night, and you really can dance on the bar!

Note: This is another of the Quintana Roo beaches sketched in for future development, so enjoy the isolation while you can.

Practicalities
The stand serves small packaged sweets, donuts, coffee, juice, and bananas, plus beer, tequila, and fresh seafood, including lobster (if the traps have lured any captives). They serve a large (very expensive) seafood platter, which includes a healthy serving of all seafood delicacies in season—fish, shrimp, lobster, and crab, enough for five to eight people, for about US$87. Although the barkeep does his best to control the cannibal flies that hover around the refreshment stand, if you're going to eat, sit at one of the colorful umbrella tables on the beach; the breeze helps a little.

For US$15 each, there are 12 screened palapa rooms. Hammocks rent for about US$2, and the huts are well supplied with hammock hooks; there doesn't seem to be a limit to the number of people you are permitted to squeeze in. The concierge claims a record of 15.

Chemuyil can get crowded during the busy winter season. Day-trippers from Cancún drive their rental cars to this beach, but only occasionally does it appear to be overcrowded with overnighters. Camp on the south end of the beach to avoid the day-trippers. Trailers can park in the lot for about US$8 per night (plus the entry fee)—no hookups, but use of showers and bathrooms is included in the parking fee.

Anyone can be a successful fisherman in this bay; it takes little more than throwing a baited hook into the surf five or six meters off the beach. If you want to fish for something special, make arrangements with Eduardo or his son Danny to take you in a launch farther out to sea—the hunting grounds for great red snapper. Other trips can be arranged, including snorkeling or a short jungle trek to nearby Maya ruins.

XCACEL

The beaches just keep coming, one right after the other—and all beautiful! Though this coast really hasn't been discovered by most of the world, some have found it and keep returning year after year. You can count on meeting some fascinating people: day-trippers from Cancún, people in camper vans, on cycles, or on foot. A few pack everything they can in campers and RVs and spend an entire exotic winter among Xcacel's (sha-SELL) palms for very little a month. For one night, a fee of about US$4 pp provides a clean shower and toilet but no hookups or electricity, and often the space gets crowded fast (this price is bound to go up). For about US$2, day-trippers can use the beach, showers, and restrooms. The small restaurant here has gotten pricey, and is open only noon-4 p.m. A hamburger is about US$6; fish is less. On certain days groups from cruise ships anchored in Playa del Carmen or Cancún are bused to Xcacel for lunch at this little restaurant and the whole place gets a bit congested. If you're cooking your own meals, bring plenty of food and water; it's a long trek to the local Safeway.

Surf And Sand
The sea directly in front of the campgrounds can be rough, but only a few hundred meters north the reef blocks large waves, producing calm water again—great swimming, fishing, snorkeling, and scuba diving on the reef. When beachcombing, wear shoes along this strip of beach to protect your feet from sharp little bits of coral crunched up in the sand. This is a good place to find shells, especially in front of the campgrounds after a storm. All manner of treasure can be found, from masses of dead coral (all white now) to sea urchin shells, keyhole limpets, maybe even a hermit crab carrying an ungainly shell on his back.

Hiking
If you're a hiker or birdwatcher, take the old dirt road which runs parallel to the shoreline from Chemuyil to Xelha, about five km in all. The road edges an old coconut grove now thick with jungle vegetation. Just after dawn, early birds are out in force looking for the proverbial worm or anything else that looks tasty. If at first you don't

see them, you'll surely hear them. Look for small, colorful parrots or brilliant yellow orioles; you may even see a long-tailed motmot. If you decide to hike to the mouth of Xelha National Park, bring your snorkeling gear, especially if you get there before all the tour buses. Don't forget sunscreen and bug repellent.

XELHA NATIONAL PARK

Xelha (shell-HAAH), a national park on Yucatán's east coast, is just five km south of Akumal. Xelha's lagoon consists of fresh and salt water inhabited by rare and colorful tropical fish. Through small openings from the sea, a multifingered aquarium has developed through the centuries, providing a safe harbor for such exotic underwater life as the brightly hued parrot fish. As a national park, the lagoon is protected from fishing, thereby preserving these beautiful creatures for all to see. Xelha gets unbelievably crowded at certain hours when tour buses bring passengers from cruise ships docked at Cancún, Cozumel, and Playa del Carmen. Come early to avoid the crowds; Xelha is open 8 a.m.-5 p.m. and admission is about US$3.50. **Note:** Do not wear tanning lotions or oils before jumping into the lagoon. These potions are hard on fish and other marinelife.

Ruinas De La Xelha

Across the highway and about 200 meters south of Xelha lies a small group of ruins. Be prepared for a bit of a stroll from the entrance. The structures are mostly unimpressive except for the **Templo de Pájaros** ("Temple of the Birds"). Protected under a palapa roof, one wall still shows remnants of paintings and it's possible to make out the tails and outlines of the original art depicting birds and Chac (the Maya rain god). To get up close you have to climb out onto a small bamboo platform, but from there you have an excellent view. Other buildings to see are the **Mercado** and **Temple of the Jaguar**. A young boy is always available to guide you around; certainly worth a dollar or so.

Along a dirt path farther into the jungle you'll find an enchanting cenote surrounded by trees covered with bromeliads, orchids, and ferns. Dozens of swallows put on a graceful ballet, swooping and gliding low over the water, steal-

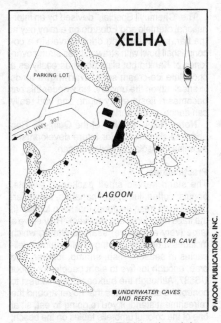

ing a small sip each time. Thick jungle and vines surround the crystal-clear water and it's a perfect place for a swim. Wear a swimsuit. It's offensive to the Mexicans to have you skinny-dipping in their country—in fact it's against the law; some Mexican police will throw you in the slammer if they catch you. And although nudity on the beach is more common now then ever before, you still run a risk of being penalized.

Museum

The small maritime museum formerly at Xelha has moved north to Puerto Aventuras, is now called CEDAM, and is open 8 a.m.-5 p.m.

Snorkeling

You can stroll around the lagoon and see the bottom through incredibly clear water. Snorkeling is allowed in marked areas, and equipment is available to rent for about US$7 per day (and a wait in a long line after the tour buses arrive). In one of many underwater caverns that punctuate the lagoon's coast, you'll see the remains of a decaying Maya temple altar. There's little to authenticate its origins, but it is believed to have been located on the now-submerged shoreline.

Xelha Lagoon

Little islands, narrow waterways, and underwater passages are marvelous to snorkel in amid beautiful coral formations and a variety of warm-water fish.

Other Activities

The lagoon is surrounded by tropical vegetation and paths that wander around the 10 square acres of water. Small platforms over the rocky limestone shore provide perfect places for the nonswimmer to study the fish and sea creatures below. There are no shallow wading areas along the lagoon edge, but you'll find frequent platforms with steps for climbing in and out of the marked areas where swimming and snorkeling are permitted. **Note:** The steps get very slippery! It's tempting and fun to feed the fish, which is okay as long as you give them the nutritious prepared food sold in plastic bags at the entrance under the large arch. Please do not throw your lunch leftovers into the water! The well-fed fish often ignore them and since the incoming and outgoing water moves slowly from the sea, the lagoon quickly becomes polluted.

Practicalities

Xelha has a cafe open during the day for lunch, snacks, and drinks. Lovers of coconut milk can buy the whole nut from a straw-hatted vendor who deftly swings his machete, preparing the fruit to order (straws included) under the cooling shadows of a palm tree. Not too many years ago, coconuts were the only refreshment available. Outside the entrance to Xelha, large shops offer a variety of Yucatecan crafts, clothing, leather goods, locally carved black coral, postcards, and other arts and crafts.

LOUISE FOOTE

TULUM RUINS

This is one of the most well-known archaeological sites along the Mexico Caribbean, largely due to its seaside location.

Five km south of Akumal on Hwy. 307, a side road leads to Tulúm, the largest fortified Maya site on the Quintana Roo coast. Tulúm, meaning "Wall" in Mayan, is quite small (the area enclosed by the wall measures 380 by 165 meters). It has 60 well-preserved structures that reveal an impressive history. The sturdy stone wall was built three to five meters high, with an average thickness of seven meters. Originally this site was called Zama ("Sunrise"). Appropriately, the sun rises directly over Tulúm, which is perched on a cliff 12 meters above the sea.

HISTORY

The Spanish got their first view of this noble, then-brightly colored fortress when Juan de Grijalva's expedition sailed past the Quintana Roo coast in 1518. This was their first encounter with the Indians on the new continent, and according to ships' logs, the image was awe-inspiring. One notable comment in the log of the Grijalva expedition mentions seeing "a village so large, that Seville would not have appeared larger or better."

Tulúm was part of a series of coastal forts, towns, watchtowers, and shrines established along the coast as far south as Chetumal and north past Cancún. The site was occupied from A.D. 1200 on, when Mayapán was the major power and this part of Quintana Roo was the province of Ecab. Tulúm's buildings, which show late Chichén Itzá and Mayapán influence, are not the most elegant structures. Many are decorated with plaster figures of a winged descending god, who in the past has been associated with a bee god and Venus, the evening star. Now some researchers believe that this figure is actually a representation of God E, the maize god. The Temple of the Frescoes contains fine wall paintings that show a strong Mixtec influence—more evidence of the Putún's central Mexican connection. One fresco portrays a rain god astride a four-legged animal that is almost certainly a horse. Tulúm evidently outlasted the conquest, because horses only arrived with the Spanish.

Although a stela dated A.D. 564 was found at Tulúm, investigators are certain it was moved

Tulúm

here, and date figures were cut into it after it had been moved.

Talking Cross

In 1850, three years after the Caste War, the Chan Santa Cruz Indians in Tulúm were a part of "Talking Cross cult." The Spanish had taught the Indians Catholic rituals, many reminiscent of Maya ceremonies; even the cross reminded the Maya of their tree of life. They believed that the gods spoke to their priests through idols. In order to manipulate the Indians, a clever revolutionary half-caste, José María Barrera, used an Indian ventriloquist, Manuel Nahuat, to speak through the cross. At a cross in a forest shrine called Chan, near what is now known as Felipe Carrillo Puerto, a voice from the cross urged the Indians to take up arms against the Mexicans once again. Bewildered, impressed, and never doubting, they accepted the curious occurrence almost immediately. The original cross was replaced with three crosses that continued to "instruct" the guileless Indians from the holy, highly guarded site. This political-religious group grew quickly and ruled Quintana Roo efficiently. The well-armed, jungle-wise Chan Santa Cruz Indians (also called Cruzob) successfully kept the Mexican government out of the territory for 50 years. Even the British government in British Honduras (now known as Belize) treated this group with respect, more out of fear of their power than out of diplomacy, and because they needed the timber trade. Around 1895 the Indians requested that the Territory of Quintana Roo be annexed by

British Honduras, but the Mexican government flatly refused and sent in a new expeditionary force to try once again to reclaim Quintana Roo.

The Mexican army was doomed from the outset. They fought not only armed and elusive Indians but constant attacks of malaria and the jungle itself. The small army managed to fight its way into the capital of Chan Santa Cruz, where they were virtually trapped for a year. The stand-off continued until the Mexican revolution in 1911, when President Porfirio Díaz resigned.

Four years later the Mexican army gave up and the capital was returned to the Indians, who continued to rule Quintana Roo as an independent state, an embarrassment and ever-present thorn in the side of the broadening Mexican Republic. This small, determined group of Indians from another time zone managed to keep their independence and culture intact while the rest of the world proceeded into the 20th century. But life in the jungle was tough, and with famine, measles epidemic, malaria, and 90 years of fighting, the Chan Santa Cruz Indians' population was reduced to 10,000. Weary, in 1935 they decided to quit the fight and were accorded the recognition given to a respected adversary. When their elderly leaders signed a peace treaty, *most* of the Chan Santa Cruz Indians agreed to *allow* Mexico to rule them. This was one of the longest wars in the Americas.

Into The Twentieth Century

One of the few pure Chan Indian villages left in 1935 was Tulúm, and today many residents are descendants of these independent people. Even after signing the treaty, the Indians still maintained control of the area and outsiders were highly discouraged from traveling through. A skeleton imbedded in the cement at the base of one of the temples at Tulúm is the remains of an uninvited archaeologist, a warning to other would-be intruders.

All of this has changed. With foresight, the Mexican government in the '60s recognized the beautiful Quintana Roo coast as a potential tourist draw, and the new state entered the 20th century. The advent of roads and airports has paved the way for the rest of the world to visit the unique ruins of Tulúm. Workers have been modernizing and enlarging the Tulúm airstrip. Tulúm's archaeological zone is open daily 8 a.m.-5 p.m. At 8 a.m. few tour buses have arrived yet, making the cooler early hours a desirable time to explore and climb the aged structures. Opposite the main entrance to the site are a number of open stalls with typical tourist curios, along with a growing number of small cafes selling soda pop and snacks. A US$4.50 pp fee (plus about US$10 to bring in your camcorder) is paid across the street from the entrance to the ruins. Parking is available directly outside the Tulúm site. On a recent visit, 29 tour buses were counted in front of Tulúm. The fumes alone will surely destroy this marvelous old site if this kind of abuse continues. At least now the buses park along the curb, away from the ruins site. The indigenous people welcome tourists and what they represent—money.

The once-thick stands of coconut trees along this part of the coast were part of an immense coconut plantation that included Akumal and Xelha and was owned by a gentleman named Don Pablo Bush. Bush initiated the CEDAM organization made up of a group of daring archaeological divers. Bush and CEDAM donated Xelha Lagoon to the government for use as a national park.

SIGHTS

Tulúm is made up of mostly small, ornate structures with stuccoed gargoyle faces carved onto the corners of buildings. In the **Temple of Frescoes,** looking through a metal grate you'll see a fresco that still bears a trace of color from the an-

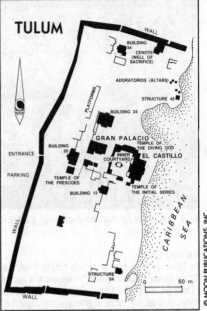

cient artist. Archaeologically, this is the most interesting building on the site. The original parts of the building were constructed around 1450 during the late Post-Classic period, and as is the case with so many Maya structures, it was added to over the years.

Diving God
Across the compound, a small palapa roof protects a carved descending god. This winged creature is pictured upside down and is thought by some historians to be the God of the Setting Sun. Others interpret the carving as representing the bee; honey is a commodity almost as revered on the Peninsula as maize. Visitors are no longer allowed to climb this ruin to view the carvings.

El Castillo
The most impressive site is the large pyramid that stands on the edge of the cliff overlooking the sea. The building, in the center of the wall on the east side, was built in three different phases. A wide staircase leads to a two-chamber temple at the top; visitors are no longer allowed to climb

1. Isla Cozumel; **2.** Chankanab Bay, Isla Cozumel; **3.** San Gervasio, Isla Cozumel; **4.** San Francisco Beach, Isla Cozumel; **5.** Isla Cozumel.

1. Akumal Bay; **2.** Akumal Bay; **3.** Ancient cannons guard Akumal

this stairway, but the view from the hill on which the Castillo stands encompasses the sea, the surrounding jungle with an occasional stone ruin poking through the tight brush, and scattered clearings where small farms are beginning to grow. Two serpent columns divide the entrance, and above the middle entrance is another carved figure of the Diving God. Until the 1920s, the followers of the "Talking Cross cult" kept three crosses in a shrine in this pyramid. It was only after the curious, as well as respectable archaeologists, showed an active interest in obtaining the crosses that the Maya priests moved the Tulúm crosses to Tixcacal Guardia, where they supposedly remain today, still under the watchful protection of the Maya priesthood.

Village Of Tulúm

Tulúm pueblo is south on Hwy. 307 about two km beyond the ruin's turnoff. It has always been the home of stalwart Maya people with the courage to preserve their ancient traditions; the descendants have vigorously chosen to enter

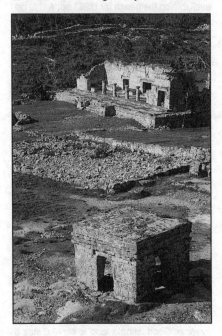

Tulúm

the world of tourism (with tiny steps), and Tulúm pueblo is becoming a viable town.

The stretch of Hwy. 307 that parallels the pueblo now has a row of glaring streetlights in its middle, while its shoulders are crowded with ramshackle storefronts. A plaza and kiosk were constructed a bit north of the traditional center and seem barren most of the time. Dirt roads extend ever farther into the jungle as more humble homes are built to house workers for the nearby resorts. The town's few services have been overshadowed by the highway businesses, which cuts down on the traffic through the residential areas. Food stores have sophisticated refrigeration and freezers, and open-air gift shops selling Mexican handcrafts are multiplying. You can get the best raw chicken from an open-air wooden stall on the side of the road. Several small markets, fruit stands, and *loncherías* line the highway. You'll spot a few mechanics on the left side of the highway just as you drive into town. There's no sign, but the large number of cars on the property is a dead giveaway. The owner and his son are good, cheap, and willing to help if they can.

ACCOMMODATIONS AND FOOD

Hotels near the site are scarce—just two at the intersection of Hwy. 307 and the access road. However, they are sprouting in bunches along Boca Paila Rd., which begins at the southern end of the Tulúm site parking lot.

Budget And Moderate Accommodations

At the intersection of Hwy. 307 and the access road that approaches the Tulúm archaeological site, you'll find **El Crucero Motel,** a 10-minute walk to the ruins. The rooms are spartan and *usually* clean, and have bathrooms, fans, and hot water *sometimes*. Rate is about US$15 d, less during low season. Reports drift in occasionally from readers that the hotel isn't always the cleanest, but then other readers report that the rooms are adequate. Check the rooms carefully before you pay your money. **El Crucero** restaurant on the premises of El Crucero Motel is definitely worth a visit. The owners, Mario and Paty Murillo, worked at various properties in Akumal before taking over El Crucero. Mario was the original chef at Lol Ha, and his talents shine here. Try the *calamar en chipotle;* the fresh chef salad loaded with meats, cheese, and eggs; the seafood crepes; or *cochinita pibil.* A large lunch costs about US$12 pp, though you can get by for much less. The restaurant's restrooms are immaculate, and there is a small market with cold drinks, some groceries, and souvenirs.

The **Hotel Acuario,** across the road, is also simple but has a/c and satellite TV in some rooms. It's clean and has a small pool; video bar in the works. The hotel seems to be constantly changing, with ongoing constuction on new rooms (now 26.) Rate is about US$35 s or d; some rooms are large enough for six persons.

On the Hotel Acuario premises, the **Faisán y Venado** restaurant serves typical Mexican dishes, and great homemade coconut ice cream. This is indeed *venado* (deer) country, but the government has cracked down on serving the over-hunted creature and there *should not* be any deer offered on the menu. On Hwy. 307 at Tulúm pueblo, **Café el Amancer** sits beside the Inter Caribe bus station, has adequate meals and prices, and is convenient for bus travelers.

Following the paved road from the parking lot south along the coast, you'll come to a series of unspoiled beaches edged by what remains of once-thick stands of coconut trees. Between Tulúm and Punta Allen, there are only simple cabanas on the beach and some basic hotels much beloved by travelers seeking seclusion and tranquility. Many don't have public power and depend on gas lanterns or small generators for part of the day; most have a good supply of cold water, though fresh-water showers are the exception; some sell bottled water, but if not, boil your drinking supply.

Osho Oasis is at the end of the paved road leading south from the Tulúm parking lot. You'll find cabanas larger and sturdier than at neighboring establishments, with hanging double beds and mosquito netting, screenless shutters that open up to the outdoors, community bathrooms and hot showers, a dining room that serves good all-you-can-eat vegetarian buffets at each meal (about US$7 for breakfast, US$6 for lunch, and US$12-14 for dinner), and a meditation room overlooking a beautiful bay. You have a choice of four different room styles: budget palapa far from the bathroom, US$25 in high season, US$15 in low season; standard

US$36 high season; deluxe US$51 high season; and super deluxe US$61 high season. Both "semi" and deluxe have private bathrooms with fancy tile. There's even a honeymoon-special room, off by itself on the beach. The owners keep making improvements; the large round palapa has a marble floor and beautiful zapote wood tables. A dive shop offers a PADI-certified divemaster and rental equipment. For reservations write to Box 99, Tulúm, Quintana Roo 77780, Mexico, tel. (987) 4-2772. The entrance to Sian Ka'an Biosphere Reserve is just across the street from Osho Oasis.

A few kilometers south of the ruins parking lot, **Cabañas Don Armandos** offers 32 very spartan cabanas with one bed and room for a hammock (mosquito netting a must!), communal toilet and showers, cold water, candles, sheets, and bottled water. A restaurant bar on the premises, **Zacil Kin** serves good food 7 a.m.-9:30 p.m. This is a family-run operation; ask for the special of the day: it's usually delicious. Cabanas rent for about US$13 for two, camping available on the beach for US$3 pp. A little difficult to find; look for the sign that says Zacil Kin a few kilometers past the ruins on the bumpy road, officially called Boca Paila Road.

Down with the old and up with the new! Just beyond Don Armando's Cabañas is **El Paraíso,** at Apto. Postal 61, Tulúm, tel. (987) 2-3636. The old huts are gone, blown away by Hurricane Gilbert, and have been replaced by 10 connected stucco motel-style rooms (set back on the property away from the sea), each with two double beds, private bath, hot water, fan (when the electricity is on), tile floors, and communal terrace with chairs. The electricity is on from sunset until about 10 p.m. Though you can't see the Caribbean from the cabanas, a short stroll along the sand and you're at the water's edge. An attractive cafe serves as a gathering spot for guests to eat, drink, or visit; open 7 a.m-10 p.m. Rates are US$35 for one or two, US$40 for three, but may be higher when demand is high.

Another small group of 10 cabanas called **Nohoch Tunich** is very primitive, but on a beautiful piece of the Caribbean coast. Expect tiny rooms, simple communal toilets, and hot-water showers; a generator provides electricity in the evening. Good, simple food is served; stay a week and get the seventh day free during the off-season. Rates for two are US$20 facing the beach, and US$15 for the other units year-round. Ask about parking an RV here; rate for two is US$11 year-round. Very pleasant managers/owners.

Just past the end of the paved road (at two km on Boca Paila Rd.), look for a sign that reads **Aldea Dzib-Ak-Tum Cabañas** and **Gatos** bar and restaurant, Apto. Postal 100, Tulúm, Quintana Roo 77780. This is a funky little place that has 17 simple palapa cabanas on the beach, communal toilets, showers (with only a curtain of strings separating you from passersby), cold water, and a laid-back, rather indifferent attitude straight out of the '60s. Dark and cool, with old upholstered couches and chairs, it's really different and has the best guacamole around. Rates for cabanas run US$20-30 d depending on size and season, or you can rent a hammock to hang in a communal area for US$5.

Continue on the same road (seven km from Tulúm), and on the left is a white wall (covered with colorful paintings and dominated by a bright yellow submarine) that surrounds small stucco cabanas. **Cabañas Arrecife** is reasonably modern and very clean, with well-kept grounds and (usually) an abundant water supply (boil your drinking water or use bottled); about US$15. The owner's wife cooks meals for guests. Another camp, **Cabañas Tulúm,** includes 18 small cabanas with beds, bathrooms, ceiling fans, and electricity from sunset until about 10 p.m. Rate is US$33 d, US$5 for an extra person. There's a restaurant on the premises and a white beach that now hosts topless visitors.

Ana y José is the nicest of the small cabana groups along Boca Paila Road. Two-story buildings house a total of 16 rooms, one with a king bed, another with two doubles, and the rest with a single and double, all with private tile bathrooms, tile floors, and fresh-water showers (with hot water in the planning stages). Rates start at US$40, less during low season. All-stone construction and red-tile roofs with pleasant little touches like hanging plants puts it a cut above many of the resorts along here. A colorful screened-in palapa restaurant overlooking the sea serves three meals a day. The food here is good and the prices moderate: burgers, US$4.50; fried chicken, US$6.25; tasty soup, US$2; *chiles rellenos*, US$6.50; continental breakfast, US$2. Bicycles are available for rent, making the

seven-km trip to the ruins easy for those without cars. Electricity is on sunset to 10 p.m. For reservations write to Box 15, Tulúm, Quintana Roo 77780, Mexico; in Cancún tel. (98) 80-6022, fax (98) 80-6021.

Nearby, **Los Arrecifes** has small, rustic cabanas and communal showers and bathrooms for about US$13 d. There is no restaurant in the low season, and sporadic service in high season.

Camping

Two combination cabana/campgrounds, **Santa Fe** and **El Mirador,** sit side by side on the beach immediately south of the Tulúm ruins. Follow the paved road going from the parking lot (about a 12-minute walk). The cabins are tiny. Bring everything—hammock, drinking water, bug repellent, mosquito netting, food (Tulúm village has a few markets and small cafes where you can find inexpensive meals). If you're camping it helps to have a tent; when the wind blows it gets mighty gritty on this beach. The fee is about US$4.50 pp.

Restaurants

Between Xelha and the turnoff to the Tulúm ruins is a special restaurant that shouldn't be missed. As its name suggests, **Casa Cenote** sits between a large cenote and the sea, where the snorkeling is superb. The cenote, Tankha, is one of the largest on the Peninsula; a family of shy manatees has been spotted in its far recesses. Lark and Gary Phillips run the restaurant, which has one of the most spectacular palapa roofs around, with no center. Sunday-afternoon barbecues are a big hit with expats living around Tulúm and Akumal, who settle in for the afternoon over heaping plates of barbecued ribs, steaks, or lobster shish kabob. The regular menu features nachos with all sorts of toppings, great burgers, and marinated chicken. Open Tues.-Sun. noon-sunset. Look for the Casa Cenote sign between Xelha and Tulúm, then follow the dirt road east along the coast until you spot the palapa.

The **Restaurant Doña Tina** under **Hotel Maya** is a popular spot serving good Mexican and Yucatecan meals, convenient for bus travelers. Turn right before the restaurant and go about a half block down a dirt road to **La Isla,** an interesting cafe run by two Italian women. The small wood-shack restaurant is nearly smothered by plants and is somewhat hard to spot, but worth a visit for the homemade pasta and sauces. Open for breakfast and dinner, closed Mondays.

TRANSPORTATION

Getting There

The best way to get around on Hwy. 307 is by car. However, public buses going north and south stop at the crossroad to the ruins every one to two hours 6:30 a.m.-8:30 p.m. There are several bus stations on the highway at Tulúm pueblo. **Inter Caribe** is on the right near the entrance to town and has first-class service to Playa del Carmen, Chetumal, and Méri-

da. **Autotransportes del Caribe** nearby has first- and second-class service to Cancún and Chetumal. The **Autotransportes de Oriente** terminal is on the left side of the road and has service to Puerto Juárez (so those traveling to Isla Mujeres needn't transfer in Cancún), first-class service to Playa del Carmen, and three buses daily that stop at Cobá en route to Nuevo X-Can and Valladolid. Both first- and second-class buses are usually crowded by the time they reach Tulúm; first class does not allow standing. Be there in plenty of time because the buses don't wait. It's always a good idea to check with the bus driver about destination, times, and return trips.

This is a busy place, so it's not difficult to hitch a ride.

KATHY ESCOVEDO SANDERS

COBA AND VICINITY

This early Maya site covers an immense area (50 square km), and hundreds of mounds are yet to be uncovered. Archaeologists are convinced that in time Cobá will prove to be one of the largest Maya excavations on the Yucatán Peninsula. Only in recent years has the importance of Cobá come to light. Though Cobá was first explored in 1891 by Austrian archaeologist Teobert Maler, another 35 years passed before it was investigated by S. Morley, J. Eric Thompson, H. Pollock, and J. Charlot under the auspices of the Carnegie Institute. In 1972-75 the National Geographic Society in conjunction with the Mexican National Institute of Anthropology and History mapped and surveyed the entire area. A program funded by the Mexican government continues to explore and study Cobá, but the time-consuming, costly work will not be completed for many years.

Cobá was perhaps the favorite Maya ceremonial site of many independent travelers. The fact that the jungle hasn't been cleared away or all the mounds uncovered adds a feeling of discovery to the visit. For the visitor, it's important to know that the distances between groupings of structures are long (in some cases one to two

km), and they're not located in a neatly kept park such as Chichén Itzá. Each group of ruins is buried in the middle of thick jungle, so come prepared with comfortable shoes, bug repellent, sunscreen, and a hat. A canteen of water never hurts.

Flora And Fauna

Cobá in Maya means "Water Stirred by the Wind." Close to a group of shallow lakes (Cobá, Macanxoc, Xkanha, and Zacalpuc), some very marshy areas attract a large variety of birds and butterflies. The jungle around Cobá is good for viewing herons, egrets, and the motmot. Once in a while, even a stray toucan is spotted. Colorful butterflies are everywhere, including the large, deep-blue *morphidae* butterfly as well as the bright yellow-orange barred sulphur. If you look on the ground, you'll almost certainly see long lines of cutting ants. One double column carries freshly cut leaves to the burrow, and next to that another double column marches in the opposite direction, empty jawed, returning for more. The columns can be longer than a kilometer, and usually the work party will all carry the same species of leaf or blossom until the plant is completely stripped. It's amazing how far they travel for food! The vegetation decays in their nests, and the mushrooms which grow on the compost are an important staple of the ants' diet. The determined creatures grow up to three cm long.

People

Thousands of people are believed to have lived here during the Classic period. Today, the numbers are drastically reduced. They plant their corn with ceremony and conduct their family affairs in the same manner as their ancestors; many villages still appoint a calendar-keeper to keep track of the auspicious days that direct them in their daily lives. This is most common in the Cobá area because of its (up till now) isolation from outsiders and low profile. The locals live in communities on both sides of the lake. Those by the ruins operate small artisans' shops and restaurants and typically speak a smattering of Spanish. The community on the far side of the lake has a small clinic and a basketball court that serves as the town plaza. The communities have electricity, but no telephone service; the only phone in the area is the cellular one at the Villa Arqueológica.

THE RUINS

White Roads

The most important reason to visit Cobá is to view the archaeological remains of a city begun in A.D. 600. These structures built near the lakes were scattered along a refined system of *sacbe* (roads). The remains of more than 50 *sacbe* have been found crisscrossing the entire Peninsula, and there are more here than in any other location. They pass through what were once outlying villages and converge at Cobá, an indication that it was the largest city of its era. One such *sacbe* is 100 km long and travels in an almost straight line from the base of Nohoch Mul (the great pyramid) to the town of Yaxuna. Each *sacbe* was built to stringent specifications: a base of stones one to two meters high, about 4.5 meters wide, and covered with white mortar. However, in Cobá some ancient roads as wide as 10 meters have been uncovered.

Archaeologists have even found a massive stone cylinder that was used to flatten the ma-

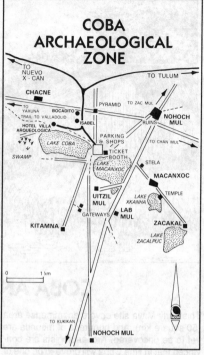

sonry. They have also discovered the mines where the inhabitants excavated the sand used to construct the roads. Sacbe #1, the longest, was an apparent attempt to extend Cobá's realm and challenge Chichén Itzá's rising aggression. It did not work, because Cobá was defeated in a mid-9th century war. Cobá had a minor resurgence during the Late Post-Classic when Tulúm-style temples were built on top of the site's pyramids and ceremonial platforms. In this last period its main function was apparently as a pilgrimage destination. (Many caches of offerings, including jade, pearls, and shells, have been found in La Iglesia and other temples.)

Most of the stelae have been found in the Macanxoc area of the site, also known Group A. Until recently, Stela 1 here has been one of the great enigmas of Mayan translation. It is covered with incredibly long date glyphs that resemble no other Mayan inscription. Now researchers believe that Stela 1 commemorates two very ancient dates. One of these is 13 August 3114

ruins at Cobá

B.C., the day on which the current era—as reckoned by the Maya—began (it ends A.D. 23 December 2012). The other, more remarkable date is the longest one ever found in the Maya world; it marks the day that creation began: 41,943,040 followed by 21 zeros. Unfortunately, like most Cobá stelae, Stela 1 is badly weathered.

The Pyramids

While you wander through the grounds, it helps to use the map. When you enter, follow the dirt road a few meters until you come to the sign that reads Grupo Cobá directing you to the right. A short distance on the path brings you to the second-highest pyramid at the site (22.5 meters), called **La Iglesia.** After climbing many stone steps (the climb gets more dangerous each year as the steps disintegrate), you'll get a marvelous view of the surrounding jungle and Lake Macanxoc. Many offering caches, including jade, pearls, and shells, have been found in La Iglesia and other temples.

Back on the main path, a short trail leads to a stela with traces of carving, covered by a palapa to protect the stone from the elements.

From La Iglesia, farther on, the main path branches to the left, leading to **Nohoch Mul,** the tallest pyramid on the Peninsula (42 meters, a 12-story climb!). The view from atop Nohuch Mul is spectacular, and at the very top there's a small temple with a fairly well-preserved carving of the Descending God. After returning to the main path, turn left and continue to another fork. The path to the right leads to

the **Grupo Macanxoc,** a collection of stelae covered with palapas.

From Grupo Macanxoc, the path to the left goes to **Conjunto Las Pinturas,** so named because of the stucco paintings that once lined the walls. Minute traces of the paintings, in layers of yellow, red, and blue, can still be seen on the uppermost cornice of the temple. This small building is well preserved, with groupings of pillars at the base and bright green moss growing up the sides of the gray limestone. It's nearly a half-hour walk from here back to the entrance to the ruins. Watch for signs and stay on the trails.

Scientists conjecture there may be a connection between the Petén Maya (hundreds of miles south in the Guatemalan lowlands) and the Classic Maya who lived in Cobá. Both groups built lofty pyramids, much taller than those found in Chichén Itzá, Uxmal, or elsewhere in the northern part of the Peninsula.

Undiscovered

All along the paths are mounds overgrown with vines, trees, and flowers—many of these unexcavated ruins. More than 5,000 mounds wait for the money it takes to continue excavation. Thirty-two Classic-period stelae (including 23 that are sculptured) have been found scattered throughout the Cobá archaeological zone. Except for those at Macanxoc, most are displayed where they were discovered. One of the better preserved can be seen in front of the Nohoch Mul group. Still somewhat recognizable, it de-

A roof has been placed over this carved stela to help preserve it from nature's constant attack.

picts a nobleman standing on the backs of two slaves and is dated 780 in Maya glyphs.

ACCOMMODATIONS

Deluxe

There's one deluxe hotel in Cobá, the **Villa Arqueológica,** part of a chain that has placed hotels at various archaeological zones in Mexico, including Uxmal and Chichén Itzá. Each hotel has a well-equipped library with many volumes containing histories of the area and the Maya people. This little sister of the Club Med resorts has an entirely different personality from what you might think. First of all, you pay for everything separately, and the food is more costly than at any other restaurants around—a lot better, also! The decor is a pleasant white-stucco and red-tile Mexican. The staff is friendly, and many are from families who have lived in the Cobá communities for centuries. The villa has *small* but attractive rooms, a/c, shallow swimming pool, outdoor bar and dining, good *típico* and French food, and a gift shop that carries quality reproductions of Maya art. It's hard to predict seasonal highs since groups from Europe are bused in all year long; reservations could be important even though the hotel is often quiet. Rate is US$70, meals extra; in the U.S. call (800) 258-2633 for reservations.

Moderate And Budget

A couple of other modest inns are located on what could be called the main street of Cobá. **Restaurant Isabel** is no longer a restaurant; instead you'll find a few simple *cabañitas* for around US$12 d; *very* spartan but clean, with electricity, two beds, and cold water only. **Bocadito's** cabins on Calle Principal, on the right side of the street as you come into town, are a little more uptown—each with a private bathroom, cold water, tile floors, two double beds, and a place for a hammock. This is a popular stop, so get here early to ensure a room. Rates are about US$10 s and US$15 d. Bocadito has the best restaurant outside the Villa Arqueológica and is popular with tour groups.

FOOD

More tiny shops and outdoor cafes are springing up near the entrance to the Cobá ruins. You'll find cool drinks and good snacks at **Restaurant Los Flamingos** and **Restaurant Cobá**. These are close to small gift shops that carry the usual, including carved wooden jaguar statues, hammocks, and pottery depicting the Maya gods. One gift shop advertises their available bathroom (there's a public restroom near the entrance to the ruins site). In Cobá you'll find the cafes at the inns clean and pleasant. The food, though limited in choice, is *típico* and can be quite good. **Bocadito** has pleasant surroundings and tasty, inexpensive food. Close by, a small market carries purified water, cold sodas, and a few groceries and sundries. The food at **Villa Arqueológica** is fairly good though pricey, with a menu that includes such unexpected treats as pate, chilled asparagus, and chocolate mousse. The bar serves a terrific piña colada and several nonalcoholic fruit drinks, especially welcome when you come out of the jungle hot, sweaty, and tired from hiking and climbing the pyramids. Soups cost about US$4.50, salads about US$9, and full meals average US$20-25.

TRANSPORTATION

Getting to Cobá is easiest by car. The roads are good, and from Cobá you can continue on to Valladolid, Chichén Itzá, and Mérida, or the coast highway (307) that goes south to Chetumal and north to Cancún. If traveling by local bus, your schedule is limited to two or three buses a day. Northwest-bound buses to Cobá (en route to Nuevo X-Can and Valladolid) depart from Playa del Carmen and Tulúm; make sure the bus actually goes in to Cobá along its route. Some buses go to the entrance of the ruins; all stop on the main road in Cobá by Bocadito restaurant. Taxis at Cobá are available to take you to Nuevo X-Can. From here you can catch a bus to Mérida. Some southeast-bound buses from Valladolid to Tulúm and Playa del Carmen stop at Cobá; again, make sure the bus actually goes into the town.

When you get on and off the bus, ask the driver about the return trip and times—the schedules change frequently! The bus skips Cobá entirely at certain times of the year. It's a three-km walk to the highway between Nuevo X-Can and Tulúm, where other buses pass. (If you're planning to spend the night, make sure you have reservations or get there very early in the day.) You'll often run into travelers on the trail at the Cobá ruins who are willing to give you a ride. Organized bus tours are available from hotels and travel agencies in Cancún, Playa del Carmen, and Cozumel.

En Route To The Coast
Tourist services are beginning to appear along the road from Cobá to Tulúm. There are small markets with cold drinks at most settlements, and a full blown rest stop called **Lolche.** You can't miss it—look for the wooden statue of a campesino bearing a rifle next to a large parking lot. Designed with tour groups in mind, Lolche has a small snack bar with cold soda, bottled water, and sandwiches; clean restrooms; and a huge souvenir shop with rows and rows of pottery, masks, hammocks and woodcarvings. Check out the carved wooden jaguars with glass eyes. Open daily 6 a.m.-6 p.m.

PUNTA LAGUNA

About 15 km northwest of Cobá on the highway to Nuevo X-Can, there is a forested area where spider monkeys can occasionally be seen. The locals have built a small palapa bar on the side of a lagoon in this area and will take you to look for the monkeys for a tip. The increase in tourist activity in the area is sure to drive the monkeys away eventually. For now, they can be seen in the early morning and at dusk.

SIAN KA'AN BIOSPHERE RESERVE AND VICINITY

MUYIL: ANCIENT MAYA SEAPORT OF SIAN KA'AN

One of the larger Maya sites within the Sian Ka'an Biosphere Reserve is Muyil, also known as Chunyaxche. Situated on the edge of the karstic limestone shelf about 25 km south of Tulúm, it has been the recent subject of a study conducted by Tulane University and the Quintana Roo Regional Center of INAH. Along with mapping the site to determine its size and settlement pattern, graduate students from Tulane and men from the village of Chumpon have been excavating for ceramics in order to provide dates of occupation and are learning the use of Muyil's seaport.

Architectural Discoveries

The potsherds dug up at the area indicate that Muyil was settled about A.D. 1 and occupied continuously until the Spanish conquest began. The report's author, archaeologist Elia del Carmen Trejo, notes that since no Spanish ceramics have been identified and because there is no mention of a settlement at Muyil in books from the period, the population of Muyil perished in the 40 years following the conquest. A large *sacbe* (roadway) at Muyil runs at least a half km from the site center to near the edge of the Muyil lagoon. The upper (western) half of the road runs through mangrove swamp.

Six structures are spaced along the roadway approximately every 120 meters. They range from two-meter-high platforms to the large *castillo*, one of the tallest structures on the east coast. All but the westernmost of the structures face westward, away from the lagoon. They have center stairways facing westward to the roadway to the west. The Maya always used directional precision involving the position of the sun and Venus. The sections of roadway between each structure are centered at the foot of each stairway, but when they arrive at the next structure to the west, they connect with it at the northeast corner, not on the centerline. It is as though you

were always meant to pass these structures along their north side; no one knows why.

The *castillo*, located in the midpoint of the *sacbe*, stands 21 meters above the lagoon's water level. At the summit is a solid round masonry turret, which is unique to ancient Maya structures. From the summit it's possible to see the Caribbean.

Getting There

Muyil is at the side of the highway about 25 km south of Tulúm; look for the sign that reads Chunlyaxche and turn left into a small parking area. The entrance fee is about US$3.50, and the ruins are open daily 8 a.m.-5 p.m.

ROAD TO PUNTA ALLEN

If you're driving south to Punta Allen on Boca Paila Rd. (south from the Tulúm parking lots and parallel to the coast), fill your gas tank at the Tulúm crossroads gas station since there's not another on the coastal road to Punta Allen (57 km). (Traveling north on Hwy. 307, the next gas station is in Playa del Carmen; traveling south to Chetumal, there's one in Felipe Carrillo Puerto.) After leaving Hwy. 307 from Tulúm on Boca Paila Rd., the road to Punta Allen appears to be paved and smooth—fooling the uninformed! The road is only smooth for about six km beyond the ruins, and then it becomes potholed, ridged, and rugged. Though it's slow going, bumpy, and uncomfortable, any vehicle can handle this all-weather road when it's not raining. Four-wheel drive may be necessary if the rains have been particularly heavy. There is usually a guard at the entrance to Sian Ka'an, about six km south of the Tulúm ruins by Osho Oasis; ask him about road conditions. Many of the fishing lodges and campgrounds along this road close in the summer months.

Boca Paila Fishing Lodge

This pricey small resort caters to fishermen looking for excellent saltwater fly-fishing for bonefish.

JUAN VEGA

Local legend has it that during the height of the post-Caste War conflict, Juan Vega was kidnapped by the Maya Indians as a young child. His entire family and young companions were put to death, but, because he was carrying religious books and could read, he was spared. The Maya had a curious acceptance of the Christian religion. Because of certain similarities, they managed to weave it into their own beliefs and would listen attentively to Juan Vega's preaching.

Although Vega was a captive, he was given tremendous respect and spent his entire life in the village, marrying a Maya and raising a family of mestizos in the village of Chumpon. Vega (nicknamed "White King of the Maya") operated a chicle business at Muyil. Chumpon is referred to by knowledgeable outsiders as the "Jungle Vatican." Vega saved the lives of many captured Mexican soldiers. They were doomed to death by the Maya, until he stepped in and read the laws of the Christian God from his worn books.

In 1961, Quintana Roo was still a no-man's land without roads and Vega was seriously ill; through a fluke, archaeologist Pablo Bush heard about Vega. Bush, acting quickly, used a small plane to spot the hidden jungle village and a helicopter to pick up the sick man (by foot it was a three-day expedition into the village). Juan Vega was rescued—but only after he asked the chief's permission to leave. After surgery and a long stay in a Mexico City hospital, the newspapers gave an account of Vega, and a soldier who had once been saved by Vega came to visit him. A recovered Vega had one request while in Mexico, to visit Abuelitas (the Virgin of Guadalupe). When able, he made his pilgrimage to the shrine and then happily returned to his isolated village and family in Chumpon. Juan Vega lived in Chumpon until his death a few years later.

Boca Paila is in the Sian Ka'an reserve, and all fishing is catch and release. Fishermen are taken to some fabulous freshwater lagoons. The resort offers eight bungalows, food, and excellent service. In some cases clients are flown in from Cozumel or Cancún. Roundtrip land transfer from Cancún or Cozumel is not included in the rate. If you fly into Cozumel, someone will meet you at the airport and take you to the ferry or air shuttle. At Playa del Car-

men you can rent a car or have the lodge van pick you up and drive you to the lodge for about US$90. If arriving in Cancún, you can rent a car or take a taxi for about US$150 for up to six persons. Rates include six days of fishing, accommodations, food, boat, and shared guide. Prices begin at US$1825 double occupancy, less for nonfishing companions. In the U.S. call (800) 245-1950, in Pennsylvania (412) 935-1577; fax (412) 935-5388; or write Frontiers, Box 959, Pearce Mill Rd., Wexford, PA 15090. In Cozumel, call (987) 2-0053.

Casa Blanca Lodge

Another great fishing lodge is located on Ascension Bay. Again this is a small resort for the fisherman, with room for 14 guests. The attractive lodge is located on a palm-covered point just 100 feet from the edge of the blue Caribbean. The modern, comfortable rooms are spacious, and an open-air palapa is a bar/gathering spot where the evening is spent telling tall fishing tales. Weekly rates begin at US$2495 pp, double occupancy of cabana and boat, including accommodation, food, boat, fuel, shared guide, fishing license, and 10% government tax. Rates are highest March-June, lower Jan.-March. The lodge is closed July-December. For further information contact Frontiers, Box 959, Pearce Mill Rd., Wexford, PA 15090, tel. (800) 245-1950 or (412) 935-1577, fax (412) 935-5388.

Qualton Club Pez Maya

The Mexico-based Qualton Club has purchased the Sol Pez Maya fishing resort and refurbished its eight cabanas, all with private bathrooms, sitting areas, and patios. As with the other fishing lodges, rates include meals; unlike the others, the Qualton includes transfers to and from the Cancún airport. Rates begin at US$1899 per week for double occupancy and double use of a boat. For further information contact Frontiers, Box 959, Pearce Mill Rd., Wexford, PA 15090, tel. (800) 245-1950 or (412) 935-1577, fax (412) 935-5388.

Across The Bridge

Another 10 km beyond La Villa de Boca Paila is the Boca Paila bridge. The new wooden bridge crosses the canal connecting the lagoons with the Caribbean. This exotic spot, crowded with tropical vegetation and coconut trees, offers

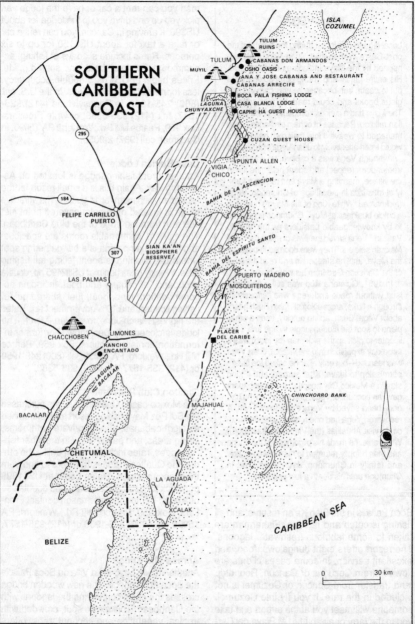

SOUTHERN
CARIBBEAN
COAST

ISLA
COZUMEL

TULUM RUINS
CABANAS DON ARMANDOS
OSHO OASIS
ANA Y JOSE CABANAS AND RESTAURANT
CABANAS ARRECIFE
BOCA PAILA FISHING LODGE
CASA BLANCA LODGE
CAPHE HA GUEST HOUSE

TULUM
MUYIL

LAGUNA
CHUNYAXCHE

CUZAN GUEST HOUSE

PUNTA ALLEN

VIGIA
CHICO

BAHIA DE LA ASCENCION

FELIPE CARRILLO
PUERTO

SIAN KA'AN
BIOSPHERE
RESERVE

BAHIA DEL ESPIRITU SANTO

LAS PALMAS

PUERTO MADERO
MOSQUITEROS

CHACCHOBEN

LIMONES

PLACER
DEL CARIBE

CHINCHORRO BANK

RANCHO
ENCANTADO

LAGUNA
BACALAR

BACALAR

MAJAHUAL

CHETUMAL

LA AGUADA

CARIBBEAN SEA

XCALAK

BELIZE

0   30 km

© MOON PUBLICATIONS, INC.

Trekkers find many campsites along Quintana Roo's Caribbean coast.

stretches of lonely beach north and south of the mouth of the lagoon. The water, though warm and inviting, is not clear enough for snorkeling or diving. The beach is open to campers. Be sure to bring all necessities, including food and water.

Continuing on the road, south of the bridge is **El Rancho Retiro,** a wonderful beach located on a picturesque bay. It reminds one of a Tahitian island before the tourists discovered it. **Note:** Since the death of the owner, the cabanas have pretty well suspended operations. Behind the cabanas the explorer will find **Laguna Chunyaxche,** a lagoon stopover for migrant birds, including flamingos, herons, and egrets. The entire area is part of the **Sian Ka'an Biosphere Reserve,** with over 300 species of birds. **Bird Island,** a small island in the lagoon, hosts two species of crocodiles and is a great place to explore and observe all manner of wildlife.

Though this is wild country, some families have lived here for many years. Most are fishermen, who will provide boat outings upon request. The setting is lovely, right on the edge of the bay where dolphins come to frolick every autumn. Visitors tell of petting the lovely creatures in the shallow water. It's necessary to travel about a kilometer around the bay for the best swimming spot.

Caphe Ha Guest House
You can't get much more secluded than this. Caphe Ha sits on a white-sand beach in a coconut grove about three miles south of the Boca Paila bridge. Guests stay in two solar-powered cottages, one with a private bath, one with a shared bath in the main house, which also has guest rooms. From here you can arrange fishing, birdwatching, and sightseeing boats trips through Laguna Chunyaxche, or just swim, snorkel, and wander the beach to your heart's content. Meals are served family style; bring along snacks and liquor if you want. Rates begin at US$75 s, US$150 d, including breakfast and dinner. For reservations, call (212) 219-2198 in the U.S., or write to Sue Brown Baker, Calle 51 #478, Mérida, Yucatán 97000, tel. (99) 23-4896.

Exploring Ancient Caves
If you're traveling with a small boat (rubber raft is best), you can explore narrow canals said to be built by the Maya that curve inland to remnants of isolated ceremonial centers—all small and none restored or even excavated yet. This is a trip for intrepid adventurers with sturdy muscles; in some spots the channel narrows, and you have to carry your boat overland or wade through muddy swamps. Caves are scattered about—some you can swim into, others are hidden in the countryside. Maya glyphs still intact on inner cave walls suggest the Indians may have lived in them. Taking along a guide familiar with the area is suggested. Bring flashlight, bug repellent, sunscreen, hat, and walking shoes that will survive in the water.

Hiking
For the hardy type with lots of time, walking the 347 km from Puerto Morelos to Chetumal or

Punta Allen can be high adventure. Requiring at least three or four weeks (or longer if you take time to smell the flowers), this trip is only for the fit. While the main highway (307) is the most direct route to Chetumal, it often veers away from the beach and is boring and flat with little to see except cars. On a trek to Punta Allen, Boca Paila Rd. sometimes disappears behind sand dunes, but it's never that long a trudge to dozens of fine beaches where you might be seduced into staying a day or a month—or forever.

In most cases there's no place to stay except the beach, where there are still some coconut trees on which to sling your hammock—a tropical paradise. Be sure to have mosquito netting with you for your nights under the stars. Simple cabana resorts are springing up as Cancún continues to spread southward down the Quintana Roo coast, but be prepared for long stretches on this dirt road with nothing but empty beach and small ranchitos.

Restaurants are also sparse on this stretch of road until you reach Punta Allen; come prepared with your own victuals and water. Once you reach Punta Allen, you either have to hoof it back or make arrangements with a villager for a ride.

PUNTA ALLEN

Punta Allen, part of the Sian Ka'an Biosphere Reserve, is a small fishing village on a finger of land that overlooks a large bay called Bahía de la Ascención. In the last century, ships would occasionally drift off course onto the dangerous reef that stands just off the coast. Maya boatmen, however, expertly navigate in and out of the submerged reefs and shallow spots that lie hidden across the mouth of the bay.

Because the area is considered the hottest lobster grounds in Mexico, wildlife groups in association with the local lobster cooperative and the Mexican equivalent of the National Science Foundation are studying the way the Yucatecan fishermen handle the spiny crustaceans. The villagers don't use lobster traps as we know them, but instead create artificial habitats from which the lobsters can come and go. The lobsters grow sheltered in these habitats, and when they reach a predetermined size, the fishermen take them by hand. For centuries the Maya built habitats from the spine of a particular palm tree, the *chit,* which

is now becoming extinct from overuse. Fishermen within the Sian Ka'an reserve have been urged to use alternative materials.

Since 1982, scientists (and volunteers from organizations such as Earth Watch) have been tagging and mapping the growth areas each summer to decide if this concentration of lobsters leads to over-harvesting, or if protecting the habitat reduces the natural mortality rate of lobsters in the open sea. Over-harvesting has already depleted lobster numbers in several areas in the Gulf of Mexico and in Baja's Todos los Santos Bay.

Sights
Along the way to Punta Allen you'll discover several beaches with white sand surrounded by thick jungle. The village itself is small and

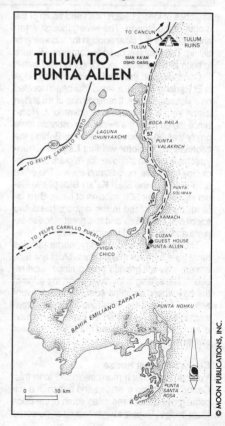

© MOON PUBLICATIONS, INC.

RECENT MAYA HISTORY

1847: The beginning of the Caste War.

1849: The Caste War goes against the Maya and they retreat, getting lost in the thick jungles of Quintana Roo.

1850: The "Talking Cross" appears at the cenote and delivers commands for reviving the war against the whites.

1850-58: The Maya warriors have their ups and downs, but life goes on for the Indians as they manage to hold off their adversaries.

1858: The Maya capture the fortress of Bacalar (just outside of Chetumal) and begin building a ceremonial city complete with church, palaces, barracks, and schools. This is the beginning of their total independence from the rest of Mexico.

1863: The British at Belize recognize the Indian state and engage in arms trade with them.

1863-1893: The Maya lose great numbers of people due to epidemics and internal conflicts.

1893: Mexico and Britain wrangle a peace treaty; the Indians no longer have their important source of arms.

1901: Under General Ignacio Bravo, the Mexican federal army takes over the stronghold city of Chan Santa Cruz and renames it Felipe Carrillo Puerto.

1901-15: While the Mexicans occupy the Maya city with brutality, the Maya in the jungle continue to raid and harrass the Mexicans, virtually isolating them from the rest of Mexico.

1915: The Mexicans give up and return Quintana Roo to the Maya.

1917-20: Influenza and smallpox epidemics decimate the Indians.

1920-29: Chicle boom. General May, the Indian leader, accepts a peace treaty with Mexico, distressing the more militant Indians.

1929: These militant traditional Maya disclaim May's "sell-out" and revive the cult of the "Talking Cross" at X-Cacal Guardia.

typical but not glamorous. Snorkeling, swimming, and fishing are good on some of the offshore islands. Walks will introduce you to unusual birds and maybe even a shy animal. Marshy areas close by are good for observing the nesting grounds and natural habitats of nearly 300 classes of birds identified by ornithologists. **Note:** Start out early in the morning for Punta Allen so that if it's not for you, you'll have time to go back.

Accommodations

All beaches are free to campers; ask permission before setting up camp in front of a local villager's house. Dispose of your trash and leave the beach clean. RVs can park on the beach, but there are no facilities. Swimming here is not the best, but the fishing is great!

Few accommodations are available at Punta Allen. For a long time the only place was **Cuzan Guest House,** a group of basic palapa cabanas, some shaped like tepees. Earth Watch expeditions stay here. If you need all the modern conveniences of the States, *don't* come to Punta Allen. However, if you're interested in learning about the culture of a Maya fishing village, and your tastes run to low-key adventure, sleeping in primitive cabanas in hammocks (a few beds are available), community bathrooms (two only), simple food that is mostly from the sea—lobster is served frequently during the lobster season (15 July-15 March)—then come along.

Arrangements can be made with Armando, if he's not fishing, to take you motoring in his fishing launch to the reef, where snorkeling is outstanding. Another popular outing is a trip to

Cayo Colebre, a small uninhabited island off the coast, where in spring you'll see hundreds of man-o-war frigates hanging like kites overhead, displaying the brilliant red mating pouches under their beaks to attract females. Fishing off Colebre, as well as several other uninhabited islands close by, is excellent. Ask about two-night Robinson Crusoe trips.

Rooms at **Cuzan Guest House** begin at US$20-50, three meals US$25, excursions US$20-100. Remember, this is a fisherman's house and not a resort! If you have any questions write to Sonia Lilvik, Apto. Postal 24, Felipe Carrillo Puerto, Quintana Roo 77200, Mexico, tel. and fax (983) 4-0383, in Cozumel tel. (987) 2-0600. Allow a couple of months for return mail.

Food
A few small cafes have opened in the town, serving basic meals with the freshest fish and lobster as the centerpiece. Try **Candy's,** one block in from the waterfront.

FELIPE CARRILLO PUERTO

Anyone who has driven Hwy. 307 from Tulúm to Felipe Carrillo Puerto in the past five years can't help but notice the varied changes taking place. Only a few years ago the main activity seen along this two-lane road was machete-swinging workers battling to keep thick jungle vines and ferns from overtaking the roadway. Today, trees have been removed and jungle has been cleared away to make room for small ranchitos. The people keep a few cattle and pigs, and grow corn, squash, and tomatoes. Also, large areas have been planted with citrus trees, a government-backed experiment to help the farmers.

From Tulúm to Chetumal, an easy drive takes you through Felipe Carrillo Puerto. For anyone curious about the past of the Maya Chan Santa Cruz Indians (also called Cruzob), it's well worth a stopover to investigate this small colonial city with some of the richest history in Quintana Roo. It has yet to be discovered en masse by tourists and remains a simple, quiet town.

Chan Santa Cruz
Chan Santa Cruz (meaning "Small Holy Cross") is now called Felipe Carrillo Puerto. Today's city folk refer to old-timers as *antiguos,* and

while the younger generation has too many modern things to enjoy to actively take part in the ancient tradition, these youngsters admire the *antiguos'* tenacity and belief in an impossible dream. When the Caste War was going badly for the Maya, the "Talking Cross" was reintroduced to the Indians, dictating tactical orders and predicting victory in their fight against the outsiders. The Talking Cross gave the Indians strength and told them they were the chosen race, true Christians, and children of God.

A few old-timers still cling to the belief that one day the Maya will once again control the Quintana Roo coast. Their fathers and grandfathers rejected the peace treaty negotiated between their leaders and the Mexicans, took their families into the jungle, and began new villages where they continued their secretive lifestyle, calling themselves *separados.*

The Talking Cross was first reported by Spaniards in the 1700s. The cross itself had been an important symbol in the ancient Maya cult, representing the four cardinal points. Studies indicate that the Maya knew full well that a human voice was responsible for the "talking," but they believed it was inspired by God. (See also "Talking Cross" under "Tulúm Ruins".)

Accommodations And Food
Faisán y Venado is the hotel on Hwy. 307 which also houses a good cafe. For anyone interested in preserving what's left of the deer population along this coast, don't order *venado* if it's offered. The hotel next to the restaurant has very basic rooms recommended only for those truly dedicated to exploring the town. The 21 rooms have hot water (sometimes) and a/c or fans; rates start at US$14 s or d with fan, US$22 with a/c.

The **Hotel San Ignacio** near the Pemex station has rooms in a two-story building framing a parking lot; all 12 rooms have private baths. Rates start at US$10 s, US$12 d. Another hotel by the main church seems suited only for the desperate. More promising is the **Hotel Felipe Carillo Puerto,** on Calle 68, one block north of the plaza. No sign, but the housekeeper says that's the name. The nine rooms have private baths, and the setting is far more peaceful than at the hotels on the main street.

24-hour Cafe, Hwy. 307 near the center of town across the road from the bus station, is still the clean, moderately priced, bustling cafe that has been bringing travelers and locals in for years. For US$5 you can get a good enchilada dish, and for US$7-8 the menu offers fish and meat dishes.

Hamburger Maya, on Hwy. 307, a clean little cafe, is two doors south of 24-hour Cafe. The burger isn't exactly a Big Mac, but it's good, and they also serve good ice cream. The bus station is close by in case you choose to continue your journey by bus.

Felipe Carrillo Puerto is an eclectic mix of modern young folks shopping for the latest hit at **Videolandia** and some of the oldest Maya (descendants of the once-violent Cruzob) still hoping for British help to conquer the Mexicans.

Transportation

Since most of the Yucatán Peninsula is flat and the primary arteries are in good condition, the Caribbean coast sees a few cyclists. When exploring off the main roads, cyclists should be prepared for bumpy, irregular, and hard-packed dirt surfaces that become a muddy morass when it rains. The main highway can be dangerous as well, since there are no shoulders to speak of, and cars travel at high speeds in isolated areas. Bring spare tires and a repair kit; few cycle shops exist.

By motorcycle you can travel almost any road on the Peninsula, but beware of the swampy shoulders near the sea.

You can expect frequent bus service between Chetumal and Cancún, and some buses heading inland to Mérida. Buses travel from all over the Yucatán Peninsula to Hwy. 307 and up and down the Caribbean coast.

Drivers should fill up at the **Pemex station,** whether you're going north or south. It sells *magna sin* (Mexico's unleaded gas), and the next station with it is 98 km distant. *Always* top off the tank when passing a gas station because there are no guarantees the next one will not be entirely out of gas. Look for the green *magna sin* sign.

XCALAK PENINSULA

This low-lying limestone shelf—bounded by the Quintana Roo mainland on the west, Espíritu Santo Bay on the north, Chetumal Bay on the south, and the Caribbean Sea on the east—is a mosaic of savannah, marsh, streams, and lagoons, dotted by islands of higher ground with dark soil and high forest, a rich refuge for Quintana Roo wildlife. The jungle has kept hidden for centuries the remainder of Maya life that once thrived on this narrow peninsula.

History

Early explorers Sylvanus Morley and Thomas Gann sailed up the coast from Belize in 1918, visiting a number of sites along the east coast. In 1926, Herbert Spinden and Gregory Mason passed by the area, and then in 1958 an amateur explorer, Michel Peissel, traveled down the coast, reporting Maya sites at San Lorenzo, San Antonio, Río Indio, and Guadalupe.

In 1988 archaeologists Anthony P. Andrews (University of South Florida), Tomas Gallareta Negron (Tulane University), and Rafael Coboa Palma (Tulane University) visited archaeological sites on the coast of the Xcalak Peninsula. They focused on the coastal strip between Punta Herrero on Espíritu Santo Bay and Boca Bacalar Chico, the canal that divides the Xcalak Peninsula from Ambergris Caye in Belize. Only sites on the shoreline and in its immediate vicinity were visited; the interior areas were not surveyed. Money and time were devoted to the most threatened sites along the rapidly developing coast. Only in recent years has a rough dirt road opened this once isolated area to home builders and a few (so far) small resorts, but many new developments are on the drawing boards.

The coastline is a series of sandy beaches and dunes interrupted by rocky promontories, some of which connect with the offshore Belize Reef. This shore is dominated by still-healthy coconut plantations planted in the early 20th century. Andrews suggests that prehistoric sites located on the high ground behind mangrove-fringed estuaries are likely to have been the parent communities of the fishing villages and camps whose remains have been found along the shoreline. Very little is known about the preconquest history of the Xcalak Peninsula because it was already abandoned by the time the Spaniards attemped (unsuccessfully) to establish a village at Espíritu Santo Bay in 1621.

However, it became a sanctuary for Maya refugees fleeing Spanish control in the interior as well as a haven for pirates, British logwood cutters, and Belizean fishermen.

The port of Xcalak was founded in 1900 as a military base for a project to dredge a canal across the southern end of the peninsula. The project never got off the ground, and instead a small rail line was laid between Xcalak and La Aguada on Chetumal Bay. In the following years, lighthouses were built at Xcalak and Punta Herrero. Large coconut plantations were established at El Uvero and Xcalak. Smaller plantations and fishing camps were set up at Tantaman, Río Indio, Benque Soya, Majahual, Río Huach, and Punta Gavilan. In 1910, Xcalak's population numbered 544 with a few additional people scattered among the *cocales* (small coconut plantations) and ranchos along the coast. Many of the original colonizers were Yaqui Indians deported from their homeland in northwestern Mexico following their resistance to the Díaz regime. In the ensuing years, the population fluctuated. The major industries—*cocales* and fishing—have been disrupted several times with the onslaught of major hurricanes.

Thick jungle still hides many sites; one local man tells of vine-shrouded structures where statues remain intact. Finding them is the realm of scientists and (sadly) grave robbers. Hopefully the development and pillage of the Xcalak Peninsula will not move faster than scientific exploration.

But tracts of land along the coast are rapidly being bought up by large- and small-scale tourism developers and private individuals seeking a last bit of undisturbed paradise. In 1993, the government of Quintana Roo began working with a major tourism developer to study the peninsula and ways it could be enhanced by tourism without destroying its fragile ecology. Naturally, rumors about the future abound and there is talk of marinas, golf courses, and other major attractions.

Sights

For the explorer looking for virgin territory, a drive along the Xcalak Peninsula is a lengthy adventure. A paved road breaks off the highway (307) just south of the Limones road and meanders toward the sea for 57 km through varied scenery. Much of this land has been

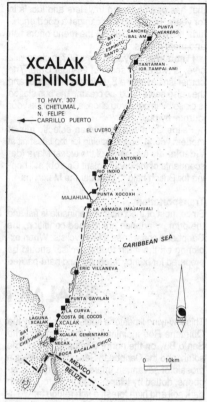

XCALAK PENINSULA

TO HWY. 307
S. CHETUMAL,
N. FELIPE
CARRILLO PUERTO

CARIBBEAN SEA

© MOON PUBLICATIONS, INC.

0   10km

cleared of jungle, and small ranchitos are scattered about. In some areas mangrove swamps line the highway and are home to a large variety of birds, including hundreds of egrets and the graceful white heron. However, in August 1989, the "rainy" season, so little rain fell that many of the swamps were dry and the birds went elsewhere. Closer to Hwy. 307, the tall trees that have been left are covered with green and red bromeliads, orchids, and ferns. In spring colorful flowers brighten the landscape.

After about 55 km on this paved road, there's a turnoff to the left (north) going to Uvero and Placer. Many getaway houses are springing up along this part of the coast as well as the beginning of a few small diving destinations. You can count on this area being fairly deserted for a long time, at least until they pave the road! Right now, the road is potholed and extremely rough. Chinchorro Bank is a virgin wonderland of crystalline water where lobster, conch, and sunken ships are just waiting for divers.

OVERLAND TO XCALAK

To go to Xcalak, don't turn off to the left onto the unpaved road as you would to get to Placer; stay on the paved road until it dead-ends at Majahual on the sea, a geographic point on the map but no town. A military camp guards the point, but they're just a bunch of friendly kids ready with smiles and information. Here turn right on the dirt road (south) to reach Xcalak, another 66 km. The jungle along this road hasn't been disturbed much and is teeming with animals and noisy birds. From Majahual, the road parallels the coast to Xcalak. This trip is especially conducive to travel in a small camper. Like an early explorer, you'll discover miles and miles of isolated beach—few facilities, just the turquoise sea, not a very pretty beach, transparent white crabs, a variety of fish waiting to be caught for your dinner, and curious birds checking out the newest visitor to their deserted paradise. It's all free—so far.

Bring plenty of food, water, and especially gasoline since you'll not see another gas station until you're back on the highway. This isolation won't last too much longer, however, as several attempts are being made to open businesses.

Costa De Cocos Resort

From Majahual, drive south exactly 52 km and you will see the sign for Costa de Cocos on a gravel road. This is a fine little resort that caters especially to divers. The resort is a diver's dream, with eight beautiful bungalows on the palm-studded oceanfront, each with a shower and hot water and lots of comfortable touches. Guests enjoy a new dining room, a PADI-trained and safety-conscious divemaster, the 30-foot custom dive boat *El Gavilan*—all this and a tropical paradise to boot. Chinchorro Bank, a one-hour boat ride away, is one of the favorite destinations; for fishermen, there are special trips to hidden caves, rich fishing grounds (permit required), bonefish, and tarpon.

Breakfast and dinner are included in room rates, which start at US$65 s, US$88 d. Diving,

Maya construction using chit *palm*

fishing, and snorkeling excursions are extra. Meals are also available in Xcalak at two different restaurants, but choices are limited. It is suggested that guests bring along a supply of favorite snacks, since shopping in town is limited. Beer and soft drinks on sale; no liquor, but feel free to bring your own. Kayak and Windsurfer rentals at the dive shop; dive instruction available there as well. A full-day dive excursion to Chinchorro Bank is US$380 for one to four persons.

If you're driving from Cancún, it will take approximately five hours (car rentals handy at the Cancún airport, advance reservations suggested). Xcalak has a 2,800-foot runway, paved and in good condition; from Chetumal, Cancún, and Belize, charter flights are available—ask at Costa de Cocos. Because of the long drive and limited accommodations, it is strongly advised that you make reservations in advance. For more information contact Turquoise Reef Resorts, tel. (800) 538-6802 or fax (303) 674-9615.

MANATEE BREEDING PROGRAM

The state of Florida, under the auspices of the Miami Seaquarium and Dr. Jesse White, has begun a captive breeding program hoping to learn more about the habits of the manatee and to try to increase the declining numbers. Several manatees have been born in captivity; they along with others that have recuperated from injury or illness will be or have been released into Florida's Crystal River, where boat traffic is restricted. They are tagged and closely observed. Florida maintains a 24-hour hotline where people report manatees in need of help for any reason. Rescues can include removing an adult male from a cramped storm drain or rushing to the seaquarium newborns that somehow managed to get separated from their mothers and have washed ashore. These newborns are readily accepted by surrogate-mother manatees and are offered nourishment (by way of a thumb-sized teat under the front flipper) and lots of TLC. Medical aid is given to mammals that have been slashed by boat propellers as a result of cruising boats. The manatee has a playful curiosity and investigates anything found in its underwater environment, many times sustaining grave damage.

Note: Another diver resort in the area is **Playa Chinchorros**. It's been around for a while, and we've had several reports that it isn't up to snuff. Let me know what you find.

XCALAK

Xcalak (shka-LAK), a tiny fishing village located across the bay from Chetumal, is the southernmost tip of Quintana Roo. Trekking there is an extraordinary expedition for those with a wellspring of energy and plenty of time. If you plan to stay for a few days, bring your camping gear even though Xcalak does have a small, simple hotel. A couple of *tiendas* sell simple food and supplies. Visitors will find two small cafes in Xcalak. One, **Commacho's**, has been around forever and serves simple meals for lunch and dinner. The newer one, **Adolfo's**, also serves lunch and dinner and maybe breakfast by now. This is a simple sand-floored cafe with good seafood and Maya specialties, run by a local family.

Note: Wind generators provide Xcalak's electricity and are not completely reliable, so be sure to bring a flashlight and batteries.

Local fishermen can be hired to take you across the reef to breathtaking **Chinchorro Bank**, 26 km off the coast, which covers a large area (43 km north to south, 17 km east to west). Scuba divers call this world-class diving, with crystal-clear water and a huge variety of colorful fish, delicate coral, and three sunken ships clearly visible from above. Xcalak is just a short distance from a channel that separates Mexico from Belize's Ambergris Caye. In days past, Mexican soldiers dug by hand the often-shallow channel to ensure border security between the two countries.

Back On The Road To Chetumal

On Hwy. 307 between Felipe Carrillo Puerto and Chetumal you'll see turnoff signs for several villages; some have small Maya sites, including **Chacchoben, Ichpaatun, Chichmoul, Tupak, Chacmool, and Los Limones**. All are minor archaeological sites off the main track but in the middle of the historical area where the Chan Santa Cruz Indians held court for so many years.

BACALAR

Thirty-eight km north of Chetumal (on Hwy. 307) lie the beautiful, multihued **Las Lagunas de Siete Colores** ("The Lagoons of Seven Colors"). Bacalar, complete with 17th-century Fort San Felipe, is a small town founded by the Spanish for protection against the bands of pirates and Maya that regularly raided the area. Today, part of the fort has a diminutive museum housing metal arms used in the 17th and 18th centuries. A token assortment of memorabilia recalls history of the area. The stone construction has been restored, and cannons are still posted along the balustrades overlooking beautiful Bacalar Lagoon. The museum, open daily except holidays, has a small entry fee.

Accommodations

Close by, built into the side of a hill overlooking the colorful Bacalar Lagoon, is **Hotel Laguna,** moderately priced, with clean rooms and private baths. Rooms each have a fan and a view of the sea. The dining room serves tasty Mexican food at moderate prices. Special touches make it an out-of-the-ordinary stopover: local shells decorate walls and ceilings, and ornate fences are neatly painted in white and green. A small pool (filled only during high season) and outdoor bar look out across the unusually hued Lagunas de Siete Colores. A diving board and ladder make swimming convenient in the lagoons' sometimes blue, sometimes purple, sometimes red water; fishing is permitted, and you can barbecue your catch on the grounds. Rate is about US$45 d. Ask about a bungalow including kitchen facilities. Reserve in advance during the tourist season and holidays. To find the hotel, turn left off Bacalar's main street and follow the shore south. For reservations, call (983) 2-3517 in Chetumal, (99) 27-1304 in Mérida; or write to Av. Bugambilias #316, Chetumal, Quintana Roo. Allow plenty of time for the mail to reach its destination.

Close by is the **Laguna Milagros Trailer Park,** with tent camping also permitted, about US$5 pp. Restrooms, showers, sun shelters, narrow beach, small store, and open-air cafe combine to offer an exotic milieu on the edge of the lagoon.

Rancho Encantado is 56 km north of Chetumal (200 miles south of Cancún), an enchanting small resort on the edge of Bacalar Lagoon. Specializing in laid-back, relaxing vacations, this mini-resort includes six *casitas* built with native hardwoods and Mexican tile and sits in a lush Eden of tropical shrubs, coco palms, and fruit trees—all just a few steps from the lagoon shore. Each unit contains a small sitting room, ceiling fan, convenience kitchen/dining room, bathroom, stove, refrigerator, and deck with a view of the garden or lagoon. A 12-meter palapa-roofed structure is the social center of the resort. Here visitors enjoy a tropical buffet breakfast and candlelit dinner, both included in the room rate. Rates (including Mexico's 10% tax) are US$110 d Nov.-April and US$88 d May-October.

Here, you can be as vigorous as you desire with a variety of activities. The archaeology buff has the rarely visited **Kohunlich** Maya site with

Rancho Encantado

its giant masks, as well as several undeveloped sites across the border in northern Belize. Take an excursion through the Quintana Roo savannah to tour Mexico's southern Caribbean coastline, or plan a scuba trip to the Caribbean's **Chinchorro Banks.** Rancho Encantado offers a variety of sporting equipment. Ask about the private villa with three bedrooms, 2.5 baths, and private dock located on the waterfront a short distance from Rancho Encantado.

Chetumal is the nearest airport, although the Corozal, Belize airport is only a 30-minute taxi ride away. Car rentals are available through Hertz at Hotel los Cocos in Chetumal. For reservations call (800) 221-6509; in Mexico fax (983) 8-04-27; or write Box 1644, Taos, New Mexico 87571.

CHETUMAL AND VICINITY

Chetumal, a good base for the many sights in the southern section of Quintana Roo, is also the gateway to Belize. The capital of this young state, Chetumal is without the bikini-clad, touristy crowds of the north and presents the businesslike atmosphere of a growing metropolis. A 10-minute walk takes you from the marketplace and most of the hotels to the waterfront. Modern sculpted monuments stand along a breezy promenade that skirts the broad crescent of bay. Also explore the back streets, where worn wooden buildings still have a Central American/Caribbean look. The largest building in town—white, three stories, close to the waterfront—houses most of the government offices.

Wide, tree-lined avenues and clean sidewalks front dozens of small variety shops. The city has been a free port for many years and as a result has attracted a plethora of tiny shops selling a strange conglomeration of plastic toys, small appliances, exotic perfumes (maybe authentic?), famous-label clothes (ditto), and imported foodstuffs. But Chetumal's days as a duty-free port are limited, and as export goods flood the country the demand has decreased for such exotic wares. Chetumal's sales tax, once far lower than in the rest of the country, is now 10%, and Mexicans from other states have little reason to shop here. The population is a handsome mixture of many races, including Caribe, Spanish, Maya, and English. Schools are prominently scattered around the town.

Climate
Chetumal is hot and sticky. Though sea breezes help, humidity can make the air terribly uncomfortable. High temperatures in August average 95° F (37° C), in Dec. 85° F (30° C). In the last 34 years, three destructive hurricanes have attacked the Mexican Caribbean coast, and Hurricane Janet all but destroyed Chetumal in 1955. Not something to be too concerned about though—these devastating blows are infrequent. The most comfortable time to visit is the dry season Nov.-April.

Flora And Fauna
Chetumal is noted for its hardwood trees, such as mahogany and rosewood. (Abundance of wood explains the difference in rural housing between the north and south ends of the Peninsula. Small houses in the south are built mostly of milled board, some with thatch roofs; structures with circular walls of slender saplings set

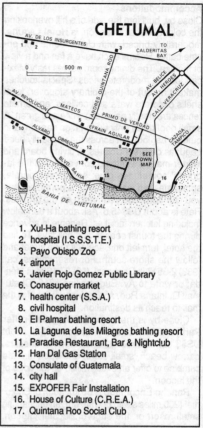

CHETUMAL

1. Xul-Ha bathing resort
2. hospital (I.S.S.S.T.E.)
3. Payo Obispo Zoo
4. airport
5. Javier Rojo Gomez Public Library
6. Conasuper market
7. health center (S.S.A.)
8. civil hospital
9. El Palmar bathing resort
10. La Laguna de las Milagros bathing resort
11. Paradise Restaurant, Bar & Nightclub
12. Han Dal Gas Station
13. Consulate of Guatemala
14. city hall
15. EXPOFER Fair Installation
16. House of Culture (C.R.E.A.)
17. Quintana Roo Social Club

© MOON PUBLICATIONS, INC.

close together are still common in the north.) Copious rainfall in the Chetumal area creates dense jungle with vine-covered trees, broadleafed plants, ferns, and colorful blossoms. Orchids grow liberally on the tallest trees. Deer and javelina roam the forests.

Calderitas Bay
On Av. Héroes eight km north of the city is Calderitas Bay, a breezy area for picnicking, camping, and RVing. The trailer park is one of the few in the state that provides complete hookups for RVs, including a dump station and clean showers, toilets, and washing facilities. Right on the water's edge, the spotless camp is in a parklike setting fringed with cooling palm trees. Even amateur divers will

giant masks of Kohunlich

find exotic shells, and the fishing is great. Nearby public beaches have palapa shelters which are normally tranquil, but on holidays they're crowded with sun- and fun-seekers.

Isla Tamalcas

Tiny Isla Tamalcas, two km off the shore of Calderitas, is the home of the primitive *capybara*. This largest of all rodents can reach a length of over a meter and weigh up to 50 kilograms; it's found in few other places in the world. The animal is covered with reddish yellowish brown coarse hair, resembles a small pig or large guinea pig, has partially webbed toes, and loves to swim. It's referred to by the locals as a water pig and is a favorite food of the jaguar. Isla Tamalcas is easily accessible from Calderitas Beach.

Kohunlich

Sixty-seven km west of Chetumal on Hwy. 186, turn left and drive eight km on a good side road to this unique Maya site. The construction last-ed from the Late Preclassic (about A.D. 100-200) through the Classic (A.D. 600-900) periods. Though not totally restored nor nearly as grand as Chichén Itzá or Uxmal, Kohunlich is worth the trip if only to visit the exotic **Temple of the Masks,** dedicated to the Maya sun god. The stone pyramid is under an unlikely thatch roof (to prevent further deterioration from the weather), and unique gigantic stucco masks stand two to three meters tall. The temple, though not extremely tall as pyramids go, still presents a moderate climb. Wander through the jungle site and you can find 200 structures or uncovered mounds from the same era as Palenque. Many carved stelae are scattered throughout the surrounding forest.

The stucco god-masks that line the steps of Kohunlich's main pyramid are obviously influenced by nearby Late Preclassic sites like El Mirador and Nakb in Guatemala's nearby Petén jungle. Kohunlich was discovered by looters in 1967, but the Mexican government was able to seize the site before they stole all the god-masks.

The first buildings you encounter upon entering the site are those clustered around the Acropolis Plaza. The largest of these is the Acropolis itself, which has several Río Bec-style rooms at the top, probably indicating the last stage of occupation. The earlier Temple of the Masks stands about 100 meters to the east. The famous masks, at least some of which represent the sun god, are well preserved because another structure was built over the original pyramid.

Walking through luxuriant foliage, you'll discover a green world. Note orchids in the tops of trees plus small colorful wildflowers, lacy ferns, and lizards that share cracks and crevices in moldy stone wails covered with velvety moss. The relatively unknown site attracts few tourists. The absence of trinket sellers and soft-drink stands leaves the visitor feeling that he or she is the first to stumble on the haunting masks with their star-incised eyes, mustaches (or are they serpents?), and nose plugs—features extremely different from carvings found at other Maya sites. The site is well cleared, and when we last visited, archaeologists from INAH were excavating a burial mound. Like most archaeological zones, Kohunlich is fenced and open 8 a.m.-5 p.m.; admission is US$3.50. Camping is not allowed within the grounds, but you may see a tent or two outside the entrance.

Kohunlich is an easy day-trip from Chetumal or Bacalar; in Chetumal check with travel agencies or your hotel for information about organized tours. **Viajes Calderitas** runs a variety of tours to Kohunlich and the nearby ruins at Xpujil, Becán, and Chicanná in the state of Campeche. The agency also offers a coastal tour to Laguna Bacalar and Akumal, auto rentals, and other services. For information contact them at Hotel los Cocos, tel. (983) 2-2540, fax 1-2006.

Tres Garantías

One of southern Quintana Roo's most impressive attempts at combining tourism and ecology is taking place at the *ejidos* in the low jungle between Campeche and Kohunlich. This area, though not virgin, is one of the state's least developed. The residents of Tres Garantías *ejido* are developing an eco-tourism project on the 45,000 hectares surrounding their settlement, including hiking trails and overnight accommodations at their **Campamento La Piramide.** Gearing their tours to groups of four to eight, the organizers introduce their clients to the *ejido* lifestyle and take them hiking on trails in the area to spot birds and other wildlife. Guests spend the night in a palapa-roof cabana raised on stilts. The well-constructed cabana has hammock hooks and sleeping platforms, but no restroom yet, and is surrounded by jungle where tapirs and other creatures roam. Only sturdy screens separate you from the outdoors, giving a true sense of being in the wilderness. It's a great chance to really experience the local lifestyle with few tourism trappings. Villagers prepare the meals for their guests, but you may want to bring along drinking water and snacks. The program was just getting underway when we visited. For more information check with the tourist office in Chetumal or call (983) 2-5232, fax (983) 2-9802.

Cenote Azul

Thirty-four km north of Chetumal (on Hwy. 307) is a circular cenote, 61.5 meters deep and 185 meters across, filled with brilliant blue water. This is a spectacular place to stop for a swim, lunch at the outdoor restaurant, or just have a cold drink. Children in the area may request an admission fee to visit Cenote Azul and will make quite a fuss until you give them a few pesos. In quite a few remote areas, locals (most of whom

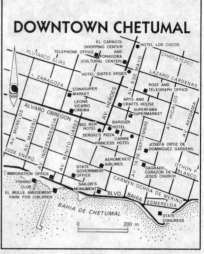

live at a subsistence level) are beginning to seek their share of the tourist dollar.

Nearby Ruins

The Maya archaeological sites of **Becán, Xpujil,** and **Chicanná** in the state of Campeche are within an hour's drive of Kohunlich. To get to Becán from Kohunlich, continue west on Hwy. 186 for about 60 km; the other sites are in the same area. (See "Campeche" for sites and accommodations.)

CHETUMAL PRACTICALITIES

Accommodations

Although Chetumal is not considered a tourist resort, its status as the capital of the state and its location on the Belize border make it a busy stopover for both Mexicans and Belizeans. If traveling without reservations, arrive as early in the day as possible to have your choice of hotel rooms. During the holiday season it's wise to reserve in advance. Most of the hotels listed are within walking distance of the marketplace, downtown shops, and waterfront.

Higher Priced: Chetumal doesn't have a true luxury hotel. The **Hotel los Cocos** (formerly the Del Prado), Av. Héroes #134 at Calle Chapultepec, tel. (983) 2-0544, fax 2-0920, comes closest with pleasant rooms, cleanliness, a/c, pretty garden, and large clean swimming pool. There is also a bar with evening disco music and a quiet dining room with a friendly staff serving a varied menu. One of the best travel agencies in Chetumal is located in the lobby, and car rentals are available. Hotel rates start at about US$55 d in the low season, US$70 in the high season. The **Hotel Continental-Caribe,** Av. Héroes #171, tel. 2-1100, advertises itself as a luxury hotel (perhaps in the past it was); has a/c, restaurant, pool, bar with evening entertainment. Though the rooms are clean, the overall appearance is not. Prices range from about US$48. **Hotel Suites Arges,** Av. Lázaro Cárdenas #212, tel. 2-9525, fax 2-9414, was new on the scene in 1993, and has 24 junior suites with cable TV and sitting areas, guarded parking lot, and a travel agency, but no pool. Rates start at US$45 d.

Moderate To Budget: The moderately priced hotels for the most part are friendly (some clean, some not; look before you pay) and usually fan-cooled; some have a/c, all have hot water. Prices range US$24-35 d. **Hotel Marlon,** Av. Juárez #87, tel. (983) 2-8411, fax 2-1065, is a newish hotel with a very pleasant staff. Rooms are comfortable and clean, with a/c, hot water, telephone, and color TV. There's a pool, a good restaurant, and the **Marquis,** a neat little piano bar. Rates start at about US$25 s, US$29 d. **Hotel Principe,** Av. Niños Héroes #326, tel. 2-4799, fax 2-5191, offers ample rooms, a/c, hot water, a pleasant courtyard, and **El Arlequin** restaurant. Rates are US$30 s, US$35 d. **El Marqués Hotel** is at Av. Lázaro Cárdenas #121, tel. 2-2888. Rooms come with servi-bar, private bathroom, and hot water; rate is US$30. **Restaurante El Marqués** is on the premises.

Hotel Caribe Princess, Av. Alvaro Obregón #168, tel. 2-0520, is very clean and has a/c, hot water, and TV. A real budget spot is **Hotel Jacaranda,** Av. Alvaro Obregón #201, tel. 2-1455. Rooms with fan or a/c are simple and cheap; rates start at about US$18. Very reasonable food available at their simple cafe.

Food

The nicest restaurant we've found in Chetumal, **Emiliano's,** Av. San Salvador #557 at Calle 9, tel. (983) 7-0267, is easily comparable to the best seafood houses in Cancún. For an all-out

*children's parade on the
first day of spring, Chetumal*

feast start with the shrimp or conch pate, followed by *empanadas* filled with baby shark, then the freshest ceviche, *pulpo en su tinto,* and don't miss the *chiles rellenos* stuffed with seafood. It's the perfect spot for a long lunch or celebratory dinner. A three-course meal will run about US$20-30, though you can get by much cheaper by ordering a heaping platter of *arroz a la marinera,* rice mixed with seafood, for about US$8. Open for lunch and dinner.

It's easy to find a cafe to fit every budget in Chetumal. Walk down the street to Av. Alvaro Obregón for several fast-food cafes. On the same street, for seafood try **El Pez Vela;** for chicken go to **Pollos Sinaloa.** On the corner of Av. Efrain Aguilar and Revolución is **Los Pozos,** a regional cafe serving typical Yucatecan dishes. Great tacos at **El Taco Loco** at Morelos #87, open 6 a.m.-3 p.m.; **Sergio's Pizza** on Obregón and Cinco de Mayo is good. **Mandinga** serves good seafood on Belize St.; usually busy, reasonable prices. **El Grill** at Hotel los Cocos is great for a special night out. The **public market** has just about everything you could need; three **Conasuper** markets can provide the rest.

Sports

A yearly event in Chetumal is the auto road race. Open to drivers from all over the globe, it's gaining prominence in the racing world. This event takes place in December, and hotel reservations should be made well in advance.

A popular sport in both Chetumal Bay and Bacalar Lagoon is sailboarding. State competitions are held in both areas yearly. What a great place to fly across the sea! Make reservations early, since many others will have the same idea. For more information, write to the Secretaría de Turismo, Palacio de Gobierno #20, Chetumal, Quintana Roc 77500, Mexico.

Services

The **post office** is on Calle 2A. You can send a telegram from **Telégrafos Nacionales,** Av. Cinco de Mayo. For any **medical** emergency, there are several hospitals and clinics. Ask at your hotel for a doctor who speaks English. One **pharmacy** is at Carmen Ochoa de Merino and Héroes, tel. (983) 2-0162. Four **gasoline stations** and at least seven **mechanics** are in town. Several **banks** will cash traveler's checks Mon.-Sat. 9 a.m.-1 p.m. First- and second-class buses use the new bus station on the outskirts of town. **Viajes Calderitas** in Hotel los Cocos is a great source of information on flights, tours, and rental cars, tel. 2-2540, fax 2-2006.

CHETUMAL TRANSPORT

By Air

Chetumal's small modern airport still has only a few flights each day. Rental car offices and the cafe seem to be open only when flights are expected.

An airport van provides transportation to hotels or downtown. Taesa has daily flights from Chetumal to Cancún, Mexico City and Mérida; Aeromexico, Mexicana, and Aviacsa serve the city less frequently.

Check with Bonanza and Aerocaribe for flights in and out of Chetumal.

By Bus

Buses from points all over Mexico arrive throughout the day at the new, modern Chetumal bus station located on the highway, 20 blocks south of town, at Salvador Novo #179. Taxis to town are available from the station. With the expanding road system, bus travel is becoming more versatile and is still the most inexpensive public transportation to the Quintana Roo coast.

Buses to Chetumal arrive from Mérida (5.5 hours) and Mexico City (22 hours), plus make frequent trips from Cancún and Campeche. Chetumal is part of the loop between Campeche, Cancún, and Mérida. Check with a travel agent for pickup point in Chetumal, usually at one of the hotels. Fares and schedules change regularly. To Cancún costs about US$30. Ask about the newish **Omnibus Caribe Express,** with deluxe service to Cancún and Mérida, tel. (983) 2-7889. New express buses are appearing in many parts of Mexico. They are modern and clean, with bathrooms, a/c, and airline-type seats. Each bus has an attendant who will serve you coffee and cookies, and some have earphones for music; these are the 747s of the road.

Frequent bus service into Belize is offered by the **Batty Bus** or the **Venus Bus,** priced at US$1-4, depending on whether or not you take an express. You will have to get off the bus when you go across the border into Belize. Have your passport handy because sometimes this takes a while.

By Car

A good paved road connects Mérida, Campeche, Villahermosa, and Francisco Escarcega with Chetumal; Hwy. 307 links all of the Quintana Roo coastal cities. There's little traffic, and gas stations are well spaced if you top off at each one. Car rentals are not yet available at the Chetumal airport; go to the Hotel los Cocos for National. Check out deals with unlimited kilometers, since most places you'll want to visit are well spread out. If you're driving, watch out for "no left turn" signs!

CROSSING INTO BELIZE

Chetumal, Mexico, is a bridge away from the country of Belize. For the explorer, the archaeology buff, the diver, or the curious, it's easy to take a side trip into what was formerly British Honduras. The Río Hondo River forms a natural border between Quintana Roo and Belize. Chetumal is the only land link between the two countries, from which Belize is easily reached by Batty or Venus bus or taxi. For someone who is close to the Mexican-Belize border, knows the ropes, and takes visitors back and forth across the border all the time, call (in Belize) **Henry Menzies Travel and Tours,** tel. (42) 2725; Box 210, Corozal Town, Belize, C.A. Henry is a good, honest guide/driver and will take you anywhere in Belize. There's rarely a problem crossing the border as long as you show a valid passport. If you look poor you'll be asked to show money or proof of onward travel. If driving you must buy insurance with Belizean dollars; moneychangers are waiting for you as you cross the border. The rates seem comparable to bank rates; however, you always take a slight risk when you buy local money from a street vendor. U.S. citizens and *most* others don't need visas, but citizens of a few countries do; check with your embassy before leaving home. Even Guatemala is now represented in Belize.

Tour Group
If you have never visited Belize, you may find the first time easier with a tour guide who knows his or her way around the country. Many are available from the States and Canada. **International Expeditions,** a company out of Alabama, offers several good trips with small groups, and each expedition is designed for your particular interest. For the nature lover an 11-day **Naturalist Quest** expedition offers all transportation and lodging, and most important, is led by a knowledgeable naturalist who takes the group into the beautiful forests and state reserves created to save the treasures of Belize, including the **Jaguar Sanctuary** and the **Howler Monkey Sanctuary.** Another expedition visits most of the country's Maya archaeological sites with a guide who knows how to bring to life the story of the Maya. Those interested in the offshore cayes will find a trip to Belize's islands a relaxing way to investigate the rich sealife of the Belize Reef. Ask about trips to nearby Costa Rica. For more information contact **International Expeditions,** One Environs Park, Helena, AL 35080, tel. (800) 633-4734 or (205) 428-1700. For details about traveling in Belize, including accommodations, restaurants, attractions, diving, and everything else you ever wanted to know about the country, buy *Belize Handbook,* another of my books published by Moon Publications (see the back of this book).

a camping tour

ESCORTED TRIPS TO THE YUCATAN PENINSULA

Vagabonders is the travel division of the **Turquoise Reef Group.** The Vagabonders' **Dive Bundle** includes seven nights and eight days. A diver's surf-and-turf splurge on the Turquoise Reef includes lodging, meals, four two-tank dive days, and more. Another special trip is called the **Vagabonder's Whole Enchilada,** 14 nights and 15 days making a circle of three countries of the Maya world (Belize, Mexico, and Guatemala) with relaxing intervals on the beaches of the Caribbean. Includes lodging, meals, guides, transportation, and more. Some of these trips are offered to guests already at a Turquoise Reef Resort in the state of Quintana Roo and originate from one of three locations along Mexico's Caribbean coast: Kai Luum, Capitán Lafitte, or Shangri-La Caribe. The **Vagabonder's Potpourri** is a five-night/six-day trip that gives the traveler an intimate look at the Yucatán Peninsula, with its Maya treasures, and a taste of village and city life. This journey includes Mérida, Uxmal, Labná, Sayil, Kabah, Chichén Itzá, Valladolid, Cobá, Tulúm, and Xelha. For more information contact the Vagabonders, Box 2664, Evergreen, CO 80439, tel. (303) 674-9615 or (800) 538-6802.

Mayaland Tours is a local travel agency in Mérida, offering outstanding packages; contact them from the States at (800) 235-4079 or in Mérida (ask for Linda) at Avenida Colón #502, Mérida, Yucatán 97000, Mexico.

Far Horizons Cultural Discovery Trips originate in Miami, Dallas, or Los Angeles. First stop is the **Museum of Anthropology** in Mexico City, where an overview of Maya prehistoric culture will be explained; from there a visit to Teotihuacán will illustrate how that ancient city heavily influenced Maya art and architecture. Other areas of Maya culture visited include Palenque, Tulúm, Cobá, Edzná, Labná, Sayil, Kabah, Uxmal, Río Bec, and Chichén Itzá. For more information write or call Far Horizons, Box 91900, Albequerque, New Mexico 87199; from the U.S. and Canada tel. (800) 552-4575.

Tropical Adventures offers a complete dive package in Isla Cozumel and other Caribbean destinations. The package includes seven nights at one of the top oceanfront resorts (choices include budget lodgings for less), boat diving, beach buffet lunches on all full-day dives, boats, guides, tanks, weights, belts, backpacks, and unlimited air for shore diving. Cozumel is considered a world-class dive site, plus offers the bonus of a multitude of archaeological sights to see on land. Low airfares available through Tropical Adventures. For more information call or write Tropical Adventures, 170 Denny Way, Seattle, WA 98109, tel. (800) 247-3483 or (206) 441-3483, fax (206) 441-5431.

Honeymoon time is anytime and the **Honeymoon Of Your Dreams Plus** is waiting at the Cancún Sheraton Resort and Towers. This special package includes a luxury suite with terrace and private jacuzzi, daily breakfast in your room or in the restaurant, domestic champagne, welcome drink, free day or night tennis, and free use of the fitness center. Three nights and four days, US$539 per couple. Another choice at the same hotel is the **Honeymoon Down Mexico Way** in the new deluxe **Towers,** where guests will enjoy a Caribbean view, welcome drink, daily continental breakfast in the lounge, bottle of domestic champagne, free day and night tennis, and complimentary use of the fitness center, along with very special butler service; three nights, four days, US$369 per couple.

Underwater Adventure Tours offers seven-night trips to Cozumel. Accommodations are at **La Ceiba** beachfront hotel and include daily dive/boat trips to Palancar Reef and vicinity, unlimited air for offshore diving, tanks, backpacks, and weights. A five-night trip is also available which includes daily breakfast, standard accommodations, four boat trips to Palancar Reef and vicinity, air, equipment, and 15% tax. For more information call or write Underwater Adventure Tours, 732 W. Fullerton, Chicago, IL 60614, tel. (800) 621-1274.

KATHY ESCOVEDA SANDERS

CHICHEN ITZA AND SURROUNDING ARCHAEOLOGICAL ZONES

From Cancún, Cozumel, Playa del Carmen, and Akumal, many travel agencies and hotels offer day-trips to outstanding pre-Columbian Maya sites nearby, and some *not* so nearby. Look into the different options. In some cases, a day-trip just isn't enough time to really absorb what you're seeing. However, it may be just what you are looking for. If you want to explore further, rent a car, take a local bus (check with the hotel concierge), or hire a car and driver for two or three days (local travel agencies can recommend someone).

CHICHEN ITZA AND VICINITY

Chichén Itzá is one of the finest Maya archaeological sites in the northern part of the Peninsula. Largely restored, Chichén Itzá is about a three-hour drive from Cancún and about two hours from Mérida—a favored destination of those fascinated with Maya culture. Chichén Itzá is a mingling of two distant cultures: ancient Maya and later-arriving Toltecs. Though there appears to be differences of opinion rising about the role of the Toltecs, scientists theorize that the oldest buildings at Chichén Itzá were good examples of Late Classic Maya construction from the 5th century to the 1100s, that the Toltecs invaded and then ruled Chichén Itzá for 200 years, and that they built new structures and added to many already in place—all bearing a remarkable similarity to those in the ancient Toltec capital of Tollan (today called Tula), 1200 km away in the state of Hidalgo.

It was believed that two centuries of mingling cultures added a new dimension to 800 years of Maya history. The carvings found on buildings of different eras vary between the rain god Chac (early Maya) to the cult of the feathered serpent (late Mexicanized Maya).

Theories

Much of the debate centers around the two distinct styles of architecture represented at the site—now known as "Old Chichén" and "New Chichén"—and whether a culture other than the indigenous Maya inhabited the city at some time.

The traditional theory formulated by Ralph Roys holds that in the 9th century, Chichén Itzá was a typical Late Classic city of the northern region, with Puuc-influenced architecture and featuring hieroglyphs to commemorate important political events. The remnants of this era may be seen in structures like the Nunnery and the Akab Dzib in the "Old Chichén" part of the site. During the 10th century, when Yucatán was embroiled in Terminal Classic wars and political strife, a king named Topiltzin Quetzalcoatl in the far-off Toltec capital of Tula (just north of Mexico City) was expelled from his realm after a power struggle with the warrior caste. He was last seen departing from the Gulf coast on a raft of serpents headings west.

In A.D. 987, the same year as his departure, *The Books of Chilam Balam* recorded the arrival on Yucatán's shores of a king named Kukulcán, identifying him, like Tolpiltzin Quetzalcoatl, with the Feathered Serpent. Kukulcán gathered an army that defeated the Puuc city-states of northwestern Yucatán and made Chichén Itzá his capital, rebuilding it in a mixed Toltec-Maya style. These Toltec traits include reclining *chac mool* figures, warrior columns, skull platforms, feathered serpents, and the cult of Tlaloc. As in Tula, hieroglyphs were absent from the art. Reliefs showed bloody battle scenes celebrating the Toltec victories. After dominating northern Yucatán for over two centuries, Chichén Itzá was abandoned in 1224, perhaps after an invasion.

Most researchers concur that the Toltecs never ruled at Chichén Itzá. The people who built the "Old Chichén" and the "New Chichén" were the same: Maya. According to one strain of this theory, Chichén Itzá was first settled by the Itzá, a tribe of Putún Maya seafarers who came from the west. In the 9th century, they fought and defeated the Puuc cities centered around Uxmal and the eastern power of Cobá and carved out a territory in central Yucatán. The Itzá gave the city its current name, "The Well of the Itza." They settled around the sacred cenote and built monuments to commemorate their victories and legitimize their rule. The sacred cenote's depths received not only human sacrifices (male and female, adults, and children) but offerings from throughout Mesoamerica until early in our own century. An internal revolt toppled the Itzá in the late 15th century, and Chichén Itzá was abandoned for good.

The city-state of Chichén was ruled by a Putún-Maya-style joint government. In other Maya cities, hieroglyphs are always associated with a sole ruler who needed to legitimize his claim to power; they are absent at Chichén Itzá, because the form of government is different, not because they were Toltecs. The Putún Maya were far-ranging traders and probably built the central Mexican cities of Cacaxtla and Xochicalco, thus Chichén's central Mexican connection. There was a Toltec influence, but Chichén Itzá probably influenced Tula more than the other way around. Perhaps the traits we regard as definitively Toltec—*chac mools,* warriors columns, etc.—actually came from Yucatán. It is certain that Chichén Itzá was a more grandiose "Toltec" city than Tula itself.

Later At Chichén Itzá

Though Chichén Itzá was most likely abandoned toward the end of the 13th century, Maya were still making pilgrimages to the sacred site when Montejo the Younger, the Spaniard who played a role in ultimately subjugating the Maya, settled his troops among the ruins of Chichén Itzá in 1533. Although they placed a cannon on top of the pyramid of Kukulcán, the Spaniards were unable at that time to conquer the elusive Indians, and after a year left Chichén Itzá for the coast. The pilgrimages continued.

Today, a different breed of pilgrim comes to Chichén Itzá from all over the world to walk in the footsteps of great rulers, courageous ball players, mysterious priests, and simple peasants. Chichén Itzá is considered one of the most orderly archaeological sites on the Peninsula. Restoration, begun in 1923, continued steadily for 20 years. After a hiatus, workers are again un-

Temple of the Warriors

covering and reconstructing buildings on the site, and there are enough unexcavated mounds to support continued exploration for many years.

Travel Tips

You can easily walk the 10-square-km grounds. Taking two days is a relaxing way to do it, but for those with less time it can be done in a day—not as thoroughly, perhaps, but you will come away with a good idea of what Chichén Itzá is about. Wear walking shoes for this entire expedition: climbing around in sandals can be uncomfortable and unsafe. For some, a short walk around the grounds is enough to say they've "been there." For a ruins nut, however, the best advice is to spend the night either at a hotel adjacent to the ruins, where you can be up and on the grounds as soon as the ticket taker is there (usually 8 a.m.), or at the nearby town of Piste with a good shot at getting to the site as early as you wish. Arrive early to take advantage of the weather (it's much cooler in the early hours) and the absence of the crowds that arrive later in tour buses. With two days, you can study these archaeological masterpieces at your leisure, have a chance to climb at your own pace, and be there at the odd hours when the inner chambers open (only for short periods each day). This also allows time to return to your hotel for a leisurely lunch (maybe

a swim), a short siesta, and an afternoon return visit (free with your ticket).

The ruins are open daily 8 a.m.-5 p.m., although some of the structures have special hours (posted on the buildings, or ask at the entrance). Admission is US$6.50 pp, US$8.50 additional if you bring in a video camera, plus a small fee to use the parking lot. The visitor center offers clean restrooms, cafe, small museum, auditorium (where short, informative films are shown), bookstore, gift shop, and information center.

SIGHTS

The large parklike area is easy to stroll. Eighteen structures have been excavated, many of them restored. The uses for these buildings are not truly understood. Archaeologists can only study and guess from the few "real" facts that have been found. Near the sacred cenote a snack bar sells cold drinks, light snacks, postcards, and a few curios. A clean restroom is available at the back of the palapa building.

Temple Of The Warriors

On a three-tiered platform, the Temple of the Warriors stands next to the impressive **Group of a Thousand Columns**—reminiscent of Egypt's

Kukulcán is also known as El Castillo.

Karnak. The number of columns actually gets closer to 1,000 each year, as archaeologists continue to reconstruct. Many of the square and circular stone columns have carvings still in excellent condition. In 1926, during restoration, a subtemple found underneath was named **Chacmool Temple.** The former color on the columns of the inner structure is still slightly visible. Close to the Thousand Columns on the east side of the plaza is a cleverly constructed sweat house with an oven and a channel under the floor to carry off the water thrown against the hot stones. Indian sweat houses are a combination religious and health-giving experience still used today throughout North America. Archaeologists are working behind this area, uncovering structures buried by jungle mounds. Within this area is the Market with a rectangular courtyard surrounded by columns. Some speculate this courtyard was covered with palm thatch and used as a marketplace.

The Platforms
Strolling the grounds, you'll find the **Platform of Venus** and **Platform of Tigers and Eagles.** The flat, square structures, each with low stairways on all four sides, were used for ritual music and dancing, and, according to Diego de Landa (infamous 16th-century Franciscan bishop), farce and comedy were presented for the pleasure of the public.

Temple Of The Bearded Man
At the north end of the ball court sits the handsome Temple of the Bearded Man. Two graceful columns frame the entrance to a small temple with the remains of decorations depicting birds, trees, flowers, and the earth monster. It's doubtful whether anyone will ever know if the unusual acoustics here were used specifically for some unknown display of histrionics, or if it's accidental that standing in the temple you can speak in a low voice and be heard a good distance down the playing field, well beyond what is normal (much like in the dome of St. Peter's Cathedral in Rome). Was this the "dugout" from which the coach whispered signals to his players downfield? Some believe that only the upper class actually watched the game, and that the masses remained outside the walls and listened.

Great Ball Court
Of several ball courts at Chichén Itzá (some archaeologists say nine), the most impressive is the Great Ball Court, the largest found yet in Mesoamerica. On this field, life-and-death games were played with a 12-pound hard rubber ball, in the tradition of the Roman Colosseum. The playing field is 135 meters by 65 meters, with two eight-meter-high walls running parallel to each other on either side of the playing field.

1. Playa del Carmen Beach; **2.** Xelha Lagoon; **3.** Club de Maya, Puerto Aventuras;
4. Chemuyil; **5.** Kailuum Beach

1. Puerto Aventuras; **2.** Roy Blom enjoying a "long" beer; **3.** Carlos and Charlies Cafe, Puerto Aventuras

On these walls note the reliefs that depict the ball game and sacrifices. The players were obliged to hit the ball into carved stone rings embedded in the vertical walls seven meters above the ground using only their elbows, wrists, or hips. The heavy padding they wore indicates the game was dangerous; it was also difficult and often lasted for hours. (In Diego de Landa's book, written in the late 1600s, he mentions in two different places, "The Indians wore padding made of cotton with salt padding.") The winners were awarded jewelry and clothing from the audience. The losers lost more than jewelry and valuables, according to the carved panels on the site—they lost their heads to the winning captain! Another theory is that the *winners*, too, were granted the "privilege" of losing their heads.

Temple Of The Jaguar

On the southeast corner of the ball court, the upper temple was constructed A.D. 800-1050. To get there you must climb a steep stairway at the south end of the platform. Two large serpent columns, with their rattlers high in the air, frame the opening to the temple. The inside of the room is decorated with a variety of carvings and (almost visible) remnants of what must have been colorful murals.

Sacred Cenote

Today's adventurer can sit in the shade of a palapa terrace and enjoy a cold drink near the sacred cenote (say-NO-tay). This natural well is 300 meters north of Kukulcán. The roadway to the sacred well, an ancient *sacbe,* was constructed during the Classic period. The large well, about 20 meters in diameter, with walls 20 meters above the surface of the water (34 meters deep), is where the rain god Chac supposedly lived; to con him into producing rain, sacrifices of children and young adults were made, evidenced by human bones found here. On the edge of the cenote is a ruined sweat bath, probably used for purification rituals before sacrificial ceremonies.

In 1885, Edward Thompson was appointed United States consul in nearby Mérida. A young writer greatly interested in the archaeological zones surrounding Mérida, he eventually settled in Chichén Itzá and acquired the entire area, including an old hacienda (for only US$75). For many years he had studied Diego de Landa's

account of human sacrifice still going on at the time of the Spanish conquest. Stories of young virgins and valuable belongings thrown into the well at times of drought, over hundreds of years convinced him there was treasure buried in the muddy cenote bottom. During 1903-07, with the help of Harvard's Peabody Museum, he supervised the first organized dive into the well. Fewer than 50 skeletons were found, mostly those of children, male and female. Precious objects of jade, gold, copper, plus stone items with tremendous archaeological value, were also dredged from the muddy water.

Thompson set off an international scandal when he shipped most of these important finds to the Peabody Museum by way of diplomatic pouch. He was asked to leave, and for years (1926-44) a lawsuit continued over the booty. Ironically, the Mexican court ruled in favor of Peabody Museum, claiming that the Mexican laws concerning archaeological material were inadequate. After the laws were toughened up, the Peabody Museum, in a gesture of friendliness, returned many (but not all) of the artifacts from Chichén Itzá's well of sacrifice.

The next large-scale exploration of the well was conducted in the 1960s, sponsored by the National Geographic Society with help from CEDAM (a Mexican organization of explorers and divers noted for having salvaged the Spanish ship *Mantanceros* in the Caribbean). As Thompson suspected before his untimely departure, there was much more treasure in the cenote to be salvaged. Hundreds of pieces (including gold, silver, obsidian, copper bells, carved bone, and other artifacts, plus a few more skeletons) were brought to the surface. In order to see in this well, thousands of gallons of chemicals (an unusual experiment by the Purex Co.) were successfully used to temporarily clarify the water. The chemicals, however, destroyed many of the blindfish and shrimp in the cenote.

Observatory

One of the most graceful structures at Chichén Itzá is the **Caracol,** a two-tiered observatory shaped like a snail, where advanced theories of the sun and moon were calculated by Maya astronomers. Part of the spiral stairway into the tower/observatory is closed to tourists in an effort to preserve the decaying building. The circular room is laid out with narrow window slits facing south, west, and toward the summer solstice and the equinoxes. The priests used celestial sightings to keep (accurate) track of time in their elaborate calendrical system.

Kukulcán

The most breathtaking place to view all of Chichén Itzá is from the top of Kukulcán, also called El Castillo. At 24 meters it's the tallest and most dramatic structure on the site. This imposing pyramid, built by the Maya on top of another, smaller pyramid, was probably constructed at the end of a 52-year cycle in thanksgiving to Maya gods for allowing the world to survive the elements—maybe even Halley's comet! Halley's swept by this part of the earth in A.D. 837 (and most recently in 1986); the construction of the second temple was in approximately A.D. 850.

Kukulcán was built according to strict astronomical guidelines. Giant serpent heads repose at the base of the stairs. There are four sides of 91 steps, with the platform on the top for a total of 365—one step for each day of the year. On 21/22 March and September (equinox days) between noon and 5 p.m., the sun casts an eerie shadow darkening all but one bright zigzag strip on the outside wall of the north staircase. This gives the appearance of a serpent slithering down the steep north-facing steps of the pyramid, giving life to the giant heads at the base. It seems to begin at the bottom in the spring and at the top in the fall. This was first noticed only a few decades ago. In the days when there were only a few people on the grounds watching, you could not only observe the serpent slithering down the steps, but also watch the shadow on the ground move toward the road to the sacred well—maybe looking for a sacrifice? Today the ground is covered with people. A visit during the dates of the equinox is a good time to observe the astronomical talents of the Maya, but be prepared for literally thousands of fellow watchers. Note: Some scientists have serious questions as to whether this was a deliberate effect of the Mayas or just a trick caused by recent reconstruction. Whichever, it's still fascinating to watch the eerie effect on those particular days!

Be sure to make the climb into the inner structure of Kukulcán where you'll see a red-painted, jade-studded sculpture of a jaguar, just as it

Chichén Caracol

was left by the Maya builders over a thousand years ago. Check the visiting hours since the inner chamber is not always open.

Others

The largest building on the grounds is the **Nunnery,** named by the Spaniards. From the looks of it and its many rooms, it was a palace of some sort built during the Classic period. **Tzompantli,** meaning "Wall of Skulls," is a platform decorated on all sides with carvings of skulls, anatomically correct but with eyes staring out of large sockets. This rather ghoulish structure also depicts an eagle eating a human heart. It is presumed that ritualistic music and dancing on this platform culminated in a sacrificial death for the victim, the head then left on display, perhaps with others already in place. It's estimated that the platform was built A.D. 1050-1200 after the intrusion of the Toltecs.

A much-damaged pyramid, **Tomb of the High Priest,** is undergoing complete reconstruction—the building is being taken apart piece by piece and then rebuilt. The ruin is intriguing because of its inner burial chamber. Sometimes referred to as **Osario** (Spanish for "Ossuary," a depository for bones of the dead), the pyramid at one time had four stairways on each side (like El Castillo) and a temple at the crest. From the top platform, a vertical passageway lined with rock leads to the base of this decayed mound. There, from a small opening, some stone steps lead into a cave about three meters deep. Seven tombs were discovered containing skeletons and the usual funeral trappings of important people, in addition to copper and jade artifacts. Archaeologists are working all around this area (commonly called "Old Chichén Itzá") and have several partially exposed ruins roped off. Work is expected to continue for several years and should result in significant findings about the Maya.

ACCOMMODATIONS

Only a few hotels are within walking distance of the ruins, all in the moderate price range; remember, most of the hotels add 10% government tax to the prices listed. **Hotel Mayaland** is a lovely colonial with 164 rooms, private baths, restaurant, bar, swimming pool, and tropical gardens. This old hotel has been around since the early 1930s and provides visitors with beauty and tranquility. A long, winding staircase from the lobby, ornate leaded glass windows in the original dining room, tile floors, tall ceilings, and overhead fans lend an exotic look.

In 1988, UNESCO declared Chichén Itzá the **Heritage of Humanity**. The Mayaland is located in the heart of this archaeological zone with over 100 acres of tropical fruit and flowering trees filled with unique species of birds. Many of the rooms have been renovated, with TVs and a/c added to those in the main building. There are 164 rooms, some Maya-type villas. Rates: about US$88-115 s or d, villas vary in price, two-bedroom Chac Mool Suite for up to four persons is about US$150, reservations suggested. These prices drop slightly in the summer. From the U.S. call Mayaland Resorts, tel. (800) 235-4079; ask about their package deals, including a family plan.

Hotel Hacienda Chichén Itzá contains original bungalows of the early archaeologists. The narrow-gauge railroad tracks used in the 1920s for transportation and hauling still go through the outlying hotel grounds. The old mule train is also still in its place, but not used today. This hotel has lots of history, plus private bathrooms, pool, dining room, and part of the rustic original hacienda. The hotel is usually closed 30 April-1 Nov., though the owners are considering keeping it open year-round. Rate is about US$87 d, reservations suggested; tel. (919) 24-2150; from the U.S. call (800) 223-4084.

Villa Arqueológica, owned by Club Med, is a pleasant hotel. "Almost" deluxe small rooms have private bath; plus shallow swimming pool, bar, covered patio, and dining room. The rooms are small though functional and some air-conditioners are noisy (listen to the air-conditioner in your room before you sign the register). But this hotel has a lighthearted ambience with a delightful garden and pool area, and the best restaurant on this side of the ruins. Don't forget to bring along your receipt, voucher, or any other communication that says you have reservations and have paid, because without it you could have a problem. This hotel has been known for

Hotel Mayaland

overbooking. Rates are about US$100; prices drop slightly in the summer. Reservations are suggested; from U.S. call (800) 258-2633.

Hotel Dolores Alba, 2.2 km east of the ruins, is comfortable, small, and clean, with swimming pool, dining room, and private baths; US$28 d. Free transport to the ruins available. Mailing address: Calle 63 #464, Mérida, Yucatán 97000, Mexico, tel. (99) 28-5650, fax 28-3163. Be sure to designate that you want a room in the Chichén Dolores Alba, since this address also takes reservations for its sister hotel, the Mérida Hotel Dolores Alba.

FOOD AND ENTERTAINMENT

The only restaurants within walking distance of the site are at the hotels. Check the hours since they're usually open for lunch only, 12:30-3 p.m. The sound and light show at the ruins was completely updated in 1993, with a new sound system and script and a computerized lighting system. The show is presented in English at 9 p.m., Spanish at 7 p.m.; French, Italian, German, and Maya versions may also be added. The fee is under US$4. Other than that there's no organized entertainment in Chichén Itzá. However, the guests of the nearby hotels are generally well-traveled people, many with exciting tales to tell. Sitting under the stars on a warm night with a cold *cerveza,* swapping adventure yarns, is a delightful way to spend an evening.

TRANSPORTATION

From Mérida, Cancún, Cozumel, Playa del Carmen, Akumal, and Puerto Aventuras, many travel agencies and hotels offer day-trips to outstanding pre-Columbian Maya sites nearby, and some not so nearby. Look into the different options. Though some travelers may think a day-trip isn't enough time to absorb the sights, it may be just what you are looking for. To see Chichén Itzá on your own, rent a car (see "Car Rental," in "Out And About"), take a local bus (check with the hotel concierge), or hire a car and driver for two or three days (local travel agencies can recommend someone).

Chichén Itzá lies adjacent to Hwy. 180, 121 km east of Mérida, 213 km west of Cancún, and 43 km west of Valladolid. If traveling by car you have many options. Newest is the eight-lane *autopista* between Cancún and Mérida, which has an exit in Piste; tolls from Mérida are about US$12, and about the same from Cancún. The regular roads to Chichén Itzá are in good condition, as long as you slow down for the *topes* (traffic bumps) found before and after every village and school. Hitchhiking at the right time of day will put you in view of many autos on Hwy. 180, but be at your destination before dark or you may spend the night on the roadside; there's little traffic on this road after sunset.

By Public Bus
Local buses leave for Piste from Cancún and Puerto Juárez (three-hour trip), also from Mérida (less than two hours). Ask about the return schedule.

By Plane
Small planes offer commuter service to Piste from Cancún, Cozumel, and Chetumal. Check with Aerocaribe, tel. (98) 84-1231 in Cancún, tel. (987) 2-0877 in Cozumel, for information and reservations. A sample price is around US$60 OW to Cancún.

Package Trips
For some, being independent and free to turn down any unexpected road is the only way to travel. However, others (maybe those who have never been to a foreign country) who don't wish to drive or take local buses, or who don't know how to go about investigating these off-the-beaten-path destinations, should look into package trips. Check with your local travel agent, or look in the Sunday travel section of your local newspaper. Several companies in the U.S. specialize in Mexico. For the area, check with **Mayaland Resorts.**

Escorted Tours
Escorted tours on modern air-conditioned buses leave daily from Mérida. Check with your hotel, or one of the many travel agencies in the city. They offer a variety of tours and prices; check around before you make a decision. The following tour is arranged by Yucatán Trails in downtown Mérida (Calle 62 #482, tel. 99-28-2582 or 28-5913, fax 24-4919), where you can get price and time schedules. This is a creative way for a traveler to make a short trip to Chichén

entrance to the Balankanche Caves

Itzá on the way to Cancún. A scheduled 9 a.m. bus stops at Chichén Itzá for a couple of hours, and again in Valladolid for lunch, then drops you off in Cancún, arriving approximately 6 p.m. Your luggage is safe in the same bus for the entire trip. So, although you don't spend a great deal of time at the ruins, you have the opportunity to make a brief visit en route while transferring from Mérida to Cancún. Fare is about US$70 pp including lunch, a tour of the ruins, and transportation to Cancún; about U$38 RT from Mérida.

Check with your travel agent either in the States or in Cancún or Cozumel; some agencies in Mexico provide a pickup service for those travelers who wish to spend the night at the archaeological zones. There are many other tours available, including custom tours.

PISTE

Piste, 2.5 km west of Chichén Itzá, has a unique tradition of providing the workforce for the archaeological digs at Chichén Itzá. Originally the men were chosen because they were the closest; now it's a proud tradition of the people. Piste is growing up. The once-quiet village is becoming a viable addendum to Chichén's services. More hotels and restaurants are available each month as the number of tourists interested in Chichén Itzá grows. Be sure to look around at the many cafes and gift shops as well.

Accommodations

The **Hotel Misión Chichén,** just a few kilometers west of the ruins on Hwy. 180 and just outside Piste, has a pool, a/c, and a dining room, and credit cards are accepted. Rate is US$85 including breakfast and dinner; rate drops slightly in the summer. Reservations suggested; from the U.S. call (800) 223-4084. Note: If you have stayed at the **Uxmal Misión Hotel,** don't expect this one to be nearly as nice.

Nearby, you'll find the **Piramide Inn Hotel.** The hotel area is peaceful, grassy, and tree shaded, and has 44 pleasant rooms with baths, a/c, and a swimming pool. Unfortunately, they have done away with their campground, but may allow RVs to park in their lot, without hookups. Dining room is open to both hotel guests and the public. Rate is US$45 s or d, plus 10% charge if you use a credit card; from the U.S. call (800) 262-9696.

Posada Olalde is a pleasant, modest place that's very convenient to the ruins, about a half-mile walk or 10 minutes on the bus. It's a little complicated to find, so ask in town for directions. Price is about US$15 d. **Posada El Paso** is another simple, clean inn with screened windows, fans, locked parking area, and (sometimes) hot water. Look for the cafe Posada El Paso; the hotel is right next door. Rates about US$16 s or d. The cafe **Posada El Paso** is inexpensive and the food is good.

Puebla Maya is a pseudo Maya village set up as a tourist attraction and rest area. Once inside the entrance, you walk along manmade rivers and lagoons to a large palapa-covered restaurant, often filled with tour bus groups. The US$10 buffet lunch is a good deal, especially since Piste's restaurants are typically overpriced, with only mediocre food. Live musicians play in the restaurant, while artisans give pottery and hammock weaving demonstrations in small Maya huts. Pueblo Maya is open daily 11:30 a.m.-4:30 p.m.

THE BALANKANCHE CAVES

Only six km east of Chichén Itzá, take a side trip to the Balankanche Caves. Here you'll descend into the earth and see many Maya ceremonial objects that appear to have been just left behind one day, 800 years ago. Discovered in 1959 by a tour guide named Gómez, the site was studied by prominent archaeologist Dr. E. Wyllys Andrews, commissioned by the National Geographic Society. What he saw, and what you can see today, is stirring: numerous stalactites, and a giant stalagmite resembling the sacred "Ceiba Tree," surrounded by ceramic and carved ceremonial artifacts. This was obviously a sacred site for the Maya—a site that perpetuates the mystery of the ancient people: Why did they leave? Where did they go? Who were they? Where did they come from in the very beginning? And what is the secret of their complex hieroglyphics?

At the entrance you'll find a parking lot, a cool spot to relax, a small cafe, a museum, interesting photos of Maya rituals, and guides; a sound and light show is offered nightly. The entrance fee is about US$6.50, sound and light show is under US$4; guided tours are offered in Spanish at 9 a.m. and 12 p.m., in English at 11 a.m. and 1 and 3 p.m., and in French at 10 a.m.; the caves are open 8 a.m.-5 p.m. Surrounding the site you'll find a botanical garden with a variety

of (identified) plants native to the areas around the Yucatán Peninsula.

Travelers Note: Remember that all museums and archaeological sites in Mexico are free on Sundays and holidays, children under 12 always free.

DZITNUP

After leaving the archaeological zone of Chichén Itzá continue on Hwy. 180 toward Valladolid. About four kilometers before you reach Valladolid, you'll see a small handmade sign that says Dzitnup. At the sign follow the road (about two km off the main road) and you'll find a delightful underground cenote. Wear comfortable walking shoes and your swimsuit in case you decide to take a swim. After a reasonably easy descent underground (in a few places you must bend over because of a low ceiling; there's a hanging rope to help), you'll come to a beautiful, circular pond of crystal-clear water. It's really a breathtaking place, with a high dome ceiling that has one small opening at the top letting in a ray of sun and dangling green vines. Often an errant bird or fluttering butterfly can be seen swooping low over the water before heading to the sun and sky through the tiny opening.

You'll see dramatic stalactites and a large stalagmite; catfish and blindfish swim in the placid water. This place is typical of the many underground caverns and grottoes common around the Peninsula, and well worth the small admission. When returning to Hwy. 180 at its intersection with the Dzitnup road, check out the southeast corner, where you'll find another cenote on private property. For a few pesos they will take you down some steps to an open-air area with a scum-covered cenote. The sight of tree roots reaching down into the cenote far below is unusual.

UXMAL

Located 80 km south of Mérida (a one-hour drive) in a range of low hills covered with brush, Uxmal is the greatest Maya city of the Puuc region. It takes its name from the range of hills that runs through west-central Yucatán. The city is believed to have been the hub of a district of about 160 square km encompassing many sites, including Kabah, Sayil, Labná, and Xlapak. The Maya word Uxmal (oosh-MAHL) means "Thrice Built," referring to the number of times this ceremonial center was rebuilt—in fact, it's believed that Uxmal was built five times. In many instances structures were superimposed over existing buildings; all are examples of the purely Maya "Puuc" style (without outside influences such as the Toltec one at Chichén Itzá). Puuc architecture is one of the major achievements of Mesoamerica. The Maya sites here all reached their apogee during the Late to Terminal Classic eras (A.D. 750-925).

The hallmarks of the Puuc architecture are thin squares of limestone veneer, decorated cornices, boot-shaped vault stones, rows of attached half columns, and upper facades heavily decorated with stone mosaics and sky-serpent monster masks with long, hooked noses.

Unlike most of northern Yucatán, the Puuc region has good soils, allowing for greater population density than other areas. Uxmal was probably the largest of many cities that lay along the hills. It emerged as the dominant city-state between A.D. 850 and 900, when the House of the Magician, the Great Pyramid, and the Nunnery were built. Few stelae have been found at the site, but we know the name of at least one ruler, Lord Chac, who could have ordered the monumental construction. Uxmal's control may have encompassed Kabah, because a *sacbe* (raised causeway) extended to that nearby city. In the mid-10th century, Uxmal was abandoned, probably after being defeated by Chichén Itzá's armies. During the Postclassic era, the Xiu clan based in the nearby town of Mani spuriously claimed to be descended from Uxmal's rulers and occupied the ruins.

HISTORY

Varied historical claims have been made about this Classic site. Some believe that it was founded by Maya from Guatemala's Petén in the 6th century. Others contend that it dates back even further, perhaps to the Preclassic period. By the time the Spaniards arrived it had been abandoned. An account of an early visit was given by Father López de Cogulludo, who explored the ruins in the 16th century, long after the Indians had abandoned the site.

Locals sell souvenirs in kiosks outside the entrance to Uxmal.

Without any facts to go on, he referred to the Nunnery Quadrangle (Las Monjas) as the dwelling of the Maya "Vestal Virgins," who kept the "Sacred Fire."

Cogulludo was followed by Jean-Fredric de Waldeck in 1836, who published a handsomely illustrated folio showing the structures of Uxmal peeking over thick brush. He compared them with the ruins of Pompeii. Only a few years later, the adventurous "dynamic duo," John L. Stephens and Frederick Catherwood, began their well-documented journey through the Peninsula in 1841. In the interim, the Indians must have cleared plots of land around Uxmal to plant corn, since Stephens commented that "emerging from the woods we came unexpectedly on a large open field strewn with mounds of ruins and vast buildings on terraces and pyramidal structures grand and in good preservation"—shown beautifully by Catherwood's sketches.

Frans Blom

The first real excavations began in 1929, led by the noted Danish archaeologist Frans Blom. Blom was involved in many archaeological digs in the Maya hinterland. Since Frans Blom, many other archaeologists have worked with the Mexican government at Uxmal; the result is a fine reconstructed site open for the enjoyment of the public. The small area (700 by 800 meters) of Uxmal presents some of the finest examples of pure Maya design, without Toltec influence.

Precious Water

Unlike most Maya centers in Yucatán, Uxmal was not built around a cenote, since there are none in this arid part of the Peninsula. Rainwater was collected by manmade installations of *chultunes* (cisterns) built into the ground, sometimes right inside a house or under a patio. Another method for saving water was the use of *aguadas* (natural holes in the ground) that in time had silted solid. Because of the almost total absence of surface lakes or rivers in Yucatán, the collection of water was of prime importance in the survival of the Maya. Most of their religious ceremonies and idols were devoted to the worship of Chac, the rain god. The constant threat of drought inspired the people to build great centers of worship, with hundreds of carvings and mosaics representing him and his prominent long hooked nose.

THE TEMPLES OF UXMAL

House Of The Magician/House Of The Diviner

This "pyramid" is the tallest on the grounds, rising 38 meters—shaped in a distinctive elliptical form, rather than a true pyramid. The west staircase, facing the Nunnery Quadrangle, is extremely steep (60° angle). Before you begin your climb do some leg stretches to loosen your muscles! Under this west stairway you can see parts of the first temple built on the site; a date on a door lintel is A.D. 569. On the east facade, the stairway has a broader slant, and though it's still a steep incline, it isn't nearly so hard on the legs. In the upper part of the east staircase you can enter an inner chamber which is Temple two. Temple three consists of nothing more than a small shrine at the rear of Temple two. Climbing the west stairway brings you to Temple four and an elaborate Chac mask with an open mouth large enough for a human to pass through. Temple five dates back to the 9th century and is reached by climbing the east stairway. From this viewpoint you'll be able to see the entire site of Uxmal and the surrounding brush-covered Puuc hills. These five temples were built one over the other!

Nunnery Quadrangle

The Nunnery, northwest of the House of the Magician, is a courtyard covering an area of 60 by 45 meters, bounded on each side by a series of buildings constructed on platforms of varying heights during different periods of time. The buildings, which contain numerous small rooms, reminded the Spaniards of the nunneries in Spain.

House Of The Turtles

A path leads south from the Nunnery to the House of the Turtles. This simple structure is six by 30 meters. The lower half is very plain, but the upper part is decorated with a frieze of columns; a cornice above that has a series of turtles along its facade. The turtle played an important part in Maya mythology.

Governor's Palace

Just south of the House of the Turtles is the Governor's Palace. Its facade is even more elaborate than those found at the Nunnery, cul-

Uxmal—House
of the Magician

minating in a portrait-relief over the central doorway that may represent Lord Chac, Uxmal's most powerful ruler. The palace is considered by some to be the finest example of pre-Hispanic architecture in Mesoamerica. It sits on a large platform and measures almost 100 meters long, 12 meters across, and eight meters high, and has 11 entrances. The lower facade is plain, but the upper section is a continuous series of ornate carvings and mosaics of geometrical shapes and Chac masks. Two arrow-shaped corbel arches add to the delicate design of this extraordinary building. A double-headed jaguar in front of the palace (presumed to be a throne) was first found by John Stephens in 1841.

The Great Pyramid

Another large structure is the Great Pyramid (30 meters high), originally terraced with nine levels and a temple on the top. According to early explorers, at one time four small structures sat on each of the four sides of the top platform, described as palacelike. The top story is decorated in typical Puuc fashion, with ornate carvings and stonework depicting flowers, masks, and geometric patterns.

Others

Walking through the grounds, you'll find many other structures a ball court. Visit the **Dovecote, House of the Old Woman,** and **Phallic Collection, Temple of the Phallus,** other small structures, and as-yet-unexcavated mounds. You can pick up a guide (or he'll try to pick you up) at the entrance to the ruins. If you feel a need for this service, be sure you agree on the fee before you begin your tour. Also something to remember: every guide will give you his own version of the history of the ruins, part family legend (if you're lucky) and part fairy tale. And let's face it, no one really knows the history of this obscure culture shrouded by the centuries. Many good books are available on the archaeological ruins of the larger sites (see "Booklist"). Grounds are open 8 a.m.-5 p.m., admission charge is about US$6.50, parking is about US$1.50, use of a video camera is about US$8 extra. A sound and light show is presented each evening in Spanish (7 p.m.) and English (9 p.m.); admission under US$3 d for the Spanish show, and US$4 d for the English show. The restaurants and shops in the visitor center and the artisan stands on the grounds are open until 9 p.m.

ACCOMMODATIONS

Uxmal is not a city; don't expect services of any kind. There are a few hotels with restaurants, and nothing else close by. To do justice to this fascinating antiquity, plan at least a full day to explore thoroughly. Because Mérida is only an hour away, it's easy to make this a day-trip by bus or car. Or continue on and spend the night in Ticul, 65 km (one hour) farther.

In Uxmal you have your choice of three excellent hotels within walking distance of the ruins. All are in the same price category. For budget accommodations a little farther out take a look at **Rancho Uxmal.** The 20 rooms have fans, hot-water showers, and comfortable beds; six more rooms were under construction on our last visit, and will have a/c. The long swimming pool is well filtered and clean, and the restaurant is great. Try the poc chuc with onions, cabbage, and tortillas; it's the best in the area. The ruins are at least a 45-minute walk from here, but the manager, Don Macario Cach Cabrera, will give you a ride if he can, or will flag down a bus for you. Buses returning from the ruins to Mérida will stop at the hotel. Rates: About US$30, and lower when tourism is down. The owners also have a small, very rustic campground next door. Other alternatives for budget accommodations are in Mérida, Oxkutzcab, and Ticul.

Hotel Hacienda Uxmal

This older colonial-style favorite has undergone some renovations in the past few years. Air-conditioning and cable television have been added to some rooms, and a spacious wooden deck built around the pool. For years it's been a favorite of visitors, with beautiful tile walkways and floors, large old-fashioned rooms with heavy carved furniture, pathways through tropical gardens, gift shop, and bar. A spacious dining room serves typical Yucatecan food and some continental dishes in fixed-price meals. There are usually four entree selections at dinner (nothing too exciting), plus a fruit salad or soup and dessert for about US$18. Snacks and lower-priced meals are available at the cafe Nicte-Ha next to the hotel's second pool, just across from the road to the ruins, open 1-8:30 p.m. Day-trippers are allowed to use that pool if they buy a meal. Rates: about US$88-120. Credit cards are accepted. For reservation information from the States and Canada call (800) 235-4079. In Mérida tel. 25-2122 or 25-2133, fax 25-7022.

Hotel Villa Arqueológica

This hotel, newest of Uxmal's three hotels, is owned by a branch of Club Med. A clone of its sister hotels in Cobá and Chichén Itzá, the hotel has small, attractive, and functional rooms, with twin beds on built-in cement platforms, a/c (a few readers have complained that the a/c can be noisy), and private bathrooms with shower. Both floors look out onto a tropical courtyard. The flower-covered patio has a sparkling (shallow) pool, outside bar and table service, covered cabana area, and complete library on the history and culture of the Maya. You'll find some French dishes along with local specialties in the large dining room. The rate is about US$70. Lunches and dinners average about US$25 pp, breakfast US$12—à la carte menu only. Credit cards are accepted. For more information and reservations, call (800) 258-2633 in the United States.

A little farther down the road (one km) but still walking distance is **Hotel Misión Uxmal,** tel. (800) 437-7275 in the United States. Transport to the ruins is available. This hotel has all the modern amenities, including pool, bar, dining room, and nice rooms with private bath and a/c. Credit cards accepted; rate is about US$80 d, including breakfast and dinner.

FOOD AND ENTERTAINMENT

All three hotel dining rooms welcome visitors for lunch. Expect to pay about US$12-16 for a complete three-course lunch; ask what light meals are available. The hotels used to allow those who paid for a meal to swim in their pools, but that practice seems to have been stopped. Ask before you dive in. The exception is the Nicte-Ha cafe at the Hacienda Uxmal; diners are allowed to use the pool by the cafe, but not the pool by the main hotel buildings. At the Uxmal Visitors Center located at the entrance to the ruins, a small restaurant serves cold drinks and light meals, and a kiosk just outside the entrance to the ruins offers cold drinks. If you're driving, another alternative is to take the road back toward Mérida (Hwy. 261), 18 km north to Muna where there are small cafes in the villages and a few on the road.

Every evening a **sound and light show** is presented in Spanish (7 p.m.) and English (9 p.m.) at the ruins overlooking the Nunnery Quadrangle. Escorted tours to the shows are available from Mérida. If you've never seen one of these shows, check it out. It's mood-altering to sit under the stars in the warm darkness surrounded by stark stone remnants and listen to Latin-accented voices and a symphony orchestra echo in stereo from temple to temple, narrating the (so-called) history of the Maya while colored lights flash dramatically on first one and then another of these stark structures. Some-

Ladies sell colorful huipiles *at Uxmal.*

Outside the entrance are kiosks where local women sell the *huipil* (Yucatecan dress). Their prices can be much better than in gift shops; frequently the garments are made by the saleswoman or someone in her family. Some dresses are machine-embroidered or made of polyester, though many are still handmade of white cotton with bright embroidery thread. Be sure you get what you want. The *huipiles* worn by Maya women always look snow white with brilliant colors. Don't forget to bargain.

The only other shopping at Uxmal is at the small gift shops adjoining the hotels near the ruins. Most of them sell the usual curios, clothing, tobacco, postage stamps, and postcards. The exception is the Villa Arqueológica, where high-quality Maya reproductions depicting ancient idols are displayed. You can find reproductions in many places, but unlike these, most are not of the best quality and have very little detail. Here, the prices reflect the excellent workmanship. Note: If you're driving or are on a tour bus (not a local bus), you will see some little shops selling *huipiles* and crafts along the highway as you get close to the ruins. Usually the tour buses make a stop or two for shopping.

times Mother Nature adds her own drama: the rumble of thunder from a distant storm, or jagged streaks of luminous light in a black sky. The already eerie temples reflect a supernatural glow evoking the memory of the Maya, their mysterious beginnings and still unsolved disappearance. Admission is about US$1.50 for the Spanish show, and US$2 for the English show; reserve and buy tickets either at hotels in Uxmal, or at government tourist offices and travel agencies in Mérida.

SHOPPING

The visitor center at the entrance to the Uxmal site is modern and beautiful. With the visitor in mind, the center offers clean restrooms, gift shops, a small museum, an auditorium where a short film promoting the Yucatán Peninsula is shown, a bookstore with a good supply of English-language books about the various ruins on the Peninsula, an ice-cream shop, and a small cafeteria.

GETTING THERE

Local buses leave Mérida's main bus station (Calle 69 #544) daily on Autotransportes del Sureste, with departures from Mérida at 6 and 9 a.m., and 12 and 3 p.m.; the last bus departs from Uxmal at 7:30 p.m. Check at the bus station in advance, since schedules are apt to change. Allow at least one hour for the trip (79 km)—be sure to check the return time to Mérida. Buses to Uxmal leave Campeche from the ADO station (Gobernadores #289).

Buses do not go onto the ruins road, but stop on the side of the highway at the turnoff to the ruins. The highway (261) from Mérida to Campeche City passes close to the Uxmal ruins and is a good road. From Mérida the drive to Uxmal takes about one hour; from Campeche allow two hours (175 km southwest). Travel agencies in Mérida offer tours of the ruins at Uxmal. (See "Travel Agencies" in "Mérida.") Check with the government tourist office at Teatro Peón Contreras on Calle 61 in downtown Mérida for more information.

VICINITY OF UXMAL

MUNA

From Uxmal traveling north, Hwy. 261 passes through the rustic city of Muna. Lovers of 17th-century architecture might enjoy a look at the large Franciscan church. In the late afternoon sun, the facade with its lacy belfries glows a mellow gold, almost hiding the decay that adds to its appeal. Early in the morning on the edge of the plaza, women sell small quantities of fresh fruits and vegetables. Opposite the plaza, a series of open stalls offers cold drinks and Yucatecan snacks, including good *panuchos* (miniburritos); for the big appetite, go for the *tortas* or tamales. Try **Katty's** for a good breakfast; clean bathroom available. **Kristie's Curios,** a handicraft store next to Muna's gas station, has good bargains for curios and clothes, but buy soda pop anywhere else—it's cheaper. The boss, a former manager at Loltún caves for INAH, speaks English.

Close by, **Yaxcopoil** (yawsh-koe-poe-EEL), a turn-of-the-century hacienda, is right off Hwy. 261 between Mérida and Uxmal and is clearly marked. A half-hour visit (about US$3.50) gives a great insight into what life must have been like in the days when Mexican haciendas operated like small fiefdoms. Hundreds of Indians provided the labor necessary to grow and harvest the thorny henequen plant which, until after WW II, made the owners of these small kingdoms millionaires. At Yaxcopoil you'll see remnants of the 1890s and 1900s furniture used in the drawing rooms and dining rooms, hinting at the gracious life the *patrones* enjoyed. Take a look into the kitchen with its unique woodstove made from white tile, pictures of the family, framed documents showing dates of events, even the old safe. This is a stroll into the past. With luck you may have Ernesto Cuitam Yam as your guide. A Maya, he was born in Yaxcopoil. His parents told of life on the hacienda when they worked there—under much different conditions than now. The hacienda is open Mon.-Sat. 8 a.m.-6 p.m., Sun. 9 a.m.-1 p.m.

Oxkintok

The ruins of Oxkintok have attracted much attention in the past few years, as archaeologists uncover an urban center at least three square miles in size. The ruins sit in a fertile plain at the edge of the hilly Puuc region, and may have been connected to Uxmal by a *sacbe* limestone road. Large pyramids have been uncovered, all including tombs with some remaining treasures (though there was considerable looting in the past and many relics have been lost). Reconstruction is far from complete, and you're likely to be the only person at the site. Still, it's fascinating to see such a large center on the verge of discovery. To reach Oxkintok drive south from Yaxcopoil to Muna; follow the signs in town for Oxkintok and Calcehtok (a left turn); once in Calcehtok, turn right at the sign just past the small town and drive down a dirt road about half a km to the ruins, which are about 30 km northeast of Uxmal.

PUUC RUINS

An entire day could be spent making a loop from Uxmal to the smaller Puuc sites of Kabah, Sayil, Xlapak, and Labná, lying in the jungle-covered hills southeast of Uxmal. On through the village of Oxkutzcab, see the Loltún caves and Mani. For the most part these are small sites and easy to see or photograph quickly, and the ornate Puuc design is well worth the time and effort. The government has reopened the ruins to anthropologists and archaeologists, and some excavation and renovation is underway. The countryside for some 15 km around Uxmal and the Puuc sites is now a national preserve, and some of the indigenous animals and birds are beginning to multiply.

The smaller Puuc sites of Kabah, Sayil, Xlapak, and Labná lie in the jungle-covered hills southeast of Uxmal. Their politics were certainly dominated by their larger neighbor. Kabah was settled as far back as the Late Preclassic (300 B.C.-A.D. 250), but the ruins we now see at all four sites date from the Late and Terminal

Classic. Although the buildings are generally smaller than those found at Uxmal, they are all fine examples of the Puuc style, and some, like the temple at Xlapak, have a gemlike beauty. Sayil, the only one which has been fully mapped, covered 1.7 square miles at its Late Classic height and had a population of over 10,000. The Puuc must have been crowded then! These sites were abandoned at the same time as Uxmal during the 10th century. Admission to each of the sites is about US$3.50, free on Sunday; all sites are open daily 8 a.m.-5 p.m.

Kabah

Kabah was constructed in A.D. 850-900. Nineteen km south of Uxmal, structures are found on both sides of Hwy. 261. The most ornate building is the **Codz-Pop,** dedicated to the rain god, Chac. This temple is 45 meters long and six meters high. Part of the original rooftop comb (at one time three meters high), with its uneven rectangular openings, can still be seen. The entire west facade is a series of 250 masks with the typical elongated, curved nose, some almost a complete circle. The Puuc architecture is colored beige, rust, brown, and gray from the oxides in the earth that engulfed the building for so many years. Small pits on each mask are said to have been used to burn incense or oil; Codz-Pop must have shone like a Chinese lantern from great distances throughout the rolling countryside. Inside the building are two parallel series of five rooms each. Archaeologists are currently doing intensive reconstruction work at Kabah; when finished, it will be a truly impressive site.

The Arch

West of the road is the impressive Arch of Kabah. It is presumed that this arch marks the end of a ceremonial *sacbe* built by the Maya from Uxmal to Kabah. A few more structures have been partially restored—look for the **Great Temple** and the **Temple of the Columns.**

Sayil

A short distance brings you to a side road to Oxkutzcab (Hwy. 184); follow the side road first to Sayil (in Maya this word means "anthill"). This is probably the most imposing site of the loop. Several hundred known structures at Sayil illustrate a technical progression from the earliest, unornamented building to the more recent, ornate **Chultun Palace,** constructed in A.D. 730. The Palace is a large, impressive building, over 60 meters long, with three levels creating two terraces, again showing the outstanding architectural talents of the Classic period. The second level is decorated with Greek-style columns and a multitude of rich carvings, including the ever-present rain god and one distinctive portrayal of a descending god (an upside-down figure referred to as the bee god). By A.D. 800 this site was abandoned.

Because of the lack of rainfall in this area, *chultunes* are found everywhere, including the sites of the ceremonial centers. One example of a *chultun* that holds up to 7,000 gallons of water can be seen at the northwest corner of the Palace. The fast-decaying **Temple Mirador** (on a path going south from the Palace) and the monument of a human phallic figure beyond.

Xlapak

Six km farther on the same road (east of Sayil) is the Xlapak turnoff. Though this Puuc site is small, do stop to see the restored building with its curious carvings: tiers of masks, curled Chac noses, and geometric stepped frets. It's easy to pick out the light-colored areas of restoration compared to the darker weathered stones that were covered with bushes and soil oxides for so many years. The word Xlapak in Maya means "Old Walls."

Labná

Another Maya arch of great beauty is at Labná, located three km beyond Xlapak. More correctly the arch should be referred to as a portal vault. Be sure to examine the northeast side of this structure to see two outstanding representations of thatched Maya huts, one on each side of the portal. This arch is one of the largest and most ornate built by the Maya; the passageway measures three by six meters.

The Palace

This Puuc-style structure was built at the end of the Classic period, about A.D. 850. The elaborate multiroom pyramid sits on an immense platform 165 meters long, and the structure is 135 meters long by 20 meters high. A *chultun* is built into the second story of the Palace and, according to archaeologist George Andrews, at least 60 *chultunes* have been located in the

Labná area, indicating a population of about 3,000 residents within the city.

El Mirador
This stark, square building stands on a tall mound with a roof comb gracing the top. The comb on the small temple was originally decorated with a carved seated figure and a series of death heads. The carvings were still in place in the 1840s when John Stephens traveled through the Peninsula. The elements and time continue to wreak their destruction on the ancient structures of the Maya.

OXKUTZCAB AND VICINITY

Oxkutzcab, a small village, is known by outsiders because of its proximity to the caves of Loltún. The town is smaller and easier to navigate than Ticul, and is a nice place to stop for a visit. Land in the area is fertile, and most mornings farmers and their families from outlying areas come to the produce market to sell large quantities of fruits and vegetables by the crate—unusual for small-town markets. Oranges are abundant, since Oxkutzcab is the orange capital of the entire Peninsula. The two-week-long Orange Festival, celebrated in late October or early November, is renowned throughout Yucatán; be sure to stop by if you are in the area at that time, but don't expect to find an empty room. Approaching Oxkutzcab, you travel through acres of healthy tall cornfields giving you the same feeling you would have in a farm town near Kansas City, Missouri. Suddenly you're surrounded by citrus groves, bananas, and coconut palms. Then you remember—you're in the tropics!

Triciclos
A large Franciscan church faces a central plaza with painted cement benches, a strange gazebo, and a painted plaster statue of a woman carrying a load of oranges on her head. A graceful arched building along one side of the plaza is the government center. While looking around, you find more examples of stark 16th-century Spanish-influenced architecture. Be careful crossing the streets—you might get run down in the bicycle traffic or overtaken by its three-wheeled cousin (*triciclo*) seen in many small towns all over the Peninsula. Similar to an Indonesian *becak*, it has a more utilitarian look and no overhead protection. But the result is the same: providing cheap transportation for the family, with dad (or paid "cabbie") pedaling in the back, mom and the kids sitting up front. When not filled with people, it's used for hauling anything from a crate of live chickens to a modern TV set. Oxkutzcab's morning streets bustle with people, coming to market, big and little trucks parked hither and yon unloading crates of healthy fresh produce. At 1 p.m. all of this activity quiets down and, with commerce completed, folks pack up and go home.

ACCOMMODATIONS

If you want the small-town experience within easy driving distance of Uxmal you might consider Oxkutzcab. **Los Tucanes Hotel** is your best (and just about your only) choice, and is popular with archaeologists and anthropologists on expedition in the area. To reach Los Tucanes drive one and a half blocks toward town from the Pemex and turn left. The two-story hotel has basic, clean rooms with private baths, painfully thin mattresses, and hammock hooks. The most popular disco/nightclub in town is on the first floor; if you're staying over the weekend choose a room far from the noise. There's also a restaurant, with pool table. Rooms are about US$20. For reservations write to Los Tucanes, Calle 64 #99, Oxkutzcab, Yucatán 97860, tel. (99) 75-0348.

FOOD

La Cabaña Suiza is one of the best restaurants in the area. To reach Los Tucanes drive one and a half blocks toward town from the Pemex and turn left. Rooms are about US$20. The owner has a fondness for birds, and keeps parrots, parakeets, and a few squirrels in cages by the tables. They make pretty music, but also attract bugs, so sit as far from them as possible. The restaurant specializes in grilled pork, chicken, and beef served with tortillas and beans;

the Yucatecan specialties are also good, and the prices are very reasonable—less than US$5 for a complete meal.

LOLTUN CAVES

Seven km southwest of Oxkutzcab, Loltún's underground caverns are the largest known caves in Yucatán. In addition to being a fabulous natural phenomenon, Loltún is an important archaeological find.

The Loltún caves were not only a crucial source of water but an important ceremonial space for the ancient Maya. They also contain evidence of humans' earliest presence in Yucatán. Researchers have found a midden of bones belonging to extinct mammals, including mammoths, dated 9000-7500 B.C. They were obviously dragged to the cave by Early Hunters. Early Preclassic ceramics (2000-1250 B.C.) have also been discovered here. One of the most interesting Maya relics is a Preclassic relief of a lord carved in the style of southern Maya cities like Tikal. Caves were important pilgrimage spots for the Maya; they represented fertility and riches, as well as entrances to the underworld.

The most important archaeological find here is the relief called "The Warrior," which is carved on a rock face just outside the Nahkab entrance to the cave. Researchers believe that it was carved in the Izapan style of Kaminaljuyú, the enormous Preclassic city near Guatemala City. The last room holds strange rock carvings that may be models of temples.

On many of the walls are decorated handprints, either in silhouette or negative outline, whose meaning remains a mystery. The earliest inhabitants of the area used the caves as a source of water and of clay for pots; their function as a religious site probably developed during the Classic era.

Loltún means "Rock Flower" in Maya and in the caves are carvings of small flowers. Hieroglyphic inscriptions on the walls are guesstimated by the guides to be more than a thousand years old. Throughout, *chultunes* are placed strategically under the dripping roof to catch water. This saved water was called "virgin water," important in ceremonies that Maya priests directed to the rain god.

A Guided Walk

No one is allowed to visit the caverns without a guide—and with good reason. Loltún is immense, and it would be very easy to get lost in the meanderings from grotto to grotto, up and down, in total darkness. (Select caverns have been wired for lights, which are turned on and off by the guide as the group moves through.) If you understand Spanish you'll enjoy a few giggles at the stories and anecdotes the guide weaves into his commentary as you stroll through chambers once lived in by thousands of Maya Indians.

Along the way the guide points out common artifacts used by the Indians, such as stone metates (corn grinders) in the "kitchen." Numerous natural formations bear startling resemblances to certain persons (like the Virgin of Guadalupe) and animals (such as the distinct head of an open-mouthed tiger). Giant columns stand from floor to ceiling and when tapped give out a resonant hum that echoes through the darkened passageway. You'll see the stone-carved head now referred to as the Head of Loltún, found by two Americans, Jack Grant and Bill Dailey, during an archaeological dig in the caves in 1959-60.

Toward the end of the two-hour tour you come to an opening in the roof of an enormous two-story-high cavern. The sun pours into the room, creating dust-flecked shafts of golden light. The gnarled trunk of a towering tree grows from the floor of the cave reaching hundreds of feet up through the sunny opening, and flocks of birds twitter and flit in and around the green leafy vines that dangle freely into the immense chamber from above—breathless sights and sounds of nature not soon to be forgotten.

Practicalities

Wear walking shoes in the caves. For the most part it's an easy two-km walk; however, it's dark and damp, and in a few places the paths between chambers are steep, rocky, and slippery. Buy your tickets (about US$6, or US$3 on Sundays) at the office next to the clean restrooms (no restrooms in the caves). Tours begin daily at 9:30 a.m., 11 a.m, 12:30 p.m., 2 p.m., and 3 p.m. Have 5-6 pesos for the guide at the end of the trip (he'll ask for it). Lectures are *usually* given in Spanish only, but ask for an English-speaking guide when you buy your ticket; you might get lucky.

If you arrive early or need lunch or a cold drink after walking through the caves, stop at the small cafe next to the cave exit. The owner is friendly, the beer is cold, the food is good and moderately priced; *poc chuc* (barbecued pork fillet) with bean soup and handmade tortillas hits the spot. Escorted tours are available from Mérida; contact Trails Travel Agency, located at Calle 62 #482, tel. (99) 28-2582 or 28-5913, fax 24-4919.

MANI

This small town, east of Ticul, was the scene of early surrender by the Xius (prominent Maya rulers with descendants still living in the state of Yucatán). Montejo the Elder quickly took over, and by the mid-1500s a huge church/monastery complex was completed in only seven months by 6,000 slaves under the direction of Fray Juan de Mérida. This old building, still with a priest in residence, is huge and in its day must have been beautiful, with graceful lines and pocket patios. Fray de Mérida also designed and built similar buildings at Izamal and Valladolid.

Historians believe it was in Mani that Friar Diego de Landa confiscated and burned the books held in reverence by the Maya. These codices, the first books produced in North America, were hand-lettered on fig bark carefully worked until it was thin and pliable, then coated with a thin white plaster sizing and screen folded. According to Landa they were filled with "vile superstitions and lies of the devil." Since that time, only four more codices have been found. The most recent (1977), though its authenticity was doubted at first, is gaining more and more credibility among archaeologists. The remaining three books are in museums in Dresden, Paris, and Madrid. Replicas can be seen at the Anthropological Museum in Mexico City. The destruction of the codices was a monumental tragedy not only for the Maya—the loss to the world is incalculable. Only a little progress toward learning the mysterious glyphs has been made; who knows, the destroyed books may have been the lost key to their language, their history, and their mystery. It is hoped that other codices exist and will some day turn up—perhaps in an unexcavated tomb still buried in the jungle. Many villages still practice the ancient rituals of their ancestors and appoint keepers of the sacred records. However, these people have learned from the experiences of their ancestors and tell no outsiders of their task.

CRUISES AND TOURS

CRUISE SHIPS

One of the fastest-growing industries in tourism is ocean cruising. What was once reserved for the idle rich is becoming commonplace for the ordinary vacationer—even the handicapped. Cruising is no longer a means of getting from point A across an ocean to point B. Cruise ships are for fun! And the more luxurious the better—though for obvious financial reasons some ships cater to fun- rather than luxury-seekers. Daily prices can start as low as US$150 pp, on up to US$700 pp.

Special-interest groups are finding a ship the perfect gathering place. For groups ranging from Smithsonian Associates' naturalists and archaeologists to theater guilds, appropriate speakers and plans are coordinated with the ship's personnel.

The Money Factor

Shop carefully if price is the most important factor; prices are competitive. A variety of ships offer mass market Las Vegas-type cruises aimed at younger passengers interested in short three- to five-day trips. Upscale luxury boats reminiscent of first-class on the "Queens"—Mary and Elizabeth—cruise for two weeks

or longer and will cost the most. These are the ones with large cabins, restaurants where one orders from a complete menu, and passengers who are pampered outrageously, with a price tag to match. For the adventurer, small, casual ships capable of traveling narrow river passages into often virgin territory where nature and people have not been exposed to the diluting effects of tourism—for a while at least—run a gamut of prices from moderate to exorbitant.

Ways To Cut The Cost

Go standby. Once you put your name on the list, you'll have no choice of cabin location or size, and airfare is usually not included. Passengers are notified two weeks prior to departure. **Last-minute travel clubs** and **discount agencies** include cruises available at the last minute in their inventories. These clubs charge a yearly membership fee, around US$50; for that, the member receives a newsletter with phone numbers, a list of trips, and other pertinent information that provides access to upcoming values. Those who are willing to pack up at a moment's notice (two weeks) can save 10-50%.

By the same token, some cruise lines will give a substantial discount to folks who book and buy passage six months to a year in advance. **Cunard,**

Princess, Holland America, and **Royal Cruise Line** are all willing to give a 10-50% discount. Often, ships offer specials for various reasons; study the travel sections of newspapers and get to know your travel agent. Let him or her know what you would like, and ask him or her to call you if and when the price is right.

Sharing a quad room generally gives you a good discount. If you don't have any roomies to bring along, some lines will sell you a same-sex quad for a set price. **Chandris Fantasy Cruises** offers a special **Single Saver** or guaranteed quad-share rate that includes airfare from your getaway city; they will give you that fare even if they are unable to find you a roommate.

Ask for **senior citizen discounts;** though not many lines give them, there are a few—Chandris is one. The Chandris Fantasy Cruises give a 50% discount to the second passenger when the first passenger in the cabin pays full fare.

QUINTANA ROO

Several passenger ships make stops at Quintana Roo's islands and ports. **Chandris Cruise Line** offers its Fantasy Cruises—budget trips on well-equipped and well-appointed older vessels sailing out of Miami, stopping at Key West before continuing to the Caribbean and Mexico's Playa del Carmen and Isla Cozumel. Tenders take passengers ashore, where they have the option of taking excursions to the Maya ruins of Tulúm, Cobá, or San Gervais, or a trip to Xelha, an inland lagoon described as a natural aquarium where you can swim, snorkel, or scuba dive among colorful tropical fish and even see an underground grotto with Mayan remnants. Other passengers opt to lie around the white beach, enjoy the turquoise sea, or shop at the many *tiendas* for typical souvenirs.

Chandris has been named by *Cruise* magazine as giving the best dollar value in cruising for 1989. For US$140 per day (depending on cabin choice), vacationers can fly from California and spend five nights aboard, enjoying the sea or engaging in a range of activities: Las Vegas-type lounge shows, bingo, a great gambling casino, good food, passenger talent show, costume party, or just a quiet corner where one can contemplate the sea or get lost in the adventure of a good book. There's even a special activity director for children. For complete information on the Chandris Fantasy Cruises, call or write for a brochure and rates, 900 3rd Ave., New York, NY 10022, tel. (800) 621-3446.

Commodore Cruise Line's Caribe I offers a large ship that sails out of Miami, frequently with theme cruises. This is not a fancy ship, but passengers have fun. Prices average US$145 per day. For

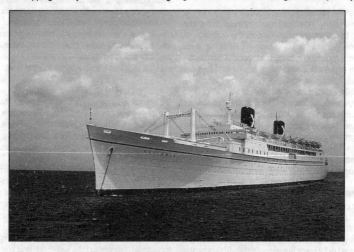

Chandris' SS Britanis *off the coast of Cozumel*

more information contact Commodore Cruise Lines, 1007 North American Way, Miami, FL 33132, tel. (800) 327-5617

Costa Cruises means cruising Italian style; everything is reminiscent of Italy, including great pasta, pizza, and gelato. The shops offer trendy Italian-label clothing, there's at least one "toga night" each sailing, and strolling tenors capture the romantics on board with Italian love songs. Night is active in the casino and the disco. Rates start at about US$232 per day, including airfare. For more information contact Costa Cruises, World Trade Center, 80 S.W. 8th St., Miami, FL 33130, tel. (800) 462-6782.

Dolphin Cruises offers the *Sea Breeze*, a large ship that is often filled with young budget-minded first-time cruisers to the Caribbean. The line specializes in seven-day cruises from Miami that average about US$225 per day. For a brochure and more information, write to Dolphin, 1007 North American Way, Miami, FL 33132, tel. (800) 222-1003.

Holland America Line sails with a gracious Indonesian staff and Dutch officers. This is a traditional ship with excellent food and exceptional service, no tipping allowed. The mix of people is varied older couples, families, and singles. Fare averages US$218 per day including airfare. For more information, write to 300 Elliott Ave. W, Seattle, WA 98119, or tel. (800) 426-0327.

Norwegian Cruise Line offers the *Skyward* for short cruises to the western Caribbean. The mid-sized ship offers a variety of star-studded entertainment for all ages. Prices average US$230 per day, including airfare. For more information, contact Norwegian Cruise Line, Kloster Cruise Ltd., 2 Alhambra Plaza, Coral Gables, FL 33134, tel. (800) 327-7030.

The **Royal Caribbean Line** offers clean, bright, and well-run ships. The cabins are small but functional. A good sports program is available, plus great entertainment and programs for all ages. Dress is casual. For more information contact Royal Caribbean Cruise Line, 903 South American Way, Miami, FL 33132, tel. (800) 327-6700.

The **Ocean Quest Line** offers a slightly different type of cruise. The line's 457-foot, 300-passenger ship, *Ocean Spirit,* sails from New Orleans and caters to the diving crowd. The seven-day voyage carries doctors, a four-man decompression chamber for treating aeroembolism (bends), and an air system encompassing two tank centers with 150,000 cubic feet of air, plus fast-filling, built-in tank systems on each of its eight dive boats. Divers can either bring their own equipment or rent on board. A US$200

certification course in scuba diving is offered as well as a multitude of water-sports equipment and events. Dress is casual and fine entertainment can be had on board at the disco, pool, bars, or cinema. A small fitness center, shop, and film-processing center make ship life convenient and pleasant. The *Ocean Spirit* combines the intimate qualities of a private yacht with the facilities of a modern cruise ship. Fare averages US$207 per day. For more information contact Ocean Quest, 512 S. Peters St., New Orleans, LA 70130, tel. (800) 338-3483.

The **Bermuda Star Line** offers the *Bermuda Queen*, which departs from New Orleans to the Caribbean coast on a seven-day cruise, US$895 to $1895 pp. Passengers will find roomy cabins and a friendly staff. This is not a regular schedule, so check with the company for more information, 1086 Teaneck Rd., Teaneck, N.J. 07666, tel. (800) 237-5361.

PLANNING A WHEELCHAIR CRUISE

by Patricia P. Gustke
A cruise can be a relaxing experience in a wheelchair, with advance planning. But it can be a frustrating daily obstacle course if you leave it to chance and pick the wrong ship.

Selecting The Ship
Accessibility for "physically challenged" travelers—there are more than 35 million of us in America alone—varies widely from ship to ship. Of course, elevators are a necessity, but many things on board can cause problems—a raised edge at stateroom doors, narrow cabin doors, a step up to the bathroom, lack of grab bars, heavy doors and steps between inner and outer decks.

The best reading resources are Berlitz's *Complete Handbook to Cruising* and Douglas Ward's *On Deck*. Then contact the Organization for Promotion of Access and Travel, P.O. Box 15777, Tampa, FL 33684. President Tom Gilbert will send a list of ships which have accessible cabins, including the cabin numbers. Send a self-addressed, stamped envelope; I always include a donation because his persistence is helping to change attitudes. More and more lines are converting a few cabins, but there are still precious few.

Planning Ahead
In wheelchair travel, it's best to accept the fact that there will be problems, but advance planning can

minimize them. Our travel agent contacts the line to explain my medical problems (muscular dystrophy) and that I must use a wheelchair full-time. I also always call the cruise line myself to point out that I cannot climb stairs (important to make clear, since buses are the normal mode of transport—fine for those with lesser mobility problems but not for "permanent occupants").

If you are fortunate enough to sign up for a handicapped cabin, insist on knowing exactly what it includes. We sometimes use a regular cabin because of better location (many adapted cabins are in the bowels of the ship!). But we take special equipment and know in detail what problems we'll find.

In selecting a cabin, remember to choose the best you can afford. It means more space, a larger bath, wider hallways. I cut back on my grocery budget to splurge on the Promenade Deck, for I love the scenic view from the big windows and the constant procession of walkers and joggers.

Try for a midship location, close to an elevator. Make your dining room selection well in advance. They want to place wheelchairs close to a door or the busy aisle, so we try to beguile the maitre d' into giving us a quiet window table for two.

Arm yourself with what reading material you can find. Most lines provide excellent shore excursion descriptions ahead of time as well as on board. Try to learn the words in local languages for "wheelchair," "elevator," "help," and "steps." I find "thank you" in the vernacular makes the difficult job of lifting a happier experience. (I've also found that it's almost always my responsibility to put others at ease. Somehow coping with a wheelchair leaves onlookers tongue-tied, and I must initiate conversation to let them know that my disability does not extend to my brain, thankfully.)

Airline reservations should be made early. The comfort of business or first class can be invaluable on a long flight. If you fly tourist class, request bulkhead seating. You'll be first to board and last to deplane. And the wonderful passenger agents become instant friends—they know all of the elevator secrets and usually whip you through customs so fast that agile passengers enviously eye your wheelchair.

If you can arrive a day or two early, all the better; or try to plan an overnight en route so you don't start your cruise exhausted. Also, remember that you're often dealing with U.S. airports and jetways, and loading and unloading can vary from traumatic to harrowing, especially in a strange language. We always ask for the special narrow chair that airlines

are supposed to have, but it's seldom available on foreign airlines, so I've learned to close my eyes, pray, and hope the men who carry me are surefooted and strong. (I once was loaded onto a 747 in Aruba via a forklift truck with no sides, and unloaded one time in Rio in a kitchen chair with no arms. So it's best to be adventurous!)

Toilet use is always a problem, for my husband Bob has to lift me. Anywhere in the world, we blithely enter the ladies' room (occasionally even the men's room)—a procedure no one seems to mind. But since the dimensions of airplane toilets were designed for anorexics, we try not to do our lifting routine there, for it leaves us face-to-face with barely room to move. So I limit liquid intake for 24 hours before a trip and drink sparingly en route. I've also used atropine, which absorbs liquids in the body, but it should only be used under a doctor's supervision. It allows me to manage eight- to 10-hour trips with no comfort stops, but it's necessary to drink large amounts of water at destination. I always try to use the terminal restrooms before we board, or sometimes on board before the plane takes off or after it lands (an easier feat than when the plane is in flight).

No matter where we travel, we must take along my special accessories. They include my "limousine," a junior-width wheelchair; crutches for the occasional step; my Roho cushion; a slide board; and Ermintrude, my folding junior walker fitted with a toilet seat which doubles as a shower chair and folds neatly into a case. There's nothing like it on the market—we just improvised. Also soccer shin guards (to protect my legs, which bruise easily) and a handicapped license plate (even in Bangkok or Buenos Aires, we've found that everyone recognizes the international symbol, and it produces effects even in taxis or rental cars). This year we added a folding bed tray and folding mirror, which made eating, doing makeup, and washing up much simpler.

We make sure my medications are in our carry-on luggage, and pack all my clothes on metal hangers in plastic bags, which fold into my 30-inch suitcase and make Bob's job of unpacking easier. And I find room for my best-looking clothes. Somehow people connect wheelchair users with hospital gowns, and I take great delight in donning chiffon, sequins, paisley shawls, gold lamé—whatever makes me feel and look stylish.

Of course, we arrange for visas, shots, passports, and a small amount of foreign currency for each country we will visit. And we always take a large supply of dollar bills; a trip through an airport or lobby with me and my accessories is quite a lesson in foreign aid!

In the future, there are other things we'll plan in advance. On our last cruise, I needed an extra mattress to ease Bob's job of lifting, and a grab bar by my bunk. I learned too late that housekeeping could have arranged for both. And there were other things on my wish list that couldn't be arranged: a stewardess bell within reach of my bunk, at least one ramped entry to the Promenade Deck without a heavy door, and elimination of that dreadful step up into the bathroom.

Once Aboard

Cruising is far less wearing than land travel, but there's no guarantee of perfect access. Chairs usually have to be junior width, so count calories and keep counting them aboard, or you may pop a rivet. The crew that has to carry you up and down the gangplank certainly appreciates it if you're a little less than five by five.

Our first chore aboard is often to remove the bathroom door so the chair fits. If there's a step or even a difficult lip, that, too, presents a problem. I've always had ample grab bars by the toilet and tub. Each wheelchair user basically has to figure out his or her own system: one man uses a slide board to transfer himself from his chair to a rolling stool in the bathroom, thence to the commode. Where there's a will, there's a way.

Our next step is to visit with our stewardess. I ask for extra pillows for propping me up in bed, for one chair to be removed for more space, and for early coffee and a late breakfast in the cabin each day. We often have afternoon tea or after-dinner coffee in our cabin too. (Do remember that extra service should earn an extra tip.)

Then we study the floor plan of the ship, for with its blueprint in mind, we can reach virtually anyplace on board. If there's a step or heavy door, crew will assist. Bob, in his usual efficient way, finds the special toggle switch on the elevator panel to hold open the door for safe loading. Even the beauty shops are usually designed so I can stay seated. If you're headed for a floor show, arrive early, for there's no such thing as an unnoticed entry by a wheelchair.

Shore Excursions

Shore excursions can be difficult if you can't handle bus steps. We confer immediately with the shore excursion director to see what's possible for me and usually use a private car and guide at each stop. The added expense of a few dollars a day is well worth it.

But you must be flexible. Debarking at a wharf is relatively simple, but at anchor is difficult. On a Cape Horn cruise last year, my greatest desire was a catamaran trip on the Beagle Channel, and somehow I was loaded—while at anchor! But it was a last-minute decision, dependent on wave conditions. And it must have looked exciting, for when the crew finally deposited me and chair inside, I was greeted by a round of applause.

If you plan pre- or post-trip excursions, let those in charge know a long time before you arrive that you'll need a taxi rather than the bus. And arrange for your own car and guide. Again, it may cost more but you learn more. I always let hotels know my special needs in advance, too.

The Personal Touch

The last cruise requirement is a physically able traveling companion. That's in the ship's rules, and I'm lucky that mine is trained as an engineer, a gentleman, and a banker. He also encourages me to be adventurous and treats me as if I'm completely healthy.

As for me, I've learned to smile no matter what and to develop an absolute will of steel, for often it's a fight every inch of the way to get where I'm going. So cultivate a politely aggressive attitude, never be afraid to ask others for help, and above all, retain your sense of humor. I put that on every day, long before I dress, and it solves most of the problems of being "physically challenged."

BOOKLIST

The following titles provide insight into the Yucatán Peninsula and the Maya people. A few of these books are easier obtained in Mexico, but all of them will cost less in the U.S. Most are non-fiction, though several are fiction and great to pop into your carry-on for a good read on the plane, or for any time you want to get into the Yucatecan mood. Happy reading.

Coe, Michael D. *The Maya*. New York: Thames and Hudson, 1980. A well-illustrated, easy-to-read volume on the Maya people.

Cortés, Hernán. *Five Letters*. Gordon Press, 1977. Cortés wrote long letters to the king of Spain telling of his accomplishments and trying to justify his actions in the New World.

Davies, Nigel. *The Ancient Kingdoms of Mexico*. New York: Penguin Books. Excellent study of pre-conquest (1519) indigenous peoples of Mexico.

De Landa, Bishop Diego. *Yucatán Before and After the Conquest*. New York: Dover Publications, 1978. This book, translated by William Gates from the original 1566 volume, has served as the base for all research that has taken place since. De Landa (though the man destroyed countless books of the Maya people) has given the world insight into their culture before the conquest.

Díaz del Castillo, Bernal. *The Conquest of New Spain*. New York: Penguin Books, 1963. History straight from the adventurer's reminiscences, translated by J.M. Cohen.

Fehrenbach, T.R. *Fire and Blood: A History of Mexico*. New York: Collier Books, 1973. Mexico's history over 3,500 years, told in a way to keep you reading.

Ferguson, William M. *Maya Ruins of Mexico in Color*. Norman: University of Oklahoma Press, 1977. Good reading before you go, but too bulky to carry along. Oversized with excellent drawings and illustrations of the archaeological structures of the Maya Indians.

Franz, Carl. *The People's Guide to Mexico*. New Mexico: John Muir Publications, 1972. A hu-morous guide filled with witty anecdotes and helpful general information for visitors to Mexico. Don't expect any specific city information, just nuts-and-bolts hints for traveling south of the border.

Greene, Graham. *The Power and the Glory*. New York: Penguin Books, 1977. A novel that takes place in the '20s about a priest and the anti-church movement that gripped the country.

Heffern, Richard. *Secrets of the Mind-Altering Plants of Mexico*. New York: Pyramid Books. A fascinating study of many subtances, from ancient ritual hallucinogens to today's medicines.

Laughlin, Robert M. *The People of the Bat*. Smithsonian Institution Press, 1988. Maya tales and dreams as told by the Zinacantán Indians in Chiapas.

Lewbel, George S. *Diving and Snorkeling Guide to Cozumel*. New York: Pisces Books, 1984. A well-illustrated volume for divers and snorkelers going to Cozumel. The small, easily carried volume is packed with hints about different dive sites, reefs, and marinelife of Cozumel.

Meyer, Michael, and William Sherman. *The Course of Mexican History*. Oxford University Press. A concise, one-volume history of Mexico.

Nelson, Ralph. *Popul Vuh: The Great Mythological Book of the Ancient Maya*. Boston: Houghton Mifflin, 1974. An easy-to-read translation of myths handed down orally by the Quiche Maya, family to family, until written down after the Spanish conquest.

Riding, Alan. *Distant Neighbors*. Vintage Books. A modern look at today's Mexico.

Sodi, Demetrio M. (in collaboration with Adela Fernández). *The Mayas*. Mexico: Panama Editorial S.A. This small pocketbook presents a fictionalized account of life among the Maya before the conquest. Easy reading for anyone who enjoys fantasizing about what life *might* have been like before recorded history in the Yucatán. This book is available in the Yucatecan states of Mexico.

Stephens, John L. *Incidents of Travel in Central America, Chiapas, and Yucatán*. 2 vols. New York: Dover Publications, 1969. Good companions to refer to when traveling in the area. Stephens and illustrator Catherwood rediscovered many of the Maya ruins on their treks that took place in the mid-1800s. Easy reading.

Thompson, J. Eric. *Maya Archaeologist*. Norman: University of Oklahoma, 1963. Thompson, a noted Maya scholar, traveled and worked at most of the Maya ruins in the 1930s.

____. *The Rise and Fall of the Maya Civilization*. Norman: University of Oklahoma Press, 1954. One man's story of the Maya Indian. Excellent reading.

Werner, David. *Where There is No Doctor*. California: The Hesperian Foundation. This is an invaluable medical aid to anyone traveling not only to isolated parts of Mexico, but to any place in the world where there's not a doctor.

Wolf, Eric. *Sons of the Shaking Earth*. University of Chicago Press. An anthropological study of Indian and mestizo people of Mexico and Guatemala.

Wright, Ronald. *Time Among the Maya*. New York: Weidenfeld & Nicolson, 1989. A narrative that takes the reader through Maya country of today with historical comments that help put the puzzle together.

MAYAN GLOSSARY

MAYA GODS AND CEREMONIES

Acanum—protective deity of hunters

Ahau Can—serpent lord and highest priest

Ahau Chamehes—deity of medicine

Ah Cantzicnal—aquatic deity

Ah Chhuy Kak—god of violent death and sacrifice

Ahcit Dzamalcum—protective god of fishermen

Ah Cup Cacap—god of the underworld who denies air

Ah Itzám—the water witch

Ah kines—priests, lords who consult the oracles, celebrate ceremonies, and preside over sacrifices

Ahpua—god of fishing

Ah Puch—god of death

Ak'Al—sacred marsh where water abounds

Bacaboob—the poureres, supporters of the sky and guardians of the cardinal points, who form a single god, Ah Cantzicnal Be-cabs

Bolontiku—the nine lords of the night

Chac—god of rain and agriculture

Chac Bolay Can—the butcher serpent living in the underworld

Chaces—priest's assistants in agricultural and other ceremonies

Cihuateteo—women who become goddesses through death in childbirth (Nahuatl word)

Cit Chac Coh—god of war

Hetxmek—ceremony when the child is first carried astride the hip

Hobnil Bacab—the bee god, protector of beekeepers

Holcanes—the brave warriors charged with obtaining slaves for sacrifice. (This word was unknown until the Postclassic era.)

Hunab Ku—giver of life, builder of the universe, and father of Itzámna

Ik—god of the wind

Itzámna—lord of the skies, creator of the beginning, god of time

Ixchell—goddess of birth, fertility, medicine; credited with inventing spinning

Ixtab—goddess of the cord and of suicide by hanging

Kinich—face of the sun

Kukulcán—quetzal-serpent, plumed serpent

Metnal—the underworld, place of the dead

Nacom—warrior chief

Noh Ek—Venus

Pakat—god of violent death

Zec—spirit lords of beehives

FOOD AND DRINK

alche—inebriating drink, sweetened with honey and used for ceremonies and offerings

ic—chile

itz—sweet potato

kabaxbuul—the heaviest meal of the day, eaten at dusk and containing cooked black beans

kah—pinole flour

kayem—ground maize

macal—a type of root

muxubbak—tamale

on—avocado

op—plum

p'ac—tomatoes

put—papaya

tzamna—black bean

uah—tortillas

za—maize drink

ANIMALS

acehpek—dog used for deer hunting

ah maax cal—the prattling monkey

ah maycuy—the chestnut deer

ah sac dziu—the white thrush

ah xixteel ul—the rugged land conch

bil—hairless dog reared for food

cutz—wild turkey

cutzha—duck

hoh—crow

icim—owl

jaleb—hairless dog

keh—deer
kitam—wild boar
muan—evil bird related to death
que—parrot
thul—rabbit
tzo—domestic turkey
utiu—coyote
yac—mountain cat
yaxum—mythical green bird

MUSIC AND FESTIVALS

ah paxboob—musicians
bexelac—turtle shell used as percussion instrument
chohom—dance performed in ceremonies during the month of Zip, related to fishing
chul—flute
hom—trumpet
kayab—percussion instrument fashioned from turtle shell
Oc na—festival of the month of Yax; old idols of the temple are broken and replaced with new
okot uil—dance performed during the Pocan ceremony
Pacum chac—festival in honor of the war gods
tunkul—drum
zacatan—a drum made from a hollowed tree trunk, with one opening covered with hide

ELEMENTS OF TIME

chunkin—midday
chumuc akab—midnight
chumuc kin—midday
haab—solar calendar of 360 days made up with five extra days of misfortune, which complete the final month
emelkin—sunset
kaz akab—dusk
kin—the sun, the day, the unity of time
potakab—time before dawn
yalhalcab—dawn

PLANTS AND TREES

ha—cacao seed
kan ak—plant that produces a yellow dye
ki—sisal
kiixpaxhkum—chayote

kikche—tree the trunk of which is used to make canoes
kuche—red cedar tree
k'uxub—annatto tree
piim—fiber of the cotton tree
taman—cotton plant
tauch—black zapote tree
tazon te—moss

MISCELLANEOUS WORDS

ah kay kin bak—meat seller
chaltun—water cistern
cha te—black vegetable dye
chi te—eugenia, plant for dyeing
ch'oh—indigo
ek—dye
hadzab—wooden swords
halach uinic—leader
mayacimil—smallpox epidemic, "easy death"
pic—underskirt
ploms—rich people
suyen—square blanket
xanab—sandals
xicul—sleeveless jacket decorated with feathers
xul—stake with a pointed, fire-hardened tip
yuntun—slings

NUMBERS

hun—one
ca—two
ox—three
can—four
ho—five
uac—six
uuc—seven
uacax—eight
bolon—nine
iahun—ten
buluc—eleven
iahca—twelve
oxlahum—thirteen
canlahum—fourteen
holahun—fifteen
uaclahun—sixteen
uuclahun—seventeen
uacaclahun—eighteen
bolontahun—nineteen
hunkal—twenty

SPANISH GLOSSARY

While on the Yucatán Peninsula, you'll find many people in the larger cities who speak English. However, once you're in rural villages and on isolated beaches, speaking Spanish becomes a necessity. Most Mexican people appreciate the effort you make, even if it's not perfect. On the Peninsula don't be surprised to find some people who speak no English or Spanish, only a Maya dialect. This group grows smaller every year.

The ideal way to prepare for your trip is to begin practicing Spanish before you leave. Most bookstores in the States sell simple Spanish-language tapes accompanied by a book. These tapes are great in the car on the way to work, or while shaving, gardening, doing the dishes, etc. Repetition succeeds.

Berlitz's *Spanish For Travelers* is a great help used along with a pocket dictionary. It is quite common in Mexico's hotel gift shops, but small English-Spanish dictionaries are not as common. Buy them before you leave home. Maya language dictionaries are not as easy to find, though limited grammar books are available on the Peninsula.

Spanish is not difficult to speak if you learn a few simple grammatical rules.

Vowels:
a: pronounced as in father
e: as in ray
i: as in gasoline
o: as in stole
u: as in crude

Consonants are similar to those in English. A few exceptions are:

g: before a, o, or u pronounced hard as in go; before e or i pronounced like an *h*.
h: silent
j: pronounced like an English *h* (with air)
ll: like y in you
ñ pronounced ny as in Spanish señor
q: pronounced as *k*
rr: rolled with the tongue (takes a little practice)
x: between vowels it's pronounced like a guttural *h,* as in Spanish Oaxaca
y: pronounced ee

GREETINGS

Hello, Hi—*Hola* or *Bueno*
Good day.—*Buenos días* (in the morning), *Buenas tardes* (in the afternoon)
Good night.—*Buenas noches.*
How are you?—*¿Cómo está usted?*
Very well.—*Muy bien.*
How goes it?—*¿Qué tal?*
Goodbye.—*Adiós* or *Hasta la vista.*
So long.—*Hasta luego.*
Please.—*Por favor.*
Thank you.—*Muchas gracias.*
You're welcome.—*De nada.*

COMMON EXPRESSIONS

Just a moment, please.—*Un momento, por favor. Momentito.*
Excuse me.—*Perdóneme. Discúlpeme.*
I am sorry.—*Lo siento.*
Do you speak English?—*¿Habla ingles?*
Do you understand?—*¿Me comprende? ¿Me entiende?*
I don't understand.—*No entiendo.*
I don't know.—*No sé.*
How do you say . . . in Spanish?—*¿Cómo se dice . . . en español?*
What?—*¿Cómo?*
Please repeat.—*Mande.*
Show me.—*Enséneme.*
This is good.—*Está bueno.*
This is bad.—*Está malo.*
Yes.—*Sí.*
No.—*No.*
What time is it?—*¿Qué hora es?*
What's going on?—*¿Qué pasa?*
How much is it?—*¿Cuánto cuesta?*

GETTING AROUND

Take me to . . . —*Lléveme a . . .*
Where is . . . ?—*¿Dónde esté . . . ?*
the road to . . . —*el camino a . . .*
Follow this street.—*Siga esta calle.*
Which way?—*¿Por dónde?*

near—*cerca*
far—*lejos*
to the right/left—*a la derecha/izquierda*
straight ahead—*derecho*
open, closed—*abierto, cerrado*
How far?—*¿Hasta dónde?*
entrance, exit—*la entrada, la salida*
airplane—*avión*
airport—*el aeropuerto*
airline office—*la oficina de aviones*
train station—*la estación de tren* or *la estación del ferrocarril*
taxi stand—*el sitio*
taxi—*el taxi*
bus—*autobús* or *camión la parada*
bus stop—*la parada*
I'm going to . . .—*Me voy a . . .*
reserved seat—*asiento reservado*
reservation—*reservación*
first class—*primera clase*
second class—*segunda clase*
I want a ticket to . . .—*Quiero un boleto a . . .*
Please call me a taxi.—*Pídame un taxi, por favor.*
How long does it take to go there?—*¿Cuánto se tarda en llegar?*
What will you charge me to take me to . . . ?—*¿Cuanto me covra para llevarme a . . . ?*
How much is a ticket to . . . ?—*¿Cuánto cuesta un boleto a . . . ?*
When are there buses to . . . ?—*¿A qué hora hay camiones a . . . ?*
Is there a toilet on the bus?—*¿Hay baño en el camión?*
Where does this bus go?—*¿Dónde va este autobús?*
When does one (it) leave?—*¿Cuándo sale? (. . . llega)*
Down! (to tell the bus driver you want to get off the bus)—*¡Bajan!*

CAR AND MAINTENANCE

gas station—*una gasolinera*
gas—*gasolina*
regular (gas)—*nova*
Fill it up, please.—*Lleno, por favor.*
Please check the oil.—*Vea elaceite, por favor.*
brakes—*los frenos*
map—*el mapa*
air—*aire*

radiator—*el radiador*
battery—*la batería*
repair garage—*un taller mecánico*
mechanic—*un mecánico*
jack—*un gato*
tow truck—*una grúa*
tire—*una llanta*
hole—*bache*
speed—*velocidad*
stop—*alto*
traffic bumps—*topes*

SERVICES

telegraph office—*la oficina de telégrafos*
public telephone—*el teléfono público*
post office—*el correo*
How much is it?—*¿Cuánto cuesta?*
postage stamp—*estampilla*
postcard—*tarjeta postal*
bank—*el banco*
Where is the ladies' room? the men's room?—*¿Dónde está el baño de damas? de señores?*

ACCOMMODATIONS

hotel—*un hotel*
a room—*un cuarto*
single—*sencillo*
double—*doble*
triple—*para tres*
with a ceiling fan—*con ventilador*
with air-conditioning—*con aire acondicionado*
without air-conditioning—*sin aire acondicionado*
bed—*la cama*
hammock—*la hamaca*
pillow—*la almohada*
blanket—*la cobija*
towel—*la toalla*
bathroom—*el baño*
shower—*la regadera*
soap—*jabón*
toilet paper—*papel sanitario*
hot water—*agua caliente*
cold water—*agua fría*
quiet—*tranquilo*
bigger—*más grande*
smaller—*más pequeño*
with a view—*con vista*

DINING

restaurant—*un restaurante*
breakfast—*desayuno*
lunch—*almuerzo*
lunch special—*la comida corrida*
supper—*cena*
dinner—*comida*
menu—*la carta*
house specialty—*especialidad de la casa*
knife—*un cuchillo*
fork—*un tenedor*
spoon—*una cuchara*
napkin—*una servilleta*
plate—*platillo*
salt—*sal*
pepper—*pimienta*
butter—*mantequilla*
bread—*pan*
French (style) bread—*pan blanco*
sweet roll—*pan dulce*
pastries—*postres*
roll—*bolillo*
sandwich on a roll—*torta*
toast—*tostada*
coffee—*café*
cold water—*agua helada*
hot water—*agua caliente*
purified—*purificada*
soft drink—*un refresco*

beverages—*las bebidas*
liquefied fruit drink—*licuado*
ice—*hielo*
the bill—*la cuenta*
tax—*impuesto*
tip—*propina*
waiter—*el mesero,* or more commonly: *joven*
to get a waiter's attention—*¡Oiga!*
Bring me . . .—*Traígame . . .*
beer—*cerveza*
a table—*una mesa*

calabash—small tree native to the Caribbean whose fruit, a gourd, is dried and used as a container on the Peninsula
chilaquiles—corn chips and bits of chicken
cochinita or *pollo pibil*—chicken baked with spices in banana leaves
conch—large edible mollusk common to the Caribbean; often eaten as ceviche or pounded and fried
escabeche—spicy Spanish style of cooking meat and game
naranja—sour orange used extensively in cooking
panuchos—small fried tortillas topped with black beans, lettuce, meat or poultry, and spices
pok chuc—broiled meat, tomato, onion, and sour orange
sopa de lima—chicken broth, lime juice, tomato, onion

HOTEL INDEX

Page numbers in **boldface** indicate primary reference. *Italicized* page numbers indicate information found in captions, charts, illustrations, maps, or special topics.

RESTAURANT INDEX

Page numbers in **boldface** indicate primary reference. *Italicized* page numbers
indicate information found in captions, charts, illustrations, maps, or special topics.

INDEX

Page numbers in **boldface** indicate primary reference. *Italicized* page numbers indicate information found in captions, charts, illustrations, maps, or special topics.

Chicki Mallan

ABOUT THE AUTHOR

As a child, Chicki Mallan caught the travel bug from her dad. The family would leave their Catalina Island home yearly, hit the road, and explore the small towns and big cities of the U.S.A. This urge didn't go away even with a good-sized family to tote around. At various times Chicki and kids have lived in the Orient and in Europe. Traveling with kids opened doors at the family level all over the world. Even when people don't speak the same language, they relate to other parents–since kids are the same everywhere. When not traveling, lecturing, or giving slide presentations, Chicki and husband Oz live in Paradise, a small community in the foothills of the Sierra Nevada mountains. She does what she enjoys most, writing magazine and newspaper articles in between updating travel books. She has been associated with Moon Publications since 1983 and is the author of *Catalina Island Handbook, Yucatán Peninsula Handbook,* and *Belize Handbook.* In 1987 Chicki was presented the *Pluma de Plata* award from the Mexican Government Ministry of Tourism for an article she wrote about the Yucatán Caribbean, which was published in the *L.A. Times.* Chicki is a member of SATW, the Society of American Travel Writers.

ABOUT THE PHOTOGRAPHER

Oz Mallan has been a professional photographer for the past 40 years. Much of the time was spent as chief cameraman for the *Chico Enterprise-Record.* Oz graduated from Brooks Institute of Santa Barbara in 1950. His work has often appeared in newspapers across the country via UPI and AP. He travels the world with wife Chicki, handling the photo end of their literary projects, which includes travel books, newspaper and magazine articles, and lectures and slide presentations. The photos in *Cancún Handbook* were taken during several visits and many months of travel.

THE METRIC SYSTEM

1 inch = 2.54 centimeters (cm)
1 foot = .304 meters (m)
1 mile = 1.6093 kilometers (km)
1 km = .6124 miles
1 fathom = 1.8288 m
1 chain = 20.1168 m
1 furlong = 201.168 m
1 acre = .4047 hectares
1 sq km = 100 hectares
1 sq mile = 2.59 square km
1 ounce = 28.35 grams
1 pound = .4536 kilograms
1 short ton = .90718 metric ton
1 short ton = 2000 pounds
1 long ton = 1.016 metric tons
1 long ton = 2240 pounds
1 metric ton = 1000 kilograms
1 quart = .94635 liters
1 US gallon = 3.7854 liters
1 Imperial gallon = 4.5459 liters
1 nautical mile = 1.852 km

To compute centigrade temperatures, subtract 32 from Fahrenheit and divide by 1.8. To go the other way, multiply centigrade by 1.8 and add 32.

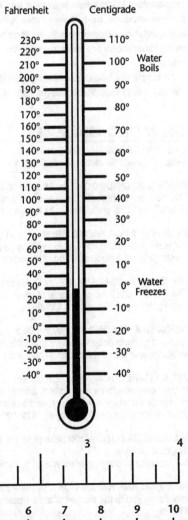

MOON HANDBOOKS—THE IDEAL TRAVELING COMPANIONS

Moon Handbooks provide travelers with all the background and practical information he or she will need on the road. Every Handbook begins with in-depth essays on the land, the people, their history, arts, politics, and social concerns—an entire bookshelf of introductory information squeezed into a one-volume encyclopedia. The Handbooks provide accurate, up-to-date coverage of all the practicalities: language, currency, transportation, accommodations, food and entertainment, and services, to name a few. Moon Handbooks are ideal traveling companions: informative, entertaining, and highly practical.

To locate the bookstore nearest you that carries Moon Travel Handbooks or to order directly from Moon Publications, call: (800) 345-5473, Monday-Friday, 9 a.m.-5 p.m. PST.

THE PACIFIC/ASIA SERIES

BALI HANDBOOK by Bill Dalton
Detailed travel information on the most famous island in the world. 428 pages. **$12.95**

BANGKOK HANDBOOK by Michael Buckley
Your tour guide through this exotic and dynamic city reveals the affordable and accessible possibilities. Thai phrasebook. 214 pages. **$10.95**

BLUEPRINT FOR PARADISE: How to Live on a Tropic Island by Ross Norgrove
This one-of-a-kind guide has everything you need to know about moving to and living comfortably on a tropical island. 212 pages. **$14.95**

FIJI ISLANDS HANDBOOK by David Stanley
The first and still the best source of information on travel around this 322-island archipelago. Fijian glossary. 198 pages. **$11.95**

INDONESIA HANDBOOK by Bill Dalton
This one-volume encyclopedia explores island by island the many facets of this sprawling, kaleidoscopic island nation. Extensive Indonesian vocabulary. 1,000 pages. **$19.95**

JAPAN HANDBOOK by J.D. Bisignani
In this comprehensive new edition, award-winning travel writer J.D. Bisignani offers to inveterate travelers, newcomers, and businesspeople alike a thoroughgoing presentation of Japan's many facets. 950 pages. **$22.50**

MICRONESIA HANDBOOK: Guide to the Caroline, Gilbert, Mariana, and Marshall Islands
by David Stanley
Micronesia Handbook guides you on a real Pacific adventure all your own. 345 pages. **$11.95**

NEW ZEALAND HANDBOOK by Jane King
Introduces you to the people, places, history, and culture of this extraordinary land. 571 pages. **$18.95**

OUTBACK AUSTRALIA HANDBOOK by Marael Johnson
Australia is an endlessly fascinating, vast land, and *Outback Australia Handbook* explores the cities and towns, sheep stations, and wilderness areas of the Northern Territory, Western Australia, and South Australia. Full of travel tips and cultural information for adventuring, relaxing, or just getting away from it all. 355 pages. **$15.95**

PHILIPPINES HANDBOOK by Peter Harper and Evelyn Peplow
Crammed with detailed information, *Philippines Handbook* equips the escapist, hedonist, or business traveler with thorough coverage of the Philippines's colorful history, landscapes, and culture. 600 pages. **$17.95**

SOUTHEAST ASIA HANDBOOK by Carl Parkes
Helps the enlightened traveler discover the real Southeast Asia. 873 pages. **$21.95**

SOUTH KOREA HANDBOOK by Robert Nilsen
Whether you're visiting on business or searching for adventure, *South Korea Handbook* is an invaluable companion. Korean glossary with useful notes on speaking and reading the language. 548 pages. **$14.95**

SOUTH PACIFIC HANDBOOK by David Stanley
The original comprehensive guide to the 16 territories in the South Pacific. 740 pages. **$19.95**

TAHITI-POLYNESIA HANDBOOK by David Stanley
All five French-Polynesian archipelagoes are covered in this comprehensive guide by Oceania's best-known travel writer. 235 pages. **$11.95**

THAILAND HANDBOOK by Carl Parkes
Presents the richest source of information on travel in Thailand. 568 pages. **$16.95**

THE HAWAIIAN SERIES

BIG ISLAND OF HAWAII HANDBOOK by J.D. Bisignani
An entertaining yet informative text packed with insider tips on accommodations, dining, sports and outdoor activities, natural attractions, and must-see sights. 350 pages. **$13.95**

HAWAII HANDBOOK by J.D. Bisignani
Winner of the 1989 Hawaii Visitors Bureau's Best Guide Award and the Grand Award for Excellence in Travel Journalism, this guide takes you beyond the glitz and high-priced hype and leads you to a genuine Hawaiian experience. Covers all 8 Hawaiian Islands. 879 pages. **$15.95**

KAUAI HANDBOOK by J.D. Bisignani
Kauai Handbook is the perfect antidote to the workaday world. Hawaiian and pidgin glossaries. 236 pages. **$9.95**

MAUI HANDBOOK by J.D. Bisignani
"No fool-'round" advice on accommodations, eateries, and recreation, plus a comprehensive introduction to island ways, geography, and history. Hawaiian and pidgin glossaries. 393 pages. **$14.95**

OAHU HANDBOOK by J.D. Bisignani
A handy guide to Honolulu, renowned surfing beaches, and Oahu's countless other diversions. Hawaiian and pidgin glossaries. 354 pages. **$11.95**

THE AMERICAS SERIES

ALASKA-YUKON HANDBOOK by Deke Castleman and Don Pitcher
Get the inside story, with plenty of well-seasoned advice to help you cover more miles on less money. 460 pages. **$14.95**

ARIZONA TRAVELER'S HANDBOOK by Bill Weir
This meticulously researched guide contains everything necessary to make Arizona accessible and enjoyable. 445 pages. **$16.95**

BAJA HANDBOOK: Mexico's Western Peninsula including Cabo San Lucas by Joe Cummings
A comprehensive guide with all the travel information and background on the land, history, and culture of this untamed thousand-mile-long peninsula. 362 pages. **$15.95**

BELIZE HANDBOOK by Chicki Mallan
Complete with detailed maps, practical information, and an overview of the area's flamboyant history, culture, and geographical features, *Belize Handbook* is the only comprehensive guide of its kind to this spectacular region. 263 pages. **$14.95**

BRITISH COLUMBIA HANDBOOK by Jane King
With an emphasis on outdoor adventures, this guide covers mainland British Columbia, Vancouver Island, the Queen Charlotte Islands, and the Canadian Rockies. 381 pages. **$15.95**

CANCUN HANDBOOK by Chicki Mallan
Covers the city's luxury scene as well as more modest attractions, plus many side trips to unspoiled beaches and Mayan ruins. Spanish glossary. 257 pages. **$13.95**

CENTRAL MEXICO HANDBOOK: Mexico City, Guadalajara, and Other Colonial Cities by Chicki Mallan
Retrace the footsteps of Cortés from the coast of Veracruz to the heart of Mexico City to discover archaeological and cultural wonders. 391 pages. **$15.95**

CATALINA ISLAND HANDBOOK: A Guide to California's Channel Islands by Chicki Mallan
A complete guide to these remarkable islands, from the windy solitude of the Channel Islands National Marine Sanctuary to bustling Avalon. 245 pages. **$10.95**

COLORADO HANDBOOK by Stephen Metzger
Essential details to the all-season possibilities in Colorado fill this guide. Practical travel tips combine with recreation—skiing, nightlife, and wilderness exploration—plus entertaining essays. 416 pages. **$17.95**

COSTA RICA HANDBOOK by Christopher P. Baker
Experience the many wonders of the natural world as you explore this remarkable land. Spanish-English glossary. 574 pages. **$17.95**

IDAHO HANDBOOK by Bill Loftus
A year-round guide to everything in this outdoor wonderland, from whitewater adventures to rural hideaways. 280 pages. **$13.95**

JAMAICA HANDBOOK   by Karl Luntta
From the sun and surf of Montego Bay and Ocho Rios to the cool slopes of the Blue Mountains, author Karl Luntta offers island-seekers a perceptive, personal view of Jamaica. 230 pages. **$14.95**

MONTANA HANDBOOK   by W.C. McRae and Judy Jewell
The wild West is yours with this extensive guide to the Treasure State, complete with travel practicalities, history, and lively essays on Montana life. 427 pages.   **$15.95**

NEVADA HANDBOOK   by Deke Castleman
Nevada Handbook puts the Silver State into perspective and makes it manageable and affordable. 400 pages.   **$14.95**

NEW MEXICO HANDBOOK   by Stephen Metzger
A close-up and complete look at every aspect of this wondrous state. 375 pages.   **$14.95**

NORTHERN CALIFORNIA HANDBOOK   by Kim Weir
An outstanding companion for imaginative travel in the territory north of the Tehachapis. 765 pages.   **$19.95**

NORTHERN MEXICO HANDBOOK: The Sea of Cortez to the Gulf of Mexico
by Joe Cummings
Directs travelers from the barrier islands of Sonora to the majestic cloud forests of the Sierra Madre Oriental to traditional villages and hidden waterfalls in San Luis Potosí. 500 pages.   **$16.95**

OREGON HANDBOOK   by Stuart Warren and Ted Long Ishikawa
Brimming with travel practicalities and insiders' views on Oregon's history, culture, arts, and activities. 461 pages.   **$15.95**

PACIFIC MEXICO HANDBOOK   by Bruce Whipperman
Explore 2,000 miles of gorgeous beaches, quiet resort towns, and famous archaeological sites along Mexico's Pacific coast. Spanish-English glossary. 428 pages.   **$15.95**

TEXAS HANDBOOK   by Joe Cummings
Seasoned travel writer Joe Cummings brings an insider's perspective to his home state. 483 pages.   **$13.95**

UTAH HANDBOOK   by Bill Weir
Weir gives you all the carefully researched facts and background to make your visit a success. 445 pages.   **$14.95**

WASHINGTON HANDBOOK   by Archie Satterfield and Dianne J. Boulerice Lyons
Covers sights, shopping, services, transportation, and outdoor recreation, with complete listings for restaurants and accommodations. 419 pages.   **$15.95**

WYOMING HANDBOOK   by Don Pitcher
All you need to know to open the doors to this wide and wild state. 495 pages.   **$14.95**

YUCATAN HANDBOOK   by Chicki Mallan
All the information you'll need to guide you into every corner of this exotic land. Mayan and Spanish glossaries. 391 pages.   **$15.95**

THE INTERNATIONAL SERIES

EGYPT HANDBOOK by Kathy Hansen
An invaluable resource for intelligent travel in Egypt. Arabic glossary. 522 pages. **$18.95**

MOSCOW-ST. PETERSBURG HANDBOOK by Masha Nordbye
Provides the visitor with an extensive introduction to the history, culture, and people of these two great cities, as well as practical information on where to stay, eat, and shop. 260 pages. **$13.95**

NEPAL HANDBOOK by Kerry Moran
Whether you're planning a week in Kathmandu or months out on the trail, *Nepal Handbook* will take you into the heart of this Himalayan jewel. 378 pages. **$12.95**

NEPALI AAMA by Broughton Coburn
A delightful photo-journey into the life of a Gurung tribeswoman of Central Nepal. Having lived with Aama (translated, "mother") for two years, first as an outsider and later as an adopted member of the family, Coburn presents an intimate glimpse into a culture alive with humor, folklore, religion, and ancient rituals. 165 pages. **$13.95**

PAKISTAN HANDBOOK by Isobel Shaw
For armchair travelers and trekkers alike, the most detailed and authoritative guide to Pakistan ever published. Urdu glossary. 478 pages. **$15.95**

STAYING HEALTHY IN ASIA, AFRICA, AND LATIN AMERICA
by Dirk G. Schroeder, Sc D, MPH
Don't leave home without it! Besides providing a complete overview of the health problems that exist in these areas, this book will help you determine which immunizations you'll need beforehand, what medications to take with you, and how to recognize and treat infections and diseases. Includes extensively illustrated first-aid information and precautions for heat, cold, and high altitude. 200 pages. **$10.95**

TIBET HANDBOOK: A PILGRIMAGE GUIDE
by Victor Chan
This remarkable book is both a comprehensive trekking guide to mountain paths and plateau trails, and a pilgrimage guide that draws on Tibetan literature and religious history. 1104 pages. **$30.00**

MOONBELTS

Made of heavy-duty Cordura nylon, the Moonbelt offers maximum protection for your money and important papers. This all-weather pouch slips under your shirt or waistband, rendering it virtually undetectable and inaccessible to pickpockets. One-inch-wide nylon webbing, heavy-duty zipper, one-inch quick-release buckle. Accommodates traveler's checks, passport, cash, photos. Size 5 x 9 inches. Black. **$8.95**

**New travel handbooks may be available that are not on this list.
To find out more about current or upcoming titles,
call us toll-free at (800) 345-5473.**

IMPORTANT ORDERING INFORMATION

FOR FASTER SERVICE: Call to locate the bookstore nearest you that carries Moon Travel Handbooks or order directly from Moon Publications:

(800) 345-5473 • Monday-Friday • 9 a.m.-5 p.m. PST • fax (916) 345-6751

PRICES: All prices are subject to change. We always ship the most current edition. We will let you know if there is a price increase on the book you ordered.

SHIPPING & HANDLING OPTIONS: 1) Domestic UPS or USPS first class (allow 10 working days for delivery): $3.50 for the first item, 50 cents for each additional item.

Exceptions:
- **Moonbelt** shipping is $1.50 for one, 50 cents for each additional belt.
- Add $2.00 for same-day handling.
- UPS 2nd Day Air or Printed Airmail requires a special quote.
- International Surface Bookrate (8-12 weeks delivery):
  $3.00 for the first item, $1.00 for each additional item. Note: Moon Publications cannot guarantee international surface bookrate shipping.

FOREIGN ORDERS: All orders that originate outside the U.S.A. must be paid for with either an International Money Order or a check in U.S. currency drawn on a major U.S. bank based in the U.S.A.

TELEPHONE ORDERS: We accept Visa or MasterCard payments. Minimum order is US$15.00. Call in your order: (800) 345-5473, 9 a.m.-5 p.m. Pacific Standard Time.

ORDER FORM

Be sure to call (800) 345-5473 for current prices and editions or for the name of the bookstore
nearest you that carries Moon Travel Handbooks • 9 a.m.–5 p.m. PST
(See important ordering information on preceding page)

Name: _____ Date: _____

Street: _____

City: _____ Daytime Phone: _____

State or Country: _____ Zip Code: _____

QUANTITY	TITLE	PRICE

Taxable Total_____

Sales Tax (7.25%) for California Residents_____

Shipping & Handling_____

TOTAL_____

Ship: ☐ UPS (no PO Boxes)   ☐ 1st class   ☐ International surface mail

Ship to: ☐ address above   ☐ other _____

_____

Make checks payable to: **MOON PUBLICATIONS, INC**. P.O. Box 3040, Chico, CA 95927-3040
U.S.A. We accept Visa and MasterCard. **To Order:** Call in your Visa or MasterCard number, or send
a written order with your Visa or MasterCard number and expiration date clearly written.

Card Number: ☐ **Visa**   ☐ **MasterCard**

☐☐☐☐ ☐☐☐☐ ☐☐☐☐ ☐☐☐☐

Exact Name on Card: _____

expiration date:_____

signature_____

F/94

TRAVEL MATTERS

Travel Matters is Moon Publications' quarterly newsletter. It provides today's traveler with timely, informative travel news and articles.

You'll find resourceful coverage on:

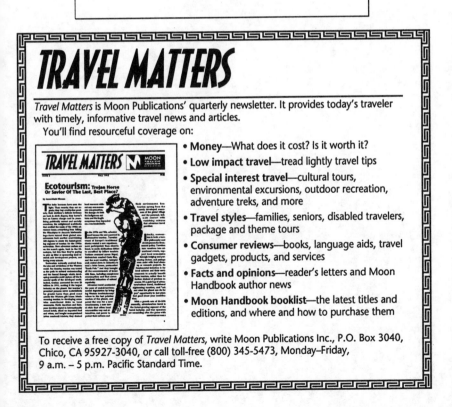

- **Money**—What does it cost? Is it worth it?
- **Low impact travel**—tread lightly travel tips
- **Special interest travel**—cultural tours, environmental excursions, outdoor recreation, adventure treks, and more
- **Travel styles**—families, seniors, disabled travelers, package and theme tours
- **Consumer reviews**—books, language aids, travel gadgets, products, and services
- **Facts and opinions**—reader's letters and Moon Handbook author news
- **Moon Handbook booklist**—the latest titles and editions, and where and how to purchase them

To receive a free copy of *Travel Matters*, write Moon Publications Inc., P.O. Box 3040, Chico, CA 95927-3040, or call toll-free (800) 345-5473, Monday–Friday, 9 a.m. – 5 p.m. Pacific Standard Time.